LONG LEGS
and
TALL TALES

a showgirl's wacky, sexy journey

to the Playboy Mansion and the Radio City Rockettes

KRISTI LYNN DAVIS

Shaw House Publishing
Dexter, Michigan

Copyright 2015 by Kristi Lynn Davis

Published in the United States by
Shaw House Publishing, PO Box 477, Dexter, MI 48130, U.S.A.

All rights reserved. No part of this publication may be reproduced, stored in, or introduced into a retrieval system, or transmitted, in any form, or by any means (electronic, mechanical, photocopying, recording, or otherwise) without the prior written permission of both the copyright owner and the above publisher of this book except in the case of brief quotations embodied in critical articles and reviews.

Cover sketch: Radio City Christmas "Bizzazz" Rockettes
by Pete Menefee (Copyright 1999)
is reproduced with the permission of Pete Menefee.

Cover Design: Annie Capps, www.swampstreetdesign.com

Interior Design: Caligraphics, www.caligraphics.net

Photos: Doug Coombe, www.dougcoombe.com

Editor: Ken Wachsberger, www.azenphonypress.com

ISBN 978-0-9964576-3-7

Library of Congress Control Number: 2015909262

Contents

Foreword by Maurice Hines
Foreword by Suzanne Sena
Don't Skip This Introduction
Acknowledgments
Dedication

Prologue: Setting the Stage 1

FINAL SCENE: Florida, July 1–August 9, 2002	2
Dolly Dinkle's School of Dance	8

Act 1: Learning the Ropes 35

FINAL SCENE: New York City, August 9, 2002	36
Scene 1: Taking a Bite Out of the Big Apple	37
FINAL SCENE: New York City, August 9, 2002	89
Scene 2: California, Here I Come!	91
FINAL SCENE: New York City, August 9, 2002	102
Scene 3: Beef and Boards	103
FINAL SCENE: New York City, August 10, 2002	118
Scene 4: The Cow's Behind (and Other Embarrassing Parts)	119
FINAL SCENE: New York City, August 10, 2002	149
Scene 5: Come and Listen to a Story About a Man Named Jed	150

Act 2: On the Road, Sky, and Sea 160

FINAL SCENE: New York City, August 10, 2002	161
Scene 1: Playboy's Girls of Rock & Roll	163
FINAL SCENE: New York City, August 10, 2002	245
Scene 2: Let Me Be Your Sugar Baby	246
FINAL SCENE: New York City, August 10, 2002	261
Scene 3: The Love Boat	262

Act 3: The Radio City Rockettes 302

FINAL SCENE: New York City, August 10, 2002	303
Scene 1: The Audition	304
FINAL SCENE: New York City, August 10, 2002	313
Scene 2: Branson	314
FINAL SCENE: New York City, August 10, 2002	353
Scene 3: Vegas	354
FINAL SCENE: New York City, August 10, 2002	426
Scene 4: Detroit	427
FINAL SCENE: New York City, August 10, 2002	447
Encore	449
About the Author	455

Foreword by Maurice Hines

When I was asked to write a foreword for this wonderful book, it brought back all the joy I had choreographing and getting to know Kristi Davis and the fabulous Rockettes. Since then, I've choreographed for many, many dancers but I must say Kristi and the Rockettes were and still are some of the best all-around dancers I've ever worked with. Pure joy, that's the only way I can explain how I felt walking into the rehearsal room and seeing those wonderful dancers all warmed up and ready to dance their hearts out. A choreographer's dream.

Kristi Davis was special in that, even though she knew how to blend in as the Rockette dancers are trained to do, individual charisma will always shine through. Ms. Davis was certainly one of those dancers. You will experience that love and charisma in every page of her story, *Long Legs and Tall Tales*. I'm proud to have been asked to be a part of Kristi's dancing life.

Kristi, you're fabulous!

— Maurice Hines, director, choreographer, and Tony-nominated star of stage, screen, and television

Foreword by Suzanne Sena

Reading *Long Legs and Tall Tales* has been such a fun and enlightening and enjoyable experience! Once upon a time, a girl from my home town was living her dream, and it inspired me to do the same. Kristi Davis takes us from her humble Michigan beginnings to her show-stopping performances in Vegas and worldwide.

From Midwestern model student to performing in the Flintstones extravaganza at Universal Studios to becoming a member of Playboy's Girls of Rock and Roll to fulfilling her ultimate fantasy as a world-famous Rockette and then teacher and mentor of "The Rockette Experience," Kristi shares the dreams, the drama, the delight, and the despair. Readers will vicariously experience her ups and downs, including the good, the bad, and the harrowing life of a professional dancer, and be grateful for the ride.

Kristi and I grew up in the same Michigan town and attended the same high school, where we both performed in musicals. Our paths crossed only during these occasions, but our lives have been forever linked by a shared mutual friend, who also went on to perform professionally.

Like most Midwesterners, and people outside of Los Angeles and New York, I didn't know that performing professionally was an option, so I pursued a more traditional career in public relations and marketing. Still, my love of performing drew me back to the stage, and soon I was being paid as a professional actor, a voice-over artist, and a television spokesperson in local and regional markets, all the while continuing my traditional "9 to 5."

One day, our mutual friend forwarded me a "newsletter" written by Kristi, outlining her day-to-day adventures in Hollywood and touring with Playboy's Girls of Rock and Roll. I was fascinated to no end; Kristi was just like me; yet, while I was working in offices, she was working full time as an entertainer. (Coincidentally, our mutual friend had just been awarded a coveted position singing professionally on world cruises.) I remember thinking, "Hey, if she can do it, why can't I?" Kristi's words reminded me that it IS possible to achieve your dreams, and, by gosh, I was going to start aiming higher with my own.

I became an entertainment professional because I admired her success. Now, it is an honor to be among the first to read of her experiences—to laugh at the humor, to join in the fun, and to empathize with the frustrations. Kristi outlines what I, too, experienced—that being catapulted "suddenly" to great heights is both fabulous and foreign. There are no overnight success stories—as Kristi and I both know, success comes from a long road of hard work and commitment, overcoming challenges and emotional roller coasters. Fame is not the objective, nor is money—which is good, because it's rarely consistent! We do it because we love it, because it's in our souls. It's not for the faint of heart, but it can fill your heart tremendously!

Whether you're an industry insider or you're still reaching for the stars, Kristi shows you what it's like to reach for them, to finally touch them, and then to savor the feel of them and go beyond them.

High kicks of praise for this behind-the-scenes memoir by the star who inspired me to follow my dreams! A page turner from beginning to end. A must-read for anyone with show business aspirations or a dancing career in the making, as well as those curious about the life of a professional entertainer. I didn't want it to end.

— Suzanne Sena, national news anchor
and Emmy-nominated host

Don't Skip This Introduction

There are three reasons you might want to read this intro: 1.) I'm going to explain how the book is written so you don't get confused; 2.) I'm going to clarify that this book is *based on* a true story (tightly, not loosely); and 3.) it's so short, in the time it takes you to think about whether you should skip it to get to the juicy stuff or just read it you could have already finished reading it. Here we go:

1.) The book includes a "Prologue" followed by 3 "Acts" within which are various "Scenes" like a theatre play (clever, eh?) plus what I call the "Final Scene." The story starts out in the final scene, which takes place a little bit in Florida but mostly in New York City and covers the last few months of my career but mostly the last two days. Everything else is a chronological flashback. So you'll read a final scene (which is short) and then you'll read a flashback scene (which is long). The final scenes and flashback scenes alternate throughout the book. You'll get the hang of it. By the end of the book, the flashback scenes catch up with the final scene, and you'll see how it all fits together.

2.) I say this book is "based on" a true story instead of is a true story, because my faulty memory could have gotten some of the details wrong (and I did purposefully alter a few details that were overly embarrassing or potentially incriminating). For the most part, and to the best of my knowledge and ability to confirm facts, it's true (at least from my perspective at the time). What is not true are some of the names. The famous people I name really were those people. So were most of the directors and choreographers. But I did change the names of my castmates and a few others (and "Celebration Magnifico" is not the real name of the company I worked for, but it's a darn good name and someone should snatch it up right away). My hope was that, if people recognized themselves in the story, they'd smile and want to shake my hand and not slap me upside the head. (Except for maybe two people, but I still tried to treat their situations responsibly and respectfully.) However, since I did not ask everyone's permission, and you can never be sure how people will respond, I just changed the names. I truly thank and honor everyone who played a role (both enjoyable and challenging) in my story. I hope I played a positive role in theirs.

3.) See, you're done. Now just read the Acknowledgments so you can see who I thank (maybe you) and you can get to the juicy stuff.

Acknowledgments

I fully recognize that I couldn't have accomplished my dreams without the help of many people. First of all, thanks to all the audience members who spent their hard-earned cash (or trust funds or stolen credit cards) on theatre tickets. Without an audience, performing a show just isn't the same. Entertaining you has been my pleasure. Thanks for applauding and cheering and laughing (mostly at the appropriate times).

Thanks to all the producers, directors, choreographers, agents, and casting people (many of whom are named in this book) for creating spectacular productions, for recognizing the value of theatre and the arts, and for taking a chance by hiring me.

Thanks to A.G.V.A., S.A.G., A.F.T.R.A., and A.E.A. for helping to keep this profession professional.

Thanks to Morningside Writers Group in Port St. Lucie, Florida for critiquing my work and being the first people who weren't friends or relatives or even my demographic to tell me my story was worth telling. (Except for that one old grumpy guy who stared at me like I was from outer space. But secretly, I think we liked each other.)

Thanks to all my dance teachers, especially my childhood dance teachers, for fostering my talent and my love of sequins.

Thanks to the visionary Russell Markert, founder of the Rockettes, for appreciating long legs and tall ladies; the fantastic Radio City Rockettes; and Radio City Music Hall for giving me a dance experience beyond my wildest dreams.

Thanks to all my fellow cast and crew members who lived the dream with me on stage and off. You've been like family.

Thanks to my gracious peer review team—Dr. Marybeth Lima, Jenny Dewar, Karen Kasteel, Steven Goodwillie, Genia A. Sherwood, Jennifer Dowdle, Cami Elen, Laura Teusink, and Phil Randall—for being my guinea pigs and muddling through the rough version of the book. Your feedback, encouragement, and emotional hand-holding were invaluable.

Thanks to the mega-talented, three-time Emmy Award-winning costume designer, Pete Menefee, for allowing his spectacular sketch to grace the cover of this book (and for creating costumes so luscious and lovely they made me swoon).

Thanks to my mentor and official editor, Ken Wachsberger, for believing in this project and for suffering through more stories about G-strings than an editor ever should.

Thanks to Kendra Englund for being my lovely and loyal best friend since high school and for sharing this love of musical theatre.

Thanks to my Grandma Elsie for suggesting to me back in the early 1990s, "You should keep a journal in case you want to write a book someday." I did it, Grandma! (I'm sure she's smiling up in heaven.) Thanks also to my writing role model, Grandma Merle, who loved to take pen to paper and continued documenting her own memoirs (15 volumes in all and she never left her small farm town in southwest Iowa) until she died a few days short of her 99th birthday.

Thanks to my wonderful parents who paid for a million dance classes, drove me to those classes day after day and year after year, sat through seemingly endless hours of dance recitals and amateur performances, babysat my kids, and traveled all over the country to see me perform professionally. You deserve a huge round of applause.

Thanks to my sister Cindy, the professional screenwriter, for her wise advice and wacky sense of humor, and sister Jen for being a smart, strong, and inspiring woman.

Thanks to my incredible children, Kieran and Kara, whom I love more than feathers and fishnets, and that says a lot.

And, finally, thanks to Dave Boutette for being The World's Best Husband and my cheerleader throughout this crazy process.

Mmmwaaaaah! I love you all.

Dedication

To everyone with a dream, may you have the courage to pursue it.

"If I ever got a chance to get a group of American girls who would be taller and have longer legs and could do really complicated tap routines and eye-high kicks...they'd knock your socks off!"

— Russell Markert, Founder of the Rockettes
(Originally the Missouri Rockets, 1925)

Final Scene: Florida, July 1-August 9, 2002

Like many Americans and international connoisseurs of culture, I have been knocked sockless by the Radio City Rockettes. But if perchance you've spent most of your life hiding under a rock on a deserted island, and upon hearing the term "Rockette" (thinking your ears need a good cleaning) you clarify, "Did you say Rock-head?" I'd animatedly articulate, "The Rockettes are the world's most famous precision dance troupe—a bevy of tall, leggy beauties acclaimed for their intricate, unison tap dancing, eye-high kickline, and gorgeous gams. They are the synchronized chorus line supreme, and their theatrical home is none other than the renowned Radio City Music Hall in New York City, where they've been amazing and amusing audiences since the 1930s." And if that weren't enough to sock it to you, I'd rave, "The Rockettes are referenced in movies, TV sitcoms, best-selling books, magazine articles, cartoons, and even the board game *Trivial Pursuit*. They are a household name and as integral a part of Americana as baseball, hotdogs, and apple pie." So enthusiastic am I about these luscious ladies that I'd continue to rhapsodize until you implored me to "Put a sock in it!"

As a devoted fan growing up in the suburbs near Detroit, I watched the Rockettes perform on national television for the Macy's Thanksgiving Day Parade every year without fail. At the end of the sparkling, spectacular performance, the camera panned across their fair faces one by one, each woman brightly beaming for her personal close-up. My sister and I delighted in discussing which dancers were the darlingest. A Thanksgiving without the Rockettes was like a Thanksgiving without turkey. In the last seven years, however, I had come to know more about the Rockettes than the average American. Let it be said with certitude that I knew the Rockettes intimately. Like you-know-the-holes-in-your-underwear intimately. For I was a Rockette.

This was a big deal to me, as becoming a Rockette was my fantasy world come true. As a kid, I used to go gaga over those old Hollywood movie dance extravaganzas (à la Busby Berkeley and the Ziegfeld Follies, circa early-ish 1900s) in which a million stunning showgirls in lavish costumes formed intricate kaleidoscopic, geometric patterns and were escorted around sensational stage sets and staircases by debonair men in tuxedos and top hats. It was a world of razzle dazzle and romance, and I loved it. Appearing as a Rockette was about the closest I could get to living my life in a magnificent musical. It meant I had made it as a dancer. The Rockettes were the cream of the crop, the top of the skyscraper, the peak of perfection. In short, they were the Big Time.

But life goes by fast, and soon, instead of getting a kick out of life, you're getting kicked out of life. Before you know it you're a ninety-nine-year-old rickety rocker in a rocking chair, about to kick the bedazzled bucket and bemoaning, "It's over already? But, but, but I feel like I just got here! Why it seems like just a blink of an eye from birth to grave, from opening night to closing night, from overture to finale. I want an encore!" In this insidious way, the end of my career snuck up, caught me by surprise, and bit me in my aging buttocks. (I was only thirty-six, but for a dancer that age meant the end of life.)

Of course, I knew subconsciously that the final curtain was about to fall, but the reality of the situation didn't hit me until I returned to perusing the audition notices after taking a year off for maternity leave. A year spent singing and dancing in my Florida home to a literally captive audience of two small children under the age of four was all well and good, but I was ready and anxious to get back to a real stage and an audience that could wipe their own bottoms.

Like a virgin, reliving the excitement and anticipation of the very first time I touched a *Backstage* newspaper in search of performance opportunities, I eagerly turned the pages only to be rudely awakened to the discovery that everyone wanted eighteen to thirty-five-year-olds. "But I was thirty-five just last year before I had the baby! What happened?" I blurted aloud, my tykes wide eyed over their ranting mommy. Time had flown by faster than I could count "a five, six, seven, eight." That's what happened. Somehow I had forgotten or failed to realize that, like a carton of milk or a can of tuna, a dancer came with an expiration date, and I was already spoiled goods. Thirty-five seemed like such an arbitrary number, but you turn thirty-five and all of a sudden you need mammograms, prenatal testing, and are no longer desirable as a dancer. The consolation prize is that you are now of age to run for president of the United States, but it's not a likely transition. (Although Ronald Reagan, Sonny Bono, and Arnold Schwarzenegger made the dubious leap from acting to politics.)

One moment I was reaching my peak and the next I was over the hill. "At least I still have the Rockettes," I reminded myself, temporarily relieved. "But I want to leave looking good and at the top of my game. I don't want to be one of those decrepit diehards the younger girls make fun of. Don't want people begging me, the crinkly old lady, to get the heck off the stage." While proud to be performing at my age, particularly post pregnancy, I preferred not to pathetically persevere past my time. I robotically retrieved my youngsters' runaway Cheerios from the floor as I continued my internal debate.

Many of my fellow thirty-something Rockettes were also getting married, buying homes, and birthing babies. We were all hanging onto our jobs by a thread trying to keep the dream (and the health insurance) alive for as long as we practically could. But our priorities were changing and so were our bodies. Dancing professionally and child rearing were like oil and water (for me, anyway). They just didn't mix. Having taken maternity leave last year when my daughter was born, this year I was required to either plop out another papoose, take a leave of absence, or actually do the show if I wanted to keep my job. As an almost thirty-seven-year-old mother of two, who was apparently too old to audition for other dance gigs (news to me), I now knew that once my Rockette contract ended, my dance career was completely kaput.

This perturbing possibility was smacking me right in the face, because the Rockettes were currently fighting to protect our positions and maintain our cushy contract with Radio City. All spring and summer long, my phone had been ringing off the hook with gossip from the Rockette cross country hotline. Being the lone Rockette outpost in the swamplands of Florida, my calls were coming in third party from New York through Vegas. My computer was bombarded with conflicting e-mails from multiple sources. My mailbox was loaded with persuasive letters from Radio City and Cablevision (who had bought out Madison Square Garden, owner of Radio City) and opposing rhetoric from A.G.V.A. (American Guild of Variety Artists), the union representing the Rockettes, and retaliation from enraged Rockettes. Our boisterous battle made the morning television news shows and CNN. Matters were coming to a head and the tension was thick. There was even talk of a strike.

One of the main issues up for discussion was Radio City's demand to dissolve the notorious "Roster." Many Rockettes had to re-audition every year to maintain their status, but, for umpteen years, there had also been a Roster of forty-one women who were considered permanent employees of Radio City. That is, they could remain Rockettes forever and ever amen, barring they didn't blow up like a balloon (in other words, as long as they met their weight requirement) or become incapable of kicking to their bifocals. So there would be "girls" pushing forty or even fifty years old, which is ancient in the dance world, still pumping out those Christmas shows and cashing in.

These rostered Rockettes had first right of refusal for any and all job offers. As such, the Roster was a cash cow and possibly one of the best gigs in New York, because you were virtually guaranteed work for approximately three months leading up to and during the Christmas season *every year*. These privileged gals could do a gazillion shows a day and get double or triple overtime. They'd make so much money they could kick back and eat bon-bons the rest of the year and then simply crash diet before the first weigh-in come fall. (That's an extreme scenario, but technically it could be done.) As you might guess, these were most coveted positions. And I had one of them.

Understandably, Radio City disapproved of having to cater to the Roster. In fact, they assured us that the very future of the Rockettes rested upon its elimination in favor of yearly, open auditions so that the creative team could choose the most capable individuals for each production. I could see their point. If I were in charge, I'd certainly want to hire the best. But the message some of us heard was, "There are younger, better models out there, and if we have to use old has-beens in the lineup, our show will suffer to such an extent that the Rockettes will decay into nothing more than a historical relic, like pet rocks." Ouch. I felt like the devoted wife of many years being traded in by my wealthy husband for a newer, hipper, prettier woman. It was an emotional issue; it hurt to be one of the few to have earned a spot on the prestigious Roster only to be told that the Roster would be the downfall of the troupe. It also hurt to have our job security threatened and our status and privileges revoked. But times they were a-changing. As compensation, Radio City was offering us each a buyout package commensurate with our respective years of service. And we still had the option of auditioning to be rehired; Radio City guaranteed that many of us would indeed be given our jobs back.

Let's be clear that I'm not here to call Radio City and Cablevision the bad guys; perhaps their actions *would* ensure a higher quality product that would keep the Rockette franchise afloat. They've employed oodles of excellent entertainers for years on end, and I'm eternally grateful and proud to have been one of them. I'm telling you what went down, because it demonstrates just how fiercely competitive and uncertain showbiz can be and how it favors the youngsters. (Thank goodness I wasn't a gymnast. My career would have been over before I got my first period.) Frankly, I'm also telling you, because this sensitive situation gives me a dramatic beginning (and ending) for this book.

So, in the name of preserving the legacy of the Rockettes, Radio City was determined to disband our cherished Roster and all its power and privilege therein. We knew that Big Daddy Cablevision and their lawyers would be a tough contender against our union that represented the pool of "variety artists." Our fight felt like a ninety-five pound weakling trying to kick sand in the face of a three-hundred-pound muscle man. I generally rooted for the underdog, but this time I wasn't placing any bets. A.G.V.A. had taken good care of us for years and was making valiant efforts on our behalf, but I sensed it was only a matter of time before my time was up.

And so it was under such suspenseful circumstances that I received a crucial call from Rockette Headquarters at Radio City. "Kristi, you're next on the list to teach the Rockette Experience. Can you be in New York in two weeks?" The "Rockette Experience" was an afternoon-long workshop open to aspiring dancers in which they would learn fragments of real Rockette repertoire from a real Rockette in the real Rockette rehearsal rooms in the real Radio City Music Hall. The participants would then proceed through a mock audition followed by a question-and-answer session with the real Rockette. I had put my name on a waiting list to lead this event, and the opportunity had arisen just in the nick of time.

This bit of business wasn't necessarily reason enough for me to be Manhattan bound. But this was a much more personal, vitally important mission, because, here's the kicker: this would actually be my first, and probably last, appearance as a Rockette in New York City at Radio City Music Hall. "What's the big deal?" you ask. The big deal is that you don't feel like a real, bona fide Rockette unless you've been on the Great Stage at Radio City Music Hall. Standing on this sacred spot is a Rockette's pilgrimage to Mecca. Even though I had logged in approximately 1,200 shows and 240,000 kicks as a Rockette, I still needed to perform at the Music Hall to feel my experience was complete.

Of course, as a rostered Rockette I had been offered opportunities to dance at the Music Hall but had turned them down, for what I thought were good reasons at the time, to perform elsewhere. In the back of my mind, I always thought I'd get around to it someday. With the contract deadline looming overhead, however, my instincts told me that someday better be *now* or it may well be *never*. When presented with a once-in-a-lifetime opportunity, it's best to stand at attention, salute your good fortune, and shout, "Yes, Sir!" Nothing was going to keep me from this final hurrah, this grand, spankin' finale, this apropos ending to my fairy-tale adventure. And, to be honest, as a mostly-stay-at-home mom, going to the grocery store alone was a thrill these days, so a solo visit to New York City seemed practically orgasmic. How could I pass it up?

Heeding the call from H.Q., I mustered the troops and briefed them on my upcoming deployment. "Kids, Mommy is being sent on special assignment and has to go bye-bye for a little bit." In response to this entertainment emergency, I left my precious progeny in the hands of my husband and boarded a flight to JFK International Airport in NYC to do the divine deed, most likely my final duty as a World Famous Radio City Rockette. I settled into my seat, took a deep breath, closed my eyes, and tried to relax for the ride. *You've come a long way, baby*, I realized, reflecting back to my humble beginnings in the world of show business.

Kristi Lynn Davis

Dolly Dinkle's School of Dance

"People have asked me why I chose to be a dancer. I did not choose. I was chosen to be a dancer, and with that, you live all your life."

— Martha Graham, *Blood Memory*

My mother would say my obsession with dance started in my infancy. She tells the story of how, as a baby, I bounced in my car seat to the beat of "Hey There, Georgie Girl" playing on the radio. I believe I first felt the rhythm long before that. Surely, I swam to the beat of my mother's heart as a mere zygote in her womb.

You see, I am convinced that I was born to be on stage. My genetic makeup dictated a life bound to the theatre. My first step on stage was an answer to a divine calling to entertain the masses: "Lo, an angel in an Armani original appeared in the heavens before me and said, 'Go forth and kick thy long legs to thine eyes and tap thy large feet loudly upon the earth, for thou shalt be adorned in sequins and glitter and all that sparkles like a star.'" Be it a call from the Hollywood heavens or a chromosomal defect, my fate was to be an entertainer. It was as useless for me to fight the urge to perform as it would be a bird to squelch the urge to fly. I only wish I had realized this from the beginning.

What I did discover early on was that I was different from most people. Never quite fitting in with the crowd, I felt special, extraordinary. Although extremely shy and insecure in many ways, I had a spark inside waiting to be kindled. Bursting to be seen, to be heard, to be noticed, I was a dreamer, and I fantasized about the fascinating people, places, and experiences that were in store for me. While I marvel that I made it as far as I did in show business, even as a small child, I knew that my life was meant for something big.

I really owe a round of applause to my mother for she had a dream, too: she envisioned her beloved preschooler on stage tip-toeing about in a frilly tutu. When I was four, she took me to the local civic center for my first ballet lesson. The classroom was located in the bowels of the dark, dingy basement, and I grasped onto her leg as we marched down the empty stairwell. All Mom's visions of twirling tulle were shattered when I was spooked by the tubby teacher in tights towering over me in the creepy underground classroom. To make matters worse, all the budding ballerinas were given star-sticker attendance books, and that creature-teacher-from-the-dark had the nerve to give me a used book left by the last defector. That horrible experience not only left my spark unkindled, but also completely snuffed out my interest in dance class for years to come.

While I had no desire to return to the "dungeon of dance," I still loved showing off for an audience. Despite having only thirty minutes of ballet instruction under my belt, I started creating and performing my own routines on the front porch of my grandmother's Iowa farmhouse. Although my mother had given up taking me to ballet class, she bought my younger sister and me black leotards, pink tights, pink ballet shoes, and pink tutus. My sister would tie her tutu on over her pants and pound on her toy drum, while I, dressed perfectly in all the appropriate dance attire, would prance around to her erratic rhythms. The hardest thing about being a dancer back then was getting my costume off in time to make it to the bathroom.

****

I continued this impromptu method of dance for five years, when, at the age of nine, I finally decided I was brave enough to try taking classes again. To be safe, I was going to take my sister and some neighborhood friends for backup. If our new teacher was as scary as the last one, at least we'd outnumber her.

This time my mother enrolled us in the illustrious Josie Grey's School, nee, "Basement," of Dance. Josie was an entrepreneurial mom who figured out how to make a few bucks underground without leaving home. A small section of her basement, with a couple of ballet barres hung on the walls, served as the studio. Josie undercut the real dance schools around town; at two dollars per half-hour class, the price was right. Plus, she lived so close that Mom didn't have to drive us. We used to walk the six blocks to her house wearing our ballet shoes and squishing fallen berries underfoot along the way.

Josie filled that "Bargain-Basement-Discount-School-of-Dance" niche for all the not-so-serious and not-so-rich kids who just wanted to dance for fun. She could have cared less if we wore our street clothes to class or even if we wore the proper dance shoes, and she accepted children of all shapes and sizes. You'd easily see a 5-foot-6-inch, 200-pound heavyweight dancing next to a featherweight nymph of a girl. Josie let us talk and laugh and giggle all through class. She offered such an affordable and relaxed atmosphere that we wanted to take everything, and we did: tap, jazz, ballet, and even baton, which we begged her to teach us.

Josie taught in her street clothes and played the accordion in class. Tap was her forte. I was sure she had been a professional tap dancer in her younger years. Perhaps she had accompanied herself on a sparkly, royal-blue accordion, her name spelled out in white felt letters down the side. I could picture the crowd going wild as she vigorously played a polka, her feet rhythmically striking the ground in time to the music. Whether or not Josie was ever paid a dime for dancing, I couldn't say, but she knew more than I did and was so unintimidating and casual that I loved going to class.

The atmosphere at Josie's was anything but serious, due to the fact that her own four rambunctious children were home while she taught. "You guys better shut up and stop that fightin'," she'd shout at them. "I ain't comin' upstairs again!" She often left class to attend to some domestic disaster generally preceded by earth-shattering crashing sounds and screams. It wasn't uncommon to have one of her three young sons or her only daughter come bounding down the basement stairs unannounced to dance a few steps with our class and then return upstairs to watch afternoon cartoons when they'd had enough.

Jazz class was a riot. We learned to twinkle, Lindy, sugar, camel, sashay and Shorty George. Josie chose the upbeat Tina Turner song, "Proud Mary," for our dance. We lined up behind the lead girl, and, one at a time, on our specific count, raised our arms up in a "V." I anxiously awaited my turn thinking, "One, two, three, four, five, six, SEVEN, eight." It was hard not to count out loud. On the part of the song where Tina sings "Rollin', rollin', rollin' down the river…," the even-numbered girls would lean right and roll their arms while the odd-numbered girls would lean left and do the same. It was more fun than I'd ever had before.

Our tap class was learning the waltz clog to the song "Daisy." The waltz clog is a simple, standard, old tap dance that has been massacred by millions of amateur tappers over the course of time. I caught on to the steps quickly. At least I thought I had gotten the steps right. It was nearly impossible to hear my own sounds in that class full of beginners, for the noise level was deafening. The walls reverberated with a hodge podge of scuffing and banging and sliding of taps across the cement floor like nails on a chalkboard.

Every kid seemed to be in her own time zone, performing some variation of the steps to the beat of her own drum. Not only that, but everyone was joyously beating the heck out of their shoes. If you stomped as hard as you could, those suckers produced some major decibels, especially in that tiny basement where the sound waves echoed off the walls. Let's face it, giving a kid shoes with noise makers on the bottoms is just asking for trouble. Getting the class to keep their feet quiet long enough to explain the next step was a huge accomplishment for Josie. Time and time again, she found herself shouting over the noise. It's a wonder that teaching tap didn't send her straight to the loony bin.

When we finally finished the dance, Josie made a shocking announcement: "For the recital you'll be doing the entire number while jumping rope, so bring one next week." Luckily, I was one of the best rope jumpers in my Phys Ed class at school. I was fairly confident about the tapping and even more secure with jumping, but tapping and jumping rope at the same time was another story. Performing the waltz clog was hard enough without worrying about tripping myself with a string.

The other challenge was to make sure I stayed on my designated spot and didn't hop-shuffle-step-step too close to my neighbor and clash ropes. I know, because absent-minded Lilly whacked mine regularly. She'd wander off her spot, tapping so close to me that her rope would hit mine. Then I'd have to get it spinning again and figure out where we were in the choreography. Lilly was a hazard on the dance floor. She was like a driver who can't stay in her own lane.

Ballet was Josie's weakest subject, but we learned to point our toes, do knee bends without sticking out our behinds, walk on tiptoe, and "sashay" across the floor. A lot of rules and numbers seemed to be involved: Ballerinas had to know first, second, third, fourth, and fifth position. For first position, we had to stand with the heels of our feet touching and our toes open to form a straight line. Our legs had to be perfectly straight and our bottoms tucked under. It was difficult to stand like that without falling over, and some of the girls tilted like the Leaning Tower of Pisa.

Josie knew nearly as little about baton as she did ballet, but we learned enough to keep us happy. She taught us how to do the majorette march, how to wrap the baton around our necks like a choke hold, and how to jump with our legs split apart while quickly passing the baton through them. Josie also showed us the one-handed figure-eight twirl, which was pretty easy, but the maneuver in which we attempted to twirl the baton using one hand and only the thumb of the other hand was so hard that we had to practice at home. Our most daring trick was lifting one leg and tossing the baton underneath it and up into the air. Fortunately, the baton wasn't too difficult to catch as it could fly only so high before hitting the low basement ceiling.

As if shimmying about in our weekly classes wasn't amusing enough, performing in the recital was about as thrilling as life could get. Our show was held one evening in June in the auditorium of a nearby middle school. On show night, the classroom that served as our dressing room hummed with restless chatter punctuated by cries of dismay from girls who discovered their mothers had forgotten some of their costume pieces.

Our cheap and cheerful costumes, ordered from a catalog, were sequined and beribboned and just to die for. Josie had instructed all of her students to buy sheer-to-the-waist nylons to wear underneath, but a couple of girls ended up with reinforced girdle nylons, which created the unsightly appearance of dark underwear hanging out below their leotards. Several dancers wore black ballet shoes while the rest of us were wearing pink, and everyone's hair was styled differently. Some girls left their stringy tresses down and in their eyes. Others had them pulled back in a ponytail or two. The dress code was a free-for-all, but Josie didn't seem to mind.

At seven to nine years of age, we were the most advanced kids Josie taught, and we felt like hot stuff on stage. Decked out in our red-and-blue halter tops and shorty shorts (which we also wore for tap and baton to minimize costume expenses), we did "Proud Mary" proud. Several of my classmates concentrated so hard they forgot to smile, and the audience could see their lips counting the beats, but I was beaming with a grin so wide I could have been a commercial for toothpaste.

Performing our jazz dance was pure joy, but our baton routine made me nervous because of the baton toss. I was worried about not catching it, and with good reason. In Josie's basement we could throw the baton less than three feet before it would rebound off the ceiling, but on stage, we could hurl it miles up in the air before it would ever hit anything. Having that super energy that comes with stage fright, half the class used way too much force and over-tossed their batons during the show. There was no way they were going to catch those whirling dervishes. Batons were flying every which way, rolling around the stage, thumping to the ground, some even bouncing unpredictably on their rubber ends when they landed hard enough. The audience members should have been advised to wear helmets in case one came spiraling in their direction. Hardly a moment went by when there wasn't a frantic girl weaving through the other twirlers trying to capture her runaway baton and return to her position. If your baton traveled all the way off stage, you could pretty much guarantee that the number would be over by the time you retrieved it. I just prayed I'd make it through the song without my baton going AWOL.

I was one of the few who survived the majorette march without incident, but I didn't fare so well with the tap. There I was, front and center, confidently clogging and rope jumping, the audience in the palm of my hand, when La-La Land Lilly took off from the back row and headed my way. I had no idea what was about to hit me. All of a sudden, her rope whacked mine and sent it flying out of my hands and across the stage. I scrambled to recover it, carefully dodging the revolving ropes around me. The sparkle left my eyes and anger set in. I was mad. I was mortified. Lilly was lucky I didn't use my rope to strangle her.

In addition to being humiliated on stage for the first time, I also had my first taste of personal stardom. Our ballet class, clad in green gypsy dresses trimmed in red sequins and white ribbon, performed the Tarantella. Being the most flexible, I got to stand center stage and hold my leg up over my head with one hand and shake my tambourine with my other hand, while jumping around in a circle. I was the hit of the recital. It was a very heady experience.

I wasn't the only one who stole the show, however. My stiffest competition came from the three-year-olds. The baby ballet class sang "I Am a Coffee Pot," which went something like this: "I am a coffee pot. I get oh so HOT! When you fill me up, have another CUP!" Their arms served as handles and spouts, and they pretended to percolate by jiggling their bodies, wobbling their heads, and smacking their lips. During the show Josie stood in the wings doing the choreography in case they forgot what they were supposed to do. Many did forget, and they were so mesmerized by the audience that it was hard to tell who was there to watch whom. The tots stood frozen in their tutus like deer in headlights until Josie, whispering loudly from the wings, broke their stupor and reminded them to point their toes once or twice and tiptoe around in a circle with their arms overhead. Most of the time, they were either spellbound by the audience or craning their necks to see Josie on the sidelines.

The tiny tap class, irresistible in their yellow-and-black striped bee attire, performed "Be My Little Baby Bumble Bee." They flapped their wings, buzzed, did a few heel steps and maybe even a shuffle or two. A couple of bees, in complete control, led the number like little troopers and shouted the lyrics loudly enough to make up for all the petrified insects. Their parents loved them no matter what they did or didn't do. The kids could have stood on stage in their darling costumes and simply farted, which was about the only thing some kids actually did, and the parents would have been elated.

Josie and her children did a family number in the show à la the Osmonds or the Jackson Five, but it took some coaxing to get all four kids on stage. The music started, and they were still waiting for the two-year-old to join the bunch. Josie rolled her eyes and shouted, "Elliot, get over here!" Someone finally pushed him on stage. The number was a real crowd pleaser.

The recital ended with Josie playing the accordion and half singing, half speaking her traditional closing song: "This is the end of our show. That's all the dancing tonight. This is the end of our show. It's been a delight." The production was quite amateur, but I didn't know any better and was having a ball being on stage with my friends. After the performance, I was swarmed by people complimenting me on my trick in the Tarantella. My adoring parents brought bouquets of flowers, and I felt like an absolute star.

****

Dancing with Josie got me off to a great start, but two musicals during that first year really rocked my world and sent me flying into theatrical heaven. The first was a high school production of *Godspell*. The inspiring songs and dances captivated me. I'd never seen or felt anything like them. The second was the movie *Jesus Christ Superstar*. I was haunted by the music and overwhelmed by the emotions stirring within me. The songs seemed to touch the depths of my soul. Perhaps entertainment was worth more than just a laugh with my friends.

Superstar so moved me that, at the ripe old age of nine, I mounted a full-scale production of the musical. I easily recruited the neighborhood girls to be cast members, but the boys were more of a challenge. I tried to coerce a few of my friends' little brothers by bribing them with cookies, which always worked when we needed a groom to play "Wedding," but even the party I promised after the performance wasn't incentive enough to get any boys to dance with us. The result was an all-girl cast for a show comprised of mostly men (Jesus and his Twelve Disciples, King Herod, Pontius Pilate, Judas). I really wanted to play Jesus but felt guilty giving myself the lead role, so I cast Frieda Snodgrass, who most looked the part and was willing to memorize all the songs and fake die on the cross at the end. Only Lynnette Bulman, who played Mary Magdalene, got to play a woman. The parents brought their own chairs and sat on our lawn to watch the production held on my front porch. I'm sure the adults were chuckling at us, but I took the show seriously. The cast party we threw at the end was almost as much fun as the show itself.

Entertaining the neighbors was a great start, but I longed for bigger opportunities so I formed the "Katherine Street Supremes" and took our show on the road. We made it as far as a talent show at a popular campground about an hour away. Sporting our old recital costumes, loads of bright pink blush, and powder-blue eye shadow, we boogied to Leo Sayer's "You Make Me Feel Like Dancin'." Afterwards, we met some other contestants in the ladies' room, and they fawned over us and told us how great we were. My fire was fueled. I was getting a rush from all the attention and adulation. I had been bitten by the showbiz bug and hungered for more.

****

By the time I was ten, Josie had taught me all she knew, and I yearned to learn more difficult moves. So I moved out of the basement and up a few steps to a real dance studio situated above ground and about five miles from my house. It was here where I met Hattie Dallas of Hattie Dallas's School of Dance.

You know those little local dance schools like "Miss Lulu's Dance Academy" or "Twinkle Toes Conservatory of Dance and Tumbling" in the middle of a strip mall between a pizza place and a dry cleaners? Those are what we in the "Biz" refer to as "Dolly Dinkle" studios. My image of the fictitious Dolly has always been modeled after Hattie Dallas: She is a dance mistress who has looked fifty for the last thirty years and has a fabulous body, perpetual tan, penciled eyebrows, and thick, Egyptian-like black eyeliner. She bats her false eyelashes and smiles too widely. Like Josie, she plays the accordion.

Hattie had a mystique about her that fed my childhood imagination. I was certain she hadn't revealed all the secrets of her past. Was she once a famous gypsy dancer traveling the world and performing in exotic places? Did some romantic liaison ultimately lead her to the Midwestern suburbs and the demise of her dance career? I sensed that she'd lived a life of adventure, and I wanted to live it, too. I could only fantasize about what breathtaking performances she'd given as I was too much in awe to ask for her resume. She was glamour personified. On the inside cover of the recital program book, Hattie was always pictured engulfed in a luxurious fur coat or swathed in a feather boa. To me, she was as alluring as any movie star.

The happenings at Hattie's were equally captivating. It would be perfectly normal, for instance, to find a girl in a red, white, and blue sequined leotard performing back walkovers in pointe shoes while twirling a baton affixed with lit sparklers. In addition to the traditional forms of dance—tap, jazz, ballet, and pointe (or "toe," as Hattie would say)—such classes as tumbling, cheerleading, Hawaiian, Tahitian, baton twirling, and clogging were also offered. Hattie's was a one-stop shop for entertainment, and I was enthralled by it all.

Referring to a show (or performer) as being "Dolly Dinkle" generally means the show (or performer) is amateur in nature and borderline corny. "She's so Dolly Dinkle!" for example, would probably be stated with an air of snotty superiority and eye rolling by a more refined professional. Technically, the Dallas productions (and performers) were amateur, but they were packed with pizzazz and had great audience appeal. Hattie loved to use all kinds of tricks in her recitals. If you could do running back walkovers, aerials (no-handed cartwheels), handsprings, or standing back tucks (somersaults in the air), if you could walk on your hands, wrap your legs around your neck like a pretzel, do the Russian splits suspended in the air by two burly guys, or perform any other form of bodily contortion, she would use it in the show every year without fail. The Dallas gals were known to utilize strobe lights, glow-in-the-dark costumes, and Tahitian dancers juggling flaming coconut shells. Anything went if it brought the house down.

Hattie Dallas's School of Dance had aspirations well beyond your quintessential Dolly Dinkle school, and the whole Dallas family was involved in this pursuit. Hattie had a beautiful, twenty-year-old daughter, Skye, who shared the teaching responsibilities with her mother and was my main teacher. She had lovely long brown hair and wore big diamond studs in her ears. Her voice was deep and permanently hoarse from shouting over the music all those years, but it sounded Marilyn Monroe-sexy on her. She and Hattie vacationed in Florida every Christmas, which helped maintain their gorgeous golden skin color (a highly coveted look back then). Skye was careful to get a perfectly even tan (including the hard-to-reach-spots like under her arms, which she tanned by lying on her back with her arms over her head), and her sun-kissed appearance made her all the more enchanting. Hattie also had a lanky teenage son who taught gymnastics classes but favored magic and was pictured in the recital program book in his goofy magician's outfit. Even Hattie's mother, who was no spring chicken, played her part by running the busy office and answering scores of inquiries.

In addition to the Dallas family, Hattie employed a small group of girls fresh out of high school to teach the classes she and Skye eschewed. These second tier teachers were young and green, but they all had tiaras and sashes and titles like "Teen Miss Southeast Main Street Deli." To me they were extremely beautiful and talented. One had a strong southern accent and was always popping her gum, a skill I desperately but unsuccessfully tried to master in order to be like her.

The school itself was nothing fancy but, oh, the tales it had to tell and the dreams it harbored within its walls! You entered the front door into a lobby, which led to one large studio and two small studios separated by a pull-out accordion partition. The lobby was festooned with trophies and newspaper clippings of Dallas students winning awards, evidence of the competitive atmosphere. "Teen Miss Tap Dancing Terror" was succeeded by "Tiny Miss Over-the-Top" who was shoved aside by "Little Miss Syrupy Sweet" all of whom lugged back trophies (some larger than they were) and gleefully displayed them at the studio for all to see. My first time entering this place, I could only imagine how glorious it must feel to have your picture on the wall of fame.

Being cute, tall, and naturally thin with long legs, I looked the part of a dancer, and the Dallas duo saw potential. (It didn't hurt that I was disciplined, polite, and well-behaved to boot.) They shoved me into ballet quicker than you can say "plie," and I started to get serious about dancing. I dove head first into rigid Cecchetti ballet training, taking two levels simultaneously. I had some catching up to do if I wanted to join the other good dancers my age who had started classes when they were barely out of diapers.

In order to move from one level to the next, I had to pass an exam in which I executed specific ballet exercises for a panel of somber ballet experts. The exams were achingly tense and deafeningly quiet. It was a stressful and solemn setting, not for the weak at heart. I had to be perfectly dressed in the required leotard, pink tights, and pink ballet slippers, my hair in a neat bun. I had to study my French terminology and know the moves on my syllabus down to the last minute detail including head and finger placement. The process was rigorous, torturous, and perfect practice for my professional life to come. I couldn't have strayed any farther from the happy-go-lucky atmosphere at Josie's Bargain Basement.

The training was undeniably tough, but something incredible happened when things finally came together, and I was properly aligned with every body part in the right place at the right time. I could balance, turn, leap, glide, jump, and soar through the air. The transformation was magical: "And unto this day, in the city of Deerfield, a dancer was born…"

By the time I was eleven, my identity as a dancer was solid, and although I continued taking jazz and tap classes, which were always a lot more lighthearted and fun than the ballet, I really considered myself a ballerina. I was ecstatic when Skye allowed me to start taking pointe, but the day I was fitted for toe shoes marked the beginning of the end of ever hoping to have presentable feet. The satiny pink slippers had ribbons that laced around my ankles and a wooden box into which I stuffed my lamb's wool-wrapped toes. The box allowed me to stand on the very tips of my tootsies. Bubble wrap would have been a lot more helpful than that meager lamb's wool. I held back the tears in class as my feet would bleed and my toenails would fall off from being bruised so badly. Soon all my toes were as callused and bent out of shape as a crusty old lady's. Oh, the agony of the feet! It's a wonder that Child Safety Services doesn't deem dancing on pointe child abuse and arrest all the ballet teachers of the world. In spite of the excessive pain, I was dancing on pointe just like the beautiful, diminutive ballerina who twirled on tiptoe when I opened the lid of my musical jewelry box.

Soon I was dancing with the favorites, the "cool" girls, and they fascinated me. They were excellent dancers and gymnasts, and some even did solos in the show. They took every class offered including

Hawaiian and Tahitian dance, which made them even cooler. They always sported the latest, trendiest, prettiest leotards and a matching ribbon or flower in their hair. They were generally good students, cheerleaders, piano players, athletes. They did it all. They would rush into the studio, McDonald's bags in hand, and stuff french fries into their Big Macs before cramming the whole concoctions into their mouths and heading off to class. The cool girls knew survival tricks I didn't know, like how to pee without taking off your dance clothes: pull leotard crotch over to the side, yank down the top of your tights, and carefully go. They were so popular, self-confident, and downright amazing, I was too shy to even try to infiltrate their clique of coolness.

****

My life revolved around the almost daily classes, but the recital fed my soul and sent my spirit skyrocketing. I could hardly wait for spring to roll around, for the end of winter signaled the beginning of performance preparations, the most thrilling of which was the distribution of costumes. I had high hopes for my jazz outfit, as my class was dancing to a hit song, "Pinball Wizard," performed by one of the greatest rock bands of all time: The Who. I held my breath as Skye tore open the precious parcel holding the much-anticipated wardrobe. My balloon deflated as she handed me a plastic bag containing a sleeveless turquoise-blue leotard, a shiny silver waistband, and matching arm and leg bands embellished in metallic fringe. That was it? A glorified leotard with tinfoil? I had created better costumes using Mom's sewing scraps and a stapler.

But it got worse. There at the bottom of the bag was the headpiece. It was a turquoise-blue, ski-mask-style hat with a silver foil fountain spewing out of the top like a whale spouting water. When I slipped it on, my entire head was covered, like a nun with a bad habit. I think we were supposed to resemble pinballs bouncing about, but I felt more like a pinhead.

Once the costumes were doled out, a professional photographer set up shop at the studio, and you could pay to have your picture taken. For an additional fee, you could have your photo included in the program book. The cool girls always had their pictures in the book.

The Dallas ladies also sold advertising space above, below, and beside the snapshots of their dolled-up performers. Your image might end up next to an ad for Angelo's Pump and Pizza, or the Cutting Edge Hair Salon, or the Legal Offices of Steele, Conn, and Lye. I felt sorry for the girls who found themselves smiling radiantly under the Paul Berrer Funeral Home. The juxtaposition of dancing cuties and a funeral parlor promo seemed inappropriate, but it certainly made death look like something to celebrate.

Even though I wasn't jumping up and down about my costume, I did get my picture taken, sans head cover, but only to stick in my own personal photo album. I didn't feel worthy of joining the beauties in the book, or think the half-page spread was worth the financial investment, so I passed on Mom's offer to pay for the spot. Still, I was a bit envious of the girls, enveloped in lace and sequins and ruffles, whose images graced the pages of the prestigious publication along with some sentimentality submitted by their adoring parents. "You're our little star! Always stay as Sweet as you are! Love always, Grammy, Gramps and Little Brother Johnnie." Hattie wrote testimonials for some of her favorites, and they were full of equally gushy prose. You knew you had made it to the top if you had a statement written by the hand of Hattie.

When the glossy booklets returned from the printer, I devoured mine like I was reading *People* magazine hot off the press. I scrutinized every word, name, face, and figure. Where did I fit in among all these beautiful, talented girls?

One student, Myrtle Hightop, was a tough act to follow. The text next to her picture claimed, "Myrtle has studied dance for 13 years. She does Ballet, Jazz, Hawaiian, Tap, and Tahitian. She also twirls baton, two batons, flags, hoop, 20 knives, and fire baton. She has 1,500 trophies, 3,000 medals, and 150 beauty titles, and recently passed her Grade III Cecchetti Ballet Exam." Wow! I was impressed by her bravery. (How many kids are fearless enough to twiddle burning sticks and razor sharp cutlery?) But her bulging collection of prizes seemed a bit far-fetched. I did the math: Fifteen-year-old Myrtle would have to have won an average of 100 trophies, 200 medals, and 10 beauty titles per year since birth. Her story didn't seem to add up, but to me the program book was the gospel; therefore, it must be true.

The recital was a three-hour marathon of semi-organized chaos, once again held in June at a high school auditorium. Dress rehearsal was scheduled for the night before the show, and my favorite part of the evening was watching the other numbers. I marveled at the precocious six-year-old soloist, a Shirley Temple look-alike, who appeared to have been swallowed by a doily, as she tapped and warbled to "Sweet Georgia Brown." I snickered at the eldest Waldorf sister, who made funny faces when she danced, mouthing "Ooooh!" and "Ahhh!" like she was judging her own performance.

One of the most memorable acts was the jazz dance by two of the unnaturally pliable cool girls in which one slowly and painstakingly bent over backwards to pick up a handkerchief off the floor with her teeth while the other did a back bend, grabbed her own ankles, and rolled around the stage like a human wheel. Their duet wasn't complete without the crowd-pleasing back handsprings and back tucks. I, too, never tired of watching them defy gravity.

The tumbling classes were the most boring, even duller than the three-year-olds who were at least funny if someone cried or wet her costume. The tumblers dressed in plain-Jane unitards and then, to music, lined up to do somersaults, straddle rolls, cartwheels, and round-offs across a row of mats. The littlest ones had to have their bottoms pushed to complete their forward rolls. The most talented kids went last and attempted to do handsprings but often ended up landing smack on their behinds, or flying out of control into the wings where the next class was waiting to go on. Sometimes at the end of this dismal display, the whole class would form a human pyramid for its bland finale.

The highlight of the show was Skye's jazz solo. As the lights dimmed, she appeared, a vision in white. Her plush halter-topped, bell-bottomed pantsuit was studded with rhinestones and perfectly complemented her sparkling, pearly-white smile. She kicked to her ear and leapt like a deer. With a magnificent face and physique and dance skills to match, Skye didn't need a gimmick to keep the attention of the audience for the entire three-and-a-half-minute song. She was stunning and captivating all on her own.

For the most part, the Dallas crew was busy dealing with the technical aspects of the show, like sound and lighting, so the army of overly made-up, restless children was corralled and shouted orders to by a bevy of stage mothers. During the actual performance, the menagerie was contained in the band room until it was time to perform. The kids who were in only one dance and waited, in costume, staring at trombones and tubas for several hours, were nearly out of their minds with boredom or stage fright by the time they saw the audience.

Many of us were in multiple dances, and a select group of kids had to change costumes so fast the stress could have given a five-year-old gray hair. Several minutes into the show, the door to the "dressing room" flung open and a flurry of crazed volunteer moms flew in dragging girls by the hand and yanking off their costumes en route. The children stood gasping for air as they were manipulated like puppets: their next outfits were thrown on, shoes were changed, hats were pinned, and hair was fixed. "Go! Go! Go!" screeched the dressers in panicked voices as they pushed the performers back on stage without a second to spare.

The music wasn't audible in our crowded holding spot; consequently, we had no way to ascertain which number was currently on. We were completely reliant upon the helpers to retrieve us when it was our turn to perform. After sitting for what seemed like an eternity, a frantic adult came bursting in and yelled, "Military March, you're on!" and my classmates and I cautiously ran out the door, our tap shoes sliding across the slippery linoleum floor. We were herded through hallways and hushed as we entered the dark, backstage area.

Waiting in the wings, I caught a glimpse of the girls smiling on stage. In a few minutes, I would leave the safety of the sidelines and step into the sacred zone of entertainment. My heart pounded; my body buzzed with nervous energy. Excited to finally take my place in front of the crowd, I was also terrified of making a mistake.

But once I hit the stage, adrenaline rushed through my veins. Wearing makeup and costumes and dancing for applause was like nothing I'd ever experienced. I belonged in that theatre. It felt right. Nothing short of being in love would ever make my heart race like it did when I performed.

All year long, we rehearsed and prepared for that night, that one chance to get it right and win the approval of the audience. Our entrance was spectacular: three perfect military time steps, turn, and lunge. I couldn't have been happier. At least I was delighted until we formed two straight lines, one of which queued up directly behind me. Where my head was when I started to change formations eight counts before the rest of the class I don't know, but it certainly wasn't focused on the show at the Southeast High School Auditorium. I flapped around toward the back curtain, but no one was following me. Then the blunder registered. Oh, God! What have I done? My face flushed and my tear ducts swelled. With a forced smile, I finished the number, devastated. After the show, I could see the look of empathy on my mother's face. I cried and cried. But my gaffe didn't stop me from wanting to keep on dancing.

****

When I was thirteen, Skye realized her dream of creating a serious ballet company in residence, the New York City Ballet of the Detroit suburbs, so to speak, which she christened the "Southeast Ballet Theatre." No doubt she intentionally and strategically spelled theatre with an "re" instead of an "er," thereby lending an air of foreign superiority to the title and making it instantly known that this was a major dance force with which to be reckoned. This fledgling troupe was intended to be as rigorous and intense as a real professional ballet company. That other Dolly Dinkle tap and jazz fluff paid the bills at the Dallas School of Dance, but the Southeast Ballet Theatre was now Skye's true passion and artistic mission.

Company placement was to be determined by audition. In order to avoid scaring away dancers from other schools, the evaluation was held offsite in a public recreational center. Having never auditioned before, I was plagued with anxiety. But I desperately wanted to be in that company.

On the big day, I donned my pink tights and my black, sleeveless leotard. I twisted my ponytail into a tidy bun secured with an extensive selection of hairpins and ensnared in a light-brown, cafeteria-style hair net, to prevent any rebel strands from escaping. My hair was tugged back so tightly I appeared as slant-eyed as a woman with a Hollywood face lift. For the final touch, I shellacked my head with a can of Aquanet, the cheapest and most powerful, impenetrable hair spray known to womankind. Aquanet was the secret weapon of ballerinas and old ladies alike. With their coifs doused in the mixture, grannies could walk two miles to church in a windstorm and still arrive looking as if they'd just left the beauty salon. Ballerinas could spin like a tornado; their hair remained unshaken and as perfect as when they'd entered the room. I discovered, in my overzealous application of the magic potion, that one too many sprays of Aquanet turned a hairdo into a helmet.

Satisfied that my hair wasn't going anywhere, I headed over to the Recreational Center. The place was drab, dreary, and deserted. I was about an hour early, so I decided to use the extra time to warm up. Stretching turned out to be a redundant gesture, however, as my nervousness made my muscles as loose and limp as a strand of cooked spaghetti. The other dance hopefuls started straggling in, and soon the entire studio reeked of Aquanet. (A whiff of the miracle solution transports me right back to my childhood dance days.) As the bewitching hour neared, I finally pulled out my pointe shoes, which I hadn't wanted strangling my toes any longer than was necessary. In my jittery state, I tried several times before tying the laces properly. After adjusting the seams on my tights to ensure that they were running straight up the backs of my legs, I was ready. There was no turning back now.

The audition was run as if we were complete strangers to Skye, even though every one of the ballerinas trying out was from the Dallas School. Skye referred to us not by name but by the specific number each of us had been given to pin onto our leotards. The atmosphere throughout the evaluation was somber, quiet, and tense; the minutes ticked by like I was waiting for water to boil. But throughout the experience I controlled my nerves enough to concentrate and pick up the ballet combinations. What a pleasant relief when the afternoon was finally over.

A few days later, a formal acceptance notice arrived in the mail: "CONGRATULATIONS! You have been selected to be a member of the SOUTHEAST BALLET THEATRE, as a Major Dancer. As you know, it is a new company, and with your help we plan on making it the finest company in the Mid-West." Not only had I been accepted into the "SBT," but I had also been selected for the Major Company, while the "minor" dancers were relegated to the Apprentice Company. Lest anyone forget their status, each subdivision had its own required uniform: The Major Dancers donned royal blue leotards while the Apprentices wore pale blue. Naturally, pink tights, pointe shoes, and a waistband made of quarter-inch elastic (used as an indicator of hip misalignment) were mandatory for everyone. Dressed accordingly, we rehearsed each and every Wednesday night for three hours. The attendance policy was strict: A measly two absences were allowed per year.

I arrived promptly, properly dressed, and a bit apprehensive for the initial meeting of the Southeast Ballet Theatre, for the first order of business was the dreaded "weigh-in." The ballerinas lined up like cattle being sized for market value, except in this case, bigger was not better. Skye stood, clipboard in hand, recording the official pounds and ounces of each dancer, measuring their worth by weight, or lack thereof. My five-foot-seven-inch frame housed a ninety-four-pound weakling. Even though I was skinny and passed inspection, standing on that scale to have my tonnage assessed was nerve-wracking, embarrassing, and felt like an invasion of my privacy.

With the amplitude of each dancer duly noted, we began work on our first annual production of the world's most pervasive ballet, that Christmas-time favorite with a title that makes every man shiver: The Nutcracker. I was familiar with the ballet, as my mother once took me to downtown Detroit to see a professional rendition. I didn't understand why the little girl, Clara, would want an ugly, nut-crushing soldier toy for Christmas instead of a pretty baby doll, but few ballet stories did make sense to me. I relied heavily on the written explanation in the program book.

Skye cast me in the "Waltz of the Flowers," the grand, climactic number performed by the "corps de ballet" (a.k.a. the "ensemble"). In the dance, we did a lot of chasing each other around in circles. The cascade of floral tulle was quite lovely to watch, but the stampede of wooden toe shoes resulted in unwanted knocking sounds masking Tchaikovsky's famous score. Silencing our steps was a skill in and of itself.

I longingly watched as other dancers were chosen for the passionate Spanish dance, the strenuous, gymnastic, Russian dance, and the exotic Arabian dance where supple girls bent their bodies in ways nature never intended. My special role was one of six "flutes" in the Danse des Mirlitons. It didn't have the spice, sultriness, or shock value of the other dances, but I loved the section where we crossed arms, held hands, and piqued as a synchronized unit. As is the prerogative of the artistic director, Skye gave herself the sweetest part of all, the Sugar Plum Fairy. During rehearsal one night, a journalist from the *Suburban Press and Guide* took photos; of all the fascinating performers, only two other flutes and I were immortalized in the newspaper.

Before long, I moved up in the ranks, rising to the top like cream, eventually even replacing Skye as the most famous of all fairies. In addition to taking over her Sugar Plum role, I played Princess Aurora (Sleeping Beauty) in *Sleeping Beauty*, pricking my finger on the spindle of the spinning wheel and falling dramatically to the floor. I played dead for so long before Prince Charming awoke me with a kiss that my leg actually did go to sleep, and I was well into my solo before the feeling in my appendage returned.

There were plenty of talented girls at the studio to play the female characters in our ballets, but it was such a struggle to find qualified dancers for the lead male roles that sometimes, at great expense, Skye even shipped in a professional. With such a dire shortage of testosterone around the place, the Dallas women were always on the lookout for unsuspecting guys they could lure in and snatch up for partners. Dads, brothers, the mailman, or any able-bodied male, for that matter, didn't dare set foot in the door of the studio, or the next thing they knew they were on stage in tights and a dance belt (the equivalent of a jock strap) bench pressing a teen ballerina. Watching a grown man attempt to do ballet wasn't half as shocking as seeing him wear tights. I never did get used to that; it was impossible not to stare at that bulge. It takes a secure fellow to tiptoe around on stage for an audience with his rear end and private parts shrink-wrapped for all to see.

That was the terrible fate of Roger, a poor, unwitting, thirty-something, long-distance runner, who made the mistake of joining our ballet class to improve his flexibility and, much to his wife's dismay, ended up as the Fairy King Oberon in our production of *A Midsummer Night's Dream*. Luckily, with his taut and toned physique, he looked about as good in tights as could be expected of any man.

Playing Queen Titania, I was Roger's partner in the ballet, and although he couldn't dance to save his soul, he was tall, muscular, strong, and could grab me by the waist and lift me over his head on cue. He held me with a death grip; my back had the bruises of his fingerprints to prove it, but at least he didn't let me fall. As King Oberon, Roger had to do some of that ballet-pantomime-acting in the show. I never did figure out what he was communicating, but I think he was supposed to be mad, because he shook his fist a lot. We attended the same church, and, when I saw him there, I blushed under the eyes of God, embarrassed that I had a pretty good idea what his family jewels looked like, having seen him in tights.

Roger also danced with Belinda, another one of our prima ballerinas, and was partnering her on stage the day it happened. No one could stop talking about it. There she was, spinning in circles, her back to his stomach, legs wrapped around his waist, arms high in the air and back arched like a hood ornament, when her breasts just plopped right out of her costume. Skye laughed hysterically. Belinda seemed to take it all in stride, but I knew if that ever happened to me I would keel over and die. Perhaps the cortisone shots she received to assuage her aching feet had numbed her feelings of modesty as well.

Like Belinda and the rest of the Dallas elite, I practically lived at the studio, taking classes four nights a week and attempting to teach tap to rambunctious toddlers on Saturdays. Dance was now my life. It gave me a place in the world. To me, the human race could be separated into two categories: dancers and normal people. Once I dubbed myself a dancer, I never wanted to be normal again.

****

The Dallas School of Dance closed its doors during the summer, so, in order to get our dance fix, a couple classmates and I attended a two-week Cecchetti ballet conference held at Michigan State University. We lived in dorms and took ballet classes all day long except for the one allotted jazz class. Jazz dance was the dessert at the end of a healthy meal of ballet. We knew it wasn't really good for us but it was a special treat after a hard day of "real" dancing.

The ballet classes were stressful and required full concentration at all times. Unlike at Hattie's, where we repeated the exact same exercises all year and could perform them in our sleep, at the conference, we were taught new and different combinations for every class, so we had to focus, pick up, and execute the steps with lightning speed. Some teachers would demonstrate the choreography using their hands as feet. Others would just tell you the moves in French without demonstrating at all: "Jeté, temps levé, jeté, temps levé, glissade, brisé, assemblé, changement!" We were separated into small groups to perform the combination for the rest of the class. You couldn't let your attention wane for a second or you'd be in the center of the room, fumbling about, looking like a numbskull in front of all the others.

The guest teachers patrolled the rooms, hunting for sickled feet, poor posture, and other violations. I got busted. "You must SEW the elastic bands to your ballet slippers. Never PIN them," scolded ballet mistress Madame Martinez. Petrified and ashamed, I completed the lesson and then ran in search of needle and thread.

My ballet classes made me so uptight I could no longer absorb the combinations and was paralyzed with fear of making a mistake. Something had to be done to put me out of my misery, or I'd never last the full two weeks. Reminding myself why I started dancing in the first place, I decided to lighten up, have fun, not worry, and try to enjoy the experience. My method worked, and soon I was dancing with more joy than fear.

Scholarship auditions to attend the next workshop were held; to placate Skye, I reluctantly entered for my ability level. Even though I hated the idea of competing and dreaded being judged on my dancing, I smiled and made the best of the situation.

The conference culminated in the Awards Ceremony and Performance during which the winning contestants were announced. Skye and Hattie attended the event, which was held in a large auditorium at the university, and we all sat together awaiting the verdict. As my category was called, my heart pounded, and my legs turned to jelly. I didn't expect to win, but, confident I had done a good job at the audition, I allowed for the possibility. "And the first runner-up is … Kristi Davis!" I could hardly believe my ears. Another ballerina was awarded the scholarship, but I didn't care, because I had won *something*. It was the first time my abilities had been acknowledged outside the Dallas School. Maybe I do have talent!

My prize was only a bouquet of flowers and prima ballerina Margot Fonteyn's autobiography, but I couldn't have been more proud. They noticed me! At our celebration dinner, I called home to tell my parents the good news, and it took a long time to convince my mother I was telling the truth.

The following fall, I took first place in a Dance Masters of Michigan competition, where we were judged not only on ballet but tap and jazz as well. Second place went to another Dallas student, Dorissa, a champion baton twirler who could spin like a top. She'd throw her baton miles up to the heavens, turn a dozen times in a second, like a blender on high speed, and catch that whirling stick without batting an eye. This girl could even maneuver her baton using only her elbows and lips!

My winning streak made me a star at the studio, but, still shy and insecure, I never felt like one. My change of status was apparent, as Dorissa and I were pictured for free in the Dallas recital program along with a caption listing our titles. In addition, Skye and Hattie requested a solo picture (also gratis) of their new celebrity. In my sequined, snow-white tutu, I posed on pointe in a beautiful attitude derriere. Hattie wrote the accompanying text, and I knew I had finally made it to the top of the Dallas School of Dance.

Having proven my competition potential, Skye and Hattie decided I should enter the Miss Suburbs Pageant. There wasn't much in this world they loved more than a beauty queen, and even I was mesmerized at the thought of garnering my own sparkling rhinestone tiara. After all, my lovely mother had been Homecoming Queen in high school, my winsome Aunt Wilma Jean had been the Iowa Beef Queen, and my darling Aunt Nancy had been crowned Iowa's Favorite Farmer's Daughter. Royal blood flowed through my veins! My dad quickly squelched the idea, however. "You're NOT wearing a bathing suit on stage?" His stern inquiry made it clear this was a rhetorical question. Ah well. I was never much interested in competing anyway, so I didn't press the issue. Ninny Boil, another girl from my class, entered, won, and had her picture (in gown, crown, sash, and with trophy) added to the collection of photos on the studio's Wall of Fame. The Dallas pair had now fostered royalty, and my measly Dance Masters triumph was a distant memory.

Unless you were being crowned something prestigious enough to get your picture in the paper along with a statement about hailing from Hattie's, the Dallas gals were not big on their students skipping class for non-dance-related activities. Missing for track meets, piano concerts, cheerleading, or anything that didn't resemble a coronation was frowned upon. So when in my junior year of high school, I landed my first lead role in a musical (Ado Annie in *Oklahoma*) and would have to forgo a few ballet company rehearsals, Skye adamantly said, "NO!" I was forced to choose between the Southeast Ballet Theatre and the Rogers and Hammerstein show about cowfolk.

Quitting the ballet company that meant so much to me was a horrifying prospect. I lived and breathed pointe shoes and tutus. But this was a LEAD ROLE IN A MUSICAL! How could I turn down the opportunity? Having already played the best fairies and other prima ballerina parts, I opted to stretch my wings and try singing and acting as well as dancing. This difficult decision did not go over well with Skye. Not at all. One thing led to another, and I realized I needed to leave the Dallas studio for good. Leaving my dance home and the teacher I had idolized for so long was heartbreaking, but it was now Oklahoma or bust.

Playing a main character in a musical was foreign territory for me. I'd waltzed around with the ensemble before, had the odd line here and there, even danced the dream ballet solo in *Carousel*, but this was real responsibility. I had pages of dialogue to memorize. I had to sing alone. Sure, I had been singing in choirs for years but not solo. And I knew nothing about acting. I begged my best friend's mom, a community theatre actress and director, for private coaching.

My character, Ado Annie, was a promiscuous, goofy, simple country girl who was always ready for a romp in the hay. This floozy sings about how she "just cain't say no" to men and ends up "in a terrible fix." The performances would have gone off without a hitch if it weren't for the not-keyed-in musical director. Perhaps his mind had wandered off to wondering why in God's name he'd relinquished his fantasy of being a famous jazz musician to teach insolent teenagers and where to numb his despondency with a stiff drink. I couldn't say for sure, but he was not paying attention and forgot to give me the starting note for my solo, which began a cappella. I waited. And waited. And waited for that critical, guiding tone. It never came. Finally I gave up hope of any musical help, and commenced breaking the awkward silence by singing. Regrettably, when the orchestra started playing, we were in different keys. Horror! Hot flash! Eventually, after some vocal floundering, I was able to sync up with the tune. I was beyond embarrassed but had to snap out of it quickly. That's part of the excitement of live theatre: Stuff is bound to go wrong, and you just can't get too keyed up about it for the show must go on.

The best part of the performance was curtain call. Lining up the length of the stage, the entire company held hands and took a bow together. The curtain lowered while the crowd was still applauding, and we all cheered. I held back tears. It felt so good! This was a team effort and a lot more fun than sitting in the corner alone after a dance recital, patting myself on the back for a job well done.

My senior year, I landed another choice part, Hedy La Rue in *How to Succeed in Business Without Really Trying*. My best friend was cast as Rose, the serious, female ingenue, and I played the sexy, dumb, funny sidekick who spoke in a squeaky voice and flitted about in high heels. Fearful of opening my mouth and releasing discordant notes in public again, I took a couple of voice lessons from a local voice teacher. Luckily, I only had one solo in the show, and it was corny so I could ham it up and hide my lack of training. I truly loved the musicals.

****

Although devastated about quitting Hattie's, I couldn't bear to stop dancing, so I moved to her rival studio, Priscilla Prescott's School of

Dance. You couldn't be more of a traitor than to leave Hattie's for Priscilla's, but Priscilla was the only other good teacher in town. I felt I had no choice. Still, the decision was difficult to make, as changing studios is like denouncing your citizenship to your native country. The instant you register for lessons somewhere, you swear an automatic allegiance to that place. You know not to become too friendly with a kid from another dance facility, and if one were to corner you at school, to reveal only your name, rank, and serial number. "They tortured me, and I told them about plies and shuffle-off-to-Buffalos! Dear God! I told them about Buffalos!" There was no telling the dance secrets you might spill if bullied, so it was best to just avoid dancers from other studios, if at all possible.

It was common knowledge that Hattie and Priscilla were arch enemies. The competition between them was so fierce, if the two somehow ended up in the same room they would surely pull each others' hair out in a down-and-dirty catfight. Back at Hattie's, Priscilla's name was spoken in hushed tones if someone dared ever speak it at all. When one of you-know-who's best students, Ninny Boil (yes, the same Ninny who won the Miss Suburbs Pageant), defected to Hattie's, the Dallas gals were more than happy to offer her asylum. Acquiring the competition's *crème de la crème* was a major coup, and there was much rejoicing. For her treason, Ninny was rewarded with the red carpet treatment and lead roles, but she could never show her face at her former studio again. So, as a deserter entering Priscilla's for the first time, I felt like I had to look over my shoulder to make sure the Dallas clan didn't have spies following me.

Surprisingly, Priscilla was not at all fearsome. She was classy, trustworthy, and not interested in having her students compete. She commanded respect, because she treated you respectfully. Her hair was perfectly coiffed, and her dancer's body was thin and toned. Someone said she had danced with the Royal Ballet in London. She could have been royalty herself as posh as she was. Her students were required to have two years of ballet before being allowed to take jazz, which annoyed some people but cut out the riffraff. The atmosphere at Priscilla's was like a library compared to the three-ring circus at Hattie's.

It was hard changing studios and starting over after all those years at Hattie's. I didn't know the girls at Priscilla's and was too shy to make many new friends. Accustomed to playing lead roles, I had to start back at the bottom and move up the ranks. On the up side, Priscilla was an extremely wonderful person, and she helped me improve my pirouettes, which had been troubling me for years. Still, I never really got into my groove there.

My momentum seemed to be fizzling out, making it all the more surprising when my mother received a phone call from out of the blue. "Mrs. Davis? This is Priscilla Prescott. I think Kristi has the potential to be a professional dancer, and I am willing to help her if she's interested." Mom and I were flattered and floored, knocked down and tickled pink. Nevertheless, I only considered this preposterous idea for a nanosecond. I truly didn't believe I was that good. Although obsessed with dance throughout my childhood, the thought of doing it for a living had never occurred to me. Dancing professionally seemed like a lark, not a viable vocation. I didn't know any professional dancers and hadn't the slightest notion of how to go about becoming one even if I were crazy enough to want to try. Hence, Priscilla's generous offer, while tremendously appreciated, was rebuffed.

Performing was my soul food and dance was my identity, but I was also an excellent student from an academic family. My parents were stable, scholarly types, and I always assumed I'd follow in their unfancy footsteps. I knew I'd become a college graduate as surely as I knew I'd grow up to be a woman. As valedictorian of my high school class, I was expected to do great things—to lead the people of this nation, earn a Nobel Prize, end world hunger, or discover a cure for cancer. At the very least, I was supposed to do something that would make my parents proud. Something as frivolous as dance, I reckoned, did not fill the bill.

So, with my passion for performing smoldering on the back burner, I ended up a stone's throw away from home at the University of Michigan where I schizophrenically flip-flopped from engineering to business school to finally settling on a degree in psychology for lack of a better option. Before long, however, I was itching to dance again, so I auditioned for and joined a student-run dance company called Impact Jazz Dance. Little did I know, this one ostensibly minor decision would cause me to meet a young woman who would jazz up my life tremendously and wildly impact my future dance career. Her name was Jenny.

On the surface it seemed that Jenny and I couldn't have been more different. She was an outspoken, lanky, 5'10", Bohemian, ultra-feminist, worldly, New York City native, who had apprenticed with the American Ballet Theatre in New York. I was a shy, curvaceous, naïve, Midwestern, Disney-esque, ex-cheerleader, sorority girl trained at a modest local dance school. It seemed we had little in common except our love of dance. She regarded me with slight disdain due to my affiliations with the Greek sorority system and my prior relationship with pom-poms, but I found her fascinating, though a tad intimidating.

As our time at Michigan came to a close, my friends and I ruminated about life after college and began preparing, like the other seniors, to get a job. What on earth was I going to do? Following the herd, I bought the proverbial interview suit: an expensive, conservative, gray wool blazer with knee-length matching skirt, high-collar ruffled blouse, and sensible black pumps. Feeling like a kid pretending to be a frumpy, middle-aged accountant, I attempted to play grown-up and get excited about finding employment, assuming responsibility, and buying a house some day.

I poured over the printout listing job interview opportunities offered by the myriad companies eager to take on Michigan grads. Do I want to be an actuarial? What the heck is an actuarial? How about a headhunter? A marketing assistant? In human resources? Sell insurance? Perhaps I should vie for one of the coveted corporate positions with Proctor and Gamble working to make neon-green dinosaur-shaped fruit roll-ups more profitable? Or apply to be a sales rep for Del Monte fighting over prominent grocery store shelf space for fruit juice and canned peaches? What can one do with a Bachelor's degree in psychology anyway?

The thought of choosing any of these careers gave me a splitting headache and put me into a gloomy funk. For the entire week following graduation, I cried. I loved my social life at school with my sorority sisters and the zany, outgoing, artistic, talented friends I'd met through Impact Jazz. My life had been full to the brim with activities, events, and parties. Every day offered a new and exciting adventure. What do I have to look forward to now? A boring, predictable existence where my sole purpose in life is to make money? Settling down with the sensible folk? My stimulating student lifestyle had come to a screeching halt. I was the proud owner of a top-rate education but had no idea what I was going to do with it.

To make matters worse, I pondered the imminent end of my performing days and distressed over whom I would be if no longer a dancer. I couldn't think of anything else that made me special, that separated me from the rest of the population, that gave me worth. Terrified of losing myself if I quit dancing, I spiraled into a deep, dark pit of despair. When Jenny asked, "Kristi, what are you going to do after graduation?" I stared blankly into space. "Move to New York to become a professional dancer with me," she commanded. Faced with seemingly dire career options, I actually considered her offer.

Jenny was abandoning her major—mathematics; she realized her true love was dance. Manhattan was her hometown, and she could always live with her parents if worse came to worse. What did she have to lose? More importantly, what did I have to lose? I hadn't the foggiest idea what would be in store for me if I flippantly threw away my stuffy business suit and college education for a sexy leotard and dance class. Was it wise to turn my back on the relatively safe, comfortable, practical world of nine-to-five and venture into the wild unknown of show business? Would I be heading blindly into a Bermuda Triangle of thespians, likely to mysteriously disappear with the other reckless showbiz wannabes, never to be seen on stage again? What should I do?

With a seemingly useless Bachelor's Degree in Psychology and no clue where my life was heading, I took a month-long, soul-searching backpacking trip through Europe. Discovering a world full of fascinating people, places, and experiences, I was impassioned, inspired, and couldn't wait to see what the next day would entail. I felt so alive and wanted that spirit of adventure to stick with me forever. When I returned home I had my answer: "God, I'm a dancer. A dancer dances!"

Final Scene: New York City, August 9, 2002

Priscilla was right: I *was* good enough to be a professional, I admitted to myself, as I shifted to a more comfortable position in my airplane seat. The clues had been there all along. I never did take Priscilla up on her offer, opting for college instead. But what if I had? How might my life have turned out differently? Regardless, I made it. Even though I didn't attend a prestigious conservatory of dance or some phenomenal university known for its musical theatre program. Even though I didn't apprentice with the American Ballet Theatre or study under the tutelage of a world-renowned instructor. On the contrary, the core of my dance schooling came from Dolly Dinkle studios, and it was pretty good training, as it turns out. After all, I managed to milk all my childhood dance lessons enough to create a pretty healthy career and recoup my parents' sizable investment.

The pilot's voice on the intercom jolted me back to the present. "Flight attendants, prepare for landing." Giving an imaginary salute to all my dance teachers, I opened my eyes just as the island of Manhattan was coming into view. New York City: the birthplace of my showbiz career and now, it appeared, the final resting place as well. I had come full circle, and this symbolic sense of completion was not lost on me.

After disembarking, I forged my way through the hustle and bustle of JFK and grabbed a cab to my dear old college friend Jenny's house in Astoria, Queens, where I'd be staying. "Hot enough for ya, today?" I said, trying to make cheerful small talk with the foreign cabbie. "That sun's been brutal all week," he replied shaking his head. I recalled the hot July day that had greeted me when I first came to New York fresh out of college.

The streets of Astoria were familiar, but I felt like an entirely different person than I did during my maiden voyage to Queens. It was hard to believe fifteen years had passed since my first professional dance gig in this most infamous of cities. So much has happened to New York, and so much has happened to me, I marveled, since that fateful summer in 1987 when I began my journey into show business.

Act 1, Scene 1

Taking a Bite Out of the Big Apple

It's a miracle that I ever set foot in New York to begin with. Growing up in suburban southeast Michigan, with parents farm-raised in Iowa, I wasn't exactly familiar with the Big City. I was so terrified of the place, in fact, that when my father traveled there once for a business trip, I truly feared for his life. When Dad boasted that he had gone to see *A Chorus Line* on Broadway, I couldn't believe he would risk leaving his hotel room any more than was absolutely necessary. I thanked God he returned home without having been mugged or worse. My family rarely even ventured to nearby Detroit, at the time dubbed "the murder capital of America," as my mother didn't want to put us in danger. Coming from risk-averse progenitors and a Waspy upbringing, New York City was sure to be a culture shock.

Consequently, I headed off to the Big Apple for a trial week to see if I really wanted to make the move. Like Frank Sinatra sang in the famous tune "New York, New York," I, too, figured, "If I can make it there, I'll make it anywhere." Jenny had generously invited me to stay with her in Astoria, Queens, wherever that was. Her old-fashioned apartment building with the squeaky stairs and interior dark wood features seemed so vintage New York. I was enthralled by her hippie, artsy, street-smart fashion and decorating style.

In addition to providing a couch for me to crash on, Jenny offered free consulting services as well. "The first thing we need to do is look in *Backstage* to find you an audition," she ordered, holding up that week's paper. *Backstage*, I learned, was the most indispensable periodical known to entertainers. This Granddaddy of weekly publications listed all kinds of auditions for singers, actors, dancers, and musicians. Even the Broadway auditions were listed there!

We scoured the pages and finally found what Jenny determined to be a suitable match: "Here's a tap dance show in Switzerland, and the audition is tomorrow. It's perfect," she exclaimed triumphantly. As a kid, I had taken tap lessons for about six years, but it had been just about that long since my last hoofing session. "I haven't tapped in forever, Jen. I don't even own tap shoes anymore," I argued. But Jenny was not about to take "no" for an answer. "Big deal. You can buy tap shoes and take a tap class before the audition to get a little practice in. Did you bring a headshot?" "You mean one of those close-up photos of your face like actors have? No. I don't have one," I responded,

Long Legs and Tall Tales

wondering if this crazy experiment was a waste of time. "We'll type up a resume for you. You can explain that you were just in town visiting and not planning to audition until you saw the notice. Make up some excuse. You'll be fine."

I wasn't so sure, but I was determined to do the audition anyway. For despite feeling extremely nervous and doubtful, I was exhilarated by the challenge and the remote possibility of getting the job. It was like my chance at winning the lottery, and I couldn't win if I didn't play the game. Jenny helped me construct my resume. Filling an entire eight-by-eleven-inch page was a challenge. We included every bit of dance training I'd had plus the college performances and high school musicals I'd done, hoping my amateur achievements would sound professional. Now what I really needed was some of Jenny's ovaries-to-the-wall personality to rub off on me so I could pull off this charade.

The next day, mustering up every ounce of courage I had, I rode the subway into Manhattan with Jenny for the big day. She went off to work, and I was left to fend for myself with nothing but a map and directions to Capezios, the world-famous dance supply store on Broadway and 51st Street, where I was supposed to buy a pair of tap shoes. Afterwards, if all went as planned, I would have just enough time to get to Steps, one of New York's most popular dance studios, on Broadway and 74th, to take a tap class before making my way down to Broadway Dance Center on 45th Street and 5th Avenue for the audition.

After getting my bearings, I began walking up Broadway. Just seeing the name on the street sign made me tingle with anticipation. BROADWAY! Soon I spotted Capezios on the second floor of the building ahead of me. Once inside, I was overwhelmed by all the colorful dance paraphernalia and the knowledge that the professional Broadway dancers buy their shoes and tights there. I was treading upon the very floor that my idols had walked before me. But there was little time to stand in awe and drool over all the magnificent dancewear. I was on a mission and time was of the essence. With the help of an experienced salesperson, I finally chose beige character shoes with two-inch heels and waited impatiently for the taps to be put on.

Purchase in hand, I quickly made my way to Steps. Being located on the third floor of the building, I had to cram into a creaky old elevator for the ride up. The heavy wrought-iron door opened, and I timidly stepped out. Immediately, my eyes became transfixed on the teachers' headshots papering the walls. It was a who's who of famous dancers. Anne Reinking's picture was there! I remembered her from that 1979 movie musical *All That Jazz*, which I absolutely adored. In the movie, Reinking did all this cool, sexy Fosse-style jazz dancing that I often tried to imitate. Already my day's quota of stimulation was nearly reached.

I found myself becoming intimidated by Steps with its famous teachers, throngs of exquisite students, and multiple studios running several types of dance classes simultaneously. It took extreme willpower to make myself stay, let alone walk to the front desk and pay my drop-in fee. There was no backing out now. I put on my spanking new tap shoes and bravely took the ninety-minute tap lesson, my only test drive before the real race. Although my performance wasn't my best ever, I made it to the finish line nonetheless. I just hoped that this brief warm-up session would be enough to dust the spider webs off my long-dormant feet.

Highly aware of the clock ticking down, my anxiety escalated as audition time drew near. I pried myself away from the relative safety of Steps and scurried south through the buzz of busy Broadway to Broadway Dance Center. My heartbeat quickened, and I felt infused with energy on my way to who-knows-what-might-happen? Now this was an adventure. The closer I got to Broadway Dance Center, the more my adrenaline kicked in. Time seemed to stand still with my heightened awareness of the momentousness of the occasion, as if every cell in my body knew this was the start of something life changing. Finding the place without a problem, I took a deep breath and walked in.

"If you're here for the audition, sign in please," instructed a toned dancer who must have been an assistant of sorts. Hand trembling, I signed my name on the paper, then looked for a spot to sit down. The lobby was already filled with dancers stretching and chatting with their friends. I scoped the competition. Skinny, beautiful, extremely flexible. What did I expect? A bunch of overweight ogres who couldn't touch their toes? And they all knew each other. What the heck was I doing here? I felt more nervous and insecure with each passing second. Squelching that negative voice in my head before its devilish derision derailed me, I invoked my inner cheerleader. "Get a hold of yourself, Kristi. You have nothing to lose. It's just for fun. The outcome doesn't matter. At least you're doing something exciting. You can do it."

After what seemed like an eternity, the moment finally arrived when we were called to audition. "As you hand in your headshot and resume, you will be given a number to pin onto your leotard, and then you may head into the studio," instructed the assistant. "I just flew into town and don't have my headshots finished yet, but here is my resume," I babbled nervously as I made my way to the front of the line. "That's fine," the assistant replied. Jenny was right. It worked. I was in!

There was no time to celebrate, I soon realized, as I watched the boldest dancers quickly claim the best spots in the front of the room leaving the rest of us to scramble for any leftover space within view of the choreographer. Once the room had filled to capacity, everyone automatically spread out and shuffled about so that they could see themselves in the mirror. Every woman for herself! By the time I figured out what was happening, I was lucky to secure a spot where I could barely catch a glimpse of my right arm in the mirror. Oh well. At least I had staked my territory. Now all I had to do was stay focused for the next few hours. I just hoped the tapping wasn't too far above my ability level, or I was going to look like a complete imbecile. "Who cares? You are never going to see these people again anyway," I consoled myself bringing out my imaginary pom-poms for one final, silent "Rah! Rah!"

The choreographer began teaching the dance combination: a smiley, cheesy, fairly easy tap number that suited my training perfectly. "I can do this! No problem," I realized, delighted and relieved. My confidence rose, and I laid on the charm. When the audition was over, I was on the high of highs. I was so proud of myself for going through with it and knew I had run my best race. It didn't matter whether I made the cut or not. Those other dancers who had frightened me so weren't that much better than I was after all.

Lo and behold, after a few days, I received the good news: I got the gig! Maybe I do have enough talent to be a dancer, I conceded. Who knew?

****

I returned to Detroit elated with my exceptional experience in the Big Apple. Plus, I was going to Switzerland to do a show! Life can change in the blink of an eye, however, and almost as quickly as I'd gotten the job, it was snatched away. "I'm sorry, but the show had to be cancelled due to work-visa problems," phoned the producer a couple weeks later. Although it was disappointing to drop my dreams of dancing among snow-capped mountains, chalets, cheese fondue, and Swiss chocolate, my immediate audition success had given me something far more valuable: the confidence to give it a go as a professional dancer. "Change of plans. I'm moving to New York, pronto," I informed Jenny, who was ecstatic.

"Come in August and we can do this month-long modern dance workshop with Jennifer Muller's company, The Works," she said enthusiastically. Not only had I never heard of Jennifer Muller, renowned artistic director of Jennifer Muller/The Works and former principal dancer with the Jose Limon Company, but I was only vaguely familiar with modern dance from the select performances I'd seen while in college. They blew my mind. The movements were bizarre, often ugly, and told a story or made some sort of social commentary. I often found myself thinking, "What on earth was that all about?" It wasn't the smiley, easily palatable entertainment I was used to. It seemed to be more of an art form and an acquired taste like Stilton cheese, which to some people really stinks. I found modern dance intriguing and refreshing.

Modern dance brought with it new names to learn: Martha Graham, Merce Cunningham, Paul Taylor, Alwin Nikolais, Murray Louis—famous modern choreographers. In spite of my lack of modern dance training, I was game to learn. Maybe the workshop was just the jumpstart I needed.

This time I vowed to arrive in New York more prepared, with headshots being my number one priority. My best friend from high school, an actress herself, turned me on to a photographer in Detroit to do the deed. I felt silly having my picture taken. Who did I think I was? "Big smile! Lotsa teeth! And tilt your head a little to the left. Eyes open wider. They look a bit sleepy. That's it!" the man coached. "Now let's try a few non-smiling ones. This would be a good time to change clothes if you brought another outfit." I jumped off the bar stool and made my way to the small dressing room. Presumably, the photographer was trying to get a few photos suitable for more serious actress roles. I had never thought of myself as a serious actress. Anything but. In my high school musical theatre experience, I had always been cast as the funny, dumb, pretty sidekick.

I took off my lime green silk blouse and replaced it with my pale pink sweater, wondering how to make a non-smiling face that wouldn't resemble a prison mug shot or my embarrassingly ugly driver's license.

"Am I supposed to make love to the camera? I can't do that!" I practiced facial expressions in the mirror: Serious. Pensive. Intense. Intriguing. Flirtatious. "Oh, God. I look ridiculous!" Finally giving up, I returned to the studio surrendering my photo fate to the expertise of the photographer.

The great thing about photo shoots is the oft-used strategy of taking a gazillion photos, so you are bound to get one that's usable. Despite my discomfort in front of the lens, I discovered a radiant smiling shot and, miracle of miracles, even a decent non-smiling one. "Hey, I look pretty good," I admitted with a slight flip of the hair and a taller stance. Then, per my actress friend's instructions, I mailed off my two favorite photos to ABC Printing in Missouri for duplication.

When those boxes arrived with five-hundred, 8"x10", black and white glossy photos of my face, I was star struck. I almost felt famous just because I existed, multiplied, in print. Still, that was a lot of pictures. Would I ever really use them all? I imagined them littering some garbage dump, seagulls leaving their droppings on my beaming smile and visions of fame. Future rubbish or not, it was thrilling to see my dreams begin to take shape. I had headshots!

Next issue: housing. An aspiring female singer who I knew from college also wanted to try New York City and agreed to be my roommate. My plans appeared to be falling into place perfectly. Until, that is, they fell out of place. The woman got cold feet and backed out at the last minute. I panicked. I couldn't afford to live alone, and Jenny already had a roommate. Would I be forced to abandon the plan and stay in Michigan? And do what? I had no plan B.

In the end, Jenny came through for me, once again. "Good news! I ran into Ashley at dance class. She and her family are going on an African safari, and you can stay in their apartment for the month of August." Not only was Ashley a college dance friend of ours from Impact Jazz Dance Company, but she was also a member of Kappa Alpha Theta, the high-class sorority envied for its beautiful, rich girls. I could only imagine how stylish her home might be. Hopefully, this apartment-sitting job would buy me enough time to find a roommate and a more permanent place to live. All signals now "GO," my parents and I loaded up their minivan with my meager belongings and headed east for New York City.

****

As suspected, Ashley's home—a two-bedroom apartment on the 16th floor of a posh, Upper East Side high rise—was gorgeous. There was even a doorman to welcome me at the building entrance. A doorman! Ashley's very thin, trendy, forty-something, divorced mom was an interior decorator, evidenced by the splendidly froufrou domicile. I was living in the lap of luxury, and all I had to do was water the plants, collect the mail, and feed the cat. What could be so bad about that?

The family had already left for Africa, so I was able to nose around at will. I marveled at the lifestyle so different from how I grew up. The kitchen appeared to be an afterthought and was about as big as a tiny, walk-in closet. On the walls hung framed menus collected from famous New York City restaurants. There was no place to sit in the kitchen and no dining room. Where did they eat? It appeared to be standing room only.

I guess that's why the kitchen was so small: They didn't cook. Oh, maybe they brewed an espresso, plopped a cocktail onion into a martini, or slathered cream cheese on a bagel. They didn't even own a regular coffee maker. All I could find was a silver metal, two-story Italian contraption that sat on the stove like a teapot, but I couldn't figure out how to use it. I assumed the family primarily ate their meals out or ordered in. Why cook when you have every restaurant and take-out delivery imaginable at your fingertips with a mere phone call? And really, New York socialites don't eat anyway; do they?

Down the hall was what I quickly determined to be Ashley's bedroom, which was where I was supposed to sleep. Her bookshelf was crammed with *Broadway Showbills*. "How lucky she is to be able to see any Broadway show she likes or pick from a smorgasbord of the world's best dance classes on a daily basis," I thought enviously. She was spoiled for culture. I sneaked a peek into her mother's bedroom, which was draped in sexy shades of lipstick red and pink. The closet was lined with designer shoes stuffed with cobblers' wooden inserts to keep them perfectly shaped. How glamorous her life was.

The living room furniture was so fancy-schmancy I was reluctant to sit on it for fear of doing damage and not being able to pay for repairs. In place of carpet, there was a rough, woven, jute floor covering of sorts that looked exotic but was scratchy as sandpaper. Everything screamed, "Look, but don't touch!" I decided it would be safest to just avoid the living room altogether. Outside on the mini-balcony sat the small window-box herb garden I was responsible for watering. Peering over the edge of the balustrade, I gasped, suddenly startled by the feel of a furry creature rubbing against my leg. "Midnight, you scared me!" I bellowed at the black cat, which smugly walked away having effectively introduced himself. Was that a smirk on his face?

Jenny phoned to welcome me and to tell me more good news: "Mirmdance needs more dancers, and I got you an audition." I was amazed and impressed by Jenny, who was already performing in two modern companies: Avodah, a company exploring Jewish themes; and Mirmdance, a fledgling troupe whose director was fresh out of NYU's Tisch School of the Arts. "Mirm," short for Miriam, the head of the company, was only a few years older than I was. I was excited and reluctant at the same time. "When is the audition?" "Tomorrow," Jenny replied. "Tomorrow? I don't think I'm ready to audition tomorrow," I stammered. Jenny, of course, would have none of it. I was going whether I wanted to or not.

When I went to bed that first night, I feared every psycho in New York knew I was there alone and defenseless–a perfect murder victim. I carefully double-checked to make sure the front door was locked. There was security at the entrance, but what if some serial killer scaled the building like Spiderman and came in through the balcony? I didn't want to become famous as a feature story on the evening news: "Gullible Midwestern Girl Slaughtered in Her Sleep."

I turned out the light and climbed into bed, trying to calm my nerves. Just as I was about to fall asleep, out of the darkness sprang the cat, which pounced directly on my head and scared me half to death. "Aaaaaa! Midnight, no!" After carefully prying his claws from my checks, I gently but firmly placed him on the floor, then laid back down and closed my eyes, heart still racing. Moments later, I was once again jolted awake by a facial cat attack. "Get off!" I shrieked, my mouth full of feline fur. After a third assault awoke me from the world's worst catnap, I locked him out of the room, feeling I had no other choice if I hoped to get any shut-eye before the big audition. The move proved pointless, however, because Midnight continually howled and scratched at the door. We had gotten off on the wrong foot or, well, paw.

The next morning, I dragged my groggy, pudgy, out-of-shape-after-a-month-of-gorging-myself-with-European-pastries body to the audition. I had never even tried modern dance before. Was I insane?

The audition was held at 33 East 18th Street on the seventh floor. My jaw dropped as I noticed the sign on the studio door: Nikolai Louis Dancespace. "Really? The famous modern choreographers Alwin Nikolai and Murray Louis?" In awe, I stepped into the sacred space of these cutting-edge artists.

Jenny was already there warming up, a comforting sight. But I was shocked when I recognized another familiar face: Adam—also a former Impact Jazz dancer. Adam was a gay male Snow White—a porcelain-skinned, black-haired Adonis. Having danced together only one year before he graduated and left for New York, we were more acquaintances than friends, but we exchanged polite greetings. I wasn't sure if he really remembered me from college or not. I was then introduced to Miriam, a sturdy, fair woman with tousled, super-short dark hair. "Let's begin with Lucy's Future," she instructed her company. The dancers groaned. I wondered why. "Kristi, just jump right in and follow along."

I was thrown into the middle of a scene showing a sexy siren surrounded by squid-like savages slinging their trailing tentacles. As members of the squid squad, we hurdled our bodies through space, threw ourselves to the floor, somersaulted, and groveled on our knees as we seduced the soloist in an oceanic orgy. This strenuous sea spree lasted for hours. My body ached, and I cringed at how ridiculous I looked trying to move like the other mollusks. As foolish as I felt flailing, failing, and even occasionally succeeding at synchronized squid gymnastics, the experience paled in comparison to what was about to come next.

"Everyone take your positions in line," ordered Miriam. "Kristi, go behind Adam and rub his butt." "Do what?" I said in disbelief. I wasn't hard of hearing, and she wasn't joking. She actually wanted me to caress the gluteus maximus of the male monster in front of me. Maximally mortified, I massaged away, trying to pretend I was a horny sea creature. Luckily, Adam was no stranger, but we hardly knew each other well enough to fondle each others' backsides. There aren't many job interviews where you are instructed to stroke someone's buttocks. (Or are there?)

I kept watching the clock, waiting for someone to tap me on the shoulder and release me from this tidal torture before I drowned. But no one did. When was this hellacious experience going to end? Unlike my first New York audition, this was an excruciating, bizarre company rehearsal into which I was blindly inserted. I felt like I had been thrown to the lions, or tossed overboard to the squids, in this case. We finally finished for the day, and Miriam announced the date and time of the next rehearsal.

By this time, I was so wet with sweat, limp, and out of breath, I looked like I had nearly gone to a watery grave. While gathering my belongings in my dance bag, I wondered to what extent I had embarrassed myself, and Jenny too. I was so out of shape, I had barely kept up with the others. Oh well. It was an experience. I had lived through it.

Jenny ran over to me. "Well, what did Mirm say? Are you in?" "Nothing. I don't know," I responded, my face red with overexertion. My mother taught me, "If you can't say something nice, don't say anything." So when Miriam didn't say a word to me, I accepted her reticence as a gesture of kindness, sparing me the scathing criticism I deserved after that harrowing performance. Jenny grabbed me by the hand. "Let's go find out." She dragged me over to Miriam and asked, "What about Kristi?" "Oh yeah, Kristi, you need to show up, too," Miriam replied casually.

I was dumbstruck. My second day living in New York, and I had already been accepted into a dance company. A modern one, at that. I phoned home to tell my parents the good news. Maybe Miriam was simply desperate for bodies to complete her choreography, or perhaps she took pity on me, or both, but I didn't care. I got the job!

****

It just so happened that the rehearsal studio Mirmdance rented was in the same building as the Jennifer Muller modern dance workshop Jenny and I were taking. So for the next four weeks, we danced with The Works from nine to five, and on our two-hour lunch break, instead of taking a much-needed load off our overworked feet, we ran upstairs to the Nikolais Louis Dancespace to rehearse with Mirmdance. It was exhausting, for sure, but exhilarating.

I began to fall into a comfortable routine. Every morning on the way to the subway, I'd stop at the Chinese fruit market for a giant bran muffin and a coffee in an "I ♥ NY" cup to go. Those fruit markets, Chinese because Chinese people run them, were one of my favorite amenities of New York. They had fresh produce, unbelievable salad bars, sushi, a small selection of groceries, gargantuan muffins, hot coffee, and an assortment of bulk Chinese junk food. There seemed to be one on nearly every block, and they were open twenty-four hours a day. I never felt completely alone in The City, because I always knew that, even in the middle of the night, I could find an Asian storekeeper awake and tending the market.

Next I'd patronize one of the most important establishments in my Upper East Side neighborhood: the H&H Bagel shop on 72nd and Second Avenue. H&H became my all-purpose meal stop, providing lunch and dinner. Their bagels were the best I'd ever tasted, with fluffy veggie cream cheese piled on as thick as the bagel itself. I could get two meals out of one overstuffed bagel by permitting myself to eat only half for lunch and saving the rest for dinner. Practically subsisting on bagels and cream cheese and bran muffins and coffee, I wasn't exactly ingesting the most nutritious diet, but at least it was cheap and tasty.

The day's meals purchased, I'd walk toward the subway, gazing up at the tall apartment buildings, amazed at how people grew trees and plants and gardens in any tiny space they could, even on rooftops. Permanent New York residents were aliens to me. Their world was so foreign and exotic. I'd read names on brass placards decorating the front gates of brownstones in disbelief that people truly called these their homes. Some even grew up here. I'd never even used the word "brownstone" before.

Neither had I much practice taking the subway, which offered its own little adventure. Apparently I needed to learn the correct way to buy subway tokens. This skill was taught to me by none other than Jenny who, after observing me fumbling about in my purse for change, thereby holding up the hurried queue of real New Yorkers, their annoyance escalating by the second, took it upon herself to correct my misdemeanor. "Kristi, you are fodder for muggers if you flounder about distracted like that. You have to be prepared, know the system, appear confident, look knowledgeable, have your money ready, and buy your tokens without pause." She showed me how to function like a smoothly oiled machine, thereby leaving little opportunity to be accosted.

Summers were sweltering, and some of the subways had no air conditioning. During morning rush hour, the stifling subways were crammed with sweaty business men and women in suits. On a typical day, as the doors were about to close, yet another New Yorker late for work would perform a kamikaze leap onto the train and squeeze into the already-packed sardine can forcing me to press my body so close to the guy next to me that I could feel the steam rising from his chest. It felt like I was involuntarily participating in one of those college pranks where all fifty-seven fraternity guys pile themselves into one phone booth, arms and legs wrapped around each other in a perverted game of Twister. The humid air hung thick with the odor of damp pressed-wool, cigarettes, cologne, and sweat.

New York City itself had its own special summer smell: a combination of subway grease, exhaust fumes, tar, sun-baked ketchup on cement, and dried urine. It reminded me of the rank aroma of my filthy jeans after I slept on train floors and park benches during my backpacking trip through Europe.

After successfully extricating myself from the subway, I'd stroll the final few blocks to the dance studio. I learned my way around Manhattan fairly easily once I realized that the avenues ran north and south and the streets ran east and west. I'd never walk more than a block in the wrong direction before being able to figure out where I was.

The Muller workshop was held at a lovely studio space called Peridance. At the entrance there was even a snack bar where you could buy yogurt, bananas, and bagels. The lobby was also where everyone hung out and stretched while waiting for class to begin. I never tired of watching all the svelte, toned, barefoot modern dancers warming up their feet and legs with their wooden foot-roller massagers and giant rubber bands.

One day, in one corner, a group of very thin but muscular men sat lacing up their pointe shoes. Is that Ballet Trockadero? It was. They were a famous men's ballet troupe, a transvestite-ish group of dancers who dressed as prima ballerinas in real tutus and pointe shoes and performed spoofs of the classical ballets like *Swan Lake*. They were incredibly skilled ballerinas. But where did they find pointe shoes big enough to fit those manly feet? And just how did they hide those manly groin bulges under their leotards? I was unable to take my eyes off them. I had seen them perform in Detroit and was absolutely overjoyed to be in the same room with these impressive, athletic, comedic performers.

The workshop was taught by members of The Works. The gorgeous girls, in their beautiful leotards, were so light and thin that they'd surely fly away like a feather if you blew on them. I wished I were thinner and had smaller breasts so I could go braless and wear lovely leos like they did, but I'd be Bouncing Betty B-cups unless I strapped myself down in a straitjacket. There simply wasn't room for boobs in the world of serious dance.

All the classes had live piano accompaniment, which was such a treat. My favorite musician was a cute, young, blond guy who sang the most mellifluous, soothing, nonsense syllables while playing. His voice and music were heavenly and inspirational, nothing like dancing to recorded music. It was like Brie versus the Cheez Whiz I was accustomed to. His magical melodies transported me into another realm of feeling and expression.

And yet, even with the inspiring accompaniment, I sometimes felt like the worst person in class, given my lack of modern dance training. The dance combinations were physically and mentally challenging and were taught at lightning speed. I had to focus and concentrate completely at all times.

There was one particular performance class I didn't care for in which we had to walk solo around in a circle, expressing on our faces our motivation for circling. We were then directed to increasingly accelerate the speed. "Something is pulling you. What is it?" probed the teacher. "There has to be a reason for you to dance. Show your motivation." I dreaded having to take my turn walking and then running the circumference of the room while being critiqued. I was not good at emoting unless I was emoting unadulterated bliss; for my entire dance career to date, I had pretty much plastered on an obnoxious, toothy smile. Feelings were not my forte. "What exactly is my motivation to dance?" I pondered. "I do it because I must. What else would I do?"

Jenny and I were in different classes because I was a beginner and she was more advanced. But we'd meet at lunch break and run upstairs together to rehearse with the seven women and three men who comprised Mirmdance. In our performance bios, Miriam summed us up as follows (The extra descriptions in parentheses are from me.):

The Men:

Compact Powerhouse (small, cute, muscular guy I never really talked to)

Southern Gent (sweet queen with a strong southern accent)

Snow White Male (my college friend Adam, who always sported a trendy scarf and toted a big bag of Chinese junk food)

The Women:

Koala (short, Jewish gal who cooked sauerbraten, journaled about her dancing, and dated a Chinese guy from Chinatown)

Trinidadian Jazzarino (flaming-red-haired temptress with six-pack abs)

Impish (petite brunette)

Resembles a giraffe (tall blond)

Ivory Girl (massage therapist in the making)

She's got legs (my leggy friend Jenny)

All American (me)

The cast of characters fascinated me. I especially couldn't wait to go to rehearsal just to see what new contraption the Trinidadian Jazzarino, Sharla, was wearing. She absolutely oozed sex. In place of a traditional leotard, she would wrap her slim, toned body in an assortment of twisted rags that just barely covered the private parts. She was so creative with clothing, she could have taken garbage bags off the street and found a way to finagle them into haute couture. Everything looked good on that woman. And she looked even better in practically nothing.

Unfortunately, I got cast in "Lucy's Future"—the squid-monster piece that was supposedly about female sexuality. (I discovered that modern dancers call a dance number a "piece." It sounded strange to me: a piece of dance?) Appropriately, Sharla the sex-goddess played the lead, Lucy. I also danced in "99 Reasons to Wear Condoms," a provocative piece set not to music but to narration about how AIDS spreads throughout a community and not just among gay males. All of Miriam's unique, creative, modern choreography intrigued me and opened my eyes to an entirely new way of moving. But my favorite piece, "Set Free," was a bluesy, hanging-around-the-front-porch-in-our-blue-jeans-type piece where I could smile and have fun and dance kind of jazzily. The company members regularly made fun of me for dancing like a jazz dancer, which I was, after all. Modern dance was a stretch for me, pun intended.

I'd arrive home in the evening absolutely spent from an entire day of dancing my heart out. My muscles were often so stiff and achy that all I could do was sink into a bubble bath before collapsing in bed. But there was something so satisfying about working hard and challenging myself at something I loved and wanted to try, even though I was quite the novice and had a lot to learn before I'd be swimming as fluidly as the other sea monsters.

Meanwhile, matters back at Ashley's apartment weren't showing any signs of improvement. Quite the contrary. The herb garden on the balcony was wilting in spite of my desperate attempts to keep it alive. Those plants must've felt like they didn't belong in the city either. I was still terrified of becoming a homicide victim during the night. To make matters worse, after weeks of being locked out of the bedroom, the cat hated me. We became bitter enemies; to spite me, he pooped right in front of me on the virtually impossible-to-clean, expensive, natural-fiber floor covering in the living room. To top that, no matter how many times I'd wash my clothes, Midnight's black, needle-like hair would be inextricably threaded through the fibers, itching me throughout the day–a permanent reminder that he was out to irritate me. I dreaded coming home at night for fear of what that pussy had planned and would cautiously peek through the doorway to see where he was poised, ready to pounce.

Feline fracas aside, I began to embrace my new identity as a modern dancer. The first thing I did was to go out and buy a foot roller, and, more importantly, knee pads for rehearsal. As squids, we were constantly, painfully crawling about on our knees. Determined to keep my kneecaps intact for future use, pads were a priority. Then I went searching for some hipper clothes, so I'd feel more like a real, artsy dancer. I bought pastel, mint-green, high-top tennis shoes that were comfy for walking in; brown, lace-up granny boots; and a black flannel jumpsuit, which I accessorized with a brown leather belt and a stylish brown fedora from a trendy shop on Canal Street. I was now able to assume the role of professional modern dancer.

The end of the four weeks with The Works culminated in an invited performance followed by a wine and cheese party. Wearing my own blazer and jazz pants, I got to dance in a piece about life on the city street. I loved performing it. My sister and her boyfriend drove all the way from Michigan for my New York debut. Performers included serious dancers from Japan, Cal Arts, and other prestigious dance academies, and here I was with little training beyond my local dance school, dancing and partying among them. I called home to my parents during the after-glow festivities. "I'm in New York City dancing for an audience and eating wine and cheese!" It was a dream come true. I was on top of the world.

Long Legs and Tall Tales

****

Meanwhile, the pressure was on to find an apartment and a roommate before Ashley returned and kicked me out. That task was reserved for evenings and weekends, my only free time. After living alone in that high-rise tower of terror, I wanted to move as close as possible to the one and only real friend I had in New York, Jenny.

Luck being on my side once again, Jenny's high school friend, Darlene, ended up needing a roommate. We signed up with a real estate agent, but it still took several weeks to locate an apartment that came with a refrigerator and a landlord who didn't bite your head off. As if I owned a refrigerator and dragged it around the country with me! We finally found a two-bedroom apartment (with refrigerator) around the corner from Jenny in Astoria, Queens. Immediately, we had to cough up three months' rent: first, last, and a security deposit. In one fell swoop, I watched a good chunk of my $3,000 graduation money disappear.

It was worth it, as I was relieved to be settled into a cat-free place I could call home. Living in Astoria was a bit of a culture shock, however, as if I'd moved to a foreign country—mainly Greece. The grocery stores were Greek, the restaurants were Greek, and the people were mostly Greek with a substantial smattering of Italians. The language of choice, therefore, was either Greek or Italian.

My landlord and landlady were among the Italian contingency. Although they spoke little to no English, I thanked my lucky stars for the affable, ample landlady in an apron-covered floral dress, who always invited me in to eat when I stopped by to pay my rent, even though they were far from rich. She, her husband, two kids, and a visiting cousin all lived together in their modest one-bedroom apartment. Every night they opened the sofa bed in the living room so the kids would have somewhere to sleep.

There was always something delicious, like breaded eggplant parmigiana, cooking on the stove, and the woman would insist I sample it. "Christina, come in! Come in! Eat!" she'd say in her Italian accent, rolling the "r" in "Christina" and motioning me in with an exaggerated hand gesture. My name isn't Christina but, somewhat fond of my special Italian moniker, I never bothered to correct her. Sometimes Mrs. Landlady would even make me sit and watch soap operas with her as we munched on her homemade, gooey, sweet, Italian dough-ball dessert. It was futile to argue with the woman, so I ended up taking my rent check to her only when I was hungry. Her husband, the landlord, was the one who did any maintenance needed on the apartment. Since he spoke only Italian, it was a game of charades telling him what needed fixing. If I were really desperate to communicate, I had to get one of the children to interpret.

My new roommate, Darlene, was a beautiful, Bohemian blond and much more worldly than I given that she had, like Jenny, grown up in Manhattan. She was a food photographer for the prominent advertising agency Young and Rubicam. Impressive. Her family and all her friends from school lived in town, so I didn't see a lot of her. Plus, I was just plain shy, so for the most part, we lived separate lives.

Even so, it was rarely quiet around our place, which was located on the second floor of a building that housed twelve units. The acoustics were perfect for amplifying the sounds of the kids roller skating in the apartment above us. And the building next to us sat so close that we could hear our neighbor gargling and spitting out his mouthwash in his bathroom sink. We probably could have reached out the window and borrowed toothpaste. It was a tad too close for comfort.

The interior of the apartment was nice enough: two bedrooms separated by a small kitchen and living room, all with hardwood floors. Thankfully, Darlene already owned furniture for the kitchen and living room, so all I had to furnish was my bedroom. The only "furniture" I had brought with me from Michigan was a cheap, blue, foam chair of sorts that unfolded and converted into a horribly uncomfortable excuse for a bed. While a testimony to the creative ways to push the limits of foam, and certainly sufficient for crashing on in a drunken stupor, as a regular resting place, this contraption only added to the discomfort of my aching body. Hence, getting a proper bed was first on my home decor agenda. But how was I going to get a bed up to my second floor apartment? Not a problem in New York. I ordered a twin bed by dialing 1-800-mattres, and it was delivered and assembled for me.

A real, honest-to-goodness bed that could give me a good night's sleep? Check. My clothes, however, were still housed in cardboard boxes, and newspapers hung in lieu of curtains. For a while, I had lived without any window coverings at all until I noticed the peeping Tom spying on me from the apartment building behind ours. Creepy! (From the safety of my current Midwestern home, my much-more-mature self now realizes that it may be perfectly natural to curiously gaze at a neighbor on display in an unadorned window; who doesn't love to observe fish in a fishbowl?) Whether he was actually a peeping creep or not, it behooved me to shell out some cash for legitimate window treatments.

Discovering an absence of any home goods stores near me in Queens, I was forced to shop in Manhattan. After an exhausting and extensive search, which would have been an easy trip to Target or Kmart back home in the Midwest, I found affordable bamboo blinds and three large wicker baskets with lids to store clothes and other belongings. Success! Ah, but then I had to get them back to Astoria.

On the interminable trudge to the N-train, my sore arms strained to prevent my precariously perched purchases from toppling out of their tower. Boarding the subway was no less an ordeal; I could barely see where I was going because of the big basket blockade. Every subway car that arrived was too full for me to squeeze onto anyway. I had to wait and wait and wait until a sufficiently empty car arrived. Once aboard, I sweated nervously as people stared disdainfully and gave me the evil eye for taking up too much space and having the nerve to move to Their City. I knew they were thinking, "Who gave you the right to come here and transport home goods on our crowded subway?" I scanned the walls for a list of rules stating that "under no uncertain terms are large hampers allowed," for that was the non-verbal communication I was getting from the other passengers. Once at home, I plopped down on my dial-a-bed, exhausted and wondering if I should have stuck with cardboard boxes and newspapers.

My neighborhood peeping Tom spooked me to such an extent that I began planning ways to save myself if he ever showed up at my doorstep. At least there was a police station at the end of our block where I could run if someone came after me, I reassured myself. Just when I was building up my confidence, Jenny and I got flashed by a stereotypic and unimaginative flasher in a long raincoat and boots with nothing underneath. Jenny shouted profanities at him, but I just stood frozen until she grabbed my arm and briskly led me away. My nerves were rattled.

Other than peeping Toms and the occasional free peep show, Astoria wasn't much of a happening night spot. So on the rare evenings when we weren't too tired, Jenny and I made our way back to Manhattan for after-hours alcoholic adventures. Jenny often preferred to patronize either the discreet, dark and shady Russian bar whose name I've long since forgotten where, like clandestine spies, we'd watch for high-class drug deals going down and Russian mafia swapping messages; or, when feeling less detective-y and more festive, a colorful Mexican joint, Tortilla Flats, for margaritas and free chips and salsa.

The downside to venturing into Manhattan was that Jenny wouldn't always return to Queens with me afterwards. I dreaded having to take a subway home alone in the wee hours, so I was forced to spend a fortune for a cab. Late one such evening, my driver was an Evil Knievel wannabe who gave me the taxi ride of death. I nervously rattled off directions, so he would know I knew the way home. My NYC friends had warned me of drivers who'd scam you by taking you the long way to hike up the fare. Unfortunately, he spoke no discernible English, or he pretended not to speak much English. When he started whizzing to Queens at speeds that would break the sound barrier, I wondered if I should demand to be let out. But I was drunk, tired, and anxious to get home, so I decided that I would either die or get home really fast. Fate was kind that night.

Just learning how to catch a taxi was tricky. There should be a school that teaches people not only how to hail one, but also how to give directions in grunts and hand signals to all the non-English speaking cabbies. You really had to be bold, wave your hand high in the air, and claim your space when the other, more experienced New Yorkers were standing alongside you competing for the next taxi. Unlike at the deli counter, on the street you couldn't take a number and be waited on in turn. It was survival of the fittest. I stood on my tiptoes to create the illusion of being larger, waved my arm wildly like everyone else, leaned out into oncoming traffic (always maintaining readiness to pull back when a raging semi was about to decapitate me), and prayed that some taxi would stop.

And the fight didn't finish when the cab stopped in front of you. Everyone within a ten-foot radius would madly dash to the cab as if it were theirs and compete for the opportunity to fling open the door and sit down. Truly, I think the rule is that whoever's butt meets that dirty, black, cracked leather first wins the cab ride. Squatter's rights. After doing the mad taxi dance for several cabs off duty or already full of passengers, I realized that only the cabs with the light on the top were available. And don't be fooled by those fancy ladies in full-length minks and high heels. They are the best and most fearless taxi hailers of all. I lost out to them every time.

While I found flagging down a taxi to be distressingly difficult, it was easy for my city-slicker friend, Jenny. Jenny grew up in a multimillion-dollar "loft" (another new term for me) on 5th Avenue and 15th Street within walking distance of New York University where her eccentric British father was a computer professor. Around the corner from their home, a mob of dark-haired men with Indian accents stood on the sidewalk in front of their stores hawking electronic appliances and knock-off designer bags and watches. Jenny's building had eleven floors, and her family's loft, which was the entire top floor, had its own stop on the elevator. Being on the top floor, they had put in sunroofs and a roof garden making their space that much more valuable. The loft's 3600 square feet included three bedrooms and a small ballroom that housed a pipe organ and other unusual musical instruments. Famous actress Uma Thurman lived in the loft below them.

I, on the other hand, grew up in a suburban Midwestern neighborhood as white as Wonder Bread. My father was a physicist at Ford Motor Company. My mother was a stay-at-home mom. Old, widowed, not-famous-in-any-way Mrs. Barnett lived next door to us.

Our dissimilarities didn't end there. Unlike me, Jenny was an outspoken feminist. She flat out refused to allow guys to hold doors open for her or pay for her meals. But that didn't stop her from appreciating men in the bedroom. "You know, Kristi, you'd be a better dancer if you had sex," Jenny said in all honesty one day. She laughed at the absence of a working male organ in my life. Her parents permitted her to have her boyfriends spend the night. In their home. In her room. With her. My parental training in sex came from a book about a boy and his puppy who grew up to be a man and his dog, and a girl and her kitty who grew up to be a woman and her cat. The man and woman ended up in the same bed and, magically, a baby appeared. I don't know what happened between the dog and the cat. Jenny learned about sex from field experience in her own home.

Jenny also constantly made fun of me, because I had been a cheerleader in high school and a sorority girl in college, two institutions she absolutely abhorred. She was stunned that I had any redeeming qualities whatsoever. Had I been homeless, black, handicapped, gay, Jewish, or Latino, she would have accepted me wholeheartedly. Having attended a multiculturally mixed high school, she was proud of her non-prejudicial attitude. But she couldn't see past the stereotype of cheerleader and sorority girl.

Maybe she saw our differences as a challenge, but she took me under her wing, like the city mouse to the country mouse. As a native New Yorker, she had an attitude of superiority and was eager to teach me about the Best City in the World, the correct way to live, and the proper way to eat pizza. "Kristi, this is *real* pizza," Jenny exclaimed leading me into a take-out pizza joint in Manhattan. "It's got thin crust, not that thick crap you get in the Midwest." She showed me how New Yorkers eat it on the run by folding it in half and nibbling from the tip up to the crust. That was the only genuine pizza and the only way to eat it. Practicing her principles, I professed that the pie was pretty tasty. Pretty tasty, indeed.

****

While I missed living in Manhattan, because everything was so close and convenient, I loved being able to ride into town with Jenny. Every morning we would meet and walk past the Roy Rogers hamburger joint to the newsstand to pick up a cup of Earl Grey tea with milk and, every Wednesday, a copy of the newest *Backstage*. Then we'd continue the few blocks to the subway station to wait for the N or the R train into Manhattan, allowing approximately forty-five minutes for the ride into The City. We performed this routine about five days a week, because although The Works workshop was over, Mirmdance rehearsals were still in progress.

For the time being, we were rehearsing for free, with promise of rehearsal pay when the official funding came through. But one day, Miriam announced to me, "I want to make sure you can pay your rent, so I got you a job as a receptionist at Joy of Movement where I work." She was trying her best to assure that I didn't bail out of Mirmdance, due to lack of funds. Joy of Movement was a high-stress, highly trafficked fitness club in a building across from Tower Records near East 4th Street and Broadway. I desperately needed the cash and also got free dance and aerobics classes. Madonna and a couple of the Village People were members, so it seemed like the place to be.

The job was high profile and I found myself attracting dates, but not good ones. First there was the massive Puerto Rican body builder on staff who asked if I wanted to go out for sushi sometime. "I don't know; I've never had it," I said, trying to weasel my way out of a date without offending Mr. Muscles. Taking matters into his own hands, he brought me a huge sampler tray of about twenty different kinds of sushi. I actually liked some of it. We never did date, but I felt safer with him and his big biceps on my side.

Next there was the fast-talking lawyer from Long Island who, I swear under oath, addressed his mother as "Babe" when talking to her on the phone. He took me to drink kir royales at a trendy bar where giant tapestries hung from high ceilings and transvestites traipsed about. I can attest to the fact that I had never before sipped a kir royale, or witnessed a transvestite in person, or heard someone refer to his mother as "Babe." To that disparaging designation, I duly objected. It was an eye-opening evening, but evidently he was too slick for me. Date adjourned.

Lastly, there was the self-absorbed soap opera star from *Loving* who couldn't stop talking about himself and took me on the subway to get to our date. "Seriously? Slumming it on the subway? A soap opera star can't afford a cab?" I couldn't say I would have been heartbroken had his TV character gotten killed off the show in a freak accident that coincidentally snuffed out his previously unknown evil twin in the process. Perhaps it was best to postpone dating for the time being. Too much drama even for me.

I found little joy in working at Joy of Movement. The clientele were aggressive and demanding, even downright nasty, and I was terrified of taking the subway late at night by myself. I'd run down the dark, deserted street to the subway at Astor Place when I finished work at ten p.m., hoping no one was following me. At the subway, I didn't feel much safer, as I was always one of only a couple people waiting to catch a train. There was nothing and no one to protect me if some villain viewed me as victim. I always glanced about nervously, scanning the deserted tunnel for lurking danger.

One day at work there was a skirmish between the Joy of Movement security guard and a man with a gun who was trying to get into the building. No doubt he was one of those insidious psycho-killers who plagued New York and scaled high rises surprising unsuspecting Midwesterners. That scare was enough to make me want to find another job ASAP.

Thankfully, Miriam's funding finally came in: a whopping $5 an hour for rehearsal and $25 for each of our three performances. A strong hunch told me that the primary contributor was Miriam's father.

The IRS would officially classify me as living in poverty, but I could finally call myself a professional dancer! I was elated.

Even so, my $5 hourly rate was admittedly small potatoes, and Miriam wanted Jenny and me to stick with her through the shows. "I thought you two might need some extra cash, so I arranged an audition on Saturday for you with Celebration Magnifico. It's a party entertainment company I choreograph for. Several of the other dancers already work for them. I'm sure you'll get in, no problem," Miriam declared. "You just have to dance at one party for free so they can check you out." Miriam was the boss, and more money sounded good to both of us, so Jenny and I agreed to audition.

On Saturday, we made our way to the party location, a moderately nice banquet hall, where we'd be entertaining a large Jewish contingency at a bar mitzvah, my first ever. We found the back room where the other dancers were noisily chatting, putting on makeup, and searching through the myriad costumes strewn about the room. Jenny and I stood, wide-eyed and unsure, holding our bags filled with an assortment of dance accoutrements.

Celebration Magnifico was an interactive audience-participation group, which meant we'd have to coerce people to dance with us. It was owned by Bart and Danny, swanky, Jewish, forty-something brothers from Long Island (pronounced "Lon Guy Lind"). They started out with a mobile T-shirt-making cart for bar mitzvahs and added a few guys dressed in costumes such as a gorilla or Richard Nixon. Now they had this impressive party entertainment company and fancied themselves Broadway producers.

For our opening set, we dressed as train cars for *Starlight Express*, the famous Broadway roller-skating show. I was the dining car; my costume consisted of a silver table, complete with dishes and lamp, fastened around my waist over a red, black, and silver spandex bodysuit. "These costumes are pretty cool," I remarked to Jenny, who didn't appear quite as enthused about playing a choo-choo.

Once everyone was dressed, Bart assembled all the train cars for our grand entrance. "Listen up, people! I want everyone to chug in to the ballroom to the beat of the music. Adam, show them how we chug." Adam (from Mirmdance) did a robotic train move. "Right! Exactly like that. Then form two lines. Watch Bobby, the D.J., for the signal, and then face each other and freeze in a pose while the bar mitzvah boy enters the room. Got it?"

He pointed at Jenny and me and continued, "You two, just follow whatever the other dancers are doing." He seemed nervous about making sure everything was going to go right. I was nervous, too, and certainly didn't want to be the cause of a train wreck.

We did as instructed and "Wow!" It was surprisingly dramatic, especially when the lights dimmed and a machine spit puffs of smoke in a field of flashing strobe lights. The crowd cheered as little Mr. Schwarzbein did a Rocky Balboa-esque victory lap between the trains, fists pumping in the air. The party started off in Grand Central Station style.

Oh, but that was just the beginning. With the help of the D.J., we fired up the crowd by teaching them simple moves to popular, high-energy songs such as "Shout," "YMCA," and "Money, Money." We formed conga lines and party trains to "Locomotion," led the limbo, and demonstrated the hand jive, the twist, and the electric slide. All activities were used strategically to keep people boogieing on the dance floor. Jenny and I never knew what was coming next, but we kept smiling and improvising until we caught on. When we weren't leading the songs with preplanned moves, we were supposed to be dancing with the patrons. Basically, it was our job to be the life of the party. And if, God forbid, the party was dying, it was up to us to pick it up and nurse it back to health.

Celebration Magnifico kept the entertainment value high by offering five different dance sets per party, the themes for which were chosen by the party givers. Theme choices ranged from musicals or movies such as *Grease, Phantom of the Opera, Starlight Express* and *A Chorus Line* to general categories like "The Fifties," "Conga," "New York, New York," "American Band Stand," "Fantasy," "Hip-Hop," or whatever one could imagine. For each set, we changed into different, elaborate costumes corresponding to the chosen theme and often performed a partially improvised/pseudo-choreographed dance number to begin the set. Between the dancing and the quick costume-changes, it was a frenzy of activity on and off the dance floor. Given that one of our themes that day was *Dirty Dancing*, the 1987 film starring Patrick Swayze and Jennifer Grey, a good portion of the afternoon found us dirty dancing (a G-rated version, anyway) with prepubescent thirteen-year-olds in yarmulkes (who kept pushing for the R-rated version).

I was truly in loco-motion, dancing like a crazy woman and having a blast. This beat sitting in an office staring at the clock any day. People really get paid for this? Yes, and paid well by dance standards. Jenny and I got the job and and a promise of $100 each for parties in the New York City vicinity and $200 plus $25 per diem for parties where we had to fly somewhere and stay overnight. I didn't even know what per diem was, but I felt like I'd hit the jackpot.

"Now I have to take you to Stage 1 for cheap stage makeup!" Jenny insisted. This store was showgirl heaven, and I bought all kinds of tacky, colorful shimmery eye shadow, eye pencils, and glitter gel. My face looked like a craft store gone bad, but it was a perfect complement to the outlandish Celebration Magnifico costumes. The downside to getting the gig was that we were required to provide a white unitard (a stretchy bodysuit that covers one from nearly neck to toes), black unitard, black character shoes, beige character shoes, flat jazz shoes, black trunks (a bikini-bottom-like undergarment), and white trunks. It was an enormous initial investment for a starving artist but, hopefully, Celebration Magnifico would help pay the bills, and at least I'd be dancing, even if a touch dirty.

****

Many of the Celebration Magnifico costumes I'd found so enchanting were created by the same costume designer Miriam was using to outfit our Mirmdance production. Gareth, the master of material, was a gorgeous, gay, punk-blond, British bodybuilder who always wore a skimpy tank top and spandex pants to highlight his flawless physique. His design studio was smack dab in the middle of the meat-packing district over on 9th Avenue on the West side of Manhattan. Miriam sent me there for what was to become, unbeknownst to either of us, the most memorable costume fitting I would ever have.

Although previously unacquainted with this part of town, it became "udderly" obvious when I had stumbled upon the meat-packing district. A lump formed in my throat as I meandered past man after man in white butchers' coats spattered with blood. They were hauling out slabs of animal carcasses to be turned into delectable steaks at some of New York's finest restaurants, no doubt. I'm surprised I didn't turn into a vegetarian that very day. This place made the Lower East Side/East Village neighborhood of Alphabet City (named for its A, B, C, and D Avenues) with its emaciated, toothless drug addicts who hung out in doorways of dilapidated buildings and glared at me as I walked by, feel like home sweet home. I was the only woman in sight as well as the only person devoid of blood stains. Learning that come darkness the meat-packing district turned into an underground world of S&M made the place that much more eerie. Animals slaughtered by day, humans whipped by night.

My heart pounded as I searched for the address on my notepaper, eager to extricate myself from the bovine body parts. Finally finding my destination, I ran up the stairs to the safety of the second-floor shop where I spotted Gareth surrounded by scraps of colorful fabric and fantastical costumes in various stages of completion. "I'm here for my fitting," I announced shakily, still catching my breath from the shocking cow-corpse display. I ogled his bulging biceps as he placed the measuring tape around my body parts, which drooped in shame at their squishiness in comparison to his rock-hardness. Spandex could have no greater friend than Gareth to show off its stretchy, shape-revealing properties, but I wasn't so sure I wanted my every nook and cranny and bulge accentuated.

Nevertheless, that is what happened. For not only would I be covered in material so form-fitting that a pimple on my rump would have been detectable to the audience, but the "Lucy's Future" sea monster costume was so hideous that I contemplated swimming as fast and far away from Mirmdance as my squid appendages could muster. The costume consisted of black and white speckled spandex that covered my entire body minus my left leg and my midriff, which were exposed. "I have to show my stomach?" The arm pieces were long gloves with three- to four-foot long, spandex tentacles that hung off the fingertips. The headpiece was a spandex, squid ski mask of sorts topped with a tall pillow mimicking a squid body. "I could not look any uglier. Even another squid wouldn't find me attractive. Why am I subjecting myself to this embarrassment?"

Fortunately, the other two costumes were more friendly: a pretty red dress for "99 Reasons to Wear Condoms" and a colorful, spandex (of course), short-sleeved, midriff-bearing (of course) top, leggings, and short, flouncy skirt for "Set Free."

As the performance dates neared, the Mirmdance company gathered for a photo shoot to make a publicity poster. To my great dismay, Miriam chose to feature "Lucy's Future," so I had to wear the dreaded sea monster get-up. Thankfully, I was hidden in the back of the group photo. I felt a little better about my costume upon seeing Sharla, the star of the number, who was virtually naked, wearing only a tiny G-string and painted in silver body paint. I gasped. "Holy cow, she's topless!" I whispered excitedly to Jenny, who was well aware of Sharla's titillating presence.

All of us insidiously sensual squids strangled Sharla's shimmering breasts in a tentacle entanglement and "Click!" the photo was snapped. The night after the posters returned from the printer, Jenny and I traipsed around Manhattan plastering them on walls next to posters of esteemed entertainers. I felt famous by proximity; in spite of looking absolutely grotesque in the picture, it was thrilling.

Mirmdance performed for three nights in October back at the Nikolais Louis Dancespace. The large room conveniently converted into a stage through the use of lights, temporary curtains, and folding chairs for the audience. Tickets were $8 each. People had to pay real money to see me perform. I was disappointed that I had no friends and family there to witness my debut as a professional modern dancer, but Jenny's family attended and even Bart and Danny, our Celebration Magnifico bosses, kindly showed up to support Miriam and the rest of their employees.

My show should have been pretty easy with only three pieces to perform. "99 Reasons to Wear Condoms" came first and, for me, predominantly involved walking around and falling over in my red dress and black high heels. There was no music, only heart-wrenching narration about the spread of AIDS, coupled with images of people from various parts of the community hooking up and then keeling over from the dreaded disease. I successfully strutted and collapsed on cue. Dance numero uno: no problemo.

"Lucy's Future," however, was not even close to smooth sailing. My costume made me feel like a gargantuan goofball and turned the number into even more of an oceanic nightmare than it already was. Every time I did a backward somersault, and there were several, my stupid squid hat fell down over my eyes, and I had to keep pushing it back up so I could see. As if that weren't aggravating enough, every blind attempt to get up off the floor was thwarted by my treading on my hand tentacles. The dance moved fast and furiously, and it was nearly impossible to keep up while fighting that darn squid costume. I wrestled with it the entire number. Perhaps Jacques Cousteau would have fared better under attack, but in my case, the sea creature won, tentacles down.

At least my last number, the finale of the show, left me dancing in my element—jazzy, smiling, and having fun. How ironic that it was called "Set Free," which is precisely what I felt having finally and forever extracted myself from that wretched squid costume. This piece, my favorite, made it easier for me to let go of my crustacean frustration from the previous piece and genuinely feel joyfully liberated. I felt redeemed as I ended the night on a good note.

The greatest thrill was being reviewed by the *New York Times*. It was a mixed critique, but "Set Free" was praised for having "gusto." Another review, in the *New York Native*, stated, "The ten dancers are affable, well rehearsed, and determined...." Only after reading our reviews in the paper did I have any inkling of what our dances were about. That's the thing about modern dance; it always has a message, and it's often a challenge to figure out just what that message is.

****

Once the Mirmdance performance weekend was over, it was back to dance classes and auditioning during the week and Celebration Magnifico gigs on the weekend. I missed the regimen of the daily Mirm rehearsal schedule, but our funding had run dry, and I was forced to relinquish my short stint as a "real artist"—a modern dancer changing the world one "piece" at a time with sophisticated social commentary—for the commercial dancing that had the potential to pay the bills.

When I spotted an audition in *Backstage* for what looked like a promising dance show to be held in Japan, I was hopeful. Always up for traveling, I thought, "Why not give it a try? Japan could be interesting." At the audition, we learned a short, choreographed combination and then were asked to do some improvisational dancing to sexy music. Having already done quite a bit of this type of dancing with Celebration Magnifico, I was on top of my game and comfortable.

I got the gig and was overjoyed until Jenny warned me, "Did you know that girls from America have been hired to dance in a what appears to be a legitimate show and then were sold into white slavery once they got to Japan?" My innocent little spirit was crushed. I didn't know if any of what she told me was true, but my imagination went wild envisioning what would happen if I took the job, arrived in Japan knowing no one and speaking not a word of Japanese, was forced to go topless, and couldn't afford a ticket back home. I would be stuck like a clump of white rice on a burnt frying pan. The company name, NBC Productions, sounded legit, like it was part of the National Broadcasting Company, but for all I knew it could have stood for "Naughty, Bare-Breasted Cuties." I decided to pass on the offer and be more discerning about what jobs I considered in the future.

In addition to auditioning and working to pay the rent, I knew I needed to take oodles of dance classes if I wanted to be fit and competitive. Let's face it: I was also determined to be prepared for the next show that required me to bare my belly or be vacuum-packed in spandex. Dance class is a world of its own, with its special structure, unwritten rules, internal drama, and colorful cast of characters. It can be extremely intimidating if you don't know the code of conduct. There is proper etiquette, and you'd better follow it or you'll be ostracized or trampled at best and kicked out of class at worst. Survival of the fittest dictated that I pick up on the protocol quickly.

First of all, most dance studios follow a standard class format. Each session is usually 1½ hours long and is traditionally broken down into three sections: 1.) a warm-up (stretching, calisthenics, strengthening, and balancing exercises) done in one place in the center of the room or at the ballet barre, followed by 2.) moving dance combinations (choreographed turns, leaps, and kicks) performed from one side of the room to the other and back again, either one at a time or in small groups, preparing you for 3.) a short, choreographed "combination" (a short dance routine). The process is not unlike athletes doing drills in preparation for the game.

Second, you must stand in a "window"—a space not directly in front of or behind another dancer—so everyone can see herself or himself in the mirror. Dancers have an interesting relationship with the mirror, which we spend an inordinately long and probably unhealthy amount of time staring into. It starts out innocently enough—we really do need to see ourselves to know if we are doing the moves properly. But at some point, the relationship gets a little warped, and we can't help but stare at ourselves in anything reflective. "How do I look as I walk by this window of the United Bank and Bust? Do I look fat?" Bottom line: Don't mess with a dancer and her or his mirror.

Third, one's warm-up "spot" in the classroom is of vital importance. The teacher's pets would always stand in the front row nearest the teacher and the mirror. It took some guts to man/woman the front line, and if you did, you probably wanted to show off. As a newcomer, you had to be either really brave or really stupid to take one of the premier spots, for it would surely cause a ruckus with the divas who had long ago staked their claim on that part of the room.

If you were somehow able to wrestle a spot away from the showoffs, you had better be fantastic at doing the warm-up, or risk looking like a dancing fool. Plus, the people in back were depending on you. I was neither brave nor stupid, so I learned to strategically place myself safely somewhere in the middle of the room. That way I had people in front to follow and also behind me if we faced the back at any point, and I could still see myself in the mirror well enough.

Fourth, when dancing combinations across the floor, you must make certain that you start on the right beat. "Get into groups of four, and go every eight counts. Pay attention, and don't miss your entrance!" the teacher would demand as we herded ourselves to the edge of the classroom and scrambled into foursomes. God forbid if you stop the traffic flow and waste everyone's time. More importantly, get it right or prepare to be stampeded like an oblivious tourist at the running of the bulls of Pamplona.

Fifth, if you talk during class, chew gum, or wear jewelry, expect to receive a public, verbal spanking from the instructor.

Lastly, regardless of how much or how little the teacher tortured or inspired you, always applaud at the end of class. The teacher earned the right to stand up front and is to be treated with respect.

Dance teachers, I discovered, are celebrities within the dance world and act as gurus with their own little following of devoted students. Each teacher has his or her own special style and warm-up, which is generally repeated verbatim at each class. The more often you attend the class, the more comfortable and proficient you become with the warm-up and the style.

My two favorite dance studios were Steps and Broadway Dance Center, which were known for their top-notch jazz and tap teachers. Between the two, there was such a smorgasbord of classes that it was challenging to choose what to try. I sampled several before settling on a few favorites. Even the worst, I rationalized, succeeded in exposing me to new and different flavors.

For one class at Broadway Dance Center, we lined up at the ballet barre for the warm-up, and I nearly jumped out of my skin at what sounded like an explosive gunshot. I turned my head to see a jazz teacher who, if I didn't know better, I'd swear was Sonny Bono whacking away on a hand-held tom-tom. The entire warm-up was done to the beat of his drum. "'The Beat Goes On' and on and on," I lamented, recalling the Sonny and Cher song of the same name. Too intense for me. It felt more like an Indian pow-wow than a dance class.

An ex-Las Vegas showgirl taught me "tipping" and Vegas-style dancing. Up until that time, I thought tipping was something one only did at a restaurant or to cows in the country. In this class, I learned that it was a sexy, stylized type of walking where you moved sideways leading with your hip. "Kind of fun, but who am I kidding? I'm no showgirl, and I'll never dance in Vegas," I said to myself.

Much more my style was the jazz class I took with the famous, funky Frank Hatchett, who had a large group of loyal devotees and even sold his own line of jazz shoes. I excelled at his high-energy, high-kicking choreography, as I could kick with the best of them.

My most unpalatable experience was the jazz class at Steps that began with a warm-up so complicated and contortionist that I'd have needed several months of practice and my bones removed to do it. The easiest part was something along the lines of splits, backbend, wrap your leg around your neck, and tie it in a knot. The regulars had these frenetic and wildly unpredictable movements memorized, so the teacher didn't bother demonstrating for a new person like me. She'd go out for a cup of coffee and casually saunter back halfway through the warm-up to find me flailing and flopping about, struggling to stay alive.

Steps should have had an agreement that the instructor had to actually be present in her classroom for so many minutes out of the hour-and-a-half to qualify as having actually taught the class. I should have asked for my money back, as a good chunk of the class I spent trying to use my dance ESP to figure out what the heck to do in her warm-up.

Natasha Baron's jazz class at Steps, on the other hand, was so much fun I absolutely ate it up. She declared, "We dance so we can eat brunch!" Sounded like solid dance philosophy to me. Her class was challenging enough to help me improve without being too frustrating to enjoy.

I ended up having a few favorite teachers, all from Steps: Natasha Baron and Denise Webb for good old-fashioned jazz and Zena Rommett, who introduced me to floor barre—essentially ballet exercises done lying down on the floor. It was the perfect way to gently and safely wake up one's muscles in the morning, particularly after a late-night margarita marathon. It was heavenly and relaxing, but still strenuous and toning and great for practicing perfect ballet technique and alignment.

Not only was I intrigued by the various instructors, but I was also mesmerized by the dance students, particularly those from local performing arts high schools. These whiz kids were a force with whom to contend. It appeared that all they did all day was take classes, and they were darn good at it. When leaping and jumping, they stayed airborne for so long, it seemed they were immune to the law of gravity. They could spin like a top and had muscles that knew no bounds of flexibility; they were Gumby in jazz shoes. These dance prodigies could have done the warm-up and dance combinations in their sleep. I was enthralled, intimidated, and thoroughly humbled.

Then there were the real professional dancers and the die-hard ballerinas (a.k.a. the "trinas") who were all skin and bones and wore pointe shoes in every ballet class. New York ballerinas duct-taped their favorite, comfy ballet slippers if they were falling apart and wore their dance clothes until they were rags. It was hard not to spend much of my class time either marveling at the amazing dancers or looking with fascination out the studio windows at the hustle and bustle of Broadway below.

One day while at Steps, I overheard the excited whispers of girls peeking into a particular classroom. "There she is: Brooke Shields!" I was star struck. I patiently waited until this famous actress's class ended, acting nonchalant and completely uninterested but secretly peering peripherally at her like a hawk honing in on its prey. Then, when she headed to the women's dressing room, I discretely followed her. When she went into a bathroom stall, I took the one next to her. Why? So I could say I peed next to Brooke Shields, of course. The next time I saw Jenny, I said, "I peed next to Brooke Shields!" You never know the famous people you might relieve your bladder alongside while in New York City.

Although I was finally becoming more comfortable with the whole dance class scenario, I was also becoming more concerned that at about $8 a pop, this expense was really going to add up. Especially if I took one or more class a day. Fortunately, I learned that some of the big-name studios periodically offered work-study scholarship auditions, and one was being held at Steps just in the nick of time. As a scholarship student, you worked the front desk or did whatever other menial labor was needed in exchange for free dance classes. It was worth a shot.

I auditioned and, by the grace of God, landed one of the highly coveted scholarships. Incredible! No more worrying about paying for classes! My assignment was receptionist-type work at Steps II—their second, smaller, less-impressive, sister studio down the street. It felt a little like being shipped off to no man's land, but I knew how lucky I was to have the opportunity, and I was not going to complain.

What left the biggest impression on me at Steps II was the sixty-some-year-old retired professional ballerina who wore a turban on her head and was still a die-hard ballet class attendee. Still continuing her craft. Still doing what she loved, even in her seventh decade of life. "I hope I'm still taking ballet class when I'm an old lady," I projected into the future. "But perhaps I'll skip the turban."

****

My fantasy life seemed to be falling into place: a nice apartment, free dance classes, and plenty of income, thanks to Celebration Magnifico, which was becoming a bigger part of my life than I had anticipated. As I learned the ropes, the idiosyncratic inner workings of the company became clearer and clearer. Bart, I discovered, was the head honcho, with his brother, Danny, playing second fiddle. Bart worked all the best parties at the nicest locations. The favorite dancers, therefore, got all the good gigs with Bart and got to travel a lot. Unofficially, this group became known by all the dancers as "the A-team." The tier below these golden guys and gals was inhabited by "the B-team." These performers worked fairly often but got the local, schlockier jobs led by Danny. The "Z-team" were the people who never worked except for New Year's Eve when Bart and Danny practically had to pull strangers off the street to cover all the parties they'd booked. I got right into the A-team, which peeved some people, and rightly so.

Being a preferred dancer, I found myself averaging about $1000 a month, so it was smooth sailing, income-wise. I could easily pay my portion of the rent—three-hundred smackaroos—and still have lots of money left for bagels. While my weekends were now relinquished to Celebration Magnifico, having neither a boyfriend nor much of a social life, I actually preferred working to sulking alone in my apartment.

Instead of being holed up at home, I danced at weddings, corporate events, conventions, charity functions, parties, and elaborate New Year's Eve celebrations. Once we even partied with patrons at a spooky mansion for an outrageous Halloween benefit. But our bread and butter came from the very lucrative bar mitzvah/bat mitzvah circuit. Being Jewish themselves, it made sense that Bart and Danny tapped into this familiar market. Hence, we made a multitude of trips out to the nether regions of Long Island—bar mitzvah country. I never had a clue where we were exactly, as I wasn't driving, and I didn't have a map. All I knew was I was thrown into a van with a bunch of tired and crabby dancers who, at the end of the long ride, would likely be accosted by a bunch of barely-teen boys.

These kids loved us, and if one kid had Celebration Magnifico at his bar mitzvah, then all his thirteen-year-old pals wanted us at theirs, too. I'm not sure if they found us entertaining so much as fair game for abuse (and, oh, they did love to push their boundaries, test the hormonal waters, and yank on our costumes), but no self-respecting parents wanted their son's shindig to be out-partied by the festivities of their friends, so we saw a lot of the same kids over and over again.

In addition to keeping me in the black financially and sparing me from becoming a pitiful *shicksa* recluse, Celebration Magnifico exposed me to a variety of settings and eye-opening experiences. It was fun to see all the elaborate parties with gorgeous flower arrangements, balloon-sculpture monstrosities, and exquisite table settings. Our gigs were everywhere from the elegant Marriott Marquis located in the heart of Times Square and the Broadway theatre district to a no-frills, drab, gray banquet hall in the Bronx, where we served as entertainment for a wedding. Those dreary nuptials were particularly memorable because we traveled there via train through the infamous Harlem. Peering out from the safety of the boxcar, I was both frightened and curious as I watched homeless people crowd around trash cans aflame for warmth.

A local highlight for me was the bar mitzvah we performed for at the Copacabana, the famous nightclub on East 60th Street that Barry Manilow sang about in his 1979 Grammy Award-winning song of the same name. My life wasn't too far off from that of the song's protagonist: Lola, the showgirl "with yellow feathers in her hair and a dress cut down to there." I was simply in love with dancing at this renowned hotspot and getting paid for it, no less.

Wherever and whenever we had a gig, there would be a specific meeting spot in Manhattan—generally in front of the home of one of the dancers, who had a list of people who were supposed to show up. We would gather on the sidewalk at the designated pick-up area until our van or limousine arrived. (Yeah, sometimes it was a limo–a nice bonus.) I got to experience all different parts of Manhattan at all hours of the day and night thanks to the varied pick-up spots. Sometimes we had to arrive at an ungodly hour like 5:00 a.m., if we had a morning start time and a long way to travel. Even in the "City That Never Sleeps" there are not a lot of people out and about that early in the morning (at least not a lot of people you would want to meet), so it could feel isolated and scary.

One such morning, a large and threatening-looking, highly inebriated, off-his-rocker man shouted at me from across the street as I waited for the other dancers. Like any typical New Yorker, I ignored him. He kept right on yelling. I continued to ignore him. His rantings grew louder and angrier. I became concerned, because I could sense the tension escalating like a boiling teapot ready to blow steam. "What do I do?" Recalling those National Geographic shows of animals in the wilderness who go into "fight, flight, or freeze" mode when they realize they are being stalked as prey by a bigger and stronger animal, I held my breath and stopped dead in my tracks figuring that, given his size and supposed speed, freeze was the logical option.

Next thing I knew, he was standing beside me, shouting defensively, "You too good for me, lady?" Ignoring him had obviously been the wrong choice, so I meekly responded, "No. I didn't mean to make you mad." Having been sufficiently validated, he nodded his head in approval and walked away. I breathed a sigh of relief, but the altercation made me anxious.

My favorite meeting spot was in front of this dumpy, twenty-four-hour Polish restaurant that served the most delicious homemade vegetable soup with thick slices of eggy Challah bread. We would sup on the scrumptious comfort food or take-out containers stuffed with chewy pierogis. If one had a hunkering for Polish delicacies at any time, day or night—even at 3:47 a.m.—this place was open for business. No wonder New York is considered one of the greatest cities on earth. The restaurant was my homey, albeit homely, safe haven.

When we arrived at our destination, we were shuffled off to our "dressing room," which was inevitably some makeshift costume-changing area, usually at a hotel or country club. Surprisingly, the guys and girls weren't separated; we were all just expected to change clothes in front of each other. I supposed this lack of privacy wasn't such a big deal, as most of the men were gay, after all. But when it became routine for our bosses, our D.J.s, and our "Schleppers" (the Celebration Magnifico term for the guys who lugged costumes and equipment around) to also roam free-range, I felt a tad violated.

It was a real challenge to get into and out of myriad garments throughout the night without mooning someone or letting a nipple peek out. Thank God for that handy trick from the movie *Flashdance* where you take off your bra without removing your shirt: pull one bra strap down and slip arm out, do the same with the other strap and arm, and then pull the bra out one of the sleeve holes. I felt like Houdini slipping out of a straitjacket. With the bra out of the way, you could sneakily slide your costume top on underneath the shirt you were wearing. Take outer shirt off and voila! All dressed without going topless and giving the guys an eye-full. These attempts at modesty took enough extra effort that many dancers gave up and let it all hang out. I didn't think I was getting paid enough for that. Still, I could see why the others didn't worry about bearing their bits, as we changed in and out of costumes a lot throughout the event.

At the gig, we'd receive the all-important costume list revealing which costumes each dancer was to wear and, hence, what parts we would each be playing for the evening. This news elicited either groans of despair or sighs of relief. The costume assignments were a big deal, as certain outfits could make or break your night; they could spell "e-a-s-y s-t-r-e-e-t" or "d-i-s-a-s-t-e-r."

While there were innumerable ways in which to embarrass oneself in Celebration Magnifico, the costumes were one of the best. It wasn't so bad if you were incognito, like when you had to wear what we called a "giant head"—a hugely oversized facsimile of the head of a famous celebrity like Richard Nixon, Joan Rivers, Sylvester Stallone, or Steve Martin. These bulbous orbs completely covered your own relatively measly head save for a minuscule peephole out of which to see. Therefore, it wasn't uncommon to bump into patrons, walls, or other giant celebrity heads. Although I didn't particularly like shoving my face into these stuffy, smelly, big balls of fiberglass with dangerously limited vision, at least no one knew it was me inside.

But on many occasions, we would have to wear absolutely ridiculous get-ups that left our faces totally recognizable. I particularly hated when we had to dress up as giant alcoholic drinks and mingle with patrons during cocktail hour. I'd cringe when my name showed up on the list of beverages, dictating that I'd have to become a super-sized strawberry daiquiri, my head serving as the cherry atop the fake whipped cream.

I was wearing just such a fruity concoction at a party once when I bumped into a big-time entertainment accountant from Los Angeles who was best buddies with a friend of mine. "Kristi? Is that you?" the man shouted from across the room. My face turned as red as my cherry head. In this case, I would have opted to take "flight" instead of "fight or freeze," but my legs were so tightly squeezed into the spandex stem of my cocktail glass that I could only slowly shuffle away. Making a run for it was out of the question. I merely hoped he'd had too much to drink already and either wouldn't remember the next day or think he was hallucinating. "Oh, hi, Mike," I said as nonchalantly as I could, smiling and trying to convince myself (and him) that there was nothing unusual or embarrassing about standing inside a large-scale libation. Who needed the drink now?

Then there was the time I was playing Carmen Miranda for an opening of a new high-rise building in Atlanta, and I ran into newscaster Dan Rather. I wished I had been there dressed in some beautiful ball gown like the other partygoers, but instead I was balancing plastic fruit salad atop my head, shimmying my shoulders, and failing miserably to fake a Spanish accent. I rolled my "R"s saying, "Arrrrrrrrre you Dan Rrrrrrrratherrrrrrrr? I'm Carrrrrrrrmen Mirrrrrrranda." He gave a socially polite chuckle, and I shimmied away in shame.

But even worse than the embarrassing costumes were the life-threatening ones, like the carousel horse. The idea was lovely: a herd of human carousel horses prancing about in a circle forming a real, live merry-go-round. The spandex leotard body suits were tolerable, but the real problem was the horsey head: a large, heavy, flat, carved and painted piece of wood into which I had to carefully wedge my face. It was such a tight fit that they practically needed a giant shoehorn to get me in and the Jaws of Life to get me out. I nearly had a nervous breakdown being trapped in that contraption.

Another headpiece horror happened at the Chicago Hilton, where we were presenting a fancy, French Victorian scene. Donning an elaborate floor-length black and silver lace gown and massive hat, my job was to pose on a pedestal and look pretty. Usually it was great if you were assigned to a pedestal because you didn't have to work as hard. While everyone else had to dance with the patrons, you simply stood on your post and did "armography," which entailed moving your arms to the music or gesturing gracefully. For some of the larger costumes, this was a matter of safety. Our "New York, New York" set, for instance, had gargantuan costumes like the Chrysler Building or the Brooklyn Bridge (which required two people: one for each pillar with the bridge draped in between) that were so cumbersome you were actually a liability on the dance floor, knocking patrons over with your big buttress.

In this case, my costume was more of a hazard to myself than the patrons. The over-sized hat cinched my head like a vice and was so heavy I got a migraine headache. It also had a tight bodice that squeezed my diaphragm like a corset and a weighty veil that completely covered my face. Consequently, I could barely see and wasn't getting much in the way of fresh oxygen either. This deadly combination made me feel dizzy and faint. I soon realized that I'd better get this costume off pronto or I was going to pass out and plunge from my perch.

The problem was I couldn't just leave on my own accord, because I couldn't see well enough to safely step off the pedestal. Even if I could, I required help climbing down. I needed both hands to hold up my long, puffy gown, or I'd surely trip on the fabric and fall to my death. And I couldn't just blurt out, "Help me!" over the roar of the music, without alarming all the patrons. How was I going to get out of this predicament without drawing attention to myself?

As I saw it, my choices were: 1.) stay where I am and eventually faint and fall to the floor (certain embarrassment plus possible major injury), 2.) attempt to climb down by myself (highly probable embarrassment, because there was no way to get down gracefully, and there was a good chance I'd trip and fall thereby possibly incurring injury), 3.) scream my head off for help (extreme embarrassment but no injury), 4.) spell S.O.S. with my hands (no embarrassment, no injury, but probably not effective) or 5.) wait for someone who worked for Celebration Magnifico to walk or dance by me, discretely grab that person's attention without being seen or heard by the partygoers, and beg for help (very minor embarrassment and no injury, but it could take a while for someone to get near enough to notice me). I decided to start with number 5, but knew I had to make this plan work quickly or I'd be involuntarily invoking plan number 1.

I desperately tried to make out a familiar figure or voice through the thick fabric covering my face. After some time, I finally recognized Bart who was ambling in my vicinity. Like a shipwreck survivor stranded on a desert island, madly trying to alert the rescue boat just appeared on the horizon, I frantically did the universal hand-signal for "Come here!" and prayed the boss would glance my way. With luck on my side, eventually he did, and I was saved in the nick of time.

Some of the costumes were so elaborate that they were traumatic both on the dance floor and in the dressing room; it was often an overwhelming job to figure out where all your costume pieces were and how to affix them to your body. Costume racks and trunks were filled with assorted pieces, but all I had to go by was the costume list, which read something nebulous like "Kristi—Gold Fantasy." I hadn't a clue what that costume looked like or that it had forty-three parts to it that I had to search for like a treasure hunt and then fit together like a puzzle. I was often forced to beg the veterans for help. This was my last resort, as they weren't necessarily obliging, especially those who as I said earlier, didn't believe I deserved a spot on the A-team.

To make matters worse, after I did find what I was supposed to wear, I never knew if I'd be able to squeeze my body into it. While by no means fat, I was one of the bigger gals in the group, and the costumes were not one size fits all. It was disconcerting and uncomfortable when my love handles would hang over the side of my much-too-tight trousers.

In spite of all the costume conundrums, they seemed spectacular to me and were unlike anything I'd ever worn. I loved getting dressed up and instantly took on the role of whatever I was wearing. Much to the annoyance of the old-timers in the group, I excitedly had my picture taken in all my costumes.

The worst part about sharing costumes with other dancers was, well, sharing costumes with other dancers. Celebration Magnifico had weekends where they were booked solid with parties on Thursday night, Friday night, Saturday day, Saturday night, Sunday day, and Sunday night. While these weekends with multiple parties were heaven for my bank account, they were hell for my olfactory system, as the company had no time to clean the costumes between jobs. Oftentimes you'd have to wear costumes that were soaking wet with the sweat of other dancers who had danced the party before yours. I cringed every time I had to don yet another outfit with moisture and dampness that wasn't my own.

Sweat swapping was one of the many issues the dancers enjoyed moaning about in the dressing room. Complaining was not only a highlight of the job, but practically a prerequisite. It was part of the company milieu. "These costumes stink like hell!" "When are they going to bring us food? I'm starving!" Usually we were offered at least a sandwich, chips, and soda pop, which I often took home in my duffel bag along with hotel toiletries. I was grateful for any free food, but the veterans complained unless it was a really nice, hot gourmet meal. "Crappy sandwiches again? I'm not eating this garbage." In between gripes, you'd often hear Southern Gent, from Mirmdance, squawking like a sick bird and calling the boss "an 'ol' buzzard" in his thick, Southern drawl.

As a general rule, the dancers were bitter and jaded and didn't appreciate anyone who was actually enjoying their job (like me). My smiling face and good attitude were poison to the toxic atmosphere they loved and in fact created. I quickly learned to squelch my excitement so as not to by lynched but found myself jaded along with the rest of them soon enough.

While I found the dancers fascinating and highly entertaining, I had a hard time fitting in at first. I wasn't used to the Jersey girls with their big hair, extravagantly painted long nails, and strong accents ("Oh my gawd...a-nuth-ah bah mitz-vuh on Lon Guy Lind? Fuh-git about it!"). Gay men were also still somewhat of a novelty to me and slightly out of my comfort zone. Many of the dancers were into crystals and metaphysics. Several even practiced Buddhism, which was completely foreign to me. They would find a quiet place to meditate and chant for money or something they needed. I didn't get it. They might as well have said they were Martians. These people and their strange ways of life blew my closed, little Midwestern mind wide open.

To make matters even more intriguing, relationship drama was happening behind the scenes. Mainly, sometimes female dancers hooked up with the Schleppers or the D.J.s, even becoming official couples. The Schleppers and D.J.s were Jersey (pronounced "Joy-zee") guys, all with names ending in "y" (e.g., Joey, Bobby, Danny, Tommy), who tended to stick with their own kind—the Jersey girls—which was fine by me, as they weren't really my cuppa tea. I also heard rumors of girls sleeping with one of the bosses to further their careers, but I never believed it. How much did you really have to gain? You got to attend a few more bar mitzvahs dressed as the Chrysler building?

If you were savvy enough to survive the backstage soap opera, your next challenge was to survive on the dance floor. The first task was learning and executing the dance number that started each set. Most of the real dance numbers we performed were taught and rehearsed only a half-hour before we were supposed to get into costume. The owners didn't want to pay for extra rehearsal time, so we had to pick up choreography fast and furiously and fake the parts we didn't know. It was mayhem.

The rehearsal scene on stage would go something like this: The choreographer would bark out orders. "Okay, we don't have a lot of time people, so listen up! Half of you pony stage left, half stage right, and then get into one straight, vertical line. Step-touch and clap moving downstage. As you get to the front, do some kind of trick, turn, kick, or jump, or something. Then peel off, every other person stage left and right. Form into a clump in the back. When everyone gets there, take three different poses and freeze in between each one." We'd all try to run through the choreographer's instructions as quickly as possible, like a movie played on fast forward.

We'd get about halfway through a number and Bart, the boss, would come running in shouting frantically and waving his arms, "Stop! Stop! Stop! The guests are coming in for cocktails. Everybody in the dressing room and get your costumes on NOW!" The choreographer would throw her hands up in the air in surrender and say, "Obviously, we didn't finish the choreography, so when we perform the number on stage, just try to follow what I'm doing. And watch for my signal about when to take a group pose at the end!"

There was no point in getting all worked up over the fact that we had only practiced half of the dance. After a while, we all learned to shrug our shoulders and laugh. "Whatever." Somehow we always pulled it off. It's amazing what we could do with great stage presence and crazy garments. We were so entertaining that the crowd never knew, or cared, that we were making much of it up as we went along.

It was a bit trickier when you were assigned a lead role like Christine from *Phantom of the Opera*, which required you to do an adage—a slow, balletic, partner dance—with the Phantom. You were expected to figure out your own choreography. If time permitted before the party started, you'd discuss or experiment with a few "lifts," where the guy picks the girl up over his head in some dramatic pose. Usually there wasn't time, so you'd improvise on the spot, even whispering in each other's ears about what to do next during the actual performance: "Run to me and grab my waist and I'll twirl you!" The entire performance was an exciting adventure into the unknown. It was all about focusing on your partner, maintaining intense eye contact, and sensing each other's movements in order to know what to do and where to go next. You really had to tune into and play off each other.

In some form or another, the Phantom would mesmerize his muse, Christine, with enchanting hand movements and a powerful "whoosh" of his mysterious cape. A tug-of-war would ensue with the Phantom and Christine embracing and pulling away from each other, lifting and lowering, twirling and standing in awkward stillness. Tormented and torn, but exhausted and weak, Christine would finally succumb to his spell, the Phantom enveloping her in a passionate kiss beneath his cape. The crowd would cheer and even the dancers would be amazed at what they were able to create in the moment.

Of course, unrehearsed dances like these were just invitations for mishaps—like the time one girl playing Christine spun wildly into a waiter carrying a tray of wine glasses. It's hard to resume the melodrama with a straight face when you've just taken out a staff member and showered the floor in alcohol and broken glass. But, honestly, some people got so good at improvising that you'd think they'd been performing the number for years. The company really relied on the talent and improv skills of each dancer. I was always flabbergasted by how we could spontaneously create such a spectacular show.

Dancing for Celebration Magnifico turned out to be great training in trusting your creative instincts, being in the moment, improvising, and becoming comfortable with the unknown. If you were terrified of what might go wrong, not knowing how the dance was going to unfold, or not being able to pre-plan your moves, you were sunk and had better quit the job or up your intake of anti-anxiety meds. Even though the performance part of the gig was often a high-pressure, chaotic, wing-it situation, I generally found it liberating and fun.

It was the second part of the gig—dancing with patrons—that didn't always jive with me. Being naturally shy, I hated having to ask people to dance. Whenever possible, I'd try to hide in the middle of the crowded dance floor and pretend I had a partner. I didn't get away with this for long, however, because Bart watched us like a hawk, always scoping the room to make sure we were paired up. I didn't want to ruffle his feathers.

At some parties it was nearly impossible to get people to dance with you—especially the corporate gigs with employees with really boring jobs. I'd begrudgingly bounce over to a table and tap on the shoulder of some random guy in a suit and tie. Plastering on my best fake smile, I'd shout over the music, "Would you like to dance?" He'd glance up from his half-consumed chicken breast and, without so much as a grin, say, "No." At the really miserable parties, you'd have to take rejection after rejection before you could successfully coerce someone into dancing with you. Eventually you had to get aggressive and grab their arms and yank them out of their chairs as they clung onto the tablecloth in a desperate attempt to remain seated.

A top Celebration Magnifico priority was that all the "important people" get invited to dance whether they wanted to or not. At a wedding, I was once sent on a mission to get the bride's stodgy uncle to boogie with me, only to receive the angry response, "I'm eating!" It was a challenge to please the boss without ticking off the partygoers.

I learned to scope the tables and use my intuition to determine who would be less likely to reject me. To make the process more fun, sometimes we held a contest to see who could be the first to get the cute guys to dance. The risk of choosing a hot babe was getting the look of death or verbal lashings if he had a jealous girlfriend sitting next to him. I danced with old men, young men, women, kids, teens, octogenarian grandmas—you name it. Anyone was fair game.

While certain aspects of the job were quite unpleasant—including harsh rejections, drunk ladies stabbing your feet with their spiked heels, and creepy guys getting fresh—letting loose and uninhibitedly dancing my heart out was cathartic and enjoyable. We were expected to put on a show and be entertaining, so the wilder the better.

On occasion, one of the male dancers would get a burst of adrenaline (or maybe he was just losing his mind) and go off into some spastic routine like kicking over his head, quintuple pirouette, jump split to the floor, and break dance. The rest of us would clap and hoot and holler at the frantic one-man-show. Unfortunately, these high-speed dance extravaganzas didn't happen often, because it was hard enough making it through the night on low to medium-speed. Most of the time, everyone was just too jaded and tired to go the extra mile. In fact, sometimes we were so exhausted at the end of the night, we'd just do energetic armography and faceography (enthusiastic arm gestures and facial expressions) while basically keeping our feet still to conserve energy.

By far the best part of the job, to me anyway, was traveling out of New York. We flew to Indianapolis, Atlantic City, Las Vegas, Palm Desert, Chicago, Baltimore, and Beverly Hills. Our time was usually so limited that we didn't get to see much of any one city, but I took my trips as an opportunity to pamper myself and at least enjoy lounging in the hotel.

To begin my hotel experience, I would check the room service menu for the price of hot chocolate and count how many different toiletries were provided in the bathroom. A high cost of hot chocolate and a high number of toiletries were sure signs of a high-quality hotel. I liked to order hot chocolate from room service while snuggled in one of the crisp, white terrycloth robes that every high-quality hotel provided. Sometimes I treated myself to an Amaretto from the mini-bar and a soak in the bath. I'd work out in the gym, tan by the pool, relax in the jacuzzi, or shop.

I especially loved our trips to the west coast; trading the gray, cement city for palm trees and sun was pure heaven. One of my favorite journeys was to Palm Desert, California, an oasis of golf courses and spas built in the middle of the desert overlooking the mountains. We stayed at the mega Palm Desert Marriott where you could actually catch little boats from the inside of the hotel and sail to various restaurants and shops, the golf course, or the spa. Most of the time I would try to save as much per diem as possible hoping we'd get free food at the party, but sometimes it just felt good to splurge. This was one of those times; I paid the $25 a day to use the spa and gym, shopped at the expensive boutiques, and dined on a gourmet dinner, spending every last cent of my per diem. I was living the dream!

Another time we stayed at the Four Seasons Beverly Hills, where I adored the complimentary Earl Grey tea with cream and honey. About twenty-five of us dancers were flown all the way across the country for a bar mitzvah, of all things. Rumors were that each dancer cost the client between $1,500 and $2,500. (Of which we only got $200, but let's not go there!) Couple that with our hotel rooms, per diem, and flights, and you are looking at a very expensive party for a thirteen-year-old. This bar mitzvah was more lavish than most weddings I've seen.

To impress the Los Angelenos, Bart played us up as Broadway performers: "Live from New York City...Celebration Magnifico!" We entered in white top hats and sexy, white tuxedo-style outfits to Frank Sinatra's famous tune, "New York, New York." We got the crowd to sing the song with us and then join us in the "world's longest kick line" for the grand finale.

The entire dance floor was covered in row after row of partiers and dancers linked arm and arm, raucously singing off key and kicking off beat. Just when it seemed the mood couldn't possibly get any more exciting, we passed out neon glow-stick necklaces, and the party reached a frenzied climax with rich people falling over each other to obtain the free swag. This was one religious initiation ritual they'd never forget.

****

More and more, I was relying on Celebration Magnifico excursions abroad to keep me sane. Life in the Big City was wearing on me, especially being regularly accosted by wackos and beggars. Before long, I began to recognize certain homeless people who consistently worked the same corner or subway line. One guy had a sign that said it honestly: "Save the winos!" Others rode the subway all day long collecting change in their five-gallon water jugs. Do I give them money or ignore them? The daily decision wore me down. Either choice made me feel bad; I couldn't donate cash for everyone's every request, but I felt guilty turning a deaf ear and a blind eye to their plight. I had a heart, which only compounded my charity confusion.

Adding to my predicament was the unfortunate fact that I was a weirdo magnet. I had "Come talk to me; I'll listen." written all over my approachable, gullible face. On the subway, one super drunk, homeless guy staggered over to me and spoke in his slurred and sloppy fashion, expelling his marinated breath in my face. Having learned that ignoring people isn't always the best solution, I succinctly answered what I surmised he had asked. Satisfied, he went back to his seat across from me and promptly puked.

I was approached by so many kooks that I eventually developed my own "Midwestern Bumpkin's Guide to Looking Invisible and Staying Safe in New York":

1.) Don't wear any clothes that might draw attention. Non-sexy, drab, cheap garments are best, preferably in black, brown, beige, or gray.

2.) Carry a purse that cannot be easily cut, snatched, or opened and hold onto it for dear life while on the subway or street.

3.) Cover your eyes. Dark sunglasses are a must at all times so you can avoid eye contact.

4.) Plug up your ears. Carry a transportable music listening device with earphones so you can pretend that you didn't hear the crazy guys ranting and raving (or begging) in your direction.

5.) Adopt an "I'm-a-tough-chick-in-a-hurry-so-don't-mess-with-me" scowl.

It was hard for me to act so hardened and thick-skinned, not to mention wear ugly attire. I wanted to be able to smile and say hello to people as they walked by. But doing that got me into trouble. So there I'd sit on the subway, clutching my most impenetrable handbag with a death grip, while wearing a boring outfit and sensible shoes, donning earphones even when not listening to music, pretending to read a book, and sporting sunglasses in rain or shine. Feigning absorption in my own private world, I clearly signaled, "Nutcases NOT welcome here!"

My disguise of indifference certainly helped, but the hoards of people I encountered daily still overwhelmed me. Traveling for Celebration Magnifico was the most stressful, and I nearly freaked out from all the crowds of scary people, destitute people, and panhandling people at the Port Authority bus terminal. Or the throngs of people at JFK Airport pushing and shoving to claim their luggage from the conveyor belt or to hail a cab. It was a shove or be shoved world. You had to fight to claim your spot in The City, and I simply didn't want to fight.

My anxiety level was getting higher and higher. The thought of braving the crowds left me cowering in my apartment on several occasions. If I didn't have to work, I sometimes stayed holed up at home for days at a time. At other times, like a pregnant woman craves pickles and ice cream, I'd crave nature and space and would escape to

Central Park to lose myself in trees, openness, and fresh air. I could see why New Yorkers tried to grow plants on any possible surface available, even a 12" by 6" ledge on their fire escape. I was becoming agoraphobic and claustrophobic in the city. To make matters worse, I felt trapped without a car. I needed to know I could get away from bricks and cement in favor of green grass and blue sky.

What was my problem? I knew that New York had so much to offer. You were absolutely spoiled for culture: food, shopping, art, music, dance, and, of course, some of the best theatre in the world—BROADWAY! As a dancer, I could choose from a multitude of performance classes taught by incredible teachers. Nowhere else in the United States offered such comprehensive training. You could take a dance class any day of the week or all day long at a wide selection of phenomenal studios. Vocal coaching and all sorts of acting classes—straight theatre, musical theatre, commercial, soap, television and film, Shakespeare–were there for the choosing. It was the place to be for the stage performer.

But there's so much more: You can walk everywhere in Manhattan. You can be inspired by some of the most incredible art in the world from its many art museums; eat virtually any type of ethnic food; be in Chinatown or Little Italy for a complete cultural change of scenery; nosh on the most delectable bagels in the world; stock your cupboards with the most glorious gourmet and deli food from Zabars, Dean & Deluca, and Balduccis; buy the best of whatever money can buy; see the Macy's Thanksgiving Day Parade and the giant Christmas Tree Lighting at Rockefeller Center; wave your silly sign on the street for *The Today Show*. You can grab a meaty hotdog or sausage with spicy mustard, a salty soft pretzel, or steamy roasted chestnuts in the winter from a street vendor. New York can meet your every desire, right? What's not to like?

Some people truly could not be happy anywhere else. They need the electric buzz of the City That Never Sleeps like they need that jolt of caffeine to wake them up in the morning. But I wasn't one of those people. To me, daily living was becoming a struggle and a chore. Apartments didn't come with washers and dryers, and I dreaded going to the laundromat. I waited until I was absolutely out of every shred of clothing before making the five block trek to the closest facility, grunting and dragging my two bulging suitcases all the way. Then I had to sit there for hours keeping guard over my precious, trendy clothes. It was always me and the fat, Italian mamas. Had I spoken Italian, I could have at least eavesdropped on their conversations to keep myself occupied. Instead, I was stuck reading or watching my laundry spin around and around.

Grocery shopping was also annoying as the only grocery stores I could walk to were the small, overpriced, and understocked Greek markets where, even if I could afford them, I could only buy what I could carry. It wasn't like home where you could fill up a grocery cart with every food imaginable and stock the refrigerator and cupboard for weeks. I decided to stick with bagels and cream cheese.

If I needed home décor or furniture, I had to schlep all the way into Manhattan, because the Astoria stores were so limited. Then if by some miracle I happened to find something I could actually afford to purchase, I had to figure out how to get it home on the subway.

Meanwhile, from my apartment, a trip to Manhattan was a forty-five-minute endeavor on the subway and enough of a hassle that I didn't want to go back and forth several times a day. I couldn't afford to keep paying for extra subway tokens anyway. So whatever I needed at any moment of the day I had to carry with me every moment of the day.

A typical day in town might include ballet class, Mirmdance rehearsal, work at Joy of Movement, and drinks with friends. Or jazz dance class, scholarship receptionist work at Steps II, an audition, and a date. Consequently, my bag was often loaded with tap, jazz, character, and ballet shoes, two changes of leotards, work clothes, toiletries, a towel for showering, a book to read on down time, address book, hair dryer, curling iron, lunch, dinner, water bottle, portable music device, sweats, headshots, sheet music, and more. I was like a homeless person or a bag lady lugging nearly everything I owned, sweaty, smelly, and grimy by evening from a day of dancing and trudging through Manhattan. If I had a hot date or plans to party with friends, I had to find somewhere to stash my substantially overstuffed satchel where no one would steal it. Such a suitable place was rare, so I usually had to haul it along. A dirty duffel is not the most attractive accessory when on a romantic rendezvous.

As if carrying around back-breaking baggage wasn't unbearable enough, I couldn't even make up for it by wearing a cute dress and high heels. I had to walk blocks in those shoes and perhaps run in them if someone questionable was following me. So I had to find comfortable, sensible walking shoes that didn't look like Grannie's orthopedics and dress down enough to minimize unwanted attention from strangers. Top this off with the fact that I was sweating from shouldering my thirty-pound dance bag for three miles, and I had exponentially decreased my sex appeal.

The most limiting factor of all was that if I wanted to go out at night I had to walk to and from the subway in the dark by myself or take a cab ride—about $15 one way to or from Manhattan, an expense I simply couldn't afford on a regular basis. To be honest, I couldn't really afford to go out in Manhattan period. It was all so expensive and such a hassle that I usually opted to stay home at night and be lonely.

Oh, I was all right when I was spending time with Jenny. On nights off in Astoria, we often ordered sesame noodles from our local Szechuan restaurant and watched a movie. But she had a boyfriend, family, and loads of childhood friends, so I didn't have her to hang out with all the time. It wasn't her job to babysit anyway.

I was particularly missing home early one morning as we rode the bus back from a Celebration Magnifico gig. It was three a.m.—perhaps the loneliest time of day—when we passed through smutty Times Square. (Remember when it used to be smutty?) I stared out the window, listening to Bruce Hornsby's "Mandolin Rain" through my headphones, and witnessed my first real, live prostitutes in mini-mini-skirts and tragically high heels. It was the dead of winter, and I knew they must have been freezing cold. I was mesmerized at the sight of real hookers. They were obvious. I couldn't imagine having sex with random, creepy strangers. Dancing with them was bad enough. I wondered if they felt lonely, too.

My stupor was interrupted by one of the metaphysical junkies sitting across from me. "Kristi, you are a star person." "A what?" I responded trying to pry my eyes off the prostitutes. "A star person sent down from the heavens to lead the people," she replied with cosmic authority. I didn't know if that was true or not, but I wondered if I was cut out to be a star in New York or anywhere else.

****

One day I overheard a conversation in the dressing room at Steps, which not only dampened my already fading quest for stardom, but also sent me into a mini panic attack. As I was changing out of my dance clothes, I heard an aging woman remark to another dancer, "I'm thirty and I'm just starting my dance career. In fact, I just got a job with a company called Celebration Magnifico." My ears perked up. "I've always wanted to dance, so I finally decided that I had to give it a shot." I loved her go-against-the-odds-screw-the-age attitude, but one terrifying thought made me sweat: "What if I'm still here when I'm thirty, prancing around hotel ballrooms in a carousel horse costume asking hormonal teens to hand jive?"

That horrifying vision sent my head spinning. Sure this whole dance adventure was fun and interesting, but where would it get me? I couldn't bear the thought of wasting my education. I wanted to move up in the world and get a respectable job that utilized my potential.

To top it off, New York City was simply overwhelming to this ingenuous suburbanite chicken. The crowds. The derelicts. The fear. The loneliness. If I stayed I might end up a mental patient escapee hiding out at McDonald's with the other defectors. Maybe they, too, had come to NYC with dreams of grandeur only to freak out and go off the deep end. I had to leave before it was too late. I ran hyperventilating to a Manhattan payphone and called my mother, sobbing, "Take me home!"

Telling my parents and Jenny that I was already giving up on NYC after less than six months was devastating and embarrassing. Going home with your tail between your legs stinks. The irony is that I had been one-hundred percent successful from the time I moved there. I auditioned five times and landed every job. I won a dance scholarship from one of the best-known studios in New York on my first try. I got into a modern dance company the day after arriving despite having never done any modern dance before. I got right into the Celebration Magnifico A-team and was traveling around the country. I never had trouble paying my rent. Really, I did "make it there." Unfortunately, I just couldn't take it there.

Next I had to break the news of my departure to my boss, Bart. I was afraid he'd be furious. I was booked solid with parties in December, a busy party month, culminating in New Year's Eve. New Year's was a big deal as performers got paid triple their usual salary and Celebration Magnifico had so many parties booked they needed each and every performer. If you turned down New Year's Eve, you might as well say sayonara to the job and leave your glitter gel behind. I was reneging on a whopping seven parties while I drove my stuff home to Michigan, but I had decided to fly back to do New Year's Eve. Scared stiff, I pulled Bart aside at a party and bravely spilled my guts. Luckily, he liked me and was overwhelmingly compassionate.

With exit strategy in order, I took advantage of the few weeks I had left to do some sightseeing. Following a book touting free things to see and do in New York City, I set out solo to see Battery Park, the view from the 102nd floor of the Empire State Building, South Street Seaport, the Frick Museum, the Whitney modern art museum, the Metropolitan Museum of Art, and the Guggenheim. Meandering down Wall Street, I sampled the street vendors' gigantic doughy pretzels and piping hot sausages draped in grilled onions and green peppers.

It was Christmas time, so Jenny and I strolled around Fifth Avenue window shopping and admiring all the bedecked buildings, some wrapped like presents or donning giant candy canes. We marveled at the lavish displays of Macy's and Bloomingdale's. We melded into the throngs of people at Rockefeller Center for the annual Christmas tree lighting ceremony, where the police surveyed the crowd from horseback like Canadian Mounties. I felt uncomfortably trapped in the crowd. "I'm really going to miss you," Jenny mourned. "Me, too," I sighed. We had become close friends, she softening her opinions and I becoming more street savvy. Somehow the city mouse and the country mouse had met in the middle.

My parents arrived, and we once again packed up my belongings. Sadly, I had to leave my nearly new dial-a-bed in the apartment, as we had no room in the van. The drive back to Michigan was icy and snowy. With my eyes closed, I sat listening to Garrison Keillor's "Lake Wobegon" stories on the radio—tales of the comforts and security of life in a small town surrounded by family and friends. I relaxed for the first time in months. Woe, be gone!

A couple weeks later, I flew back to New York, as I had promised Bart, and rode the Celebration Magnifico bus to Atlantic City for our New Year's Eve gig. As I limboed in the New Year with drunken strangers, I knew the coming year would be very different for me. And that's about all I knew.

Final Scene: New York City, August 9, 2002

"I certainly never expected to end up back here again," I thought, staring out the cab window, my eyes squinting from the glare of the summer sun. I had gone to New York a youngster, but was coming back a star. "We've been through a lot," I whispered to The City. I wanted to hug the place like an old friend. "Sure our relationship was short and somewhat rocky, but thanks for everything," I silently offered in sincere gratitude. "I'm not the same scared, naïve girl I was fifteen years ago, and I wish I could have seen you back then like I do now." Because, in spite of its involuntary, 9/11 maniacal make-over, New York looked better to me than ever before. The City shone brightly, and I could clearly see the diamond beneath the rough—the excitement, splendor, and beauty of this place of extremes, its wealth, poverty, and everything in between.

The yellow taxi cab dropped me off in front of Jenny and her musician husband's four-story, red brick brownstone. "Have a beautiful day and keep cool," I said, over-tipping the driver in honor of this special occasion. "Thanks very much. You, too, Ma'am. God bless." *The people here are so nice.*

Jenny was at work when I arrived but she had left a key for me under the flowerpot in the charming, tiny, back garden. This place was a palace compared to the small, two-bedroom apartment she and her friend rented back when I lived there. I set my suitcases down in the living room and plopped down on the comfy sofa. A cat wandered in to check me out. "Well, who do we have here?" I bent over to pet her. "Nice pad, kitty," I said as I scanned the room. Jenny had done well for herself here. She had abandoned her performing career, opting for stage management instead, and had worked her way up to the pinnacle of the profession. How impressive that she was a Broadway stage manager for *Chicago* (the steamy, jazzy, Kander and Ebb and Bob Fosse musical about Prohibition-Era murderesses). It didn't get much better than that.

"New York's not so bad; is it?" I asked the cat, who started to purr from all my petting. "What if I would have stuck it out a little longer? I didn't even audition for any Broadway shows. I should have taken more advantage of my scholarship at Steps and trained hard with all those amazing teachers. What do you think, kitty-cat?" No answer.

"Cat got your tongue?" I chuckled at my own stupid joke. "Woulda. Coulda. Shoulda." Second guessing my decisions was pointless and a waste of precious time and energy. Had I stayed in New York, I would have missed out on some pretty bitchin' California adventures. My rad move to the West coast had gotten me where I was today. "Cowabunga, Dude!" I kicked off my shoes and laid down on the couch for a quick catnap while I waited for Jenny to come home.

Act 1, Scene 2

California, Here I Come!

New York wasn't for me. I loved dancing, but that wasn't enough to overcome my fears and the challenges of life in the Big City. Plus, becoming a professional dancer was a tremendous shock to my system having come from such a sensible, academic, risk-averse family. Tossing my education out the window to do something so frivolous and insecure seemed selfish and foolish, two characteristics I did not wish to possess. My parents didn't discourage my wacky dance adventure, but I knew they'd sleep more soundly (as would I) if I went to graduate school. Consequently, I decided to get my PhD in Social Psychology. "Dr. Davis." Now that sounded respectable. What a relief to be doing something that seemed like the intelligent, practical thing to do—a decision that would bring sincere support from my parents and a guaranteed paycheck.

While waiting to get accepted into graduate school, I took on mundane jobs in retail and fundraising. They were the perfect reminder of how the real world and I did not get along. I did not thrive in a practical life of nine to five, suits and nylons, weekends off, one-week vacations, and bottom lines. Working an office job, I felt like a piece of cheese sitting undiscovered, molding away in the back of the refrigerator. If I didn't get out soon, I'd shrivel up and die from a life of missed opportunities, wasted potential, adventures not experienced, and what ifs. I didn't want to be eighty years old thinking I had never really lived. This "normal" existence was killing me. I stared at the clock, watching the time tick slowly by, wishing my life away. After a few months, I noticed my saggy derriere in the mirror and decided it was time to start working out again. I missed the dancing, so I auditioned for and was accepted into a modern/jazz dance company in Ann Arbor. It kept me somewhat sane for that year.

In August of 1989, I left Michigan and my humdrum routine for graduate school at the University of Minnesota. At first, it was exciting to be doing something supposedly worthwhile with my life. I was successful there, too—got a full teaching scholarship, earned good grades, had a nice apartment in a fun neighborhood, made friends, and even dated a bit. Still, it was lonely living all by myself in a new city, so I bought a beautiful, blue, Siamese fighting fish to keep me company. Once again, I missed dancing so I started taking classes at a reputable dance school downtown. Grad school turned out to be terribly stressful, and the chain-smoking assistant professors seemed more overwhelmed than the students. "This is what I have to look forward to?"

I was at a loss. I sat down by the fishbowl and confided in my fish, "I am miserable here. All I do is study until midnight and then wake up and study again at five a.m. It's interesting stuff to learn, but I hate statistics and I don't really want to do social psychology research for a living. It's too stressful and not fun for me. But I just moved here. What will people think if I abandon yet another career plan? What will my parents think? More importantly, what am I going to do with my life if I give up on this, too?" My fish stared back in silence with a look that said, "I'm stuck alone swimming circles in this tiny bowl for the rest of my God forsaken life. You think I give a rat's patootie? Stop your whining. At least you've got choices."

The thought of quitting was so embarrassing and horrifying, however, that I mustered all my willpower and forced myself to stick through another semester and make it work. I chose to keep right on swimming circles, feeling alone in a tiny fishbowl. But, once again, I nearly had a nervous breakdown. This time felt even worse than the time in New York. When would I learn to follow my heart and do what I truly loved?

Apparently, this world of academics wasn't for me either. I had tried the business route, the academic route, the safe and secure and practical route, the route that garnered parental approval. "Now what?" Hoping to find some clarity, I pulled out my credit card and booked an emergency trip to San Diego, California, to visit my sister, Cindy, who was in transition herself. She was abandoning her PhD program in Oceanography to pursue a sexier career: screenwriting.

There is no better place for soul searching than by the ocean. As I walked barefoot in the sand, I asked myself, "How do I really want to be spending my twenties?" The most exhilarating, thrilling, exciting, passionate, enticing, challenging, rewarding, inspiring idea I could come up with was to be an entertainer traveling the globe. The reasons flowed like the ocean waves: "I want to meet unique, interesting, artistic, creative, outgoing, talented, famous people. I want to go to places I'd never go to on my own. I want to be learning, changing, growing, and challenging myself on a daily basis. I want to stand out in a crowd and be fascinating. I want to live on the stage, being paid to do what I love most: sing and dance, wearing exotic makeup and glitzy costumes."

What it boiled down to was I wanted my twenties to be a thrilling adventure, and I was finally willing to take the risk. The truth was, everything else made me so miserable that I was forced to do it as my last option. I was afraid to try again, but what did I really have to lose? I had no money, no house, no husband or children. I could only move up in the world. If I failed, I would have wasted some time and felt like a fool in front of friends and family. But if I never tried, I would regret it for the rest of my life. There's nothing worse than wondering, "What if?" I could always go back to school later, but this was something I had to do when I was young. It was now or never.

The hardest part of this new game plan would be telling my parents about another seemingly flippant, haphazard choice. All I knew was that I had to find myself, discover the world, and fill the void of dissatisfaction that was gnawing at me.

"Move out here and live with me," Cindy offered. I felt relieved at the thought of having my sister around, plus California seemed like a logical place to relaunch my entertainment career. And it's sunny California, for goodness sake.

So, much to my parents' chagrin, after finishing the semester, I quit school and moved back to Michigan, where I spent two months working as a secretarial temp at Ford Motor Company to bank some cash. I was headed off to California with $5000 and no idea how to make my dreams come true. All I knew was I wanted to be an entertainer. And this time, I meant it.

****

When I announced the impending move to my Midwestern friends, their response was, "Are you crazy? You're moving to California with all those weirdos?" They were sincerely scared for me, worried I'd end up practicing naked yoga, consuming tofu and wheat grass juice, and shaking a tambourine at the airport with the Hare Krishnas. I left with slight trepidation, wondering if they might be right.

Mom and I repacked my possessions, this time into my new Ford Escort. With my precious pet fish in its fishbowl, wedged between the seats, we ventured west. It was California or bust. In the Rocky Mountains, we nearly did bust. My underpowered and overloaded car labored up the steep, snow-covered roads at a maximum of thirty-five miles per hour, semi trucks whizzing dangerously past. I kept a vigilant watch for runaway vehicle lanes on the downward slopes, as I never knew if my brakes were going to work. My poor, gorgeous, royal blue fish sloshed about so violently in his fishbowl that he turned a pale, deathly gray. I would have thought it impossible, but my fish appeared to be seasick! Eventually, a blizzard forced us to stop for the night. Hotel staff and patrons pointed and laughed as I carried in my fishbowl wrapped in a pillow to keep the traumatized little passenger from turning into a frozen fish stick.

When the snowstorm abated, we continued on to Las Vegas. The casino scene was smoky, seedy, and swarming with slimy people. "How can anyone stand this place?" I asked my mother. Even the one-armed bandits and cheap, all-you-can-eat buffets weren't enough to entice me into staying any longer than absolutely necessary. I couldn't wait to get out of there.

It was such a relief when we finally reached our destination: sunny Del Mar, California—a charming, little, tourist town situated on two square miles of picturesque Pacific coastline. At the sight of the sparkling, blue water, a wave of peace and calm washed over me. "Ah … freedom, hope, and new beginnings!"

Since my last visit six months ago, Cindy had moved from La Jolla to Del Mar. Her four-unit apartment building, surrounded by palm trees and built on dramatic bluffs bordering the shoreline, sat smack dab on prime ocean-front real estate. How on earth did she score such a superb top-of-the-line location? I quickly discovered how: Her abode was a bit on the ramshackle side and clearly in need of repair. I was tempted to hammer in a few nails on the spot. We knocked on the door of the weathered wooden building. "Kris! Mom! You made it!" Cindy squealed as she hugged us. "Come on in. You can put your stuff in my room." Cindy shared her two-bedroom apartment with another young woman, and now I was adding all my belongings to their already cramped space.

"I call this place 'The Crap Shack,'" Cindy chuckled, as my eyes scanned the scuzzy interior. Her jesting only slightly softened the blow of the shocking sight of my new living quarters. The grungy, brown living room contained two shabby sofas—one placed on the floor in the usual manner conducive to sitting and the other propped up on its end, leaning against the wall, as if she was saving it as back-up in case of a couch emergency. In addition, a towering, ceiling-high, ratty, dirty-beige carpet-covered cat scratching-pole stood in the corner.

This place was a pigsty (or catsty), thanks mainly to Cindy's roommate—a quiet, pencil-thin, plainly pretty PhD student from the

University of Southern California—and her two cats. To call her a slob wouldn't do her justice. She was the slobbiest slob I've ever seen. You could not walk through her bedroom without scaling mountains of clothes and junk. Even her bed was completely covered in rubbish, and the bathroom shower curtain could have served as a science experiment, growing mold and an assortment of fungus in its thick layer of grime. I envisioned the roommate twenty years down the road as one of those crazy cat ladies you see on the news, with forty-seven cats and a condemned home filled with their feline feces. She had started her collection with two pets we nicknamed "Psycho" and "Pee-Pee." Psycho was afraid of everyone but her owner and would run around like a maniacal scaredy cat. Pee-Pee would climb into your clothes and urinate on them. We had to make sure the closet was shut and the door to our bedroom locked at all times.

Pee-Pee also preferred to whiz on the stove while you were cooking or on your leg when you sat down to eat. When he was in a good mood, he'd walk up to you and vomit a hairball, but that was about the friendliest he got. He just didn't want us in his home. As if that weren't disgusting enough, the living room became infested with fleas from the cats. We had to sprinkle Borax everywhere to combat the little buggers. It was all I could do to keep from crying, "What was this recurring problem with cats? Had I been a cat-abusing dog in a previous life?"

To make matters worse, my fish died not long after settling in California, because the public drinking water he was swimming in was so bad. He disintegrated before my very eyes, more chunks falling off him every day. Distraught, I called a San Diego pet store for help. "How often are you changing the water?" the man inquired. "Every few weeks, like they told me when I bought him in Minnesota," I replied. "You need to change the water every few DAYS here, Lady," the man replied shocked at my mistreatment. I made that fish endure motion sickness, the frigid cold of Colorado, and the oppressive heat of the desert, only to be placed in toxic, flesh-eating water. I could have done that poor, little guy a favor and simply flushed him down the toilet before I left Michigan.

I started feeling buyer's remorse. You know, like when you make a big decision such as moving across the country with no job and no home of your own, and you get there and your beloved fish dies and you end up living in a hell hole? Even a good night's sleep eluded me because the sound of the ocean waves crashing on the shore was so loud. This wasn't what I thought I was buying when I purchased a one-way ticket to Cali.

Fortunately, my life situation was about to change again, and this time for the better. First, after a few weeks I became used to the sound of the waves and even learned to take comfort in their tidal rhythm. Then Cindy made a discovery.

Cindy had been searching the want ads of the local paper for jobs, since she was currently out of hers, having bailed on grad school. "Kris, there's a notice for salespeople for an art gallery called Intarsia Gallery. It's at The Plaza, which is great, because we can walk there if we want." The Plaza was a three-story, high-end, open-air shopping plaza that had opened in the heart of the main street, Camino Del Mar, just after I arrived in town. It was a heavenly, peaceful shopping and eating oasis overlooking the ocean.

The art gallery was just as magnificent. Tucked away on the top floor in the back of the building, it was a classy, eclectic boutique that housed everything from faux Southwestern Indian pottery waterfalls, to unique jewelry dripping in amethysts and silver and turquoise, to colorful hand-painted silk clothing. Cindy and I both got hired there, and with careful counting of our pennies, eventually earned enough change between us to move to a very nice one-bedroom apartment a few blocks away from Le Chateau du Merde. "Au revoir cats! Au revoir fleas!"

****

Once adequate income and hygienic housing were acquired, I began to acclimate to my new surroundings. I had moved to Del Mar during peak time—summer—when it was flooded by tourists, many coming down from Los Angeles to rent beach houses or hit the Del Mar race track for racing season. The one main street in town included a delightful mix of funky little shops, cafes, coffee houses, art galleries, independent bookstores, boutiques, seafood restaurants, expensive gourmet dining establishments, and waterfront luxury hotels, to support the influx of people with deep pockets. The city's oceanfront also offered some "gnarly waves, dude," so you could walk down the street any day and find buffed, tan, young surfers changing in and out of their wet suits by their cars on the side of the road. It was good to keep an eye on them as occasionally one would accidentally let his towel slip.

In addition to all the surfers, famous triathletes were a dime a dozen given the superior training conditions: year-long gorgeous weather, mountains for cycling, and the ocean for swimming. Famous or not, it seemed that everyone ran races or mountain-biked on the weekends, worked out daily, juiced, practiced yoga, got massages, and saw a therapist. Many women sported fake sets of perfect, perky, bulbous breasts. Clearly, the body was highly revered here. There was no shortage of buffed physiques. As a result, every untoned muscle on my body suffered from low self-esteem. Something had to be done. And quickly.

Working out became high on my list of priorities, not only so that I'd fit in, be accepted, and be beautiful like everyone else, but also because there was so much I wanted to eat, without getting fatter. The influence of nearby Mexico was as strong as a Habanero chili pepper, and there was plenty of fabulous Mexican food to be found: savory fish tacos made of flaky white fish nestled in a bed of crispy cabbage slaw with a squirt of lime juice and salsa verde all pocketed in a soft corn tortilla, crisp and salty tortilla chips to dunk in salsa fresco (diced tomatoes, onion, peppers, and cilantro), and overstuffed burritos with garlicky shredded beef, refried beans, rice, and guacamole smothered in cheese and sour cream and washed down with a tangy margarita. Olé!

The word "cilantro" became an important addition to my vocabulary, and if either cilantro or some type of hot pepper wasn't in my meal it was probably only my morning scone. I cranked up the heat on my taste buds and craved spicier and spicier foods. Having grown up with such gastronomic delicacies as Jell-O, Velveeta cheese, Oscar Meyer bologna, and casseroles based on Campbell's Cream of Mushroom soup, these fresh, foreign foods blissfully expanded my palate.

I enthusiastically soaked myself in this exotic culture like I was basking in the warmth of the sun. Spanish was the second language, and I wished I knew how to "hablar español." Southern California was a place where Mexicans, who had risked their lives crossing the border illegally, slaved away as fruit pickers or worked secretly in the kitchens of popular restaurants. Homes had roofs made of terra cotta tiles and were often decorated in Southwestern turquoise and salmon colors. Even the vegetation spurred my soul: palm trees galore; beach areas covered in thick-leaved, green ice plants with magenta blooms; masses of large trumpet-shaped hibiscus flowers in red, orange, yellow, pink, purple, and white; spiky Mojave yucca plants; fences lined with vibrant, papery Bougainvillea; cheerful flocks of Bird of Paradise flowers proudly displaying their orange plumes; night-blooming jasmine seductively scenting the air. Even the freeway medians and roadsides were lush with lemon-yellow and hot-pink flowering bushes. This piquant, tropical paradise felt worlds away from the gray, frigid Michigan, of my youth.

The people scene enthralled me as well. I was fascinated by anyone who had shunned the normal life of nine-to-five jobs, broken all of the rules, and risked everything to find something better. Many of these people were artists who showed their artistic creations at Intarsia Gallery where I worked. Take Molly, for instance. She was a handsome, thirty-ish, tall, leggy, tan runner with a short, black, pixie haircut, who painted abstract designs on silk neckties and scarves. When hanging out in Paris some years earlier, she had seen an advertisement for silk-painting classes in the back of a magazine. She learned the trade and now made a living selling her hand-painted ties and scarves in shops around San Diego. She also cooked for a family or two and would travel with them on their boats as their private chef. I collected delicious recipes from her: basil beer bread, mint-chocolate brownies, carrot cake with cream cheese frosting, and ginger-soy chicken (chicken breast marinated in soy sauce, lemon juice, fresh grated ginger root, minced garlic, and a touch of sugar and then grilled).

Another quiet, unassuming, librarian-like artist who intrigued me sold Chinese brush paintings, which consisted mainly of graceful, purposeful, abstract, thick, black brush strokes with a splash of red. She taught classes from her beautiful home so, out of curiosity, I joined in. The mood was very zen. We meditated while mixing our black ink in slate dishes, counting every stir. After reaching some ridiculously high number (it felt like one million), we were allowed to stop the stirring ritual and start painting. By this time we were in a self-induced trance. Fresh, whole strawberries were served along with Chinese tea in delicate Chinese porcelain cups. We ended the afternoon in the artist's lovely, peaceful, flower garden with a session of tai chi. I was a tiger.

Del Mar also had a captivating dating scene, peppered with men unlike any I'd met in the Midwest. My boss, twenty years my senior, had been wooing me—a flattering prospect, but not the wisest choice, perhaps, given our age difference and the fact that he had the ability to fire me. I decided I needed the job more than the dalliance, so I passed on him and instead dated Matt—a hunky, long-haired, thirty-something artist whose work was displayed at the gallery. His big-ticket items were stunning, large, plaster wall hangings—bas relief sculptures of wild horses made to look like antique relics using paint and fake cracks. Being situated in a horse-racing town, horse art was a big seller. But what really intrigued me were Matt's travels down to South America to make plaster replicas and rice paper rubbings of Mayan and Incan designs. He gifted me a rice paper rubbing of a pregnant woman and a miniature sculpture entitled "Bondage" of a long-haired slave in a loin cloth kneeling with an arched back. Matt's accent was a mixture of Stanford-educated academic and California surfer dude. He was also a runner, of course. He took me to Tijuana to shop, eat, drink tequila, and be accosted by small, pesky, insistent Mexican children selling Chicklets. I returned home chewing gum, carrying two bottles of cheap Kahlua, and covered in a layer of grime. Matt was certainly captivating, but the relationship didn't make it much past Tijuana.

For a short time, I dated an extremely handsome Top Gun fighter pilot and even got to visit the officer's bar at Top Gun air force base where they filmed scenes from the Tom Cruise-Kelly McGillis film *Top Gun*. One of my date's instructors actually flew a plane in the flick. Having spent many a movie drooling over Tom Cruise since high school, I was in awe of it all. My date was debatably as hot as the diminutive movie star. Sadly, even though his gun may have been the tops, the relationship didn't fly.

Aside from meeting groovy new people, I spent most of that first year working at the art gallery while taking the odd dance class. I found a professional studio in downtown San Diego, but getting there was inconvenient, finding parking was a pain, and the lack of instructors who satisfied my needs made the effort not worth my while. I tried a studio a few towns north of Del Mar that had a couple of excellent teachers, but I was too tired to travel all that way after working at the gallery all day. At either studio, fitting classes into my schedule was a task, and my motivation was weak. Finally, I started teaching aerobics and a few dance classes at a nearby gym, figuring I might as well get paid to workout. For the most part, I was spending all my energy paying rent and getting adjusted to my new surroundings.

To be honest, I had also become highly distracted by my persistent boss, Adam—a forty-five-year-old, tan, athletic, Jewish, ex-hippie— who finally persuaded me to go out with him. In addition to designing and owning a gorgeous art gallery, he was a woodworker who handmade exquisite furniture adorned with colorful, Southwestern inlaid designs in the studio behind his house on the hillside overlooking the ocean. He was both creative and energetic, a combination of personality traits that compelled him to constantly reconfigure the interior and exterior of his stunning home, which he embellished with a collection of provocative African and Southwestern artifacts.

Adam wasn't afraid to try whatever intrigued him. At one point in his life he studied to become a psychotherapist. At another, he spent a few years on an Ironman team, just training—running, biking, and swimming—for the Ironman race in Hawaii. He even started a health-food restaurant back when I was just a toddler. Now he owned a retail art gallery, and his daily work attire was khaki shorts and a good-quality Hawaiian shirt. Adam was a native Los Angeleno; his father had been the agent to Willie Shoemaker—one of the most successful and famous horse jockeys in history. Adam's family had a box at the Del Mar Race Track, where he took me on the momentous Opening Day. Adam knew everyone in town and was extremely sociable. He lived life the way that made him the happiest, disregarding the opinions of the outside world. I envied that.

So, I gave in to his advances, against my better judgment of dating a man so much older. It was gratifying to be desired by this worldly man about town, and being on some tenuous mission to find myself, I allowed myself to experiment. Let's face it, I was lonely, too. My free time was now spent hanging out with this long-time Del Martian who wined and dined me; taught me about running and cycling and art; and took me on exotic trips to Hawaii, Banff, and Las Vegas, on gallery art-buying excursions to San Francisco and Scottsdale, and on ski vacations to Whistler and Mammoth. The man had exquisite taste and bought me wonderful gifts as well. Once we hooked up, I was immediately welcomed into Adam's circle of fascinating friends. This gossipy, slightly dysfunctional, small town functioned like a soap opera, and I was now part of the melodrama. My new social life kept me from wallowing in unsolicited solitude, as my sister Cindy was deeply focused on her writing and often unavailable. I was living the high life.

And yet I was discontented. I wasn't doing anything in entertainment like I had envisioned. This would've been a great retirement lifestyle, but I still wanted to make something of myself and utilize my potential. But how?

Final Scene: New York City, August 9, 2002

The sound of a key in the door lock awakened me from my slumber. Jenny and I greeted each other like long-lost sisters, squealing and hugging. "J-Dancer!" "K-Dancer!" We picked up as if no time had passed. Jenny poured two generous glasses of chardonnay. "I'm so excited to have you here! Do you want to come to my show tomorrow night after your Rockette thingy? You can sit backstage with me and watch me call the show if you'd like." I was overjoyed at the opportunity to see a top-notch stage manager in action. Plus, a behind-the-scenes peek at Broadway actors was sure to be highly entertaining.

"Cheers, Jen," I toasted, raising my glass. "If it weren't for you I would have never become a professional dancer." It was true. Not only had she talked me into moving to New York, but even after I left town, she kept getting me gigs. She was like the Pied Piper, and I followed her wherever she led me, even to Indiana. This woman believed in me when I didn't believe in myself. She got me dance jobs when I didn't have a clue what to do or where to go with my life. As far as I was concerned, she was my guardian angel and divine guide, disguised as a dancing, feminist, Bohemian, hippie, New Yorker. We stayed up far too late laughing, sipping vino, and recalling moments from our crazy, musical theatre days together.

Act 1, Scene 3

Beef and Boards

When out of the blue, after more than three and a half years, I received a phone call from Jenny, I nearly fell to the floor. "I'm in Indianapolis doing *Funny Girl*," she said. "One of the chorus girls is breaking her contract to do a cruise ship gig, and they need a replacement. I want you to come and do the show!"

Serendipity or destiny? "You're just about her size and will fit the costumes. I told the stage manager about you. You need to fax him your headshot and resume, and mail a vocal demo tape right away," Jenny insisted. "I don't have a demo tape," I wailed. "Just throw something together quickly, before they find someone else. It would be so much fun! You have to do it!" She begged me, but it was unnecessary. I wholeheartedly agreed.

In haste, I bought a karaoke tape of James Taylor's "You've Got a Friend," taped myself singing the vocals atop the canned background music, and threw it in the mail. "It's not the best, but at least they'll know I'm not tone deaf and can carry a tune," I rationalized. You'd have thought I'd been smoking some bad Tijuana marijuana when I made this decision, as this song wasn't even remotely appropriate for the gig I was trying to land. But, sometimes you get the job simply because "you've got a friend." Jenny laid her credibility on the line, begged, pleaded, and promised her first born to the stage manager to get him to consider hiring me. In the end, he did, mainly because I was immediately available, likely to fit the costumes, and saved him from having to spend time auditioning people. Jenny can be very persuasive.

"Your room and board are free, and we can pay you $275 a week," the stage manager informed me over the phone. I didn't care if I got paid $75 a week. I was going to do a professional musical! This was living! He didn't want to pay to fly me out there but gave in at the last minute. Here I was in Del Mar, California, population 4,000-ish, plugging away at the art gallery and going nowhere with my entertainment career when unexpectedly, no audition necessary, a dance job comes my way. I thanked my lucky stars. I thanked my tall angel, Jenny. That's how I landed my first professional musical theatre job: It was handed to me like a gift.

The next thing I knew, I was on a plane bound for the Midwest. "Goodbye, Hollywood. Hello, Hoosierville!" I settled in for a long day of travel, with multiple layovers and an overload of peanuts and Diet Coke. They had obviously scored the cheapest flight option available, but at least I wasn't footing the bill. The travel time across country gave me plenty of opportunity to think about *Funny Girl*. As a kid, I had seen the movie version starring Barbra Streisand as Ziegfeld Follies star comedienne, Fanny Brice, and Omar Sharif as her gambling husband, Nicky Arnstein. I recalled that Fanny and Nicky had a tumultuous relationship that ended sadly, and Barbra sang renditions of "People" and "Don't Rain on My Parade" that gave me goosebumps. But that's about all I could remember. "Wonder what I'll be doing in the show?"

It was fall when I arrived in Indianapolis, but the leaves had already fallen off the trees. So mainly it was cold, brisk, and gray—the familiar look, smell, and feel of football season in the Midwest. "Ahhhhhh….home sweet home." Made me want to put on a sweatshirt and make a big pot of chili. The theatre was located just off Indiana interstate 465, exit 27, among hotels and office buildings, and, oddly enough, just down the road from my college sorority national headquarters. That was a good sign. If I needed support from my sisters-in-the-bond, they were only a secret handshake away.

The name of the venue, "Beef and Boards Dinner Theatre," should have alerted me that I'd be in for a unique experience. "Beef" stood for the dinner they served and "Boards" for the stage. The most unique facet of the "gig"—a showbiz term meaning "job" that I started throwing around casually—was that I lived at the theatre in a second-floor room that I shared with Jenny, who served as my tour guide. Our bedroom, which doubled as our dressing room during the show, was full of costumes and wigs resting on white Styrofoam heads. A young chorus guy named Brent and an older character actor named Belinda lived down the hall from Jenny and me; everyone else lived in apartments a short drive from the theatre.

The rest of our home for the next few months was downstairs at stage level. It consisted of two smallish, no-frills rooms adjacent to each other (and conveniently located next to the stage left entrance) that served as our kitchen and the green room. (The "green room," I learned, is a room backstage that provides a place for the actors to hang out before, after, or during a show. There are many opinions on the origin of the term, but suffice it to say that the room is rarely actually green.) She then led me into the theatre, which could hold up to 450 patrons sitting tableside, surrounding centrally located, portable buffet carts that were covered in sneeze glass. "We get first stabs at the dinner buffet before the audience descends upon it, but we have to fend for ourselves for breakfast and lunch," Jenny informed me. "Bonus! Free chow!" I applauded. I would soon tire of seeing the same salad bar, beef, chicken, and baked potatoes night after night, but it certainly saved on the food bill. The lobby was adorned with posters of the previous shows that were performed there. The next poster would be for a musical that featured me. And people were going to pay to see me!

After the tour, it was time to stop dilly-dallying and get down to business. We had a lot to do, and quickly, as I had only a week to learn how to fill the shoes of the girl I was replacing. First order of business: try on costumes. Luckily, nothing needed alterations except for the shoes, which I filled and then some, as they were two sizes too small. Being young and naïve, I stuffed my tootsies into them anyway, like the ugly stepsister pretending to fit into Cinderella's glass slipper. My feet could have been permanently damaged, and my career permanently ruined, but I was afraid to ask for new shoes. Not wanting to lose my first job, I grinned and beared it.

Second order of business: placate (pay off) the union. "This is an Equity theatre," the stage manager announced, "so you have to pay $100 to the Actors' Equity Association. This allows you to become a candidate for Equity eligibility." I didn't know what he was talking about, but if I didn't do it, I wasn't going to be working there, so I wrote out the check. (So far this gig had cost me money.) He explained that "Equity" was the nickname for Actors' Equity Association, the labor union representing live theatre actors and stage managers in America.

Third, fourth, and fifth order of business: The stage manager handed me a pile of sheet music and said, "You will rehearse during the day with Sandi, the dance captain, to learn your track. At night, you need to watch the show to get a better idea of what you will be doing on stage. Oh, and here's your music for the pre-show with Brent and Jenny." My eyes widened. "Jenny didn't say anything about a pre-show!"

As directed, I watched the performance that night, terrified about the pre-show. "Can I sing well enough to pull this off?" I would have to don a blond wig and black sequin gown, hold a microphone, and sing a Broadway medley for the geriatrics as they filled their bellies before the main production. I was simultaneously thrilled about using a mic for the first time and petrified that I would have everyone wondering who I slept with to get this part. "Most of the audience probably can't hear too well," I reasoned, "and maybe no one will recognize me in disguise." *Funny Girl*, on the other hand, was totally within my realm of capabilities. Not willing to let a little pre-show rain on my parade, I encouraged myself that I might actually be good. Being a part of this show made me feel like one of the luckiest people in the world.

The next day I reported for rehearsal with Sandi, the "dance captain." The title sounded intimidating. Unlike what the name implied, she had no military training whatsoever, although that probably would have helped her in her pursuits. Apparently every musical theatre show had a cast member who served as commander. It was the first time I'd heard of such a role. Jenny explained, "Someone has to keep the show clean after the director and choreographer leave." "Aren't there maintenance men to mop the stage?" I asked, but she wasn't talking about that type of clean. "Clean" meant keeping the original directions and choreography intact. Over time, if someone didn't keep a close eye on it, choreography had a sneaky way of morphing into moves unapproved by the choreographer. Since the director and choreographer skedaddled out of the theatre for good after "putting up" the show, the dance captain was needed to maintain the proper moves and grooves.

The dance captain also was in charge of settling choreographic disputes—a customer service representative of sorts, listening to performers' gripes about one another. If you saw someone on stage doing the choreography incorrectly, it was taboo for you to tell that person directly. You were supposed to tell the dance captain, who would then relay the message to the offending dancer.

Finally, the dance captain assumed the monstrous responsibility of knowing everyone's individual "tracks"—their choreography and "blocking" (where to move to at specific times during scenes). Hence, Sandi was the one to whip me into tip-top shape in only seven days time. Thankfully, she was about as sweet as dance captains come, so I could let down my guard and rest at ease. She was a beautiful girl a few years older than I, who had done oodles of shows at Beef and Boards. Her handsome hubby Matt was in the show, too. Sandi loved performing, meeting people, and socializing with her showbiz friends. I envied how she made the most of her job and enjoyed the journey.

Fortunately, she wouldn't allow me to dwell on the dreaded preshow, as I had plenty to focus on for the real show. My numbers included an opening rehearsal scene; a military-style tap dance; "Sadie, Sadie, Married Lady," a simple number sung by Fanny and the girls about how glorious it was to be married; and "Beautiful Bride," a fashion show of sorts in which we glided around stage in ridiculously over-the-top, extravagant, designer wedding gowns with towering head pieces, escorted by debonair men in top hats and tails. This is the song where Fanny Brice, decked out in a wedding gown and roller skates, turns to the audience to reveal that she is hugely pregnant. I also did a couple bit parts, and my character even had a name: "Polly." My first real role! I had only two speaking parts—called "lines"— in the show, but it was a start.

Once I learned my track, a portion of the cast was brought in for a quick "put-in." A put-in is a rehearsal where the new, replacement actor is plugged into or "put in" the hole left by the original actor who vacated it. The cast consisted of the two leads (Fanny and Nicky), a group of older character actors (one man and three women), and the ensemble (three men and four women) who did the heavier dancing. Since my role required little in the way of direct interactions with the leads or the seniors, they were allowed to lounge at home in their pajamas and rest their voices while the ensemble gave up their time off to rehearse with the new chick. Jenny, Sandi, Matt, Brent, Steven (a debonair tenor), Harriet (a tall, statuesque redhead in her early thirties), and I comprised the ensemble. Everyone was warm and welcoming except for Harriet who offhandedly commented, "I was the prettiest one here until you came along." The words sounded like a compliment but the tone made me tremble. I treaded carefully around her after that, not wanting to step on her toes, literally or figuratively.

For the put-in, I had to do all my costume changes and numbers "full out"—at performance quality with a big old smile plastered on my face—while the rest of the cast "marked" the show in their sweats. In other words, they went through the motions without really performing, so they could conserve their precious energy for the real deal. The numbers I wasn't in were bypassed to speed up the process. I basically got a rough idea about where everyone else would be on stage relative to me and where I might crash into someone or trip over a set piece.

The put-in also prepared me for my "traffic patterns." "Traffic patterns? Are you going to be driving cars on stage?" you might ask.

Not usually. The term refers to how and where and when people move around on and off stage relative to each other. Performers are required to strictly adhere to their specific sequence every night, every single show, without fail or exception, or there's bound to be an accident.

The problem with a put-in is that, without running the entire show at regular speed, you don't get any idea of the pacing of the show and how much time you have to change costumes or how out of breath you'll be between numbers. That pleasure is saved for the first time you do the show for an audience. Scaaaaaary. With our "dressing room" located on the second floor, Jenny and I were constantly running up and down the stairs to change costumes and wigs. I didn't know how it would all pan out come show time.

Being wigged the entire show and having no prior experience wearing fake hair, I was grateful when Jenny took it upon herself to teach me about pin curls and wig caps. "Take small chunks of hair and curl them, like you'd wind a hose, into tiny buns all over your head," Jenny demonstrated. "Then secure them with two bobby pins placed in an 'X' formation." When I finished, my head looked like I'd been attacked by cinnamon rolls.

All these mini-cinnabuns and any leftover wisps of hair were then further secured by covering the entire hairdo with a wig cap. Our wig caps were sections of pantyhose tied into a knot on the top to form stretchy caps like criminals wear. After the show, all we'd need to do is pull the wig cap all the way down to hide our faces, and we'd be ready to moonlight as bank robbers. "I'm a sperm head!" I screamed as I grimaced at my hideous image in the mirror. Jenny burst out laughing, grabbed her camera, and took my picture. While I certainly did not feel glamorous, I was learning a vitally important lesson. The beautiful secret of pin curls is that they provide something you can anchor your wig into with hairpins. I didn't want to take a chance on a wig mishap, as I did not look attractive in a wig cap. I learned to love wearing wigs, because I could be having the hair day from hell and it wouldn't matter.

After "Wigs 101," I was ready to hit the stage and shine like the star I was meant to be. I plugged into my part with no particularly troublesome problems. The songs and dances were pure joy to perform. Once I got into my show routine and knew the ropes, I felt quite confident that I was doing a bang-up job. The exception was the pre-show, of course. Even after banging away at it for several weeks, I still couldn't tell if my singing was passable or even tolerable. I was too mortified to ask. They weren't firing me, so I left well enough alone and had fun faking it as best I could. Eventually, I became so comfortable with the show that I was able to play cards in the green room between scenes with the other actors waiting to go on stage.

The most hazardous part of the show was running through the kitchen of the theatre for certain entrances and exits during the performance, being careful not to slip on spills on the tile floor. I wasn't too stable to begin with in my much-too-tiny, used shoes. The smell of steam and industrial dishwashing soap mixed with a collage of leftover buffet food became etched in my olfactory memory.

Our performances were Tuesday night, Wednesday matinee and evening, Thursday, Friday, Saturday, and Sunday matinee and evening. The matinees were overrun with senior citizens. You could tell by the glare of all the glasses. Those two-show days were tough for me. Coupled with the show the night before, I felt like I never left the theatre for days. I was in and out of make-up and costume over and over and over. I loved dancing and singing and wearing the costumes, but running up and down stairs for fast changes scene after scene, show after show, day after day got monotonous.

The saving grace was Monday—our "dark" night at the theatre. A "dark night" sounds like a moonless night or a night when everything goes insidiously wrong, but it really refers to a night in which the theatre is dark, as in no lights, no audience, no show. In other words, it was our precious day off. While *Funny Girl* was dark, however, there was always something else booked in the theatre. Acts as famous as Marie Osmond (who made her own beet juice, by the way) performed there. Once there was even a male strip show, which, of course, Jenny and I eagerly attended. The muscular, young men stripped on stage and then circled the room, dancing and caressing for tips. I bravely and carefully stuffed a dollar in one guy's G-string and received a kiss on the cheek. It was revolting in one sense and stimulating in another. The smell of the strippers' cheap cologne lingered in our green room for days. It felt like slimy strangers had invaded our home.

Barring the striptease, my time off was often ho-hum, as I was essentially trapped at the theatre without transportation. The cast members from out of town did have one company car to share, but it stayed parked near the lead actors' apartments several miles away from Beef and Boards. Consequently, those of us living at the theatre had to beg for rides to the grocery store and were at the mercy of the people in control of the wheels. The theatre was within walking distance of a few mediocre restaurants, but otherwise there was just an exit off the highway and a few office buildings.

Thankfully, the cast learned to make our own fun by organizing activities we could drive to together, like racquet ball, gymnastics classes, progressive dinner parties, and bowling. Sandi served as the unofficial extracurricular activities coordinator and, being a local who had her own car, also kept the ball rolling by giving us rides to the various events. She was a big proponent of continuing Beef and Board's post-performance Friday night bowling tradition, for which cast members would buy a bona fide bowling shirt and sew on a patch for every show they had done at the theatre. I'm sure we were a hoot to watch as we dance-bowled our way through the game doing crazy ballet/jazz moves before, during, and after the ball toss.

A couple of times the cast ventured to downtown Indianapolis to a sing-along piano bar where we played pool, shot baskets, drank beer, and ate peanuts, throwing the shells on the floor. Occasionally a group of us made the exciting trip to a popular pancake house that served "dutch babies"—a puffy pancake the size of a large plate, topped with cooked cinnamon apple compote. On Halloween, our leads hosted a costume party at their apartment, and Jenny and I went as headshots of the Doublemint Twins. I was "Wanda Job" and Jenny was my twin sister "Anita Job." We drew our oversized headshots on poster board, cut holes out where the faces were, and stuck our faces through. On the back we created funny, mock resumes. Socializing with the cast was a highlight of my experience at Beef and Boards. Fortunately, I liked my castmates (even Harriet and I had made peace), because ours was a pretty closed world, and I spent most of my time hanging around these same few people. We rarely even got to fraternize with the techies, as they were local and scooted straight home after the show.

Speaking of going home, it was a bit eerie living in that theatre when the crowds, waiters, staff, and the rest of the cast had gone home for the night. "Rumor has it that the theatre is haunted," Jenny informed me. When the lights were out, those ghastly white Styrofoam wig heads looked pretty creepy. It felt like we were living on a Scooby Doo mystery set and at any time would find Scooby, Shaggy, Velma, Daphne, and Freddie bursting through the door with flashlights on their search for the ghost of Beef and Boards.

****

Word spread that *A Chorus Line* was being performed in Chicago. Auditions were going to be held on a Monday, which was perfect, since that was our dark night. Many of us didn't have gigs lined up after *Funny Girl* ended, so this was a prime opportunity. Actors are constantly looking for work. No sooner did they start one show then they were already auditioning for the next show, at least with short stints like this one. This musical theatre world was all so new to me; I hadn't given any thought to what I would do once the show closed. But my success in *Funny Girl* had proved to me that I wanted to continue pursuing a career in entertainment. Who knew how many auditions I'd have to go to before landing a part? It behooved me to get a head start on the process. Our run at Beef and Boards was only three months long. Time to pound the pavement.

"We can drive after our Sunday show and stay with my aunt. Her house used to be a bed and breakfast," Jenny suggested as she rallied the troops. I was excited and extremely nervous to go. *A Chorus Line* was the epitome of dance shows, and this was my first professional musical theatre audition. The very first. Ever. I was going to audition for the chorus line in a show about an audition for the chorus line in a show. "Rumor has it that they are going to do the original Broadway choreography," Sandi informed us. "I know it and can teach anyone who wants to learn." I welcomed her gracious offer, thrilled to be learning the real Broadway choreography, and *before* the audition, no less. I could use all the help I could get.

My enthusiasm slightly dampened, however, when I realized I would have to sing at the audition. "You could always be Kristine. She's the girl in the show who really can't sing," Jenny reminded me. The apparently tone-deaf character Kristine spoke her solo (which was all about how vocally challenged she was), except for her few ear-splitting, painful, failed attempts at reaching an actual note. "Yes, but I really can sing and I want to sing," I countered. "I just need more training, more practice, and a lot more confidence." I got up the guts to ask Belinda—the eccentric, heavyset, jovial, middle-aged actress and voice teacher who lived with us in the theatre—if she would give me a couple of voice lessons. She was a gypsy of sorts, traveling from show to show with all her personal belongings, including sheet music. Thankfully, she agreed to help.

When the time came immediately following our Sunday evening show, Sandi, Matt, Brent, Harriet, Jenny, and I piled into Sandi's car and drove the 180 miles from Indianapolis to Chicago. We pulled up to Jenny's aunt's gorgeous home at about three a.m. on Monday. Auntie served us a quick cup of Earl Grey tea with milk, kept warm in a ceramic teapot snuggled in a quilted tea cozy, one of her large collection of pretty and unusual teapots on display. Then it was off to try to get some sleep, each of us in our own room warmly decorated with antiques. The few hours of sleep I managed to get were restless with anxiety about the audition.

Morning arrived all too soon. Auntie gave us the royal treatment and served the big, gourmet breakfast she used to make for her paying guests: Eggs Florentine baked in individual custard cups, sausage, homemade biscuits, and more delicious tea. I had a feeling I shouldn't eat so much when I had a leotard to squeeze into, but it was all so wonderful, and I didn't want to offend Jenny's aunt. Also, I tend to overeat when nervous.

The audition was held at the theatre where the show would be performed. The lobby was packed with dancers stretching and catching up on the latest gossip. Many of them knew each other because they lived and performed in Chicago. I felt anxious beyond anxious. My voice needed warming up, but where? And that decadent breakfast had left me bloated and uncomfortable. My stomach was so nervous and full of heavy food that the combination gave me the runs, so run I did, continuously, to the bathroom to relieve my churning intestines. The bathroom seemed as good a place as any to try singing a bit, especially since I was spending so much time there anyway, but I was too embarrassed to allow anyone to hear me, and girls kept coming in to primp. "In less than an hour, I will be singing solo in front of the casting people," I realized. I could have died just thinking about it.

After giving up on the vocal warm-up, I joined Jenny in the lobby for a much-needed session of stretching out my body's stiffness from a night of riding in the car. Sometimes your muscles freeze up from cold and exhaustion. Sometimes the anxiety and nervousness make them relax to the point of near liquidity, like a guy getting wobbly knees when he asks a girl to marry him. I hoped for the second situation, and, sure enough, I was instant Gumby. I could easily kick myself in the face or drop to a perfect split on the floor. The price paid would come the next day when my muscles would retaliate from being over-extended. My extreme flexibility reminded me of those miraculous stories where some poor guy is pinned under a car about to be crushed and a ninety-pound weakling passerby suddenly turns into Superman and singlehandedly lifts the car and saves the victim's life. Of course, the next day our unlikely hero has to be hospitalized for muscle stress. "Tomorrow I might be sore as all get out, but today I get to be Superwoman," I determined.

My body was ready and so was my resume. Thanks to Beef and Boards, this time my resume had a bona fide professional gig on it, one that didn't require beefing up to disguise me as someone better than I really was. Jenny said I could hand write in my latest show, *Funny Girl*, instead of typing up a new resume. "It actually makes you look more professional by showing that you're currently working and too busy to print new resumes," she explained. I could even list my character's name, "Polly." I was lucky. Usually chorus girls didn't get actual names. Perhaps it was only a small step, but I was definitely moving up in the world of showbiz.

The choreographer collected our headshots with resumes stapled to the back and handed us each a paper number to pin onto our leotards. I was now a number, not a name. I glanced at some of the other headshots and found them to be much more glamorous than mine. I was certain those girls could sing, too, and wondered what I was doing there. "I can only do my best and leave it at that," I reminded myself.

Sometimes you sing first at an audition and sometimes you dance first. We danced first, and I was relieved when the choreographer taught the exact same choreography we had learned from Sandi. At least I was familiar with it, but so was everyone else in that room. It killed my knees, because I wasn't really in dance shape, having not taken classes regularly since I lived in Minneapolis. Still, I loved to dance and felt fantastic when I got it right.

Then came the moment of truth: the singing audition. I prayed to God that I wouldn't have to sing in front of all the other auditioners. The first number was announced, and the young man went into the room all by himself. Thank goodness! But as soon as the door shut behind him, people began peeking through the crack in the door and craning their necks to hear. The room wasn't completely soundproof. "Great. The other performers are still going to be able to hear me, but," I rationalized, "at least not at full volume." Every time they got closer to my number, I wanted to run away and never look back. I could have bailed and not gone through with it. No one was holding a gun to my head. If I were really that distraught, I could have grabbed my bag and bolted outta there. But a braver, wiser, dream-filled part of me made me stay and go through this ordeal I knew would be painful. It just wouldn't let me back out and quit.

When my number was finally called, I walked into the room and handed the pianist my sheet music (properly taped together, so he wouldn't have to fumble with turning the pages). I cleared my throat, greeted the casting people seated at a table with my headshot in front of them, and, trembling, announced, "I am going to be singing, 'You Can Always Count on Me.'" As the musical intro played, my heart began beating faster and faster. Adrenaline pumped through my veins. A wave of heat flushed through my entire body. My nerves took me hostage. By the time my entrance cue arrived, I had no breath support and could barely make a peep. After a seeming eternity of awkward silence, by sheer willpower, I broke free and managed to squeeze out a note. The sound that emanated from my lips was like nothing I'd ever heard, my voice cracking and shaking like a mini, oral earthquake. The same nervous energy that allowed me to kick to my forehead had left my vocal chords careening out of control. Nevertheless, I kept right on singing to the very end of the required sixteen bars, all the while horrified at what I was hearing. I knew everyone within earshot was completely uncomfortable and mortified for me.

"This was my first singing audition," I blurted out apologetically before the casting people had a chance to comment. My statement was a waste of breath, as my inexperience was painfully obvious after they heard, or didn't hear, my first few notes. (Never apologize or make excuses for a rotten audition. It just makes you look worse and certainly makes you look unprofessional. Ugh. What humiliation.) Fortunately, instead of being appalled and rude, the casting people were compassionate and kind, and took pity upon me. After all, I had just given a real-life performance of the vocally challenged character Kristine. And I was pretty convincing, if I say so myself.

I walked out of the room terribly defeated and embarrassed in one sense but slightly triumphant in another. Sure I was absolutely atrocious, but I had gone through with it. I had overcome my fear and lived to tell about it. I resolved to take voice lessons, confident that I could only get better.

Once everyone had sung, the choreographer came out and, just like in *A Chorus Line* after an arduous day of auditioning, announced which people they would like to have stay. He shuffled through the deck of headshots naming the chosen ones. Only after his polite dismissal, "Thank you all for coming," did we know for sure that those of us whose names hadn't yet been announced hadn't been called back. I was disappointed, but certainly not surprised that I got cut after that dreadful singing disaster. Still, I held out hope that they would consider me for the part of Kristine. Unfortunately, none of my castmates had gotten a call back either.

No sooner had we returned to Jenny's aunt's house, foiled in our attempt to secure employment post *Funny Girl*, when the phone rang. It was the choreographer calling for me. "We accidentally put your headshot in the wrong pile. We'd love for you to come to the callback." I couldn't believe my ears. The victory was bittersweet, however, as my Beef and Boards buddies hadn't been invited back. Competing with your friends stinks. It's the nature of the beast. Even when you make the cut, it's hard to be completely happy for yourself when you are glum for your chums.

Cut to the chase: I attended the callback and didn't make the final cut, but I felt proud that I had made it that far. As far as I was concerned, my "failure" was simply a step closer to future success. I wasn't convinced that I wanted to live in cold, windy, gray Chicago anyway. I missed sunny California. I missed my sister and friends.

Back at ye olde Beef and Boards, I started to feel that five weeks of the same show, no matter how much fun initially, would be tedious. I had never repeated a performance more than three times total in the past, let alone eight shows a week for five weeks. Getting settled in a long run—this wasn't even long by industry standards—was a whole new experience for me. Soon after getting comfortable in the show, I began beefing about being bored. I didn't know how to relax and enjoy the ride.

The restlessness didn't last long, however, thanks to one especially effective boredom breaker: visits from family and friends. Indianapolis was a drivable distance from Detroit and Chicago, so parents and pals ventured down to witness my professional musical theatre debut. Having loved ones in the audience was like a jolt of caffeine giving me just the buzz I needed to perk up my show.

Another monotony savior was mistakes. My first big onstage mishap was a costume malfunction that happened in the "Beautiful Bride" number. The wedding dress I wore had a heavy, wire-framed skirt à la eighteenth century France, which protruded several feet to either side of me and dripped strands of beads and white doves. As my partner paraded me around, the clasp holding the marital monstrosity around my waist broke. I was horrified as I felt it plunge to the ground, and I quickly grabbed it with both hands. The number was about "taking the plunge," but this wasn't the plunge the songwriter had in mind. Instead of holding my partner's hand and attempting any semblance of choreography, all I could do was try to hold up the awkward, weighty bird cage and keep my rear end covered until the end of the number. Of course, the rest of the cast found this hilarious. Even I could giggle about it later.

My five-week stint at Beef and Boards culminated in the traditional playing of pranks at the last performance. We ladies opted to abuse and amuse the guys with the old "lotion in the hand" trick: put a glob in your palm before going onstage, and when your partner grabs you he gets a slippery surprise. Everything that happens on stage then is exponentially funnier because 1.) you know your victim has to keep a straight face in spite of having been slimed; and 2.) you know you yourself are forbidden to break character while pulling off such hijinks. The boys were so shocked by our gooey gifts that I had a chuckling fit on stage that could have gotten me fired. As a final bonus, we girls put on thick layers of fiery red lipstick for kissing attacks on the guys when they came off stage. Smothering their faces in crimson smooches, I kissed Beef and Boards "goodbye" and my future in showbiz "hello!"

Although *Funny Girl* had been funny and fun both on stage and off, bidding farewell to Jenny and my new friends was no laughing matter. I would miss everyone. But I refused to allow the gloom of parting with my performing pals to overshadow my enthusiasm for the entertainment adventures that surely awaited me in sunny California.

Final Scene: New York City, August 10, 2002

The next morning, I walked the few blocks from Jenny's place to the nearest subway station and caught the N train from Queens into Manhattan for my farewell performance as a Radio City Rockette. I was an emotional cocktail—a heavy dose of excitement, invigoration, and anxiety with a splash of melancholy, grief, and regret. I was proud of myself for all I had accomplished, regretful of the risks I never took, and grief stricken by the fact that my dance career was ending. It was hard to imagine leaving showbiz behind after all these years. "The theatre feels like home," I thought. "It's where I feel most like myself, most passionate about life." Throughout the course of my adulthood I had taken brief forays into other jobs, but, like a boomerang, I always returned to show business. Whenever I felt lost, I could step back into a musty, dusty dance studio and feel safe and comforted. Dance fit me like an old shoe.

Most jobs are what you do. Dance is who you *are*. Dance was at the core of my being. "Who am I if I stop dancing?" I wondered. Ironically, throughout the majority of my career I had worried about how I was going to break into showbiz and sustain a living in entertainment. Now, I was wondering how to break out of showbiz and create a lucrative career doing anything else. My duffel bag sat heavy on my lap. Saying goodbye to the theatre felt like breaking up with a lover when it wasn't my choice.

Quit depressing yourself, Kristi, or you'll never get through this day. Focus on all the fun you had. Be grateful for the adventure. The familiar "ka-chung, ka-chung, ka-chung" rhythm of the subway soon lulled me into a trance with memories of my past continuing to pierce my awareness like a barrage of fantastic dream images.

Act 1, Scene 4

The Cow's Behind
(and Other Embarrassing Parts)

Upon returning to California, I plugged myself right back into the life I'd left behind almost as if I'd never left, with one important exception: My intention to follow through on my dream of becoming an entertainer was cranked up a notch. *Funny Girl* had left me even more enamored of the theatre and all its trimmings and had given me the boost of confidence I needed to forge ahead.

Alas, I still didn't have a plan on how to accomplish my goal. So I went back to working at the art gallery, teaching aerobics, and dating Adam. Then one glorious day, I got the break I was hoping for. While casually sipping my morning cup of java and flipping through the newspaper, I spotted an ad. It jumped out from the pages, grabbed me by the collar, and pulled me in close. Auditions were being held for Starlight Musical Theatre's Summer Series at Balboa Park in Old Town, San Diego. Five different musicals were being presented at the Starlight Bowl amphitheater over the course of the summer–practically in my own back yard!

When I laid eyes on that audition notice, I became a three-year-old begging for a cookie: "I want it! I want it! I want it! I want it!" Unfortunately, I hadn't been taking dance classes and wasn't in top-notch shape. Looking at myself in a leotard made me cringe. Since leaving Indianapolis I hadn't been singing at all either. But I was absolutely determined to be in a show, and I still had several weeks left to prepare. I could picture it so clearly: the thrill of being up on that stage singing and dancing for a live audience. It was almost too much to bear. I had to audition, and, more importantly, I had to get hired.

This time I practiced and practiced and practiced my audition song until I could sing it in my sleep. "I can sing this measly amount of music without making a fool of myself. It's not that big a deal," I counseled myself, knowing I needed to be much more emotionally prepared than I was for my last, disastrous audition. I was a woman on a mission. No piddling sixteen bars of little, black notes were going to stop me from my dream. I showed up at that audition, danced as best I could, and belted out my song. That *Chorus Line* catastrophe must have shocked the stage fright right out of me, because I sang my solo without incident. I didn't freeze up, shake uncontrollably, hyperventilate, implode, or spontaneously combust. Hallelujah! Victory was mine. Lo and behold, I made it into one of the shows: *The Wizard of Oz*. I was ecstatic.

Long Legs and Tall Tales

The Wizard of Oz was one of those films that I both loved and hated as a kid. I loved the music, the magical Land of Oz, Toto the dog, and glittery Glinda the Good Witch. The Munchkins left me mesmerized, being my first encounter with midgets. I joyfully imitated Dorothy, Scarecrow, Tin Man, and Lion frolicking down the yellow brick road while singing "We're Off to See the Wizard." To this day, I find opportunities to exclaim, "Lions and tigers and bears! Oh, my!" or to liquefy, like the Witch, into a puddle on the floor while screeching, "I'm melting!" But parts of the movie scared the pantaloons off me. Who doesn't recall those terrifying scenes where the tornado came spinning toward Dorothy Gale's Kansas farmhouse? How about when the Wicked Witch threatened Dorothy, "I'll get you, my pretty, and your little dog, too!" "Not the dog!" I'd protest tearfully as a child. And the Witch's evil, ultra creepy, flying monkeys were no barrel of monkeys. The show was a recipe for nightmares.

Thankfully, there were no nightmares involving our directors. On the contrary. The Mom-and-Pop team of Don and Bonnie Ward were a dream to work with. The Wards were a fifty-something, former dance duo who brought the house down in the Catskills. These happy, light-hearted souls played off each other and corrected each other like any married couple might. Their easygoing nature was reflected in their practical, comfy, street clothes—Bonnie in a flowery dress and ballet flats, and Don in a collared Polo shirt and khakis. They truly cared about the cast and were glad to have us on board. It was like working for doting parents. They seemed to enjoy directing *The Wiz* and held no bitterness about The Biz. Don and Bonnie were a refreshing introduction to the world of musical theatre.

With a mere two weeks to put up the show, the cast rehearsed long days, six days a week. It was like having a real job, only doing something fantastically fun. Rehearsals were held in a brick building on a deserted street near downtown San Diego. The rehearsal room had high ceilings and lots of light. I loved being there. Another room, for costume fittings, came complete with wardrobe people to take our measurements. My favorite was the funky woman in her twenties who wore different wigs of varying lengths and colors. New and interesting people were everywhere.

Many of our leads—Lion, Tin Man, Scarecrow, Wicked Witch, and the Wizard—as well as a portion of the ensemble were Equity professionals, some imported from out of town. The remaining cast consisted of local, non-union performers. The Equity members made about three times as much moolah as the rest of us (who received about $200 per week) and got more time off throughout the day. I marveled at the clandestine union meetings to which I was not privy, their rules and regulations, election of union reps, official breaks at specified times, and higher wages. "I'm working as hard as they are. Why do they get more time off and more money for doing the same job?" Basically, they earned more because they had paid their dues, literally and figuratively, and were extremely talented, seasoned professionals. Still, it was easy to get annoyed with the inequity. The theatre was required to hire a certain number of Equity performers at full price, and then were free to fill in the rest of the cast with bargain-priced, non-union, less experienced entertainers like myself. The musical required a large cast, mainly due to all the townspeople needed to populate the Emerald City—capital of the Land of Oz—so it made sense for the producers to cut costs this way. Who was I to complain, when it got my foot in the door?

A crowd of kids also got their feet in the door, as they were used to play "Munchkins." The whippersnappers were a lot more prevalent than bonafide little people and easier on the payroll. Toto, on the other hand, was a consummate professional and probably cost a pretty penny. Toto came with his very own trainer who taught Dorothy how to get the dog to follow her on stage: click a hidden clicker in her skirt then reward Toto with a small treat. The process was fascinating to behold. Animals and children can be unpredictable, so having them in the cast made the show all the more exciting.

While dancing was my forte, I absolutely adored singing. I looked forward to the point in the day when we were all exhausted from jumping about, and we grabbed folding chairs and gathered around the piano. I brought my tiny tape recorder to record our sessions and my pencil and score, so I could circle my harmonies and note any changes from the musical director. It really helped that I played piano and could read music. Plus, having spent years singing in the choir in high school and church, I was comfortable singing harmony and finding and holding my note while others around me sang different parts of the chord. Doing that can be a real chore for someone who hasn't done it before. Picking your note out of an eight-note chord can be like finding a needle in a haystack. It's all too easy to gravitate toward someone else's note or switch to an easier part.

When the musical director asked what part I sang, I said I sang alto. That was what I sang in high school, more so because I could sing the right harmonies than because I had a low voice. "First or second alto?" he inquired. I could have been a mezzo soprano, for all I knew. Those sopranos always had to screech notes so shrill and high only a dog could hear them. I didn't think I could reach the rafters. "Can you belt a high E in your chest voice?" he asked. "You have a nice blend of head and chest voice." I appreciated the compliment, although I was unschooled in differentiating between the two. Exasperated, I finally accepted that I was a first alto for lack of a better idea. I should have known what part I sang. How embarrassing. I was just relieved he didn't make me sing solo in front of everyone to determine my vocal range.

Not only was I thrilled to be at rehearsals, but I was ecstatic that I was going to be performing at the San Diego Civic Theatre in downtown San Diego. It was a big theatre (about 2,500 seats), and I had seen the Broadway tour of *Les Miserable* there, so the venue itself overwhelmed me with delight. To top that off, I got to enter through the stage door—the "secret" backstage entrance for cast and crew—instead of out front with the rest of the ticket-carrying crowd.

My main role in the show was as one of the green-clad citizens of the Emerald City. The show didn't require much of the ensemble, but our most exuberant number was more athletic than an aerobics class. It culminated in thirty-two frog jumps while sustaining a high A note—the kind of note that would make a dog whimper in pain—as part of a magnificent, climactic chord. Thirty-two frog jumps would exhaust even the most athletic frog. I could barely catch my breath, so trying to sing and hold any note, let alone a high A, was worse than having a frog in my throat.

Much more traumatic was my first appearance in the show, near the end of the first act, when Dorothy and her entourage approach Oz. They happen upon a field of poppies that lull them into a drug-induced, sleep-like trance. My big debut was as a giant flower in a field of singing poppies. We poppies wore black, spandex suits with hoods that covered our heads like a bathing cap, over which we clasped enormous red petals around our necks. Our heads were the flowers and our bodies the stems. I felt like a complete moron. When my friends came to see the show, I prayed they didn't discover me. To make matters worse, later in the production, a girl named Dana and I had to dress up like giant birds and run across the back of the stage flapping our wings.

Why we didn't get to actually fly as birds is beyond me, because theatrical flying experts, Flying by Foy, flew in from Vegas to rig the cables for our many airborne performers. The Wicked Witch flew, the flying monkeys flew, several people flew inside the tornado, and the Wizard flew off in a hot air balloon at the end. To add to the magic, pyrotechnics illuminated the appearance and disappearance of the Witch; she entered and exited in an explosive flash of flames.

The first time the entire cast saw the staging of the tornado scene, it blew our minds. Everything got swept up by the twister and spun through the air, including the nasty Miss Gulch on her bicycle with Toto in the basket and Auntie Em in her rocking chair. The whirlwind reached a frenzied pitch ending with Dorothy's house landing on the Wicked Witch, her red and white striped legs extending out, wearing the ruby slippers. The cast cheered and applauded wildly. There is so much about a show that you are in that you don't know about, as you rarely get to see the show in its entirety. If you ever get a chance to watch it from out front, you are always amazed at how the production looks from the audience's perspective.

My four weeks rehearsing and performing *The Wizard of Oz* were simply enchanting. The theatre had become my "somewhere over the rainbow" where "troubles melt like lemon drops." There was no stopping me now. I had found me a home, and, as Dorothy Gale proclaims, "There's no place like home."

****

After *The Wizard of Oz* ended, I got more serious about show business and decided to take steps to move my career forward. Step #1: It was clear I would benefit from finding a voice teacher. I figured that by the time I was thirty-five, I could have ten years of voice lessons under my belt and possibly become a singer. Plus, if I wanted to get anywhere in this business of entertainment, I needed to be able to sing for auditions. My boyfriend Adam, who loved connecting people, knew some local women who sang in an all-female quartet called "The Fabulous Earrings." One of the women in the group, Marcia, was also a voice teacher. Perfect.

My first lesson with Marcia was unnerving, because I was still self-conscious about singing solo in front of someone. "What's the worst thing that could happen?" I asked myself and then answered myself right away: "I could make unpleasant sounds, and she'd know my singing stinks." I decided I could live with that. Using the same karaoke cassette tape of James Taylor's "You've Got a Friend" that I used for *Funny Girl*, I pathetically, meekly, eked out the lyrics atop the background music. I was relieved when it was over. "Okay, so you can see where I'm starting from," I said. She nodded. So began my vocal training.

Marcia was a pretty, single woman in her forties who dressed in comfy, worn beach clothes and wore her wavy, blond hair long and natural. She played the acoustic guitar to accompany me except when she plunked out scales on her small, portable keyboard. Singing with the guitar was heavenly. We'd do songs by Linda Ronstadt, Bonnie Raitt, and Janis Joplin. Her hippie/folksy bent was not exactly ideal for musical theatre coaching, but if I lived near her now, I'd still want to sing with her.

My lessons were held in La Jolla in Marcia's small studio apartment built atop the garage of a large house that she watched over while its owners were out of town. Her apartment had windows running the entire length of the back, which overlooked the ocean. I would sing while gazing out at the waves coming into shore. The room had a tiny bathroom and a little kitchenette where a mini coffee maker was always brewing in case I wanted a cup. Her sleeping area was a bed-sized loft, reachable by ladder. A small TV sat on a shelf, but I doubt Marcia watched it much, because it had a sign taped across the screen announcing "twenty-four hours notice needed for lesson cancellations." I'm not sure the set was even functional. Sometimes she had a vase with a few flowers sitting on the counter. At other times, her sewing machine would be out, so she could stitch costumes for her quartet. Besides teaching voice lessons and performing with The Fabulous Earrings for private parties and shopping mall celebrations, she played guitar and sang standard, tropical vacation repertoire at oceanside restaurants. In the winter, her large family convened at a California ski resort where she would sing in the chalet to pay for her vacation. Her life seemed so serenely simple. Marcia herself took lessons from a famous teacher all the way up in Los Angeles and would come back and share the skills she had learned with me. Thanks to Marcia, my singing improved by leaps and bounds. I cherished my weekly lessons with her.

Step #2: Update my photos. A new showbiz friend of mine recommended a good, local photographer for professional, theatrical headshots.

Step #3: Get an agent. Isn't that what entertainers do? It would sound so cool to say, "My agent this and my agent that." But where would I find an agent? I grabbed the Yellow Pages, located one of the few legitimate talent agencies in San Diego, and bravely called the number.

Surprising to me, joining the agency was a piece of cake—no audition, no rigorous resume examination, no screening for super model status. They didn't seem particularly selective; I think they took anyone with professional photos. I just had to bring in a healthy supply of headshots for them to add to the towering stacks covering the floors of their cramped, tiny rooms. I really didn't know what to expect of an agent, but what did I have to lose? Apparently, about 15% a gig, that's what. They gave me agency address labels to stick on my headshots in place of my personal address. I now had "representation!"

My first agency job was serving as an "extra" in the movie *Mr. Jones* starring none other than the incredibly debonair Richard Gere and alluring Lena Olin. I was eager to find out what it was like to be on a movie set. How were the scenes filmed? How did the director work with the actors? Did acting look like something I was capable of doing? More importantly, what did a sexy superstar look like in person?

Lucky for me, the movie industry was filming more and more movies in San Diego as they were saturating L.A. locations. I also heard that the Los Angelenos were sick and tired of being regularly inconvenienced by movie studios and their recurring demands to close off streets for filming. As a result, this particular scene was being filmed in front of the San Diego County Courthouse. My agent instructed me to dress like a lawyer, meaning to wear a skirt suit and high heels.

As did all the other extras, I spent the day outside in the sun with the "Second A.D." (assistant director) and "Third A.D."—a young man and woman who wore headsets and shuffled us around like cattle herders. "Okay, when I cue you, you four walk across the sidewalk to the other side of the building and wait there," the Second A.D. said. We'd hear the "snap" of the clapboard and the "Take 10!" Then it was "Back to one!" which meant back to our starting position. The harried A.D.s were constantly running to shove real pedestrians, as opposed to the hired movie extra pedestrians, out of the way or to stop traffic or stop something that was going to ruin the shot. As a consequence, sometimes we had to repeat the same moves over and over and over again: "Take 11! Back to one!" "Take 12! Back to one!" "Take 13! Back to one!" It was like a real-life version of pressing rewind on your DVD remote and then pressing play…rewind…play….rewind…play.

As extras, we were treated more like props than people. I felt subservient and powerless, but I actually had the ability to spoil the shot, thereby wasting time, thereby costing the movie copious amounts of money. Feeling rebellious after hours of slave labor, I was tempted to do cartwheels instead of my quick-paced lawyer stride but decided I wasn't ready to give up showbiz just yet.

Most of the time, I stood way out in the boondocks waiting for something to happen. Waiting. Waiting. Waiting. I kept watching for Richard Gere but was so far from the action that I needed binoculars to see the stars for any positive identification. At one point I got close enough to see the directors and "their people." They actually sat on directors' chairs labeled with their names, just like in the movies. Cool. Later in the day, the extras were all abuzz exclaiming, "There's Richard Gere!" I turned in time to gaze upon his famous pepper-gray hair. He was extremely handsome. I craned my neck to hear what was going on in the scene and to decipher the directions given by the director, but, alas, I couldn't hear much. While certainly fascinating to witness the workings of a movie set, it was also a long day, which got boring quickly. Especially since we did a whole lot more standing around waiting than we did acting. By definition, we were extra. What did I expect?

As luck would have it, I got called a second time to film for *Mr. Jones*, this time in Mission Beach at a casual, little restaurant not far from the ocean. My big acting assignment was to be a restaurant patron who would stir some fake coffee at a table and try not to attract attention. "Pretend you are conversing or eating or drinking but don't stand out and pull focus away from the stars," ordered one of the A.D.s. This was a little more fun, because I was right in the heart of the scene and could watch the action. But did I really think my lot in life was to feign beverage mixing while remaining unnoticeable?

The best part of the job was, by far, the free food. A food trailer that the actors and crew referred to as "craft services" provided a selection of drinks, fruit, yogurt, bagels, muffins, and more as well as an extensive, short-order, hot menu. I wasn't getting real acting experience, but I certainly was well fed.

****

The following spring when auditions came around again for Starlight Bowl's Summer Series, I was poised, ready, and waiting with a year of voice lessons under my belt and a new song prepared. Happily, Don and Bonnie Ward were at the helm again. "Your work on your singing has paid off. You've improved a lot," they announced after my vocal audition, like proud parents giving their nod of approval. Between my audition and my work on *The Wizard of Oz* the previous year, I must have done something right, because this time I was cast in all five shows for the summer stock season. They even cast me in *Camelot*, which everyone knew was a singer show not a dancer show. I was on cloud nine, my feet barely touching the ground. I was going to be performing and only performing—no more teaching aerobics or selling art—for the whole summer! Being one of only three gals and three guys cast for the entire season, I felt like I had won the lottery.

Summer stock—a series of plays performed over the course of the summer, mostly outdoors—served as an intensive musical theatre immersion course for me. Once the first show was up and running, we'd started rehearsing the next show during the day while performing the current one at night. Talk about a way to learn the ropes lickety-split. My salary—$200 a week per musical—didn't get me far, but with paychecks from working two musicals at a time overlapping, I could get by. It was enough dough that I could afford to move into my own studio apartment in a two-story, eight-unit building in Hillcrest—a fashionably funky neighborhood in San Diego close to where I'd be performing. Hillcrest was a charming town chock full of cute shops, swanky restaurants, and flocks of gay men. Hence the charm, cute shops, and swanky restaurants! I adored it.

Every morning I'd cheerfully make coffee and put on my leotard, aerobics shorts, and terry cloth head band, channeling Olivia Newton John from her 1981 hit, "Physical." I'd juice some apples, carrots, and celery in my juicer—a healthy California practice I had adopted—to take along with my sack lunch. I'd load up my large duffel bag with every type of dance shoe I owned plus a book, magazine, small tape recorder, pencil, notebook, and water bottle and joyfully head out to WORK at the rehearsal hall. I was happy to get up in the morning, to be able to dance and sing and hang out with outrageously fun people. I felt so alive!

Our first show of the season, *Gypsy*, was performed at the San Diego Civic Theatre where I'd done *The Wizard of Oz*. *Gypsy* is the true story of a famous stripper named "Gypsy Rose Lee" and is based on her memoirs from 1957. It tells the tale of the obnoxious stage mother, Rose, who pushes her two daughters to become famous vaudeville performers during the depression.

One daughter, Louise, is very shy and always takes a backseat to her outgoing sister, June, who is the highlight of the act in which they sing "Let Me Entertain You." Eventually, June has enough of Mama Rose's demands and runs off with a boy. Now all of Rose's dreams of stardom fall upon poor Louise. Pathetically, Mama Rose sings "Everything's Coming Up Roses" to convince herself and Louise that they'll be okay without June.

Everything comes up more thorns than roses, as vaudeville venues fade away, until Louise's act ends up at a burlesque house and she is introduced to the seduction of stripping. When one of the main strippers is arrested, Rose makes one last, desperate attempt to turn Louise into a star by making her fill the vacant stripper spot. It works, and Louise, who takes the stage name "Gypsy Rose Lee," becomes famous for baring her body.

In an uncanny similarity to my real-life situation, I got cast as one of the Hollywood blonds—an entourage of peroxide blonds attempting to become starlets in Hollywood. In one dance number, I was asked if I could hold my leg over my head and jump around in a circle. "Are you kidding? That's my specialty!" I replied, this being the very move that had garnered me adulation as a kid in the dance recital at Josie's. Unfortunately, this time my costume consisted of pajamas and a hideous hairpiece rolled up in curlers—not exactly the glamour-do I would have preferred.

Unfairly, I also got cast in every other embarrassing part in the show. At rehearsal, our choreographer Toni Kaye called over to Dana (the gal with whom I'd flapped around as a big bird in *The Wizard of Oz*) and me. "What have we done?" I wondered. "I want you two to be Dainty June's cow, Caroline, for the farm boy number," Toni announced. "Dana, you will be the head and Kristi will be…" "The cow's behind?" I blurted out in horror. My excitement about the show suddenly took a dump. I had to bend over and hold onto Dana's waist, my head resting inches from her rear end, underneath a cow costume, and do a dance number with June. I could see the entire cast snickering, the cow and butt jokes formulating in their brains, and the relieved looks on their faces that they were not chosen to be bovine buttocks.

Staying crouched beneath a sweltering cowhide, into and out of which we had to be snapped by wardrobe, was extremely uncomfortable. My part was certainly easier—Dana had the tricky job of maneuvering the animal's mouth and blinking eyes while dancing—but far more dangerous being in such a precarious face-to-fanny position.

Toni was apologetic and tried to ease the pain by promising to never make us be animals again. In spite of her asinine assignment, she became one of my favorite choreographers of all time. She was talented, kind, and respectful. I was thoroughly spoiled with my bosses. The funny thing is, being the cow's caboose was the highlight of my show in the end. The part garnered us so much attention from the rest of the cast that it became a wonderful ice breaker. Cast members gave me cow-related gifts including a cow magnet for my fridge, and, in return, I made everyone cow-shaped cookies for opening night.

As if being the udder half of a cow wasn't bad enough, Dana and I were also chosen to be Roman gladiators. Set in a burlesque house, we were no ordinary gladiators, however. We were strippers dressed loosely as gladiators, wearing little more than a feather-bedecked helmet and knee-high lace-up heels. As does any warrior worth her weight in gold, we carried a shield and spear for protection. Other than that, we were fairly vulnerable and exposed to the elements.

When the wardrobe mistress handed us our costumes, I butted in, "Where is the rest of it?" The top was a shrunken, pseudo bikini top with clear plastic straps, so we would appear nude behind the shield. For the bottom, we were to wear a gold G-string, which consisted of a one-half-inch strip of fabric that went around the hips, embellished with a few, minuscule, dangling sequined decorations, connected by another half-inch strip that went under the crotch and butted up against a tiny triangle of fabric concealing the front. I'm no astronomer, but I'd say this was about as close to a full moon as one should ever get. During the show, we walked across stage safely hidden behind our shields until we turned around to exit, at which point the audience caught a view of our bare backsides. Great. Once again, I was the butt of jokes. Why me? Why was it always me? Shouldn't the degrading bits have been doled out more fairly? It was amazing how many crew members managed to show up in time to see us strut across stage every night. We fought them off left and right.

I was mortified at having to prance around half naked while being leered at, but eventually I learned to make the most fun out of an embarrassing situation as possible. Everyone else was having a good laugh at our expense; we might as well join them and throw it back at them. Herbie—the lead male and Mama Rose's love interest—had to wait in the wings for his cue at the same time we were there for our gladiator cross, so he always got an eye full. He was a sweet, sexy, blond guy close to fifty who had done soap operas and TV shows. I thought, "Wow! Here is a real star!" To counteract our embarrassment, Dana and I would try to embarrass him instead. One night we drew heart tattoos on our heinies with black eyeliner and red lipstick that read "Herbie, TLA (true love always)."

In addition to the cringe-worthy roles, the directors were kind enough to offer me several tasty bit parts including that of Gypsy Rose Lee's French maid. Although I had only one line, which consisted of two words, "Oui, Madame," I agonized over how to say it. Should I use a French accent? Should I put the emphasis on the "Ma" or the "dame"? Should I use Method acting and dig deep into my previous travels in Paris, recalling all my conversations with Parisians? When I was fifteen and visiting a McDonald's fast food joint in Paris while on vacation, I tried ordering dinner for my family in French, being the most proficient speaker of the bunch with two years of middle school français under my belt. My request for "*deux Big Macs et un cheeseburger*" received the response, "That will be 75 francs," spoken in perfect English by the French cashier. I felt incredibly stupid. The real question is, what on earth were we doing eating McDonald's while in one of the greatest culinary cities in the world?

I had two simple words to say in the show, and I struggled with how to perform them. What a disaster. Acting did not come naturally to me. Maybe I should have stuck with stirring fake coffee and trying not to attract attention. In any case, I was too shy to ask the directors how to perform my line, so I just said the words as fast as I could and got it over with. "Perhaps I should take some acting classes," I advised myself.

Besides turmoil over the dialogue, the French maid bit presented another challenge—the quickest, fast changes I had ever experienced or witnessed. In a matter of seconds I had to get out of one costume and into the maid costume, dash on stage, and say my line. Then I had seconds to rush off stage, get out of the maid costume and into another costume, and return to the stage for the next scene. And every costume included a different wig. To save precious time, these transformative miracles had to be performed in the wings as close to my entrance as possible. As such, modesty was not an option. With a team of five dressers poised to strip me down and build me back up, I was like an Indy 500 race car running off stage to take a pit stop where my pit crew descended upon me, fixed me up, and sent me off in record time. I was amazed at and completely dependent upon their skills and "presets." I held my arms out like a scarecrow while they unzipped, unsnapped, unhooked, and unpinned. One group yanked off the costume, while another disassembled the wig and hat. They'd signal me when to step out of and into shoes and pants or skirts. Shoes were preset directly under the leg holes of rolled-down pants or skirts, so all I had to do was step in, and they'd pull up and zip up the next costume. It was a masterful process.

After the quick change, I would run to the stage, my heart beating wildly, hoping I was fully clothed and that my wig wasn't too far askew, which it occasionally was. What an adrenaline rush. Missing my entrance meant leaving the star, Gypsy Rose Lee, on stage in a deadly, awkward silence. Talk about pressure to be on time for work! As soon as I opened the set door and walked into her boudoir, I had to act calm, cool, and collected and smoothly deliver my line, "Oui, Madame," regardless of whether or not my hairpiece was hanging off the side of my head. Actors need to have complete control over their autonomic nervous system.

Our costumes were from the original Broadway production, and I felt like a star simply wearing the same clothing as the talented performers who had donned them before me. As far as I was concerned, it was the next best thing to being on Broadway. Our "Garden of Eden" scene get-up caused me consternation, however, being that it was yet another microscopic bikini. This time it was adorned in cloth apples and leaves, but there was no shield to hide behind. The long, bleach blond wavy wigs we women wore provided more coverage than the entire rest of the outfit put together. I was far too modest for the theatre but was relishing my first opportunity to be seductive nonetheless.

The guys in the "Garden of Eden" scene were also nearly naked—the effect desired—except for a pair of small, nude-colored trunks (that were little more than skimpy underwear) and a stuffed cobra in Mardi Gras colors that wound all the way from one ankle, around the midriff, and ended with the reptile head atop their human head. It was hard not to stare at these young, serpentined, hot bods and easy to see why Eve gave in to temptation and ate the forbidden fruit.

Lesson learned: When signing a theatre contract, one never knew exactly what one might be getting oneself into (the back end of a cow costume) or out of (nearly all manner of clothing). It was painfully obvious I needed to be prepared for anything if I planned to stay in show business. This career was stretching me out of my comfort zone, indeed. Unlike Gypsy Rose Lee, however, I hoped my future shows would be far less revealing.

****

Shortly after *Gypsy* opened, we returned to the rehearsal hall to begin work on our next show, *No, No, Nanette*. For about ten days, we rehearsed *Nanette* during the day while continuing to perform *Gypsy* at night. It was a busy time of round-the-clock rehearsing and performing. After completing our thirteen-show run of *Gypsy* at the Civic Theatre, we moved to the Starlight Bowl outdoor amphitheater for technical rehearsal, followed by dress rehearsal, and, finally, performances of *No, No, Nanette*.

The Starlight Bowl, located in Balboa Park in San Diego, would be home to the final four shows of our summer season. Balboa Park, which claimed to be "the nation's largest urban cultural park," housed fifteen museums, the San Diego Zoo, and many other attractions in addition to the theatre, all set amidst 1,200 acres of lush gardens and beautiful Spanish Revival architecture.

Moving from the rehearsal hall to the theatre was exciting not only due to the lovely change of venue, but also because we got our own dressing tables and could settle in and make the place feel like home. The phrase "home is where you hang your hat" could never be more true than for performers whose gypsy lifestyle forces them to become adept at making wherever-they-are-at-the-moment feel like home. In a flurry, the mirrors above our dressing tables were taped with photos of friends, family, lovers, and pictures of ourselves in other shows. We could even leave a few non-valuable items there; I left my Gumby slippers, a water bottle, a coffee mug, and some makeup.

Performers also make whomever-they-are-working-with-at-the-time feel like instant family. If you look at performers' photo albums, every photo shows them with their arms around people in big bear hugs grinning from ear to ear like they are best friends. In reality, they may have only met the people the day before. An actor can be sent on assignment to Boondocks, Idaho, to perform with a group of completely unfamiliar cast members. "Okay," she (or he) says, "This will be my family for the next four months, and this will be my home." The assimilation happens that quickly.

Upon relocating to the theatre, my first mission was to run to the box office to reserve tickets for my friends and family and purchase a souvenir show shirt for myself. So exciting! The shirt became the uniform I'd wear to the theatre on show nights.

With tickets and the latest show shirts in my possession, I was ready to focus on the task at hand: tech rehearsal—the time when the crew, lighting designers, and sound engineers work their magic. Prior to this, I had no clue about tech crew and little contact with them. For some reason, during this particular rehearsal week, I suddenly noticed these men (and women) in black roaming about backstage. They weren't hunting aliens like Will Smith's *Men in Black*, but they did seem to be awfully busy doing something important. So self-absorbed and in my own little world was I that I couldn't have identified our stage manager in a line up or accurately described what a stage manager does. Did I think the show could just run itself? All I knew was the men in black were the ones who screamed at you during tech rehearsal when you were about to be killed by a heavy set piece zooming in like a locomotive.

Tech rehearsals tested my patience like waiting in a long, slow-moving line at the grocery store check-out counter. They consisted of endless hours standing around under the searing stage lights while the lighting designer and director worked out all the lighting cues as we proceeded through the show "cue to cue." The incessant glare of lights in my eyes gave me a migraine, which I learned to counteract somewhat by wearing a baseball cap. The process became so dull that it was nearly impossible not to whisper and joke around with the other actors; we were all entertainers, for goodness sake. To the delight of the cast, a dancer overrun with ants in his pants might finally break out into a Michael Jackson impression doing the moonwalk and grabbing his crotch. We would all bust up laughing until the director shouted, "Stand still and be quiet, please!" It was like kindergarten when the teacher tells the whole class to sit and wait quietly, but after a while the kids have to say something or do something goofy, because they can't stand all the silence and boredom.

Tech rehearsal was also a likely time for injuries, because some directors required us to dance full out until the next change in lighting. Then we'd stop and stand there for so long that our muscles would tighten up, especially on cold days. After waiting forever for the lighting to be worked out, the director would have us resume dancing at performance level once again, but our muscles would still be in a deep freeze or completely asleep.

The schedule was particularly grueling, because we were there for several "ten-out-of-twelves"—ten hours out of a twelve hour day. It wasn't as bad being outside, but when you do this inside in a dark theatre, you begin to feel like a mole stuck deep underground. Moles, of course, seem perfectly happy with this arrangement, but I needed sunlight and fresh air once in a while.

Tech rehearsals were also by far the most dangerous point in the theatrical process. The entire theatre should have been wrapped in yellow police caution tape. If we did venture into the danger zone, it would have behooved us to wear a hard hat with a miner's lamp attached and steel-toed shoes and preferably flame-retardant clothing. Backstage, there were black cables running everywhere underfoot. They were supposed to be taped down and marked with glow tape (tape that glows in the dark), but inevitably someone would trip over a wayward cord while running to make an entrance. Stairs were also supposed to be marked with glow tape so that when the lights were off backstage we'd be able to see the edge and avoid tumbling down to our death or, worse, embarrassment. Glow tape was our friend! Even scarier, sometimes "pyro" (pyrotechnics) was used for special effect, so we needed to be prepared to "stop, drop, and roll" to put ourselves out should we get too close to open flames.

The most hazardous safety issues, however, commonly involved the set pieces and overhead drops flying in and out at rapid pace. These scene changes could be so perilous for those in their path that the backstage "choreography" became every bit as important as the on-stage choreography. If we didn't know where to be and where not to be backstage at every moment in the show, we could get bowled over by a massive set piece or have a seven-hundred-pound drop dropped on our head. We had to be alert and have our heads up at all times. We hoped, should we find ourselves in the wrong place at the wrong time, that the crew would yell or push us out of the way in time, but it was really our responsibility to steer clear. This was the first time it dawned on me that tech rehearsals could mean the end of my life if I weren't vigilant and careful.

Back to the show: *No, No, Nanette* was a 1920s, glitzy, cheesy, tap dance extravaganza first performed on Broadway in 1925 and famous for the songs "Tea for Two" and "I Want to Be Happy." The show features Nanette, a young lady who wants to go to Atlantic City to indulge her wild side but is told "No, No, Nanette!" by her companions in an annoying attempt to keep her wholesome and respectable. (Kind of reminded me of how my Midwestern friends implored me not to move to kooky California.) It's a crazy comedy of romantic entanglements and misunderstandings all set in that silly, early twentieth-century musical theatre world where everyone acts like a doofus.

Lucky for me, this was a huge dance show with a chorus of eleven guys and eleven girls. It was so sugary sweet and sappy it made your teeth ache to watch it. The *Los Angeles Times* said that while the show technically had a plot, it was really about "spangles and beads, tap dancing, dancing through hoops (literally), dancing on beach balls and glorious candy store colors that drape its chorus from hats to spats and be-ribboned feet." An accurate assessment.

I especially loved the exuberant group tapping in "I Want to Be Happy" and the soft-shoe partner dancing with frilly parasols in "Tea for Two." In one number, called "Peach on the Beach," we all dressed in old-fashioned, colorful bathing suits, and some of the girls had to walk atop giant wooden beach balls. That was one balancing act I'm glad I wasn't chosen for, because I certainly didn't have the balls to do it, and I wanted to stay injury free for the three remaining shows.

My biggest headache was "Two Many Rings Around Rosie"—a song about how having too many boyfriends will "never get Rosie a (wedding) ring." In this number, we danced with giant hula-hoop-like hoops to represent the ring theme. The hoops weren't my problem, however. It was the blasted hat toss. Although never very good at Frisbee, I was somehow chosen to Frisbee-toss a barber-shop-quartet-style hat to one of the leading men all the way across the entire length of the stage. The rest of his choreography involved the hat, so it was imperative that he catch it. Talk about a pressure position! Every night, I'd wind up and watch that hat fly across the stage, praying to the theatre gods to let it land somewhere within his reach. Sometimes it would arc over the orchestra pit threatening to decapitate the conductor. (He was such a pro and so focused on the music that he never skipped a beat. Whether he was ducking for an airborne chapeau or being buzzed by a bumble bee, his baton kept the orchestra playing in perfect time. My hat was off to him.) Amazingly, I never once missed my intended target, but my nerves were on edge every show.

"Two Many Rings Around Rosie" seemed to be the directors' downfall as well. They re-choreographed it over and over and over. We finally had to quit and go with what we had because the show was opening, and we were out of rehearsal time. The directors weren't getting what they wanted and were frustrated. So was I; I had a hissy fit every time the number was changed. What's the lesson? Don't marry the choreography. Expect changes up until and sometimes after opening night. Even directors and choreographers have writer's block, so to speak. It doesn't pay to get all worked up over it.

Fortunately, the vivacious finale more than made up for the "Rosie" debacle. It was a dazzling dance party made all the more spectacular by the bubbles spraying out of bubble machines à la Lawrence Welk, as we tapped our way to the end of the show in our colorful, sequined flapper dresses. It was a delightful, effervescent champagne finish.

Due to the abundance of dance numbers, the ensemble had loads of costume changes, including hats and bows and wigs. Between numbers we all stampeded en masse down the stairs to our dressing rooms to quickly change clothes. Between the onstage dancing and the offstage sprinting, it was a great overall workout—better than interval training at the gym.

We also had a ton of choreography to learn. I panicked one day when I realized my head no longer knew what steps came next, especially for the tap numbers. Before each show and before each number, I tried to review the choreography in my head, but it was pointless; the choreography had already migrated from my brain to my muscles. At first, when performing, I'd have to make a concerted effort to remember the step sequences. After enough rehearsals, however, I danced on auto pilot and couldn't have told you in words what came next even if you offered me a million dollars. When another performer asked me, "What comes after the kick ball change?" I replied, "I don't know. Let me find out." Then I had to do the dance in fast forward and let my body show me, because the show had settled in my muscle memory.

My brain had delegated the job to my muscles, thereby freeing up precious space in my mind for new information. I was then free to think about other, more important matters, like what to buy my friend for her birthday, where to go out for drinks after the show, or whether there were any cute guys in the audience. The process became second nature, like driving a car. Once you've done it enough, you can listen to the radio, talk to passengers, drink a smoothie, make phone calls, and fix your lipstick while the car seems to drive itself.

The problems came when I got nervous or distracted, or second-guessed my muscles. Thinking about the choreography too much sabotaged my performance. Once during "I Want to Be Happy" I started to consciously wonder what came next, and I didn't know what to do. It was terrifying, and I had to glance at my castmates next to me to get back in step. I learned that I had to quiet my mind, relax, and trust my muscles to do their job.

The lead actors in *No, No, Nanette* awed me, as did anyone who could really sing, act, and dance, for that matter. Alan Young was one of the leads in our production, and he had been a real, live television star! From 1961 to 1966 he starred as Wilbur Post in the popular *Mister Ed* series about a talking horse by the same name who only talked to Wilbur and liked to cause trouble. I was thrilled to introduce my parents to him, as they used to watch his TV program back in the old days. Alan was very kind to my parents and in front of them said to me, "You should keep performing. You have what it takes to make it." I was honored to have his seal of approval.

Two of our other leads were none other than the directors' son and his wife. Sure it was nepotism, but they were both incredible talents and well suited to their parts. The daughter-in-law had given birth to two children and was still able to wear short shorts and wow the cast with her perfect legs. I was inspired. Maybe having babies wouldn't ruin my figure forever. If she can do it, why can't I? Eventually the couple went on to star in *Crazy for You* in London's West End. Another young female lead in our show went on to star as Eponine on

Broadway in *Les Miserable*. At least two of the ensemble members went to Broadway as well. So I was thrown in the midst of a group of very talented people with bright futures ahead of them.

The Starlight Bowl was a unique place in which to perform, not only because of its setting within Balboa Park, but also because it sat in the middle of the San Diego Airport flight path. As the story goes, some time after the Starlight Bowl was built, the San Diego airport decided to redirect all incoming flights directly over the theatre. I'm sure the musical theatre directors were none too thrilled. Of course, a few singers and an orchestra were no match for the deafening jet noise. It was impossible to perform as airplane after airplane roared overhead. Audience members would have been highly disgruntled had they bought tickets to *Oklahoma* hoping to be moved to tears by Curly and Laurey singing their tender, romantic love duet "People Will Say We're in Love" only to see the star couple open their mouths and hear nothing but jet engines. They'd surely want to boo, throw tomatoes, and demand their money back.

The ingenious solution was a stoplight system visible to performers at the back of the orchestra pit. As long as the light was green, the show proceeded normally. A yellow light warned that a plane was approaching, and we should prepare to stop. A red light signaled that all performers were to "freeze." We watched the orchestra conductor for the exact cut off point. Whenever possible, he tried to pick the end of a musical phrase or an appropriate moment in the dance, hopefully not while our partners were holding us up in a lift.

We'd be frolicking around stage, singing and tap dancing and suddenly catch a glimpse of a plane in the distance. Oh boy, here it comes. The jet noise would become audible, "I want to be happy..." (triple time step right, triple time step left). The yellow light would come on, "but I can't be happy..." (triple time step right, add arm swing, triple time step left, add arm swing and move one spot to the left). We'd try to discreetly take a peek at the conductor without breaking character, "till I make you happy..." (triple time step right, bigger arms, triple time step left, bigger arms, and move one more spot to the left). The conductor would bring his baton to sweeping halt, "... too!" We'd strike a pose using whatever dance move we were in at that moment.

If we remained there for an inordinately long amount of time, the situation could get pretty hairy, depending on the pose we were in.

After a while our muscles began to quiver with fatigue. (Try lunging deeply on your right leg with one arm up above your head and one straight out to the side with your head and eyes looking skyward. Hold that pose for a full minute.) And we'd have to remain frozen with whatever goofy face or toothy grin we had plastered on at the pausing point. If I got stuck gazing directly into the eyes of another performer I'd feel like I was in a childhood staring contest not wanting to blink or laugh first. The entire wait we'd have to watch the conductor with our peripheral vision to see when he waved his baton and the green light "Go!" signal returned to resume the show. We'd try to remember where we'd left off, but the lag time could seriously disrupt the flow if we were already dancing on autopilot.

Some nights we stopped and started again and again. It seemed like every few bars of music we'd have to freeze, like someone was constantly hitting the video pause button. It wasn't unusual for audience members to become annoyed, perhaps a reason the company struggled with patrons.

The other challenge had to do with dancing outdoors and braving the elements. In June, San Diego was loaded with, appropriately named, June bugs. June bugs were half-inch long, brown, winged, hard-shelled beetles that looked pretty scary the first time I saw them. They'd fly in our faces while we were dancing, but we couldn't swat them away, or we'd distract the audience and mess up the choreography. Those insects seemed to know that we were helpless and took advantage of our predicament. Accidentally, I got revenge on plenty of those creepy crawlies. When tap dancing, I'd hear an awful crunching sound beneath my feet and know another one bit the dust. Or I'd do a cartwheel, my hands crushing their brittle shells. Yuk! Believe me I tried, but I couldn't always avoid them. The temperature outdoors was also out of our control; we might sweat to death or freeze to death. There wasn't much we could do about it.

Working at The Bowl definitely offered its pluses and minuses, one big plus being the live orchestra, which, of course, is better than working with a dead orchestra and infinitely better than working with recorded music. Dancing and singing to that full, rich, magnificent sound was a real treat. As performers, we relied on a competent conductor for the right tempos and on competent musicians for a clean sound. A change in tempo either faster or slower than what we practiced with in rehearsal made a considerable difference in the ease or difficulty of performing the choreography. As such, the orchestra could enhance or botch up the show. Regardless, the first rehearsal with the orchestra was always a big day. The glorious sound infused us with energy and excitement.

Opening night was also a thrill, not only because it was our first night to perform for a real audience and hear their response, but because opening night meant presents, flowers, and a party. The performers passed out cards and small gifts to the other cast members. I could barely afford to pay my bills, but that didn't stop me from making cutesy little trinkets for everyone. For *No, No, Nanette*, I filled plastic champagne glasses with party streamers and bubble gum balls to look like glasses of bubbly champagne. Many cast members received bouquets of flowers from friends, family, and lovers. It almost didn't seem fair that we got gifts for simply doing a job we loved to do—but that was tradition in the theatre world. For closing night, we all chipped in to get presents for the conductor, director, choreographer, and stage manager. It was a love fest from beginning to end.

Life in Southern Cali was moving along splendidly. Then, one morning around five a.m., I was awakened by the alarm clock from hell: an earthquake. Good morning, Mother Nature! My entire two-story building was grinding back and forth like we were being carried on ocean waves. My heart beat wildly as I waited for the wild ride to subside. I never slept well after that, always anticipating another tremor. Talk about feeling out of control. While California was certainly famous for its entertainment scene, it was also notorious for natural disasters. Earthquakes came with the territory. I was going to have to shake, rattle, and roll with the punches.

****

The second show at the Starlight Bowl was *Chess*—a rock musical about American-Russian relations, illustrated metaphorically through a competitive professional chess match between an American and a Russian chess master. Also thrown in was a love triangle between the brash American, his female manager, and his Russian competitor/nemesis. I had seen the show in London and was blown away. I absolutely loved the music, which was co-written by two of the singers from the famous pop group ABBA. "One Night in Bangkok" was a radio hit dance tune from the eighties, and I knew it well. Rock musicals seemed to move me more than any other type of musical. Music was this show's strong point.

This was the first show of the season not directed by the Wards. Instead, a middle-aged, silver-and-gray haired guy named Jamie Rocco directed with his sexy sidekick choreographer, Donna Drake. It appeared that I left little impression on Mr. Rocco, because he paid me next to no notice. Donna, on the other hand, left a big impression on plenty of us. At thirty-some years of age, she was still a babe with a bodacious bod. She would nibble on cold hotdogs during rehearsals making all the straight guys salivate. I never had an inkling what the backgrounds of the directors and choreographers were until the *Playbill* came out, at which point I would eagerly flip through to find their biographies. It turns out that Rocco had starred on Broadway in *Cats* and had directed and choreographed in many theatres around the United States and in London as well. Donna had been in the original cast of *A Chorus Line*. Now I was really impressed.

Our two male leads—the Russian and American chess competitors—were both handsome, sexy men. The American guy looked like a smokin' hot rock star with streaky, spiky blond hair and tiny, gold hoop earrings in his ears. Boy, could he wail. I stood mesmerized as I watched him sing his solo, gyrating like a true rock star and ending dramatically on his knees, his back arched, head facing heavenward. I wished I had an ounce of his vocal talent. He was jaw-droppingly captivating. The Russian was attractive in a more stately way and belted out those ABBA tunes with the power of a proud Soviet.

Yet again, I was thrown for a loop when I heard a rumor that another super cute guy from the ensemble who had been dating one of the female cast members dropped her like a hot potato and hooked up with one of the other babe-alicious dudes instead. Hold on! Not fair! That took two of the prime dating possibilities out of the running in one fell swoop. Figuring out who to flirt with became confusing, because these guys did not look or act like stereotypical gay men. But really, was it fair for so many gorgeous, talented guys to play for the other team? I was partially disappointed that the women's team had lost two good men and partially excited by witnessing what may have been my first bisexual in action.

Along with our amazing superstar talent, we had the perfect set for a show entitled *Chess*—a giant chess board, of course! Ours covered most of the stage. What made it particularly interesting was that its squares could be lit in different patterns and the whole board could be tilted on an angle or rotated. Very cool and effective visually. The set was so treacherously slick, however, that it was more like an ice rink than a game board. I had been slipping in rehearsal and asked wardrobe for some help. They gave me rough-surface stickers to adhere to the soles of my shoes. The stickers were cheap and ineffective and peeled off when I danced, but that's all wardrobe would offer.

On opening night, during our big dance number, "One Night in Bangkok," I proved just how inadequate those measly stickers were. The choreography included an exuberant Indian war-dance step where we hopped on one leg and punched one arm in the air. Of course in all the opening night excitement I gave an extra-high-energy punch, which was too much for the slippery floor. The resulting unfortunate occurrence I witnessed in slow motion like a movie special effect: leg sliiiiiiiiiips out from under meeeeeee, faaaaaaaaallll baaaaaackwaaaaaaards onto elboooooows, leeeeeegs appear in front of faaaaaaace and over heeeeeeaaaaaad, skirt of very short dreeeessss in eyyyyyyyyyyyyeeeeeees. The spill seemed to last an eternity as each detail was etched into my brain. In reality, it all happened in a fraction of a second. In an instant, I resumed the pow-wow with the rest of the cast. Like a shot, I popped back up and punched and hopped, punched and hopped.

The humiliating experience reminded me of those Olympic ice skaters who, in a failed attempt to do some gravity-defying quadruple-turn jump, instead land smack on their bellies, sprawled all over the ice, legs spread-eagled. A couple seconds later they are back skating with smiles on their faces as if nothing happened. Let me tell you, it's embarrassing. And, after the initial shock and embarrassment wear off, it hurts, too.

Kristi's Law: Your biggest mistakes and mishaps will happen when you have the most important people in the audience. Of course, my catastrophic collapse had to happen the night my entire family had flown in to see my performance. "You bounced back very quickly," Mom said reassuringly. But I was still horrified, and with my (literally) bruised tail between my legs, I finally mustered up enough courage to confront the director before he beat me to the punch. "So, how about my accident in 'One Night in Bangkok'?" I asked, dreading his response. "What accident? I didn't see anything," Mr. Rocco replied casually. Maybe it wasn't the tragedy I had made it out to be. Sometimes it's better not to be noticed.

Had I had the proper rubber on my shoes to begin with, the disaster probably would never have happened. It wasn't until our Equity female lead fell during the show and ended up with a bloody knee that stage management did something to rectify the situation. They mopped the floor in Coca-Cola to make it stickier, and I was given permission to get my shoes properly rubbered by a shoe cobbler under wardrobe's threat that "nothing had better happen to those shoes." Thankfully, nothing did happen, and I finished the remaining shows on my feet.

Slippage aside, I enjoyed this "game show," which was made even more interesting by playing some games of my own. In particular, one of our highly intelligent male dancers and I tried to finish a crossword puzzle by the end of each show. After each of our numbers, we would race downstairs to the dressing rooms as quickly as possible, change into our next costumes, and rush to rendezvous at my dressing table so we could figure out what to write for seventeen down. "Hurry! What's an eight-letter word meaning "puffed out; full?" "Um, um, um … bouffant?" "Yes! It fits!" "We gotta go; that's our cue!" Then we'd run up the stairs just in time to make our entrance. Perhaps this wasn't the best way to stay focused on the show, but it definitely helped the night go by faster.

****

Game over! With our Chess match complete, we moved right into *Paint Your Wagon*—a show about the California gold rush back in 1853. It opened on Broadway in 1951 and featured the famous ballad "They Call the Wind Mariah." Clint Eastwood starred in the movie version. Along with this new endeavor came yet another new director and choreographer.

You can't have a gold rush without prospectors, and since there weren't enough real men to fill the bill for the opening scene, all the ladies got a lesson in cross-dressing. Our transformation from females to males generated uproarious laughter, as we donned scruffy wigs, beards and mustaches, ratty old clothes, hats, and boots in an attempt to disguise ourselves as male miners. It was the best gender conversion we could muster without a mega-dose of testosterone. There was much guffawing from the guys in the cast. "You look like Michael Landon!" they told me. "Oh, really? Well, he was very handsome, so I'll take that as a compliment," I replied remembering that Michael Landon made a pretty sexy "Pa" in the TV show *Little House on the Prairie*.

Every night, we prospectors embarked on what felt like a secret reconnaissance mission. About ten minutes prior to show time, after most of the audience members were seated, the stage manager gave us the "Go!" to head to the hills. In order to avoid being prematurely discovered, we crept and crawled, tip-toed and snuck, stationing ourselves behind bushes, trees, and hills immediately surrounding the theatre. I crouched behind a shrub and tried not to attract attention for so long I felt my brown beard turning gray. When the opening number finally began, we popped out of our hiding spots and journeyed to the stage as if we were really traveling to California. I mustered up my manhood as much as possible, but I could feel the audience eyeballing me and doing a double-take.

The most annoying part about being men was that we couldn't wear any makeup, except for perhaps a little base, until the opening scene was over. Then we had to hurriedly metamorphose into beautiful women. I yearned for my pre-performance hour of makeup time, as that was when I'd relax and get my mind out of my day and into my role. It was my calming period which gave me the opportunity to switch gears from normal life to entertainment mode.

As surprising as it was to see myself transgendered, the real shocker came at rehearsal when the choreographer announced, "Kristi, you will be doing the dream ballet adage with Fred." My jaw dropped to the floor. Now you would think that I would have been thoroughly elated to be doing the slow partner dance, especially since 1.) Fred was a strong, tall, handsome, straight, blond guy, and 2.) this was a featured dancer spot!

However, getting selected for the special part was bittersweet, as I worried that other cast members would scrutinize my performance and think they should have been chosen instead of me. I was nervous, as it had been over ten years since I had done any partnering or serious ballet, but I was determined to do my best. Even so, I was a slightly unsettled settler, never feeling completely confident about the adage. Plus I found out that Fred was married. Another one bites the gold dust.

No Wild West is complete without a bevy of raucous dance hall girls in a brothel-esque saloon setting. Naturally, I was one of them. While fun at first, after a while too much Can-Can can do a girl in. It required so many kicks and jump splits that I wondered if I'd permanently stretch my inner thighs to the point where they'd stay in the splits and never go back. I liked kicking well enough and was good at it, but it certainly took its toll on my body.

Our big dance hall dance number was a 911 call waiting to happen. It was organized chaos, with multiple partnering tricks happening simultaneously in close proximity to one another. As I dutifully cartwheeled holding onto my partner's thighs with my head in his crotch, other duos whizzed and whirled around me, their spinning, kicking bodies too close for comfort. Yikes! "I think my partner and I are too close to the couple next to us. Would you mind moving us?" I pleaded with the choreographer. "You look fine to me. Just stay where you are," she rebutted. Easy for her to say. She wasn't the one trapped upside down with her face exposed, vulnerable to the flailing feet. Still concerned but too shy to push on, I chose to trust the choreographer and not make a big stink about it.

Sure enough, one night, in the midst of all the hootin' and hollerin', I put my head down toward my partner's privates in preparation to cartwheel, and the guy next to me spun around and kicked me right in the temple with his heavy boot, like a football being punted toward the goal posts. Somehow I finished the number, then ran off stage and burst into tears. I cried all through intermission and then miraculously pulled myself together enough to finish the show, even with what was surely a mild concussion. One of my best friends in the cast was the culprit. "I'm so sorry! I'm so sorry, Kristi!" he apologized profusely. But really the choreographer should have taken me seriously.

I was too clueless to know about accident reports or to have stage management take me to the hospital. Had I suffered permanent injury from the incident, I would have needed the accident report in order to claim disability or file a lawsuit. I should have insisted that the choreographer move my partner and me to a safer spot. But it's hard to pull rank when you are a newbie and a peon.

Although *Paint Your Wagon* was my least favorite show to perform, I had the most fun in the dressing room and got a reputation for causing people to laugh soda pop out of their noses. A couple gals made *Paint Your Wagon*-themed backstage activity books (word games, crossword puzzles, hangman) for everyone. It was becoming apparent that backstage is where much of the best entertainment happened.

****

The summer was winding down and those of us who had done the entire season were both exhausted and sad to see it end. We finished off with *Camelot*—that romantic tale of King Arthur and the Knights of the Round Table, Sir Lancelot, Lady Guinevere, and Merlin the Magician. The Wards were back at the helm for this knightly pursuit. Yes! I was extra excited to get cast in *Camelot*, because it was primarily a singer show. In other words, you could pretty much be a "singer who moves well" (a showbiz classification term) and do all the choreography without a problem. Unfortunately, I had one *grande battement* (a high kick) to do in the show, so I still had to stretch every night. Even more unfortunate was that I pulled my hamstring by overstretching or stretching incorrectly or stretching when my muscles were too cold. Whatever the case, I was in pain and didn't know enough to rest my muscles and give them time to repair. It was good that this was our last show of the summer, because my legs needed a siesta.

In *Camelot*, I also learned one of the greatest showbiz secrets of all time: "underdressing"—hiding one outfit underneath another. Sometimes, costume changes were so quick, portions of our costume for the next scene had to be worn underneath our costume for the current scene. Of course, it felt bulky and uncomfortable, but it was the only way to make the fast change in time. More importantly, in an effort to get home (or to the bar) in record time, performers also underdressed their "street" clothes. That is, they took off as much of their costume gear (tights, socks, G-strings) as possible and replaced it with as much of the clothing they wanted to wear home as possible. Oddly, while everyone was dying to get cast in the show, once actually in it, after the show ended for the night, they couldn't seem to get out of that theatre quickly enough. Those ladies really in a rush to leave removed false eyelashes and all their hairpins except for the bare minimum required to maintain the hairdo, and some even scrubbed off some of their makeup. Because the costumes in *Camelot* were floor-length gowns covering our arms, legs, and feet, the women could underdress their T-shirts, jeans, and sneakers. Fantastic! I'd never seen anything like it. Once the curtain went down, it was a race to the finish, that is, the parking lot. Entertainers turn into Olympic sprinters after a show and can reach their cars faster than most audience members.

Over the course of the summer, I became fast friends with two castmates who did all five shows with me: Ronnie, a manly straight guy with a steady girlfriend, and Matthew, a charming gay guy. Neither of the men were dating prospects, but the three of us bonded beautifully and hung out together. For some reason, Ronnie ended up calling me "poophead." For the duration of *Camelot*, it was his mission to play poophead jokes on me. I'd find notes in my shoes, on my costumes, and taped to my mirror calling me a poophead. I even found a rubber poop under my wig on my Styrofoam wig head. Before going on stage, I had to search my costumes to make sure they weren't carrying some sort of fake dung on them. The mischief and camaraderie of our unlikely threesome was a highlight of my time at the Starlight Bowl.

Even more exciting than the doo-doo shenanigans was the baby shower the female ensemble threw for our newly pregnant cast member. We welcomed any excuse for a party. This was no ordinary baby shower, however. It was a high-speed extravaganza held during the show's twenty-minute intermission in (What better place?) the dressing room shower! (Water off, thank you.) There were gifts and cake and snacks, and then we hurried back to stage to finish the show. Power shower! More and more, the backstage entertainment was rivaling the onstage entertainment.

Summer stock really propelled me into the world of show business, showed me the ropes, and dug me in deep. My New York experiences got my foot in the door, but summer stock left me fully living in the house. I felt connected to, enthralled with, and enchanted by entertainers. I fell in love with the theatres, the dressing rooms with mirrors edged by light bulbs, and the whole process of putting together a show. I thrived on the quick learning curve and getting to do so many different types of musicals in such a short time. I adored the costumes and how they instantly changed me into someone else. I lived for the dressing room camaraderie and conversations and the social events, like opening and closing night parties and all the gatherings for drinks in between. Like King Arthur at the end of the show, lamenting the demise of his beloved Camelot, I mourned the thought of leaving this fairytale existence behind. This was one summer full of shining moments that would not be forgotten.

Final Scene: New York City, August 10, 2002

My thirty-five minute trip on the "N"ostalgia train flew by in a New York minute, and before I knew it we arrived at my designated stop—the 49th Street station at 7th Avenue. I exited the subway and made my way onto 49th Street where I found a street vendor. What fun! A street vendor! I bought a cream-filled donut and a cup of coffee in a paper "I ♥ NY" cup for old time's sake. "I really do love New York today," I thought to myself. "What was I so scared of before?"

I walked east on 49th to 6th Avenue and headed north toward 50th Street, sipping my hot beverage and obscuring pedestrian traffic flow by stopping to crane my neck for a glimpse of the mammoth skyscrapers. Up, up, up they reached higher and higher toward the heavens. I recalled my 1987 visit to the Empire State Building—it was exhilarating to be on top but also terrifying, because it was a long, long way to fall. I felt both exhilarated and terrified that very moment—exhilarated to be at the top of my profession and terrified that the fall from stardom would be devastating.

Why wouldn't I give a hoot about losing my little claim to fame? Starring as a Rockette had been one rip-roaring adventure. Heck, working with bonafide stars had been an absolute ball, too. Performing alongside Buddy Ebsen made me happy as a pig in a mud hole. That gentleman was a top-notch celebrity—the real McCoy. I hope I'm still happily hoofing away in my eighties like Buddy. I may not be a professional my whole life like he was, but I'm still going to keep right on dancing. I punctuated that thought by taking a big, determined bite out of my donut, as a yellow taxi sped by.

Act 1, Scene 5

Come and Listen to a Story About a Man Named Jed

It's all about who you know. Being the cow's rump without complaint must've won me points with our *Gypsy* choreographer, Toni Kaye, because when Buddy Ebsen phoned her looking for two singer-dancers for his stage show, I was on her list of recommendations. Buddy Ebsen was a showbiz legend, hoofer, and star of the silver screen having played opposite such leading ladies as Judy Garland and Shirley Temple. On television he starred in the miniseries *Davy Crockett* (1954-1955) as Davy Crockett's sidekick, as detective Barnaby Jones in *Barnaby Jones* (1973-1980), and most recognizably as ultra-rich hillbilly Jed Clampett on that hilarious hit, *The Beverly Hillbillies* (1962-1971). I absolutely loved *The Beverly Hillbillies*. Working with Buddy would be my first brush with real fame, and I desperately wanted to perform with him. Still, I didn't want to get too excited about the possibility for fear that I wouldn't even be called let alone chosen. The golden carrot dangled in front of my nose. I tried to forget about it and went about my daily business.

Unfortunately, I also went on vacation to Hawaii with my boyfriend, and that is where I was when the call came. (These were the olden days before cell phones.) I returned home golden tan and a little plump from one too many piña coladas by the pool and found this message on my answering machine: "Hello. I am calling on behalf of Buddy Ebsen. Toni Kaye recommended you for his upcoming show, and we would like you to audition on…" I nearly had a heart attack, as I reached for my calendar. It couldn't be! The audition date had already passed. I had missed my big chance.

I was sick with grief at having missed the audition and phoned back right away, my voice shaking. A woman with a German accent answered the phone. "Hi, this is Kristi Davis returning your call. I am so very very sorry that I didn't call sooner, but I was in Hawaii. Is there any chance I could still audition? I was so excited about performing with Mr. Ebsen." "Oh, I'm afraid not," the woman replied sounding sincerely compassionate. "We have already cast the show." "Oh, no! Really? Oh, that's terrible. I really really wanted to do it. (Sigh.) I…I hope you'll accept my apology for not responding earlier. Please, please feel free to call if anything comes up in the future." I was devastated. Why was I off gallivanting around the Aloha state when I should have been home, available for auditions? What was I thinking? Why hadn't I taken my career more seriously? I could have kicked myself for leaving town when such a prime job was at stake. "This kind of mess up will never happen again," I vowed.

Miracle of miracles, the mess cleaned itself up. As luck (or destiny) would have it, a week later I received another phone call from the same woman: "I'm Buddy's wife, Dorothy. I'm calling because one of the dancers had to back out, and you sounded so disappointed on the phone that I called you first to fill her spot." I could not believe what I was hearing. "We would like you to come audition at our home this weekend," she continued. Not at some studio or theatre, but actually at their home! I was beside myself with excitement. This was too good to be true!

On audition day, I drove north from San Diego to Buddy and Dorothy's home near the Pacific coast. My mind was awhirl with "Ohmygod, ohmygod, ohmygod, I am going to Buddy Ebsen's house!" I couldn't believe when I actually rolled into the driveway of his mansion. So this is how the other half lives. His beautiful brunette, decades younger, German wife greeted me at the door. "You must be Kristi. I'm Dorothy," she said warmly. I stepped into the foyer beyond which stood a grand spiral staircase leading to the second floor just like in *The Beverly Hillbillies*. "And this is Darla," Dorothy continued, introducing me to the one remaining dancer who had already been cast from the first audition. I wondered where Buddy was and half expected to hear trumpets blaring, announcing his grand entrance down the magnificent staircase. Or maybe he would shoot off his rifle and say, "Weeeeeell, Doggies!"—his famous Jed catch phrase.

Instead, this spry, white-haired eighty-four-year-old, who could have easily passed for my grandfather, casually sauntered out of his office, shook my hand, and said a kind hello. I immediately recognized him as a vintage version of Jed Clampett. The whole experience felt surreal. No longer just some fantasy television character, he was a real live person who was talking to little ol' me. Buddy shared that he had always dreamed of creating his own, live stage show. Branson, Missouri, was the perfect place to welcome an old hoofer, and when famous country music star Roy Clark invited him to perform at his theatre there, Buddy accepted. "What could possibly be in Branson, Missouri?" I wondered.

"So, do you know the shim sham?" Buddy inquired as he took off tapping right there in the foyer. Stomp brush step, stomp brush step, stomp brush ball change, stomp brush step. "Yes," I replied, and Darla and I began to imitate his feet as he skillfully demonstrated a few standard tap steps. We stayed in our street shoes so as to not scuff his floor. "Good. Now this," Buddy instructed as he continued to throw fancy footwork at us.

"Let's have you try singing some back-up vocals," Buddy said as Dorothy produced the sheet music to "The Ballad of Davy Crockett"—a catchy tune about the American folk hero known as the "King of the Wild Frontier." I was considerably more nervous about the singing than the dancing, but it wasn't anything too difficult, and Debbie was singing with me. I faked it as best I could. This was beginning to feel much more like a rehearsal than an audition, and it soon became clear that I was going to be in the show!

Finally, it was time for a break. I was stunned when Dorothy ushered us into the kitchen where she had prepared a German feast for lunch. It happened to be Buddy's birthday, and he loved German food. We all sat there devouring the tasty vittles. I was in absolute heaven. Getting my PhD in psychology would have been great, but how can you beat dancing, singing, and eating German food with Jed Clampett in his very own mansion in California? Life just doesn't get much better than that. I was overwhelmed by the Ebsens' generosity. What a day this had been.

Subsequent rehearsals were held at a local dance studio during the day, when it was empty and free of potential paparazzi. The show was essentially a series of songs, skits, and dances. It highlighted the various roles Buddy had played during his television career, including Jed Clampett, Barnaby Jones, and Davy Crockett's sidekick, Georgie Russell. Some songs Buddy had written himself. Darla and I practiced our part of the act with Buddy, which consisted of 1.) a *Beverly Hillbillies* skit with Buddy playing Jed Clampett and Darla and I taking turns playing "Bonnie Sue"—cousin of the character Ellie Mae, Jed's daughter in the show, 2.) singing backup for many of Buddy's songs, and 3.) a little soft shoe dance with Buddy. "I also need you two to do a dance number by yourselves to give me time to change costumes. I want it to be some type of dance challenge where you try to outdo each other," Buddy declared. "Can you do that?" Darla and I assured him we could, and we set off choreographing our dance duel to the "St. Louis Blues."

Buddy observed and often interjected pearls of showbiz wisdom, old tricks of the trade. "Ya gotta leave the crowd wanting more!" he said one time. "Do this with your hands on the exit. This always gets them," he said another time as he put his hands out to the sides with palms to the audience and, with fingers spread, shook them like crazy. "And put a move on the 'button' (an accentuated beat at the end of a song) to drum up even more applause," he added as he did a sharp body pose mimicking the emphatic musical finish.

"Now we've gotta get you gals some costumes, because we want to take some publicity photos before we leave for Branson," Buddy decided. Darla announced, "I think I can get us these gorgeous costumes that we wore when I was a Love Boat Mermaid." I was thoroughly impressed. Love Boat Mermaids were a group of sexy dancers who performed weekly on the hit TV series *The Love Boat*, which ran from 1977 to 1986. As a teenager, I adored the show's romantic adventures on the high seas, especially when they brought on dancers. "As far as shoes are concerned, we'll need the silver, open-toed, t-strap, ballroom dancer-type shoes, with two-and-a-half-inch heels. And we definitely must have rubber on the soles and braces under the arches," Darla strongly advised, espousing exactly what was required to make our legs the safest and the sexiest. I certainly concurred on the rubber.

True to her word, Darla delivered the goods: high-quality, handmade costumes from *The Love Boat*. They were white and silver rhinestone-studded spandex leotards, low cut in the chest and high cut in the legs with spaghetti straps that crisscrossed in back. Over the leotards we wore matching silver-sequined, waist-length jackets that opened in front. The costumes were appropriately sexy, and Buddy and I approved. The ballroom shoes were beautiful but took me a while to get used to, as I was accustomed to dancing in sturdier character shoes with only one-and-a-half-inch heels. I was glad Darla had taken charge, because, being a more seasoned dancer than I was, she really knew the business. I liked her a lot and looked up to her as a mentor of sorts.

Darla's expertise was even more obvious when we finally had the professional photo shoot. The publicity shots were taken at the dance studio and consisted of several poses with the two of us flanking Buddy on either side. "You ladies kiss Buddy on the cheek," the photographer directed. I never in a million years would have dreamed I'd be smooching Buddy Ebsen. Upon seeing the developed photos, I noticed how Darla angled her body to look great for the camera, while I was in one unflattering pose after another. I had no idea how to bevel properly—how to place my feet to make my feet and legs look pretty—or how to pose for photos to maximize my assets.

Dorothy and Buddy flew to Branson ahead of us to get settled, as Buddy was also preparing for an exhibit of his paintings in St. Louis (he was an artist, too). Darla and I didn't fly in until the day before the show opened. We landed in St. Louis and then boarded an eency, weency, super-bouncy, nearly-make-you-throw-uppy commuter plane to Springfield, Missouri, from which we would have a forty-five-minute drive to Branson. The Springfield airport was small and manageable, but if you arrived at 11:00 p.m., there weren't a lot of folks on duty to help you. The place was absolutely deserted, so when Darla and I realized our luggage had not made the trip with us, we had no one to turn to for help. Our first show was the next afternoon, and if our luggage didn't arrive we'd be dancing without costumes. (Note to self: Always carry your costume on board with you in case of such a mishap. It's luggage you can't afford to lose.) All we could do was grab a cab and call the airport in the morning.

Driving through the hills into Branson, we noticed all the billboards advertising shows featuring old country stars: Anita Bryant, Glen Campbell, Tony Orlando, Wayne Newton, Jim Stafford. As we entered the main drag on Highway 76, we saw theatres sporting the same names. "There's the Roy Clark Celebrity Theatre!" I shouted, a chill of excitement running down my spine at the sight of the place where we'd be performing and staying. I remembered the banjo-picking Roy Clark from the country music and corn-pone TV show *Hee Haw* that my family and I watched when I was a kid.

The next day, after a good night's sleep in our very own rooms with kitchenettes (yes, folks, this was the lap of luxury), Darla and I headed to the theatre to prep for the show. Upon entering the backstage door, we couldn't help but notice that the walls were covered in graffiti—signatures of the many, famous musical acts that had played there. "That is so cool!" I exclaimed, in awe of our predecessors. We then met the band that would accompany us. They eagerly presented us with their headshots, which they signed, of course, as well as their demo tapes. These good old country boys all had their own individual musical projects and dreams. There was a lotta talent in them thar halls and more musicians than you could shake a stick at in Branson. Luckily, while we were introducing ourselves to the band and getting settled in our dressing room, our costumes arrived from the airport.

We hadn't come up with a good backup plan, so Darla, Buddy, Dorothy, and I were relieved, to say the least.

We performed two shows daily (2:00 p.m. and 8:00 p.m.) on Thursday, Friday, and Saturday following the popular *Jennifer in the Mornings* show—a post-breakfast production for all those earlier risers and/or theatre maniacs who wanted to squeeze in as many shows as they could in one day. A spunky blond singer-dancer, Jennifer woke up the crowd with her high-spirited clogging. She was a tough act to follow, but Buddy was a well-loved TV and movie celebrity who knew how to work an audience, milking every last bit of laughter and applause. Plus, at eighty-four, he could still tap dance circles around the best of them. After each show, Buddy stood in a little booth where he signed autographs and greeted his adoring fans (a must in Branson). The whole experience was such a hoot.

During our shows, we noticed a mysterious, shady, skinny, acne-faced young guy slinking around and taking pictures. Later I discovered he was a reporter from *Star* magazine. *Star* ended up running a one-and-a-half-page story on Buddy, which was, surprisingly, quite complimentary and well written. The best news was that Darla and I were in one of the photos. We didn't look too shabby either. Buddy, in a long-haired wig and holding an electric guitar, was featured on the cover with a decent-sized photo and caption that read, "Buddy Ebsen turns rock star—at 84." Although he was trumped by a much larger picture of Sarah Ferguson, Duchess of York, and the headline story "Fergie bought pot from palace guard," it still wasn't bad for an octogenarian. We three were pictured in the *National Enquirer*, too, which noted that Buddy was "definitely still alive and kicking!" I never dreamed I'd end up in the tabloids without birthing a three-headed alien baby or spotting Elvis at a Kentucky Fried Chicken in Kalamazoo. An article in a local Branson newspaper mentioned how Buddy's act "will feature two new dance partners, adding to Ebsen's extensive list of renowned leading ladies including Shirley Temple and Judy Garland." Judy Garland and I both danced with Buddy Ebsen! It was almost incomprehensible.

One night, after our show, the band kindly invited Darla and me to a spontaneous cast party. "Why not?" we thought, game for some fun. The grand festivities consisted of a case of beer and a pick-up truck parked in the parking lot, doors open, country music blasting on the radio. Nothing was too good for us Los Angeles girls. We partied

Branson style. "You gals are the most professional people we've ever worked with," the guys agreed. Well, shucks. I could toast to that. This wasn't your typical showbiz shindig, but it seemed fitting, all the same.

My parents drove all the way from Michigan to see me perform and to see Branson for the first time. I was thrilled to have them in the audience and to be able to introduce them to Buddy and Dorothy. After all, I was on a first-name basis with somebody famous, and that was too extraordinary not to share. To top it off, on our last day in Branson, Buddy and Dorothy invited my parents and me to have breakfast with them. I just about flipped. They were such kind, gracious people and a joy to be around. I felt privileged to be giving my parents this rare and exciting experience.

During our minimal time off, Darla and I were able to see a couple of the other shows in town. Amazingly, we were allowed in for FREE when we told them we were performing at the Roy Clark. There was some sort of generally accepted reciprocity agreement whereby performers of the various shows could see the other shows without charge. How fabulous! First, we saw the Osmond Show, which was very exciting, as I had been a Donnie and Marie fan as a youngster. While I was disappointed that my favorite duo weren't actually in it, the remaining brothers had enough vocal talent and pizzazz to get by without their superstar siblings. The second show we saw featured a man the Osmonds can thank for discovering them—Andy Williams. Andy was an old pop star well known for his rendition of "Moon River," and he now performed at his very own Moon River Theatre. As a kid, I was especially fond of his cozy Christmas specials which were as heartwarming as a hand-knit sweater and a cup of hot cocoa.

Branson was, without a doubt, like no other place I've ever been. Praise God if you were a white, heterosexual, patriotic American Christian. If not, you may have been more comfortable elsewhere. This was the Bible Belt and Ku Klux Klan country, and we felt the influences. I was shocked to see a sign on the side of the highway stating that the KKK had sponsored that portion of the road. Being more or less a white, heterosexual, patriotic, American Christian, I was treated like royalty.

This little town in Missouri, I learned, was a viable growing family entertainment destination. Who knew? Set in the heart of the Ozark Mountains, its beauty was unrivaled in the fall when the leaves changed to vibrant red, orange, and yellow hues. Chock full of road-kill paraphernalia, down-home cooking, and old country music stars, the city drew in busload after busload of tour groups looking for some good, clean fun in a small-town atmosphere. It was the one place in the country where roadkill was big business and you could create and star in your very own show. The whole place comforted you like a bowl of Grandma's homemade chicken soup and buttermilk biscuits—good old Southern hospitality at its finest.

Branson could feel like a nursing home where antique country stars performed out their final days. Instead these luminaries brought vitality and a passion for their art to busloads of senior citizens who loved to meet and greet the stars of their day in person. The stars were old, but the audiences were older. With many celebrities, it was popular to have their families join them on stage for a number or two, and if they didn't include a patriotic song in their finale, why, they were missing the standing ovation they deserved. A "God Bless You!" at the end of the performance was nearly a prerequisite for everyone as was shaking hands and signing autographs. They aimed to please, and it seemed to be working. Branson was a show factory where many of its stars performed six days a week, two to three shows a day—a heavy schedule for even the hardiest of the bunch. But they got to keep doing what they loved, and that's what it was all about.

Buddy, too, did what he loved, for well over sixty years, and had plenty of stories to share about his adventures in the world of entertainment. Not only was he a versatile performer and artist, but he was a writer, too, and the following year his autobiography was released. He entitled it *The Other Side of Oz*, because he had actually been the first Tin Woodman cast in the film *The Wizard of Oz*. Sadly, while filming he became hospitalized from the silver aluminum dust makeup he had to wear, which made him seriously ill. After inadvertently poisoning him, the movie studio didn't even wait for Buddy to recuperate before hiring another guy to play the part. The rest is history, and Buddy's final words of the epilogue beautifully sum up what he learned over the years:

> *I wanted to tell this story for the millions of young men and women—and the grownups, too—who start out bravely every morning prepared to sell something, whatever it may be. I wanted them to know the story of someone, like themselves, who has been confronted by negative people who are secure behind polished desks, and who listen doubtfully as your pitch flops.*

So what do you do then? Ring up "no sale" and walk out of the office defeated? Never! Refuse to accept it! Just call it a temporary postponement of success. The difference between success and failure is often no wider than the thickness of a cigarette paper. Just as Dorothy, the Scarecrow, the Cowardly Lion, and the Tin Woodman stood up to the Wizard and won—so can you! Life's a brand-new ball game every day! Remember that of all the elements that comprise a human being, the most important, the most essential, the one that will sustain, transcend, overcome and vanquish all obstacles is—Spirit!

Now those are words to live by, spoken by a man of triumph over adversity. As soon as Buddy's autobiography came out I bought and mailed two copies to Buddy's home. He signed one for me and one for my uncle who loved *The Beverly Hillbillies* and was going nuts about me working with Jed Clampett. In my book he wrote "To Kristi—with great affection from Dorothy and me and a strong belief in your future—Buddy." For several years following the gig, I received Christmas cards from Buddy and Dorothy. One was a photocard of Buddy's original artwork. I really cherish them and my time with the legendary and memorable Buddy Ebsen. "Weeeeellll, Doggies!"

Act 2
On the Road, Sky, and Sea

Final Scene: New York City, August 10, 2002

Buddy had been good to me. The Rockettes had been good to me. Showbiz had been good to me. I wandered down the 6th Avenue "skyscraper alley" toward my destination: 1260 6th Avenue—Radio City Music Hall, "showplace of the nation." When I finally arrived near the famed Music Hall, the sight of the massive marquee sent a chill down my spine. It covered an entire city block. The luminous appearance of this uberglamorous New York icon, world's largest indoor theatre, and home to the Radio City Rockettes, took my breath away. I snapped a photo from across the street, but it couldn't capture the magnificence and magic of what this place meant to me. Seeing Radio City Music Hall felt like a reunion with a close relative I was meeting for the first time. I was an alien returning to the mother ship.

Taking a deep breath, I headed over to the stage door on 6th Avenue and 51st Street. I loved stage doors as they always made me feel like I was going through a secret entrance privy only to the VIPs. Today I felt even more privileged than usual. A security guard manned the entrance from his booth. "I'm here to teach the Rockette Experience," I announced to him, trying to sound confident, despite being certain my heart was beating out of my chest. After checking his notes to make sure I was the real deal, he phoned the person in charge. Shortly an enthusiastic man arrived to escort me. He gave me a special badge to wear. *Whoa…I'm in!*

The nice fellow walked me through the building to show me the pertinent spots. "Here's the green room where you can hang out before the workshop starts," he said as we approached the first open door on the right. I stepped in for a brief look around. The green room had attractive wooden furniture, leather chairs and sofas, drink dispensers, a refrigerator, and a coffee maker. I read the notices on the bulletin board, envious of all the girls who danced here.

We continued down the hall, past a couple of rooms where the Rockettes could relax with professional massages. Finally we stopped by a brightly lit dance studio with mirrors covering an entire wall. "Here is the small rehearsal hall, and over here is the large rehearsal hall where you'll be teaching. Any questions?" I was impressed by the beautiful facilities. "I do have one question. If it's all right, I want to take the Radio City tour before I have to teach. Can you tell me where to go?" He kindly took me to the lobby to wait inside with the tour guides for the tour to begin.

None of the tourists knew I was an undercover Rockette. We all took photos of ourselves standing on the great stage. I pictured what it would be like to dance there, to look out on the audience of six thousand people, to ride the elevators and run through the halls backstage to make my entrances.

The tour guide led us to a holding area in front of the dressing room door, which, naturally, had a star on it. "Now we are going to meet a real Rockette! Is everybody ready?" the tour guide asked, as she knocked on the door. "They've been walking and talking with a real Rockette for the last half hour," I thought, keeping the secret to myself. A lovely young lady appeared, decked out in her cute red costume and perma-grin. Acting on her best behavior, she happily posed for photos and answered questions with politeness and sweetness that would have made a Disney princess proud.

While certainly fine, upstanding citizens and consummate professionals with the best of intentions, the Rockettes couldn't be expected to be that wholesome and pure *all* of the time. Could they? I'm sure even Cinderella wanted to let her hair down and let loose now and then. Constantly having to be perfect can drive a person crazy and, perhaps, even call in one's naughty side to balance oneself out. That perfect, good-girl image required of the Rockettes was the polar opposite of how I was expected to behave in one of my earlier jobs—a member of the "Playboy's Girls of Rock & Roll." Oh, the freedom of being the "bad girl" and embracing my inner floozy. If dancing with the Rockettes was my superego, then dancing for Playboy was my id in wild abandon. It was the angel versus the devil in me, and the devil can be very tempting.

Act 2, Scene 1

Playboy's Girls of Rock & Roll

I wasn't really Playboy Bunny material, and, even if I were, I hadn't the slightest clue how to get my buck-naked body on a centerfold nor would I want to bare my birthday suit for friends and strangers alike to critique. Nevertheless, it seems I was destined to be associated with those famous, fuzzy rodents because, like a free lap dance, the opportunity to work with Playboy simply landed in my lap.

(Note: So my parents don't have heart attacks, I'm telling them right now to skip this whole Playboy section and resume reading when the next section begins. That goes for the rest of you who have a low tolerance for talk about breasts and G-strings. I confess this book is no worse than a PG-13 movie, so those who were hoping for some X-rated material should skip it altogether. I'm still a goody two-shoes even if the shoes are stilettos.)

****

It happened like this: A few months after my Branson stint with Buddy Ebsen, I got a call from Celebration Magnifico, as they had recently expanded their operation and opened a West Coast office. Jenny had told them I was living in California and that they should contact me. With reluctance and a bit of nausea, but needing the cashola, I rejoined the ranks of party dancers. I was grateful for the opportunity to make more money but wasn't all that jazzed about having to ask strangers to tango again. Oh well, I'd make the best of it, and at least I'd be dancing. The downside ended up being less the job itself and more the extensive driving, as parties could be located anywhere from San Diego up to L.A. and its surrounding area. Unlike New York City where we were transported everywhere by the company, here we were expected to have a car and get ourselves to the gig. A party could easily require a two-hour drive up the coast. Still, it was $100 that I wouldn't have had otherwise.

Celebration Magnifico actually booked us some decent trips that included transportation, like the one-night gig at the Golden Nugget in Las Vegas. My first time performing there, I was excited in spite of the fact that I still thought Vegas was sleazy. As we flew into the city, I saw the shiny black pyramid of the Luxor hotel rising up from the desert. We learned a dance to "One" from the musical *A Chorus Line* and opened for the infamous, brash, insult comic, Don Rickles, who was as entertainingly obnoxious in person as he was on stage. We returned to Vegas another time to dance at an extravagant, black-tie New Year's

Eve party thrown by Caesar's Palace. Getting paid triple overtime was a terrific way to ring in the New Year, and it was fun to be a part of all the action. My absolute favorite trip was to Maui, Hawaii, where we stayed at the luxurious Hilton Wailea in $500-a-night rooms. The service at the hotel was impeccable: Too hot as you lounge in the sun? A pool boy would spray you with an Evian spritzer. Too sweaty as you run on the treadmill in the open air gym overlooking the ocean? A gym servant would offer ice cold, wet towels and Evian water to drink. This was the life! We ate from sumptuous breakfast buffets loaded with succulent, tropical fruits and rode bicycles into town to shop for chocolate macadamia nut candies. It was heavenly! The decadent setting more than made up for the fact that I had to dance as half of the Brooklyn Bridge.

My enthusiasm for the job had certainly waned since those initial days in New York, but the California dancers were cordial and relatively laid back. The pool of performers was much smaller than New York and, consequently, without the distinct A, B, and Z teams. Here, the Jersey girls were replaced with nipple and navel-pierced, tattooed, vegetarian Valley girls, and I even made a few friends. An aspiring actress, who trained with the famous improvisational group called the Groundlings, invited me for a night out with a couple guys she knew. One guy, Jonathan Elias, a successful movie soundtrack producer, gave us a tour of his gorgeous home/recording studio in the Hollywood Hills and handed out copies of his latest C.D.—a compilation of film scores he had written. His impressive resume included creating music for the motion picture trailers for *Alien, Altered States, Bladerunner, Gandhi, Ghostbusters,* and *Back to the Future,* scoring scenes for *Nine to Five* and *Still of the Night,* writing the title song for *9 1/2 Weeks,* and working with such artists as Duran Duran, Grace Jones, and Yes. At the time, however, I had no idea who this composer was. Call me clueless. Call me naïve, but this is the caliber of amazing person you can run into in Los Angeles.

Jonathan and his buddy took us to chichi Club Tatou, where we were supposedly on the VIP list. As VIPs, we had to wait in line at the "secret" back door entrance with the thirty other trendily dressed "Very Important People" and convince the big, scary bouncer—an ex-con from the L.A. County Prison, no doubt—that we were worthy. The bouncer/security guy eyeballed us up and down, assessing our grooviness. Concerned we might be turned away, my new guy friend assured the man with the requisite name dropping, "We're friends of So-and-So. We're cool." Jonathan most certainly was cool, and finally Scary Security Guy bought it. Mind you, we still had to pay the $25 cover charge. If we VIPs had to beg to be let into a nightclub, I felt sorry for the Very Unimportant People. Maybe you have to be a VVIP to walk in free of charge and without groveling. On the way to the dance floor we passed Rod Stewart and his model wife, Rachel Hunter, dining with their large entourage. "I bet they never stood in the VIP line," I whispered to my friend. It bothered me that you had to be somebody famous or know somebody to get into these places. You had to look the part, or forget it. Yuck. Of course, I pretended not to be impressed by Rod and company. I was just that cool.

But I digress. What I'm really getting at is through Celebration Magnifico I also met the super-hot, Italian, dream boy, Gino. With his wavy black tresses and abs of steel, he was as charming as his muscles were solid. I didn't stand a chance with him, as he was gay, of course. *Sigh*. But, over time, we became buddies, and he offered me something else I couldn't refuse. "I'm going to be choreographing a show for Playboy," he announced, "and I thought you would be perfect for the job." "Say what? The *real* Playboy? As in *the magazine*? As in *Playboy Bunnies?*" I asked incredulously. He assured me it was the real deal. The next thing I knew, I had an audition with the executive producer of Playboy's Girls of Rock & Roll.

****

I must admit, I was nervous walking into Playboy Enterprises for my initial interview. Would this be the last we'd see of a once-wholesome Midwestern girl? Would I suddenly want to throw all caution and clothes to the wind? The success of *Playboy* magazine made me question the validity of the phrase "If you've seen one, you've seen them all." Apparently, men never tired of looking at mammaries, at least not at those resembling full-grown melons. Hugh Hefner—the founder of this fruitful empire—had the money to prove it.

The multi-story glass office building looked perfectly normal from the outside. What did I expect? Giant breast-shaped domes and a phallic tower? It wasn't until I walked through the hallways past oil paintings of scantily clad women that I sensed any sexual overtones. I suddenly felt a bit overdressed and concerned about what my interview would entail. When I met the producer of the show—former modeling agent Valerie Craigin—I was slightly comforted by the fact that she was a woman. Rumors had it that Valerie was in her mid-sixties but she looked like a well-preserved fifty. She had short coiffed brunette hair, professional attire, a deep smoker's voice, and a nervous laugh. She took the liberty of saying "Hef" instead of "Hugh Hefner" although I don't know how well they knew each other. Valerie seemed harmless enough and, thank God, had no intention of making me take my clothes off. We chatted a bit and that was it. I had the job! She mainly held the interview in order to get a good look at me and make sure I wasn't a heifer, so I could be a "Hefer."

"We'll be touring all over Southeast Asia, so be sure to get your shots," Valerie advised. "I'll be sending you an itinerary as soon as our travel plans are confirmed. We'll start out in Indonesia and then we may go to Singapore, Malaysia, India, Japan, Australia, Germany, Puerto Rico, who knows? There are so many possibilities, it's driving me nuts! Plan to be gone for six months." I tried to remain calm and professional but inside I was thinking "Ohmygod! Ohmygod! Ohmygod!" I was so excited: dancing for Playboy, traveling to exotic countries. *Now this was something to call home about. Or not. What would my parents think?* "Oh, I almost forgot," Valerie continued. "Next week we'll be doing a photo shoot with all the girls to be used for posters and promotional items to be sent overseas."

I went home incredulous about the job I had just landed. Then the doubts and fears and insecurities set in. *I'm not a model. I don't know how to do a photo shoot. I don't have a perfect body. I wish I had better abs. I wish I were thinner. I wish I were prettier. I wish…*

Did I condone magazines that flagrantly promoted women's bodies as mere sex objects? No, I can't say that I did or do, and perhaps, if I had put any serious thought into it or been more enlightened, I would have taken up a feminist stance, stomped my foot, and shouted defiantly, "How dare you even ask me to be associated with a company that is degrading women by shamefully displaying them as play toys!"

Instead, I was eager to get a firsthand look at the debauchery behind this famous furry icon. It was more of a sordid curiosity—like wanting the forbidden fruit simply because it's forbidden. My inner Tigress was roaring and ready to be let out of its cage. This was just too much of an adventure to pass up. After all, I wasn't going to be doing anything *really* naughty; was I?

****

In the days leading up to the photo shoot, I may have appeared relaxed and confident on the outside, but on the inside I was a nervous wreck because, horror of horrors, over the course of the week a boil had sprouted out on the middle of my forehead. I was casually glancing in the mirror while brushing my teeth when, all of a sudden, my eye was drawn to a raised, red spot on my face.

"What's that? That wasn't there before!" I said in disbelief, touching the bump to make sure it was real. "NOOOOOOO! I have the photo shoot in three days!" I panicked for a few minutes, then quickly began pulling out my blemish-eliminating tricks. "Okay, maybe there's still time to get rid of it," I thought, hopefully.

I used lotions, potions, zit creams, and a steaming hot washcloth, but I think I only made it madder, because it grew. And grew. And grew. Bigger than any pimple I had ever seen. It was a dime-sized lump that birthed from my face like I was trying to grow a second head on top of the one I already had. There was nothing there to squeeze or pinch. Nothing short of surgical removal could have helped. I had no bangs (the fact that I wouldn't even consider cutting some to cover that monster was evidence of how much I hated bangs) and no way to hide it.

And so it was that my new "friend" and I returned to Playboy Enterprises for the important photo shoot. As if I wasn't nervous enough already about the photo shoot and meeting the cast for the first time, I was now also horribly self-conscious about my dermatological nightmare. Valerie's eyes bugged out when she saw me. "Oh my. Uh, you'd better get yourself over to the makeup artist right away, dear," she insisted, laughing nervously.

I agreed with Valerie, and I prayed the makeup artist would have some special pancake makeup to disguise that blasted boil. When I showed her the mountain on my face and, in desperation, asked her, "Can you do something to fix it?" she gave me this incredulous look like "I'm not a miracle worker, you naïve, acne-faced bimbo!"

Of course, trying to cover that sucker was about as easy as trying to make my nose look invisible. Even the best makeup artist in the world can't hide Mt. Vesuvius. She made a valiant effort by piling on the thickest cover-up she had. It was the best we could do.

Back in the main room, I joined the rest of the all-female cast of Playboy's Girls of Rock & Roll, which consisted of three singers, two dancers (myself and another girl), and three *Playmates*. Satin, Mallory, and Taffy were the three nude models who were willing to sing and dance in this show. They had taken their clothes off and been photographed for the most famous girlie magazine in the world. I was going to be dancing with them, talking to them, socializing with them. Word was, they made twenty-some-thousand dollars or so for posing for the magazine. I don't know if that was true, but even that sizable chunk of change wasn't enough to make me want to bare it all. Meeting the Playmates was like going to the Big Top of the Bizarre to see the woman with three eyes or the rubber man who could twist himself up like a pretzel. I stared at those real Playboy Bunnies like they were circus attractions. I was enthralled.

Taffy was an ultra-petite beauty with long, wavy blond locks and a tiny, taut body. She starred in a Playboy video where she did naked rhythmic gymnastics while twirling a long, satin ribbon attached to a stick into mesmerizing circular, spiral, and figure-eight patterns around her delicate figure. She was light and airy and not extremely friendly. She didn't need to be; she was just that hot, and boy, could she give a look to kill when she was in a sour mood.

In contrast, Mallory was an enormous, blond, athletic, Canadian kick boxer with exquisite, fake D-cups and an "I'll kick your ass!" attitude hovering beneath the surface. I wanted her on my good side; she could most certainly beat the tar out of me if she felt like it.

Satin was a voluptuous gal with lusciously long, blond hair. Under that soft, sultry exterior, however, was a tough little cookie. I'm sure she could hold her own, if not entirely slaughter almost any woman, in a mud wrestling contest.

Callie, Jasmine, and Rhonda were our well-seasoned singers. All three had performed in the Playboy Show at the Maxim in Vegas and were so well acquainted with Valerie they called her "Val." Callie was a riveting seductress who reminded me of a young Morticia from "*The Munsters*" with her waist-long, brunette hair parted in the middle. On stage she had a dark, sorceress aura about her, but off stage she was as fun, funny, and lighthearted as a person can be. An L.A. native, she was always sporting some funky, ahead-of-the-trend clothing and was game for just about anything.

Jasmine, a nice girl from New Mexico, was an aspiring country singer and guitar player. She was tall, thin, flat, and wholesomely beautiful with waist-long, stick-straight blond hair. She did her best to put on a rock and roll vibe for the show, but underneath you could tell she was a country sweetheart. At thirty-something, Rhonda was our most senior and most experienced performer. This rowdy rocker from Vegas sported big, black, wild, frizzy hair, and a curvaceous, womanly body. She had found salvation in her Mormon church and was proudly counting the days she'd been sober. Rhonda had a rough edge about her, having lived on the wild side for so long. All three singers were amazingly sexy performers in their own way.

Besides yours truly, Porsche was the only other real dancer Valerie hired. The two of us were the only Playboy virgins, the rest of the cast being Playboy veterans in some respect, either on stage or in print. Porsche was a talented dancer with short, strawberry-blond hair and a fantastic boob job that was her pride and joy. She had married a sensible guy with a normal job and was the only wedded one of the bunch.

I was nervous and shy around these stunningly beautiful, overly sexy, talented, and worldly women. I felt like a frumpy housefrau in comparison. Many of them knew each other and chatted away as they dug through a box of old black leather, silver-studded S&M mix-and-match costume pieces claiming their favorites from previous shows.

"Remember this ugly thing? I'm not wearing that again." "Hand me that belt. It's mine." "Here, Jasmine, this must be your tiny bra; I'd never fit into it. What is it: triple A?" "Very funny. Ha ha." "Satin, this would look good on you." "Does this make me look fat?"

The costume box contained as assortment of thigh-high black boots, black halter tops, black bustiers, lacy black bras, black leather gloves, dog-collar chokers, and wide black belts to wear over black thongs. It was Harley Davidson meets harlot. *Gulp.*

"Find something to wear, dear," Valerie said to me. "These are the costumes for your opening number." I pawed through the scraps of black, black, and even more black, hoping to find something that would cover up my flaws and accentuate my assets.

The veteran girls seemed to take over, leaving Val in the dust. A couple of them emerged from a closet where they hauled out another box to rummage through. "I'm sick of those old costumes. How about these, Val? These would look better," Rhonda said holding up a colorful, sequined spaghetti-strapped mini dress in one hand. "We have five of these and three of these," she added, grasping a midriff-bearing sequined halter top and sequined shorty shorts in the other hand. "The singers can wear the dresses, because I'm not showing my stomach, and this would look better with my boobs."

The veteran girls grabbed their picks, and I was stuck with a halter top and shorts, which meant I was going to have to show *my* stomach. I kept wishing I weighed ten pounds less and had washboard abs. Still, I guess this was better than a black thong, motorcycle mama bra, and studded dog collar. We were given black fishnet tights and black stiletto boots to finish off the look.

For our photo session, we grouped together for a sexy pose that would lure those Southeast Asian men away from their bowls of rice and toward our bosoms. Sure that a massive pimple wouldn't help our marketing efforts, I tried to part my hair so that a few strands hung over my forehead. Then I watched as the other girls instinctively arched their backs, stuck out their chests, cocked their heads, and pouted their lips for the photo. I had no clue how to make love to the camera, so I just sucked in my stomach, held my breath, and smiled. *I am way out of my league here.*

Next, we changed into super-short, simple, sexy spaghetti-strap black dresses with long, white satin gloves that came up to the elbow. It was a classier, more romantic look. Having no cellulite showing and being fairly hidden in the back of the group, I had a much easier time posing like a lady of the boudoir.

Glory be! The promo pictures actually turned out pretty nice. I was relieved that one had to look very closely to see that boil I had sweated buckets over. Anyway, no one was going to be looking at me when there were professional sex kittens offering an eyeful. Meow.

****

Once the photo shoot was over, it was time to get down to business and learn the show. Our rehearsals were held in Santa Monica at the studio of producer/director/choreographer Anita Mann. Sadly, my fabulous friend Gino was ousted as choreographer before we even started. He was replaced with Anita, who was much more experienced, but I felt terrible for Gino and am forever grateful for his recommendation. If you are out there, Gino, I hope when this door closed, a better one opened for you.

Anyway, Anita was this forty-something, super sexy blond dancer/actress who used to choreograph for the 1980s TV show *Solid Gold*—a musical countdown in which the sultry Solid Gold Dancers would move alluringly to the top ten pop hits of the week. These women knew how to work the camera and were always shown in their close-ups making seductive faces for the people watching at home. Of course, I loved the show, which aired when I was a teenager, so Anita was a celebrity to me. Her work there even got her nominated twice for Primetime Emmy Awards for Outstanding Choreography. (She later earned a Primetime Emmy Award for Outstanding Choreography for her work on *The Miss America Pageant* and continued to produce phenomenal productions for stage, screen, and television, even garnering recognition by the Academy of Television Arts and Sciences as "one of America's top five contemporary choreographers." Anita was also born in Detroit. What an amazing talent hailing from my neck of the woods!)

To stay young and gorgeous, Anita was game to try a facial peel or some Hollywood miracle beauty treatment or a special diet. Whatever she did, it worked. She also sported stylish clothing, especially shoes. Dancers are very trendy; when her dancers would come in wearing the latest cool duds, she had to have them right away. She looked sensational.

Scads of distractions, however, kept Anita spread so thin that they made it hard for her to focus on one task. When she first started her business, she actually choreographed shows herself. You'd learn two sets of eight, and she'd have to answer a phone call about another project or her boys would come in or someone had to know if she wanted Chinese take-out or chicken burritos for lunch or one of a hundred other questions had to be answered. She'd return to rehearsal wondering where we'd left off. This was the way she worked, and you could count on her projects being tweaked and perfected up until the last moment.

Used to working television where she choreographed on the spot, Anita seemed to thrive best with the push of a deadline looming in her face. To succeed with her, you had to be able to work with organized chaos, rehearse yourself, do your homework, and be flexible and prepared for last-minute changes. She was extremely kind and friendly and happy to have you, but if you could steal a minute to talk to her it was probably while she was on hold on her cell phone, in between bites of chop suey and running to her next meeting. She was like an espresso shot in Doc Martens. I wanted to be her, looking Hollywood hot and sassy in jeans, black leather jacket, and with cell phone, before cell phones were popular.

Anita often critiqued her choreography as she created it, saying, "This isn't right." I thought, "How can it be right or wrong?" She was attempting to work the choreography so that you didn't have odd weight changes or "cheats"—where you have to quickly switch to another foot to be prepared to go in another direction. Her attention to these sorts of details made my job easier and less disjointed. I learned a lot from Anita and thoroughly dug working with her.

Anita had her hands full in teaching the show due not so much to her business juggling act as to the impulsive Playmates. These unpredictable Bunnies didn't have the same work ethic as did the professional singers and dancers. Everyone held their breath wondering if they would show up on time, if at all, for rehearsals and, once there, if they would agree to do what was asked. The choreography had to be amended to fit their abilities, as they weren't professional dancers. In general, reliability was an issue. Perhaps some ladies weren't used to the daily discipline required to practice and perfect a production.

In fact, partway through the rehearsal process, Taffy, a Playmate who came with a designated talent (gymnastics), up and quit on us. I was disappointed, because she really spiced up our act. She was replaced by Kylie, a professional dancer from Anita's talent pool, who was another sexy, petite blond with a fantastic body and the ability to be provocative. Sadly, we were now down a Bunny. Gladly, we were up a real dancer.

My track was easy—no difficult choreography or challenging singing. It was all fun and few worries. Between performing and changing costumes, I was busy the entire show—no time to sit down and take a coffee break—but the pace was comfortable enough.

Some of our show consisted of slightly altered and patched-up hand-me down numbers from Anita's other shows. Being a smart business woman, Anita recycled her work when appropriate. The numbers were entertaining and energetic, seductive and flirtatious, but they weren't particularly pornographic; this was no XXX Adult Girlie show like you'd see in Vegas. For me it was just the right amount of risqué without crossing over into sleazy. I could do this show and still show my face in church. Maybe.

In retrospect, I feel extremely lucky that the show was as respectable as it was. Being an adults-only production, I could have shown up for rehearsal and been required to do lord knows what with lord knows who. What would I have done? I was just that naïve that the thought never crossed my mind about what trouble I might be getting myself into.

****

February rolled around, and before we knew it, it was time to leave the U.S. for foreign lands! Val was constantly on the phone with the booking agent, but we still didn't have a definite itinerary. All we knew was that we were starting out in Indonesia, and the rest was up in the air. We were prepared to be gone for six months to places including Singapore, Malaysia, Japan, and India. After that, maybe we would visit Germany or other venues in Europe. There were so many options on the table. We didn't know where this journey might take us, but it was sure to be exciting.

Half a year was a long time to be gone from those we loved, so Callie planned a bon voyage party at an Italian restaurant in L.A. for all of us and our friends. We were Playboy's Girls of Rock & Roll, but we hadn't gotten paid yet, so the invitation had a disclaimer:

Due to the current economic climate,
we can only provide location, fun & good looks.
Not grub.
Simply put, if you're hungry – bring money.

My boyfriend, Adam, also threw a big farewell party for me. All his friends came, and they even brought presents. I was uncomfortable about it because I didn't know these people well, and they were probably ambivalent about my leaving. I'm sure they came mostly to support Adam. It was a little embarrassing to have all that attention lavished upon me, but what the heck. I was leaving on a grand adventure and wouldn't see these fine folks for many months. Why not celebrate?

Unfortunately, during all the hoopla and preparations for the trip, I came down with bronchitis. I was so sick I finally went to the doctor, afraid that he would tell me I wouldn't be able to fly. Luckily, he gave me permission along with a prescription for antibiotics. I stocked up on meds and Sudafed day-time and night-time decongestant.

****

Playboy's Girls of Rock & Roll packed their bags for Jakarta—the capital of Indonesia and its largest city. For going away gifts, Val presented us all with Playboy T-shirts and blue jean jackets each with a huge bunny logo emblazoned on the back and our names embroidered on the front. We were to wear these on our trip. Forget about going incognito; we were shamelessly and conspicuously advertising our affiliation with Playboy. At the time, I just thought it was exciting to be part of the club. And it sure beat wearing bunny ears and a fluffy tail.

It was unbelievably thrilling to be standing in the ticket line at Los Angeles International Airport in the Southeast Asia terminal. I never thought I'd visit that part of the world as a tourist let alone a star with Playboy. I felt like I was embarking on an exotic adventure. I was.

Besides Val and the eight of us girls, we were also traveling with one very important man—Malcolm. Val had the smarts to hire this 6-foot 5-inch tall, dark, and handsome, fortyish-year-old bodyguard and company manager of sorts. The Asians were used to dealing with men as authority figures, and Malcolm was better suited than Val to being the tough guy. He helped us with anything and everything from making sure our huge costume trunks made it on the plane to protecting us girls from overzealous fans. Having Malcolm's brains and brawn along was a big bonus.

The flight to Indonesia was a whopping twelve hours. By the end of it, my hair was a grease pit, my eyes blood shot, and my mascara smeared. My clothes were wrinkled and smelly, and I desperately needed a shower. My throat hurt terribly and my head throbbed from congestion. Achy all over, I felt like hell.

I went to the airplane bathroom to try to spruce up a bit before arrival. I brushed my teeth, wiped under my arms with a wet towel, applied deodorant, and layered on more perfume. I washed my face and reapplied my makeup. The hair was a lost cause. No matter how much brushing or spraying I did, it still looked like it was plastered to my head.

Jakarta is fourteen hours ahead of Los Angeles, so while it was the middle of the night L.A. time, the day was in full swing in Indonesia when we arrived. Driving into town from the airport, I felt like I was in the middle of a page from *National Geographic*. Indonesia was a beautiful, lush, green, developing country.

Looking out the van window along the side of the highway, I noticed mini shanty towns made from all types of refuse including cardboard and corrugated metal. These structures weren't much better than the play forts we used to build as kids from discarded appliance boxes. I was shocked to see the poverty. It was a real eye opener.

In stark contrast, we arrived at the plush, modern high-rise President Hotel in the heart of downtown Jakarta to an entourage of Indonesian sponsors who warmly welcomed us with bouquets of flowers. Here we were a group of scraggly, stinky girls who looked like we stayed up partying all night and then fell asleep in our clothes, and we were supposed to be the alluring Playboy's Girls of Rock & Roll. I tried to smile and be gracious to our hosts but, feeling deathly ill and going on only four hours of sleep in forty-eight hours, all I wanted to do was crawl into bed. When I found out we were to go straight into dress rehearsal at the nightclub, I thought I was going to die.

We headed to our rooms to quickly change clothes. I was ecstatic that we each got our own room; at least I wouldn't have to worry about getting along with a roommate. I looked out my hotel window and marveled at what an exotic and extremely foreign place I was in. My view revealed a thriving metropolis, including an impressive, massive circular fountain—the center attraction of a five-lane roundabout, chockablock with small whizzing cars. Across the busy street, over ten lanes of traffic, was the lovely Hyatt Regency.

All in all, I was pleased with the beautiful hotel, which offered all the amenities of a western hotel except you couldn't always find someone who spoke English. I just hoped I would get a chance to actually sleep there someday soon.

I grabbed my makeup case and met the rest of our group in the lobby. The air conditioning in the hotel was on full blast. I found out why. The second we set foot outside, sweat began pouring out of every one of my pores. I've never felt air so hot and humid that it sucked the liquid right out of you. The humidity was unbearable.

We climbed aboard our private state-of-the-art bus complete with TV, VCR, and male tour guide—a young, twenty-something English-speaking Indonesian who had the dubious honor of escorting us to and from hotel to venue. While the Bunnies downed massive amounts of Twizzlers red licorice, our host enthusiastically educated us about his country.

Our rehearsal and shows were held at the most enormous nightclub I'd ever laid eyes on. The name of it, "Dynasty," was a testimony to its large scale. Even the stage was huge. We looked like eight tiny peas on a massive turkey platter trying to look like a full meal. While it was a job for us to fill the stage, all the black and silver and colored lights gave it that hard edge that any self-respecting motorcycle mama would be proud of. We looked hot.

First things first: The show would not go on unless we first passed government inspection. Our hosts assured us we were not to worry. The government censors "can be paid off here. No problem." Thanks to Malcolm, they were, and we got the all-clear to perform. Sure, corruption was prevalent, but there was no shame attached, nor did they try to hide it—a refreshing change from our country.

Malcolm, being tall and imposing by American standards and positively gargantuan relative to the Indonesians (think Gulliver versus the Lilliputians), was the perfect person to troubleshoot the governmental red tape and look out for our interests. He dwarfed even the tallest of Indonesians and, therefore, did not look like a man to be messed with. Val was brilliant for bringing him on board. Plus, I just felt safer having him around.

Everything was big at Dynasty including our huge dressing room—something we would soon no longer take for granted. What a luxury. Mirrors all around and plenty of space to each have a seat, spread out our stuff, and even stretch out before the show.

The girls' dressing room talk was an education like no other. I sat quietly, applying my makeup and absorbing all kinds of interesting information. "Back in the old days, when I sang back-up for Wayne Newton in Vegas," Rhonda said, "Wayne, Dean Martin, and Sammy Davis Jr. always played pranks on each other. Once Wayne snuck a real horse onto the stage when Dean was singing!" I loved listening to her stories.

"So, how did you end up becoming a Playmate?" I finally asked Satin, intrigued by her racy lifestyle. "My mother was a centerfold in the 1960s." "You're kidding!" *My mother was baking cookies and teaching Sunday School in the 1960s.* "When I was sixteen, I sent a telegram to Hugh Hefner that said, 'Bunnies do multiply.' As soon as I turned eighteen and was legal, he allowed me to screen test." They were one of only a few mother-daughter pairs to both earn the prestigious title of Playmate of the Month. (Of course, when I got back to the States, I searched the bookstore and found a collectors' edition of Playboy Bunnies over the years. There she was, pretty in pink lace and white anklets, skillfully and beautifully baring all the inappropriate parts.)

Satin soon became my favorite Bunny in the show. She was no pushover and could beat the living daylights out of you if she had a mind to but also had a heart of gold when it came to old people, babies, and pets. Volunteering to clip toenails for an elderly lady or rescuing a stray dog seemed to be as second nature to her as popping you one if unduly provoked. "I want a tattoo right here," she said pointing to her privates, "of the Pink Panther pushing a lawn mower. Then I'm going to shave a strip where the lawn mower supposedly mowed. Wouldn't that be cool?" You just don't meet fascinating characters like that in an office job. She taught me how to put my hair in a quick bun using only a ballpoint pen, for which I will be forever grateful.

"I love my girls!" Porsche exclaimed giving both of her enhanced breasts a little squeeze. "I was so sick of being flat. Your boobs are nice, too, Mallory. They look great on you, but I could never go that big." We all stopped to examine each others' knockers. There were several people with implants in the cast. I glanced down at my size 36 Bs, which now looked somehow measly. I decided they would have to suffice. Funny how as a "real" dancer, I always thought my breasts were much too big and hindered my dancing. Now I was questioning whether or not they were too small to be sexy. We had everything from grape-sized to peach-sized to grapefruit-sized to Mallory's plump melons—she by far out-bosomed everyone else in the group. There was something on the menu to please every preference.

Then Callie and Jasmine started doing this Farmer Bob imitation where they'd stick their front teeth over their bottom lips and talk like hicks. It soon caught on and the whole cast was doing it. It was Gomer Pyle meets Goofy with an extreme overbite. We laughed and laughed. It's good not to take yourself too seriously no matter how large and luscious your bust is. (Bear in mind, I actually have an Uncle Bob who was a farmer at one time, and I can assure you he is quite sophisticated and well-spoken.)

We began our Indonesian tour thanks to Lions International, who call themselves "the world's largest service club organization." They were sponsoring us for a Valentine's charity night. We performed February 13th (8:30 p.m. and 11:30 p.m.), 14th (8:30 p.m.), and 15th (8:30 p.m. and 11:30 p.m.). The advertisement was in Indonesian but I could understand a few words—"romantik" and "erotis." It hardly seemed like an event appropriate for the Lions Club—a group who pride themselves on serving needy communities. Perhaps this community was in need of a few stiff drinks and an evening of romantic erotica. Our hosts lovingly presented each of us with a Styrofoam heart with a rose inserted into it.

****

While managing to avoid performing pornographic maneuvers, I wasn't so lucky when it came to the opening costume. In order to raise the raciness of our show, we threw a bit of indecent exposure onto the bargaining table. Mainly, we had to bare some buns by dancing in G-strings. This was my first time performing in a G, and it was quite an experience.

No conventional underwear fits under G-string trunks, so our lead singer, Rhonda, brought us handmade "under-Gs" (a.k.a. "personal Gs") from Vegas, like the real showgirls wear. They were basically tiny triangles of soft cloth held up by quarter-inch elastic. By design, the under-G covered the bare minimum and nothing more, because otherwise it would peek out from the skimpy G-string costume trunks we wore over it. The trunks were essentially thong bikini bottoms.

Under the trunks we wore black fishnets. (Fishnets are mesh stockings that look like what they're named after: netting for catching fish. For some strange reason, making one's legs look like ensnared sea creatures was supposed to be sexy.) For added support and coverage, under the fishnets we wore nude tights, which prevented any jiggly bits from over jiggling. Although they kept us from feeling buck naked, it was in our best interest not to have too many layers underneath, or the tights acted like a trampoline and the bikini bottoms would just bounce around on top of them, revealing the parts we wanted concealed. Before the show, we gave ourselves wedgies to anchor the trunks in place as best we could.

It was surreal walking on stage in a G for the very first time. After a while, however, I forgot all about the fact that my rump was on display. Or maybe I just pretended it wasn't really happening to keep myself in denial that I was voluntarily inviting people to leer at my bum. It takes a fine, tight derriere to look good in a G, and I never did feel quite right about flaunting it.

****

Our opening number consisted of the entire cast singing and dancing to the original tune "The Girls of Rock & Roll," written specifically for the Playboy's Girls of Rock shows. Clad in black fishnets, thigh-high black boots, black thongs, bust-boosting tops, and assorted sordid accessories from that stash of black leather costumes, we strutted, air-guitared, flipped our hair, and rocked the house. Posing for sexy photos wasn't my forte, but dancing sexy was another story. I had rock and roll in my blood. The number was almost Disney-esque compared to the blatant bumping and grinding that's done on stage nowadays, but, thankfully, we got away with it.

When I was thirteen, the movie *Grease* came out, and I loved the part where Sandy (played by Olivia Newton John) transformed from a cutesy, goodie two-shoes in poodle skirt and conservative sweater into a cigarette-smoking babe in black leather and stilettos, driving bad-boy boyfriend Danny Zuko (played by John Travolta) crazy. I always related to the Sandy character—my college boyfriend, who adored Olivia Newton John, even said I reminded him of her. Being a Playboy's Girl of Rock & Roll felt like my fantasy transformation into that babe in black. It was a role I got a real kick out of playing.

Except for the opening and closing numbers, which included everyone, Anita wisely organized our show so that the singers alternated with the dancers and Bunnies, allowing time for costume changes. Our three singers remained onstage after the opening to sing a sizzling hot version of "Free Your Mind" (En Vogue's hit single) while Porsche and the Bunnies and I changed into hip-hop clothes with black baseball hats, on backwards, of course.

The five of us did a watered-down hip-hop dance to C&C Music Factory's "Everybody Dance Now." It was pretty pathetic as the Bunnies were choreographically challenged, and I was hip-hop challenged. Porsche was in her element, but I had to fake it as best I could. Hip-hop wasn't even taught back when I was in dance class. Now it was all the rage, and I found myself trying to Running Man, Roger Rabbit, and Cabbage Patch like a home girl and not a lame girl.

Rhonda, Callie, and Jasmine followed with a girl groups medley, which included the Andrew Sisters' "Boogie Woogie Bugle Boy," the McGuire Sisters' "Sincerely," and "I'm So Excited" by the Pointer Sisters. They looked beautiful in their long, slinky gowns and long, white gloves, doing jazzy and elegant armography and singing chanteuse style into mics on mic stands. Singers' envy set in, and I wished I had their vocal abilities. I so badly wanted to do their numbers.

Next came my favorite number to perform: Rod Stewart's "Hot Legs." Playmate Mallory spoke-sang the lead, and Porsche and I danced back-up. Sporting red fringed shorty shorts, red fringed bras, and long, red satin gloves, we danced seductively with chairs, arching over them and coquettishly showing off our hot legs. It was the sexiest dance I got to do, and I worked it.

The singers returned to present a sixties medley—one of Anita's high-energy cruise ship show favorites. They were dressed in funky black and white sixties garb and did famous dances from that era, including the mash potato, the alligator, the watusi, and the hand jive. "I could easily do that number," I thought, wishing I were up there twisting with the go-go girls.

Instead, Porsche and I flanked yet another Bunny. This time it was Satin as she confidently belted out "It's Raining Men," by the Weather Girls. We began in bright yellow raincoats twirling umbrellas as we ran around stage and then stripped down to our costumes: short, spandex, spaghetti-strap, rhinestone-studded disco dresses with fringed skirts. Satin's dress was light blue and ours were black. While she showered the crowd with her sexy song, Porsche and I finally got to show off with more challenging choreography. Hallelujah!

Satin's singing really took the audience by storm when she did her kittenish rendition of "Makin' Whoopee." She'd sit on a male audience member's lap, stroke his hair, and otherwise embarrass him with her advances. That was the closest performance we had in the show to a lap dance (although much classier), and it was always a big hit.

Callie showed off her legitimate vocal talent by raising the rafters with her show-stopping rendition of "I Will Always Love You"—the Dolly Parton song made famous by Whitney Houston. I was blown away by her versatile voice and sultry stage presence.

To add some variety and to highlight Jasmine's specific talents, the show took a country turn. For her solo, she sang "Achy Breaky Heart"—that goofy tune made famous and then infamous by mullet-haired Billy Ray Cyrus. Callie, Rhonda, Porsche, and I backed her up with some country line dance-type moves and a lot of improvised "Woos!" and "Yee haws!"

Our costumes were cute: cowboy hats and cowboy boots, gold lamé bras, fringed brown suede armbands, and little brown suede fringed skirts that were open in the front so our gold bikini bottoms would show. Jasmine's, on the other hand, was stunning. She wore a brown suede fringed bra, fringed suede armbands, and gorgeous custom-made suede cowboy chaps studded in rhinestones. The chaps were so superb I was tempted to buy a pair to wear out dancing.

Instead of wearing the chaps over jeans like a cowboy does (and like I'd do if going out for a night on the town), Jasmine wore her chaps over G-string trunks. This created an interesting effect as the back of the "pants" was completely cut out. Consequently, when she turned around, the audience got a panoramic view of the landscape, as the opening revealed a lot of bare behind and only a little thong with her song. She was very cheeky, indeed.

Back in L.A., Anita had sent us to Elaine's—a famous Hollywood costume shop—to get fitted for our cowgirl costumes. While there, we had a star spotting: "That's Nancy Sinatra! That's Nancy Sinatra!" we whispered excitedly. Frank Sinatra's daughter, famous for the hit "These Boots Are Made for Walkin'," was there for a costume fitting, too. Unlike some of us, I'm sure she opted to have her derriere fully covered.

Back to the show. Kylie and the Bunnies kept the mood lighthearted with "I'm Too Sexy." (Remember that narcissistic Right Said Fred song about being too sexy for everything from one's own love, shirt, car, hat, and pussy cat to Milan, New York, and Japan?) The lovely ladies took turns strutting sexily on the runway in their lace teddies and fur stoles à la a fashion show. It was a Playmate parade of sorts in which they got to shake their little tushies on the catwalk.

In addition to prancing around in lingerie for "I'm Too Sexy," Kylie was also required to do what was supposed to have been Taffy's solo: an acrobatic dance to Madonna's song, "Erotica." Kylie wasn't exactly a gymnast so, instead, she seductively rolled around on the floor, tantalized with her extreme flexibility, and did straddle splits all while spinning a long ribbon on a stick. At times, the ribbon was purposefully used like a whip, so anyone with an appreciation for dominant women got a little teaser.

After Kylie had finished whipping the audience into a frenzy, the singers reappeared with their Aretha Franklin medley, which included "Respect" and "You Make Me Feel Like a Natural Woman." This was Rhonda's chance to shine as soloist. With her booming, gritty, powerful voice, she did Motown proud. She was the most authentically rock and rolliest of the group, so when she said to give her a little "R-E-S-P-E-C-T," you knew you'd better do it.

For our closing, all the girls reconvened to sing the sappy, happy Michael Bolton tune "Love Is a Wonderful Thing." We wore our gold bikinis from the cowboy number with gold sequin blazers over top and did simple, subdued dance moves. The number was tame enough that we could have performed it at a nursing home or an elementary school PTA fundraiser. This sentimental song led right into a rousing reprise of "Girls of Rock & Roll," and tha-tha-tha-that's all, folks.

When we walked around the club between shows, we noticed that there were a multitude of tiny private viewing rooms situated around the perimeter. Through the darkened windows, I could see what looked like a large bingo board. "What game are they playing in there?" I wondered innocently. On closer inspection, I realized this was not some mild form of recreational gambling for senior citizens. The numbered board corresponded to numbered women for sale for the night. BINGO! We termed such viewing rooms "the Zoo." Kind of made us sick to our stomachs. There was blatant prostitution on the premises and yet the government censors insisted on inspecting our show. Quite the double standard.

I still felt horrible from the bronchitis, but I had made it through the show. Everyone had, and it seemed to go as well as could be expected. I was elated to finally go to bed and get a good night's sleep.

****

In addition to being a night club, Dynasty also claimed to be an "international restaurant," which I think meant that it served Chinese food. That's what they gave us anyway. Each evening we were escorted to a private dining room where our own private wait staff would serve us dinner. As word spread that it was feeding time for the Bunnies, much commotion would ensue; the employees would gather en masse, following us down the hall, more staff members joining the parade as we made our way to the dining room. Like animals observed at the zoo, we were stared at and spied on as we ate, people's heads poking through the doorway to watch these foreign creatures in their unnatural habitat.

A beautiful and generous spread of what appeared to be Chinese food was placed on the table. Famished, I eagerly dug my fork into the pile of breaded fish nuggets only to discover the unwelcomed crunch of fish bones in my mouth as I began to chew it. I completely lost my appetite.

It seemed that everywhere we went, our food contained animal body parts, rubbery skin, bones, and slime that we wasteful Americans usually discard. By the end of the first week, I was ravenous and on the verge of tears when we were taken to yet another "parts-is-parts" restaurant. Finally, I found fresh pineapple juice on the menu. It was exquisite, and I drank it all evening while shuffling the rest of my meal around on my plate so as not to offend our hosts.

Even the most adventurous eater might be surprised at how unappealing the food can be after a few weeks of finding chicken parts and fish bones in your food. Usually, I love to try the native cuisine, but here I was squeamish about the animal remnants and was quickly becoming a vegetarian. More accurately, I was turning into a Pop Tartian—saved from starvation by the stash of Pop Tarts, instant oatmeal, and hot chocolate mix I'd brought with me. Thankfully, some wise, old showbiz sage had warned me that Asian breakfasts were unappealing to American taste buds, and it would behoove me to bring along morning munchables. Fortunately, I heeded her advice and devoted a considerable amount of precious suitcase space to pseudo astronaut food.

Ironically, I reserved these sugary, non-nutritious treats for dinner, as the hotel breakfasts were absolutely divine. The room service menu actually included a traditional American breakfast complete with cornflakes and milk, buttered toast and jam, bacon or sausage, two fried eggs, and the most delectable, dark, rich coffee I had ever tasted. I guess I should have expected some tasty java; we were in the capital city of the island of Java, after all. But this was heavenly coffee as if roasted and brewed by God himself/herself. I relished those morning feasts and ate every last morsel in case the rest of the day proved to be a fast.

Ordering was sometimes an ordeal, however, and it was always a surprise to see which items made it onto the breakfast tray. Typical American that I am, I didn't speak a word of Indonesian and had to order in English. It was hit or miss whether or not the person taking room service orders on the phone understood any of what I was saying. No matter how loudly and clearly I annunciated "C-O-O-O-RN-FL-A-A-A-KES," if they didn't speak English, the higher volume and slower speed wasn't going to help. Miraculously, most of the time, I got pretty close to what I had asked for.

Luckily, the hotel also housed a restaurant with open air courtyard seating and a delicious truly international menu, which we were able to eat at if we were there at lunch time.

****

If I had really wanted to complain about something, it shouldn't have been the food; a far greater problem was the water, which was unsafe for us to drink. Ice cubes or anything washed in the water (like fresh fruits or vegetables) were strictly off limits. At one club, I was relieved to receive real Coca Cola in glass bottles instead of a cup of Coke on the rocks, which would have been a digestive disaster. We drank the precious liquid with a straw so as to not touch our lips to something that might be contaminated from the water.

While we did our best to not ingest the unsanitary H2O, other unexpected ramifications were unavoidable. After a few days in Indonesia, for instance, I noticed that my sweaty costumes smelled like the worst body odor ever. I was mortified and embarrassed, worried I'd be forevermore labeled the "smelly girl"—like the poor middle school kid who reeked with B.O.

Thank goodness, as it turned out, everyone's costumes were rank. It's not unusual for costumes to get ripe after repeated uses, especially when wet with perspiration. Still, Valerie was appalled and had us all hand wash whatever items we could in the travel packets of laundry soap we'd brought along. Playboy's Girls of Rock & Roll were supposed to be funky, but this was ridiculous. And highly repugnant.

The washing hardly helped at all, however. We still smelled repulsive. What was going on here? Then one day I detected a terrible stench in my room, surprisingly similar to the one emanating from our costumes. Sniffing around my room like a police dog hot on the trail, I traced the scent back to my bathtub drain. Horror of horrors! The water smelled like sewage. We were dousing ourselves daily in this bacterial soup, soaking our skin and our costumes in filth. Case closed.

Unfortunately, there was little we could do to rectify the situation. The more we showered, the more we marinated ourselves in microorganisms and pollution. We smelled worse than a men's locker room after football practice on a hot summer day. It was disgusting. You really learn to appreciate the luxuries you take for granted—like good water—when you no longer have them. I LOVE CLEAN WATER!

While our *"eau de excrement"* effluvium may have repelled the audience, it appeared to attract rats and roaches like an alluring perfume, for we found both scurrying about our dressing rooms. Screams and shouts of "Oh my God, I saw a rat!" "Ewwww....cockroaches!" and "Get your stuff off the floor!"

launched a flurry of activity as we fast and furiously hung costume pieces everywhere to avoid becoming a rat or roach motel. As if roaches and even rats can't climb walls. I cringed at the thought of stepping my foot into an insect-infested cowboy boot.

Finding places to suspend our outfits and elevate our accessories was particularly tricky at the second club where we performed, because, unlike the palatial expanse we enjoyed at Dynasty, this dressing room was akin to a teeny, tiny closet. It probably was one at one time. All of us could barely fit in the space simultaneously; there was no room to spare. But we did the best we could, were careful not to leave food around, and made sure to check our costumes for critters before putting them on.

Of all the possible performance problems I anticipated, rats and roaches never crossed my mind. The constant vigilance required to avoid unwanted contact with these vermin far outweighed the extreme challenges of eight women attempting to fast-change in our cramped compartment. Here again, I had taken sanitation for granted. I LOVE SANITATION! Perhaps we should have traveled with an exterminator instead of a body guard.

While I'm talking about privileges I'll never take for granted again, I'd like to also mention good teeth, because most of the Indonesians had horrible, rotten teeth. Even twenty-year-olds. Can you imagine being a youngster, hot on the prowl for dates, and smiling your sexiest smile only to reveal a mouth full of black holes and decay? I don't know if it was the bad water, lack of proper nutrition, dearth of health services, or something else entirely, but those poor people were in serious need of dental help. I LOVE GOOD TEETH!

****

Once the show was up and running, we had free time during the day to do what we wanted. The girls decided we would treat ourselves to massages and an afternoon at the hotel spa. The spa had a room filled with massage tables separated only by some flimsy curtains to offer a bit of privacy. Consequently, we were all able not only to be massaged at the same time, but also to hear what was going on in the rubdowns next to us.

Not knowing how they did massages in Indonesia, we stripped down to nothing but our underwear—a typical practice when getting massages in California. When the tiny Indonesian masseuses walked into the room and saw that we were wearing G-strings, they burst out giggling. I didn't know what to think. Were their clients usually completely naked? Or did they find it funny that our underwear appeared to have been swallowed up by our buttocks?

The laughter in the room gave way to intense curiosity and amazement when the ladies discovered Mallory's perfectly round, gravity-defying, D-cup breasts. They had obviously never seen anything like them, and, frankly, neither had I. They were a wonder to behold. I could hear the excited chatter as the women gathered to marvel at her delightful domes. Like a pair of Mt. Everests, you wanted to scale them, conquer them, sit atop their peaks, and view the world from their mighty mountaintop perspective. They could almost compete for the title of one of the seven wonders of the world.

But the real surprise came when those same masseuses started massaging body parts we never knew we had, as well as other familiar parts, all of which were strictly off limits. We politely declined their supplementary services. No bonus round for us, thanks.

****

In addition to our "relaxing" spa day, we managed to squeeze in some hot and sticky shopping in Jakarta. The bustling center of commerce included small businesses that closed up at night with what resembles our roll-down garage doors. People often crouched like frogs while waiting on the street, instead of standing or sitting in a chair. Smoking was popular; the distinct, pungent smell of clove cigarettes hung in the air, co-mingling at times with an assault of sewage stench emanating from the bowels of the underground. The occasional gigantic rat sighting heightened the thrill of the experience.

In addition to housing stores much like any American strip mall, downtown also displayed a lot of what we would call poverty. However, the people seemed to be working hard selling food and drinks off little street carts shaded by colorful umbrellas, cycling rickshaw-like contraptions, and selling all kinds of magnificent Indonesian crafts and imposter designer items, such as watches, sunglasses, and purses, which hung plentifully from outdoor racks.

Ironically, *Playboy* magazine was illegal in Indonesia, but the Bunny brand was on everything. That logo is so world famous that, even in the most remote parts of the earth, you are sure to find human beings who recognize that black-and-white bunny head sporting a bow tie. There was a definite obsession with this iconic fur ball; we got a kick out of spotting our company symbol on item after item. Either

Indonesians really loved rabbits or, more likely, *Playboy* had been elevated to star status simply because the dirty magazine was contraband, and, therefore, extra enticing.

I could take or leave the unauthorized *Playboy* merchandise, fake Rolexes, and faux Gucci bags, but I went crazy over the beautiful hand-woven blankets, wood carvings, elaborate dolls, painted wooden masks, and exotic batiks, which could be purchased for next to nothing. My boyfriend Adam had turned me on to ethnic artifacts; numerous items decorated his home and were sold at his art gallery.

I took advantage of the bargain prices and bought a totem pole-like carved stick as tall as I was, that sported human faces, figures, and creatures and was topped with feathers—a perfect accessory should I find myself engaged in a tribal ceremony. I also purchased an intricately carved bleached-white bone for Adam; a hand-painted black, gold, red, and white mask whose bulging eyes, fangs, and long, protruding tongue could scare the dickens out of you on a spooky night (perhaps it was designed to ward off evil spirits), and a blue, red, and cream-colored blanket woven with Indonesian designs.

While there were certainly great deals to be had, it was a little scary walking around town, as we large Caucasian beauties stood out like sore thumbs against the backdrop of small, dark Indonesians. We were a foot taller than the tallest man and were the only fair-skinned blonds to be seen. Consequently, the natives followed, stared at, and even touched us everywhere we went. There was an element of danger in the air; attracting so much attention from the locals made me feel uncomfortable and unsafe, and with good reason. When visiting a large indoor shopping area at the Hyatt Regency hotel across the street from our hotel, I nearly got pick-pocketed. We were going up the escalator when I felt a slight tug. A guy standing behind me had started to unzip my purse. I turned around just in time, and caught him before I lost my wallet. I didn't make a scene or alert the authorities, but I became a lot more cautious and aware of what was going on around me. We were not in Kansas anymore.

On a more pleasant note, at a restaurant in the Hyatt we discovered mango, papaya, and avocado smoothies. In Indonesia, avocados were treated like a sweet fruit, a practice I found strange and intriguing. And also quite delicious.

The most exciting or, more accurately, terrifying part of our outings was the taxi rides to and from our destination. New York taxi drivers were wimps compared to the fearless Indonesian taxi drivers, who either had a death wish or were missing the part of the brain that discerns danger. The Indonesians zipped around in their miniature cars at speeds that would break the sound barrier, not bothering to slow down as they made death-defying, last-minute changes in direction. They made even Indy 500 drivers look like pansies.

Feeling like I was in a Hollywood high-speed chase scene, I covered my eyes and prayed. The taxi drivers, along with everyone else on the road, believed they had the right of way and proceeded with confidence as they missed a fatal collision by a hair. Their feathers weren't ruffled a bit, but those rides scared all the feathers clean off me.

****

The second week of our Southeast Asia tour was spent in Bandung, Indonesia's third largest city and the capital of West Java. We gathered our suitcases and hopped aboard our plush bus for the 180 km (about 110 miles) journey through the countryside, heading southeast from Jakarta.

We kept ourselves entertained on the ride by eating more Twizzlers and taking pictures of ourselves wearing the long, blond wig that Jasmine had brought along for when her hair grew out and her dark roots started to show. Even Malcolm tried on the hairpiece, and I have the picture to prove it.

I spent a lot of time gazing out the window at the exquisite views of the spectacular, lush green hillsides—evidence of the extreme beauty for which Indonesia is famous. The old was integrated with the new as donkeys and people bearing massive bundles of twigs tied like a barbell to a large stick across their shoulders trod by small, modern, palm tree-flanked houses and telephone poles. But mostly we saw mile after mile of gorgeous, thriving vegetation. Seeing all that green growth was soothing for the soul.

We stopped for lunch and a bathroom break at a lovely little restaurant/pool/gift store destination in the middle of nowhere. Every bathroom we came to was a guessing game as to whether or not we'd be sitting or squatting. Sometimes we found eastern "toilets," simple holes in the ground, each with an ashtray at ground level (how thoughtful); and other times "western" toilets, namely, your basic American porcelain gods.

Eastern toilets took some getting used to. In particular I didn't like my face being so close to the waste, as I crouched like a frog and tried not to soil my clothes. At least I didn't have to worry about my body touching a germ-ridden toilet seat. I suppose all that squatting up and down kept folks more fit and flexible. Many older people in our country would never be able to get down into that position let alone get back up out of it. In spite of the possible benefits, I counted myself lucky to sit on a good old-fashioned potty. No more taking my toilet for granted. I LOVE WESTERN TOILETS!

Every time we stopped to get off our bus for a bathroom or meal break, we were swarmed by Indonesians with handfuls of souvenirs, necklaces, and *tchotchkes* to sell us. They were so persistent and annoying that we'd buy something just to get them off our backs. I seem to recall a similar sales strategy used in Tijuana, Mexico. It worked.

Our hotel with its carved wood, marble floors, and crystal chandeliers was a welcome sight. We entered to the unique, percussive sounds of an Indonesian Gamelan orchestra consisting of costumed musicians sitting cross-legged on the floor and playing ornate xylophones, drums, and gongs. Very nice accommodations once again.

We had only been in Indonesia for a week, and already the jet lag, late-night performances, and busy schedule were wearing on all of us. Moreover, I was still trying to knock out the last of the bronchitis. Our tour was especially exhausting, because every time we changed venues we had to take time to rehearse and rework the show to fit the new stage, which varied from the others in size and proximity to the dressing rooms.

At one club in Bandung, I was shocked when the club owners casually asked us if we would like to "book private clients" after the show like some of their other "performers" did. Callie was even offered $10,000! Saying yes would have turned this job into an entirely different profession as far as I was concerned. None of us took up the offer, as far as I know.

At that same club, Satin had all her jewelry stolen out of her makeup kit. An element of shadiness and seediness accompanied this whole Indonesian experience. But what did I expect when being sponsored by a pornographic magazine?

On the upside, Bandung, situated in a river valley surrounded by volcanic mountains, offered a prime opportunity to view a volcano up top. We ventured out to take a sightseeing tour of this potentially explosive natural attraction.

Once again, upon our arrival at the tourist site, we were accosted by young Indonesian guys—one wearing a Harley Davidson baseball cap—trying to sell us stuff. Having already endured a couple weeks of this type of incessant pestering, our resources were depleting and our nerves were getting frazzled. We simply couldn't take one more person hounding us.

These boys, on the other hand, could teach a sales course in never taking "no" for an answer. Although they weren't skilled in customer service, and probably wouldn't get a lot of repeat business, they knew they probably had one shot to sell you something because they'd never see you again. So they weren't worried about maintaining a good relationship.

We politely shook our heads and said, "No, thank you, we do not want your goods." They kept after us. Again, "No, thank you." We continued walking. They pressed on, shoving their necklaces in front of our faces. A little more forcefully, we declared, "NO." Not a bit discouraged, they followed, knowing they would break us eventually. Nothing short of buying their whole inventory stopped these people.

Like a volcano, the pressure got so great that we finally exploded. "NOOOOOO!" we screamed at the top of our lungs as we took off running. They thought this was hilarious and just laughed and ran after us, even going so far as to jump aboard the little tour shuttle—basically a glorified golf cart with extra seats— and join us on our sightseeing tour. We never did give in and buy anything, but we took some adorable snapshots with our new friends.

As our mini-bus approached the top of the volcano, the rotten-egg smell of sulfur became overpowering. Staring down at the steaming, milky interior, I wondered how long this pressure cooker would remain dormant. Would we end up like those unfortunate victims of Mt. Vesuvius in Pompeii, buried under lava, our traumatized forms discovered thousands of years later—young men with arms outstretched offering strings of jewels to the big-breasted volcanic goddesses? What theory would future archeologists dream up about that scenario? This volatile vent in the earth's crust was an impressive site to see, but I felt better once we were safely back down in the valley.

While it had certainly been a fascinating experience, our Indonesian itinerary was also grueling. We had had enough of cockroaches, rats, corruption, polluted water, fish heads, and animal carcass in our food. It was time to move on.

****

Our next stop was the Republic of Singapore, located on the southern tip of the Malay Peninsula, and just over an hour's flight from Indonesia. I didn't even know Malaysia was a country, and Singapore itself only sounded faintly familiar. There was so much more to the world than I ever knew existed. I couldn't begin to know what to expect.

Soon I got a little taste of Singaporean culture when the pilot's voice came over the loudspeaker kindly warning everyone on the flight, "Anyone bringing drugs into the country will be killed." "WHAT? Did he say 'KILLED?'" I whispered in disbelief to Porsche, who was sitting beside me. Well, they could have told us this BEFORE we boarded the plane. It was a little too late for all the smugglers unless they could run to the bathroom and flush their contraband before we landed.

Studying my travel book, I learned that Singapore was a fascinating cultural mix of predominantly Chinese, Malay, and Indian people; Buddhism was the most popular religion; and, by decree, there was little unemployment. I also discovered that the government was strict and, apparently, wanted their country clean, clean, clean. Hence, chewing gum was illegal. Spitting was, too. And toilet flushing in a public bathroom was an official requirement, not an option. No joke. In Singapore, I'd be considered a gum-chewing, non-flushing, saliva-spitting criminal, as I had performed all three of those acts at certain points in my life. Yikes! In America, I would simply be considered impolite and uncouth. Or normal.

Suddenly I became nervous about my Sudafed and my stash of Juicy Fruit used to pop the pressure in my ears on our ascents and descents. Would I be arrested for possession of prescription-sinus-pressure-and-congestion-relief not to mention for carrying a sizable cache of that bane of Singaporean society—chewing gum? I could picture one particularly ticked-off government official stepping on one too many gooey globs of gum on the sidewalk. "This is an outrage! Gum is banned for good!" It was scary.

But not as scary as our descent. It felt as if the pilot had been daydreaming and flying on "autopilot" so to speak, only to suddenly realize we were directly atop our destination. "Oops...there's Singapore. Almost flew right past it. Better land this baby pronto!" He abruptly proceeded to nosedive the plane straight down. In a matter of seconds, the plane went from a comfortable horizontal position to a hair-raising vertical one—the world's longest rollercoaster plunge. All you could see whizzing by outside the windows were green-gray clouds the color of our petrified faces. I really felt as if we could be plummeting to our deaths. Porsche was a fearful flier to begin with and this was taking her fears to an entirely new level. I would have been twice as terrified myself had I not needed to be strong for her and keep her from panicking. Porsche sunk her fingernails into my arm and didn't let go until we were safely on the ground.

I was thrilled that I lived, albeit with nail puncture wounds in my arms, because Singapore was absolute heaven. Our hotel was gorgeous and we got our own, plush rooms. We swam in the palm tree-lined pool and dined on fresh, tropical fruits. The restaurant had an exquisite international menu. We no longer starved. I was on an exotic vacation.

Our show venue was The Heartthrob Club (Wasn't the name apropos?)—a trendy, tiny disco bar within a stylish high-end hotel complex. Monday through Friday we had a 9 p.m. and a 12 a.m. show; on Saturday we had only a 12 a.m. show. Let me tell you, it's not easy getting cranked up to perform at midnight, especially if that's the first show of the evening. By that time, I was ready to snuggle up in my p.j.s in my cozy bed. But such is the nocturnal life of a performer. You have to find a way to turn it on at all hours. Actually, that's a great life skill: no matter how tired, sick, depressed, bored, or afraid you may be feeling, when the show must go on, you have to find a way to look entertaining. Most of the time, I found a way.

The stage, a four-foot-high carpeted, raised platform built to house a few musicians, was barely big enough to fit the eight of us at one time. Had the puny Heartthrob seen the ample Dynasty in Jakarta, it would have certainly had stage envy. Once again, we had to creatively adjust our choreography to fit the reduced space.

The house band didn't even bother to move their instruments so we had to perform in front of their setup. This left us with a depth of about four feet—an extremely tight squeeze for dancing. Depth-wise we could maybe fit three people standing one behind the other if we held our breath (possibly only two people if Mallory and her protruding D-cups were in the back row). This made passing each other and changing locations like two cars going in opposite directions on a one-lane mountainside road. You must travel with care or risk falling off the edge. Width-wise we could just fit the whole cast if we stood straight with our arms to our sides like pencils. Not exactly ideal for a dance show. It was a challenge not to whack your neighbor in the face or step on each other's toes when doing the moves.

If you wish to experience something similar, try cramming as many people (all in bathing suits and high heels) as you can into your smallest bathroom, and then do jumping jacks as you switch places (without hitting each other, of course). Now try to look sexy enough doing it that people would pay lots of money to watch.

Even more of a challenge was our "dressing room," which had probably once served as a small storage space. We needed a shoe horn to wedge all eight of us in. Changing costumes in such close quarters gave the term "press the flesh" a whole new meaning. Talk about the cast becoming close.

The bigger problem was that the dressing room was located on the opposite end of the club from the stage, so we had to push through the patrons to get to and from stage as our body guard, Malcolm, cleared a path and fended off touchy-feely fans. This was no easy task as the bar was packed so tightly with people that there was barely room to walk. Bodies were even pressed against the stage. The fire marshal must have been paid off, because there were far more people packed into that venue than could legally be served. People could easily reach out and grab us at any time. Plus, it made it difficult to time entrances—you never knew for certain how long it would take you to reach your destination. You just had to change costumes as quickly as possible and get right back out there.

Being a Bunny certainly had its perks: Wealthy businessmen presented us with $400 bottles of Dom Pérignon, which we felt obligated to drink or risk offending them. Not that I had a problem with sipping some of the world's finest champagne now and then. We were also given dozens of roses, brooches made of real orchids dipped in twenty-four-karat-gold, and gold pens inscribed with our names. We even signed autographs. I felt like a star.

The gifts, all the spoiling, and having men wrapped around our little fingers were fabulous fringe benefits of being famous (mind you, this was low on the totem pole of fame). Star treatment was not always amusing, however. Did I actually say presents, pampering, and men at my mercy weren't enough to keep me blissfully happy at all times? I can hardly believe it myself. But the truth is, being "famous" meant that, when we were in public, we had to be careful what we looked like, did, and said. We were essentially on stage all the time.

People never left us alone. We had about an hour of free time in between our 9:00 p.m. show and our midnight show, and since all eight of the cast members plus Malcolm and Val in the dressing room would have been about as comfortable as ten people and eight piles of laundry jammed into a phone booth, the only place we could hang out and put our feet up was at the restaurant downstairs. That being the case, we were in the public eye and fervent fans would barge in on us throughout our breaks. We had to be "on" even when we were off. It was exhausting. While extremely thankful for the enthusiasts (they bought tickets and were the reason we had a job after all), we would have preferred they give us some space to rest and rejuvenate before our second show.

We also felt like we had to be made up and looking attractive every time we left our hotel rooms, for we never knew when a crazy fan would show up at the hotel to snap pictures of us. There was no jumping out of bed, throwing on a wrinkled T-shirt and jeans, putting the hair in a ponytail, and grabbing a quick breakfast. Not unless we were okay with being the subject of one of those tabloid-type photos where the unsuspecting star is caught looking—God forbid—anything less than perfectly coiffed and gorgeous. Then the truth would be out that we were human and had bad hair days and the occasional zit. We even had to have our calls screened. It was my little taste of fame. I now understand why celebrities end up punching paparazzi.

****

In Singapore, too, we were subjected to government censors. They watched our show during rehearsal to make sure everything was kosher. It wasn't. We had to tame down certain moves they considered too sexy, like Kylie's deep knee bend with legs apart in front of a bar stool. In ballet, it's a standard warm-up step called "plié à la seconde" but it is done at the *barre*, not the *bar stool*. It hardly seemed a bend worth banning. Then again, Kylie could make even the ultra goofy Chicken Dance look seductive (and I mean to humans, not just to chickens), so maybe the censors had a point. Regardless, it was frightening; you never knew when you were going too far or what you would do that would offend or be illegal.

The police also objected to Satin going into the audience and greeting men during "Making Whoopee." No physical contact between performer and patron, they told us, and please keep the action on stage. Like the M.C. Hammer song, "You Can't Touch This," one newspaper article title summed it up: "You can see, but you cannot touch." Rhonda, too, caused a big ordeal when she indecently exposed herself, according to the government censors: For our finale we wore gold bikinis with gold blazers over top and her blazer button came undone, thereby revealing the bikini. We were in trouble and had to talk our way out of it by claiming it was an accident—a spontaneous costume malfunction of sorts.

Later Rhonda admitted, "I did it on purpose just to tick them off!" She wasn't about to be told what she could and couldn't do by some foreign guys with ridiculous rules and regulations. While I certainly admired her spunk, I wouldn't have pulled that stunt for anything. If chewing gum was illegal, I wasn't about to risk getting thrown in a foreign jail for purposely antagonizing officials. Wanting to make sure I safely returned to the good, ol' U.S. of A., I thought it prudent to follow the laws when in another country, so I vigilantly checked the security of the buttons on my blazer every show. What I learned: I LOVE OUR COUNTRY! We truly have freedoms other countries don't. God Bless America! And let me pop my buttons in peace!

The hoopla over the inappropriateness of our show continued to dumbfound me, as it was much more tasteful, decent, and mainstream than what one might expect of Playboy. It wasn't a show a teenage boy would have to hide under his mattress for fear of his parents finding it. The performers got high marks for sex appeal, certainly, but Playboy wasn't giving it all away in their stage show; you had to buy the magazine to get the entire package. And yet the government censors preferred it even more watered down. Some of the audience members, however, were hoping for more excitement. One newspaper quoted a "disappointed banker" who lamented, "I thought the girls would take their tops off. Now that we have R-rated movies, I thought maybe the authorities might let the girls go topless."

The poor guy. I felt for him. But not enough to dispose of my shirt. Just thinking about all those poor Singaporean men who are missing out on those "Hot, Live, Nude Girls!"-type of establishments brings a tear to my eye. Or not. I bet the native men in those "primitive" villages in Africa where the women have never worn a shirt in their lives (You know the ornately bejeweled females with free-range bosoms who are always photographed for *National Geographic*?) are not obsessed with breasts. They get a free peek 24/7. No need for topless dancers.

Newspaper articles also devoted column inches to wondering whether or not the wives of the husbands who attended the show knew they were there. "No, she doesn't, but I'm not doing anything wrong!" one man angrily defended himself. Many claimed their wives had given permission. A small contingency of wives even joined in on the fun.

Not all of them were impressed. Some newspaper quotes included "I expected something more. I thought the show would be more erotic and the girls more gorgeous," and "The girls are very attractive, like the contestants for Miss World, but I thought the show was only just passable." I'm sure I would have come in with high expectations myself.

In general the newspaper reviews were positive, most agreeing that we were stunningly beautiful (I'll take the compliment!) and that there truly was talent among us. As if physical beauty precludes any other abilities. Although, maybe it should. It doesn't seem fair for some to get not only jaw-droppingly good looks but talent as well. Perhaps the "beautiful" people should naturally be dumb as a donut just to even the score a bit.

The title of one article read, "Song and Dance Bunnies: Who says Playboy bunnies can't sing and dance? We talk to seven who can. And their sizzling show bears testimony." (Side note: It wasn't that only seven of the eight cast members had talent and one was a dud; rather, the night the article was written, we were down a performer—see below.) Kylie and I were pictured in our black leather outfits combing our hair in the dressing room, serious looks on our faces as if we were about to go out and prove we were more than just pretty.

Another paper claimed the audience was "mesmerized by the leggy, voluptuous and scantily-clad women." Yet another read, "Playboy Girls bowl over a mostly-male crowd." The accompanying photo was the revealing rear view of Jasmine in her open-air chaps during her country and western solo. Perhaps not Jasmine's first choice of how she'd like to see herself represented in print but, lucky for her, she was extremely photogenic from all sides.

My antibiotics had finally started kicking in and I was feeling much better. Unfortunately, our lead singer, Rhonda (the missing performer I mentioned above) had become frighteningly sick with malaria, probably contracted from a mosquito during our trip through the countryside to Bandung. Let's not even entertain the idea that her purposeful bikini exposure had given her some sort of bad karma. She truly looked like death—ghastly white with blue-gray lips. Malcolm sent word of her grave illness to her church back in Vegas, and before we could even find a doctor who made house calls, there were faithful Mormons praying at her bedside.

The combination of the Church of Latter Day Saints and *Playboy* seemed odd. "Let us pray for sister Rhonda, so that she will quickly be back on her feet dressed like a tart and gyrating to rock and roll, spreading the good news of *Playboy* throughout the land..."—but I gave the Mormons a lot of credit for suspending judgment and offering her loving support in spite of what some might consider a sinful career.

Not only were we deeply concerned about our dear friend's health, but we were also down a lead singer. Remember how I had yearned for the singer's spot? Well, be careful what you wish for; you just might get it. I did. "Kristi, you'll be taking over Rhonda's track," Val informed me, and I immediately began rehearsing her lyrics and choreography for that night's show. It was a crash course—like cramming for a test in school. Talk about pressure.

Luckily, Val had the foresight to bring a backup vocal tape in case of just such an emergency, so all I had to do was lip sync, thank goodness. I was in no position to learn to sing like Aretha Franklin if I practiced for a lifetime let alone just one afternoon. I felt conspicuous, however, because no one with decent hearing and eyesight would believe Rhonda's raspy rock voice was coming out of my mouth. But the show must go on.

The experience was crazy and intense, particularly because I was doing not only her numbers but mine as well. Simply figuring out the costume changes proved perplexing, as I usually changed clothes while the singers were singing their songs. Val was holding her breath the entire show hoping I would successfully fake it through and not completely crash and burn.

Praise be to God, I did triumph without incident or accident. Val was thrilled and utterly impressed at what a quick study I was. My dream had come true, even though I was only lip syncing. Still, I was relieved when Rhonda got better, for her sake and mine.

****

During our free time, other than the short stint Playboy's Girls of Rock & Roll did on a television game show called *It's Your Move* and a performance on the TV show *Rollin' Good Times*, we snuck in a bit of sightseeing. Callie, Jasmine, Porsche, and I rode a cable car from the Southern precinct of Singapore over the water to Sentosa Island—an amusement-park type attraction. Porsche's fear of flying pertained to riding cable cars as well as airplanes and, frankly, I was a bit nervous being suspended in a little box hanging from a measly cord. We were, after all, traversing a large body of water with nowhere to go but down. The 360-degree view, however, was spectacular: over the water and freight docks, and with views of the city skyline, harbor, and lush green vegetation and sandy beaches of Sentosa Island. Once safely back on the ground, we walked the trails through the forest to the Imbiah waterfalls, where we stopped for a swim at one of the lovely beaches and visited a small aquarium complete with touch tank where you could handle starfish and other sea creatures.

Our exotic, one-week stay in Singapore was short and sweet. Before we knew it, we were back in smoggy L.A., noshing on bagels and fighting traffic.

****

Showbiz can be a flaky business, one in which you might not want to count your chickens until they are hatched. Val had promised an entire coop full of poultry and only two birthed from their eggs. In other words, you may think you have work for the next six months only to find yourself unemployed three weeks later. Such was the case for the Playboy's Girls of Rock & Roll. We were in Indonesia for two weeks and Singapore for one week and then we flew back home, as all the rest of the potential bookings fell through. In addition to being a huge disappointment, it was also embarrassing, as my friends had thrown me a big, emotional farewell party, and here I was back home shortly after I'd left. *Should I give back all the going-away gifts?*

These unpredictable work circumstances can be a financial and emotional nightmare. *Should I try to get other work right away or hold out with the hope that more Playboy gigs will come through soon?* I didn't want to commit to a dull day job or to a less desirable showbiz job to pay the bills and then be unavailable if and when the show got up and running again. But I couldn't afford to wait around too long not making money. It takes real fortitude to handle this kind of uncertainty. It's especially hard for the people who have given up their apartments, put their stuff in storage, stopped their mail indefinitely, and otherwise closed down shop on their previous lives. *Do I start my old life back up again or remain in limbo, and for how long?* Luckily, I was living with my boyfriend at the time and didn't have to worry about finding new housing at the last minute.

I decided I would stay hopeful and ride it out for a little while to see if more Playboy work came through. Soon I received this lovely letter from Val assuring me that we'd be performing again in no time:

Dear Kristi:
Enclosed are some photos of some of my favorite people in the whole world. I couldn't have asked for a better cast. You certainly had some challenges. We went from "Huge" to "Tiny" stages...had quick substitutions for Rhonda, etc. Was I ever impressed by your amazing quick study in the "Free Your Mind" number in Singapore. You know I couldn't even tell that you were lip synching...but someday, I hope you'll be in the show with a live mic? The girls were really the best group with whom I have ever worked...and it wasn't always easy... (Will YOU EVER FORGET the stench of that street in Jakarta or the size of those rats?) but none of you complained or got bitchy with each other. And the quality of the show was enhanced by your terrific relationship with each other. I always hope for and expect the best from my cast; but I don't ever take things for granted. Thank you so much for everything you did to make the show wonderful and the trip memorable. We'll be taking off to God only knows where in about two weeks. PLEASE GO TO THE DOCTOR to get your shots; AND you might ask your doctor about the pills (think it's quinine derivative) that they advise you take a week before traveling and during travel. I certainly don't want you to ever get sick. Right now, the plans are for us to go to Hiroshima, Bangkok, --then possibly over to Germany and back to Puerto Rico...then to Australia. There are so many "maybes" that I'm going nuts! The Tokyo show has not been cancelled...but it has been delayed. But promise that you'll know the same day that I know. Think we'll take the '50s number out (because it really belongs to Anita) and put back our Motown number. So there will be a minimal amount of rehearsal before we leave. I'm also hoping that we can replace the "Hot Legs" number with something that better suits Mallory. If the final plans turn out that the time away becomes too much for any of the girls, we will replace those girls...one by one. But it's nice to be working again. And I really hope you'll be able to stay with the show as long as possible.

Anyway, it's not a bad way to see the world!
Much love and a big hug...
Valerie

Although Val certainly gave the impression that there were all kinds of possibilities in the works and that our World Tour would be continuing shortly, after this last debacle, I never fully believed we would be performing in a country until we were actually standing in that country. Even then I had my doubts until we were actually on stage and approved by the government censors. But I loved Val, and she loved us, and I also loved doing the show, so I was going to hold out for as long as I could with the hopes that some gigs would come through.

I didn't have to wait long because, sure enough, so popular was our first show that we soon got invited back to the Heartthrob in Singapore for a two-week repeat engagement. It wasn't the whirlwind, multi-country, six-month tour we had expected, but at least it got us back on the road again for another mini-adventure. Besides, what happened in our downtime was worth coming back home early for.

****

If someone had told me that someday I would visit the Playboy Mansion—Hugh Hefner's most infamous party palace—I would have thought they were as loony as a loony bird. But one day Valerie announced, "Ladies, we will be having another photo shoot for new publicity pictures. This time we will be shooting at The Mansion." *The Mansion?* I nearly swallowed my tongue. "Everyone knows where it is, right?" she continued. "I don't," I said, raising my hand. "10236 Charing Cross Road. It's in the Holmby Hills area not far from UCLA." Val explained.

Grabbing a pen, I hurriedly wrote down what felt like one of the world's greatest secrets. I now knew the address of the Playboy Mansion. Never mind that so did anyone who went on one of those stars' homes bus tours for which Hollywood is famous. Those poor tourists could only stare out the bus window and imagine what lasciviousness went on behind that blockade of walls and shrubbery. I was actually invited in!

The first time I visited the Mansion felt like a dream. I kept double checking my piece of paper with the address scribbled on it, making certain I had found the correct location. Hefner's extravagant soirees of the 1970s put this place on the map and earned it its notorious reputation. My heart pounded in anticipation as I approached this haven of horniness. Would there be fornicating on the front lawn? Copulating on the kitchen counters? Massive orgies in the master bedroom? Debasement in the basement? Who knew what titillating experiences lay ahead?

Naturally, I arrived in my sparkling white Mercedes convertible, sporting a low-cut, high-slit designer dress, strappy stilettos, and stylish sunglasses, the warm breeze gently blowing my bleach-blond hair extensions off my sunkissed face. I was Malibu Barbie with hot lips, hot legs, and hot wheels. Well, in my fantasy, anyway.

In reality, I drove up to the impressive iron-gate entrance in my well-worn little blue Ford Escort, wearing jeans, a T-shirt, and cowboy boots. I rolled down my window and announced my name and purpose for being there into a fake rock that housed a microphone and speaker. Magically, the gate slowly opened, like a chastity belt unlocked, and I was free to enter and explore the previously forbidden territory.

While there were certainly bigger and grander estates in the world, Hef had no need to possess Mansion envy. The approximately 22,000 square-foot Gothic-Tudor style home, built in 1927, sat on about six acres of prime Los Angeles real estate. It reminded me of a mini medieval castle. I half expected a knight in shining armor to come jousting out of one of the heavy wooden doors.

The gorgeous grounds housed not only a waterfall pool and an incredible indoor/outdoor hot tub inside the "grotto" (a man-made, stone cave), but, more surprisingly, peacocks and other exotic birds, rabbits, and monkeys, as well as a pond full of exquisitely striped ducks and koi fish. It was a zoo. Literally. If you heard someone in the heat of love making on the lawn shouting, "You animal!" it may have merely been a response to one of the freely roaming menagerie.

There was also a Game Room separate from the main home, and this was where Satin, Athena, Porsche, and I were to have our first pictures taken. Athena—a tall, fleshy, long-haired brunette Greek Bunny-to-be—was the replacement Playmate for Mallory, who bailed out of the show. The room housed a juke box, pinball machine, and pool table. The entire place, floor and walls included, was cushioned, assuredly so you could comfortably fall to the floor in a fit of passion (and the more the merrier). One could sense the ghosts of psychedelic shagfests past. The room, reminiscent of the 1960s, was clearly in need of an update. Austin Powers would have felt right at home.

For the photo, we wore one of our hip-hop dance costumes from the show: red crushed-velvet shorts with a thick black vinyl belt, a long-sleeved black spandex top with the shoulders cut out, tan fishnets, black combat boots, and a black, floppy beret with an oversized daisy on the front.

I still felt like a complete imbecile next to the professional models, Satin and Athena, who knew just how to stand, arch their bodies, lift their breasts, twist at the waist, crane their necks, and flip back their hair to get the perfect sexy shot. I tried to imitate them and learn from what they were doing, but the poses felt so unnatural and ridiculous on me. One of their special tricks was lowering the bottom lip to show a little bit of teeth. While steamy on them, I looked like a snarling dog.

Next we took individual headshots outside in front of the veranda of the Mansion, which offered a nice backdrop of stone pillars. I was given a black fur stole to wear over, well, nothing. They wanted me to appear naked underneath, so I wore the stole below my bare shoulders. But being modest, I kept my bra on, pulling down the straps so they wouldn't show. My shoulder-length blond hair hung down, softly and naturally, and I accessorized with long, dangly rhinestone earrings. This glamour shot really made me feel like a movie star—very Marilyn Monroe. Now this was something to tell the grandkids about.

When the official photo shoot was completed, we all got out our own cameras and took pictures of ourselves in front of the Mansion's main entrance as proof that we were actually there. I probably wouldn't believe it myself if I didn't have the photos. And even with the picture to prove it, I'm still not sure I believe it.

This wasn't my only visit to the Mansion; later we also held rehearsals in the guest house. Sometimes the out-of-town performers—like Rhonda, who was from Vegas—were allowed to stay in the guesthouse. I was so envious. The guesthouse had a room with a wall covered in mirrors. While I'm sure the mirrors were really intended to heighten one's arousal during a carnal liaison, they made a perfect setting for our dance rehearsals.

Although jealous that I didn't get to stay in the guesthouse, I did get to eat dinner at the Mansion one night. We were seated at a table in a small, bare nook just off the kitchen—probably the staff dining area. It felt stone cold and stark, like the interior of a real castle. But the kitchen was always stocked with a tray of generously cut crispy rice and marshmallow treats from which we were allowed to help ourselves.

Perhaps the biggest treat, however, was our surprise visit by the Queen of the castle—Hef's wife, Kimberley. Whether she was protecting her palace or simply being friendly, she was certainly pleasant and kindly chatted with us as we ate. I can hardly imagine how she felt having a husband who was constantly surrounded by nude models, many of whom could offer her stiff competition. Did she feel tremendous pressure to be a dynamo in bed? I didn't envy her as matriarch of this empire of lust. I can make my own marshmallow munchies, thank you very much.

****

A month after we had returned home, we found ourselves once again on the airplane flying the thirteen hours back to Singapore. What were we, crazy? Yes. Not as crazy, however, as the fifty-two-year-old Dutch man who thought he could get away with smuggling in drugs. They hung him immediately. They are serious. Rules are rules.

The whole repeat experience felt like déjà vu in many ways, with one major exception: our accommodations went from five-star to no-star. The Ritz to the pits. No self-respecting star would set foot in that dumpy hotel. There had obviously been some bargaining done for this engagement. We had become a discount show—plucked off the clearance rack, brought back at bargain prices. Either that or Val hadn't been made aware that they were going to cut costs by tremendously lowering the housing standards.

Whatever the case, the end result was the same: no more lavishing in luxury. The rooms were drab and dingy and mine smelled musty. I searched for the location of the smell and found that my mattress was moldy. Disgusting. In keeping with the theme, the restaurant was a dreary brown, no-frills café with unappetizing food. The place had an odd odor —a combination of Asian spices; a hot, damp basement; and a stale, men's locker room. We forced ourselves to eat from the mediocre menu but didn't enjoy the experience.

Another mentionable change was our new body guard. Malcolm had already booked another job, so Billy—a big thirty-something, long-haired, red-headed redneck, good-ol' country boy—took over his position. I was fascinated by Billy's past; he claimed to have been a pro football player and cocaine smuggler in his earlier, rougher, tougher days. Good thing he had dropped the drugs sometime back, or he may have ended up swinging by the neck next to the Dutch man. I had never known a cocaine smuggler before; it just goes to show you that you can't stereotype. Not that I approved of his previous profession, but I preferred to have him and his sizable body on my side. He loved to play guitar and sing country western music and was as loyal a friend as they come. He was a big teddy bear to us gals.

****

Back at the Hotel Melia, where our gig was located, I picked up a postcard advertisement for our show, which read: "Heartthrob presents…Playboy's Girls of Rock & Roll. The Sexy, Sizzling And Sensational Beauties Are Back Here By Popular Demand!" On the back: "A Week of Hot Sweaty Night!" (Yes, it said "Night" and not "Nights"). "Don't Miss! Limited Season! See & Hear Them! LIVE!" There was also an R rating noted: Restricted. Above 18 years admittance only.

As if the nights weren't already hot and sweaty enough in Singapore, as it turned out, we were in town at the same time as our sexy male counterpart: HotBod—six white, muscular, male strippers also imported from the States. With their long hair and bulging biceps, six-pack abs, and firm pecs, they were the perfect diversion for Singaporean women while their men were gallivanting off to our show.

Of course, the newspapers played off this fortuitous synchronicity, comparing our sultry shows and noting that both were exciting Singaporeans with the tantalizing possibility that the authorities would finally allow more flesh to be seen. "Nightspots go for hot stuff. One strips the other struts…" "For the first time, Singaporeans will be seeing men stripping to their briefs." There was also a lot of hype about us performing in see-through lingerie and possibly even being the first show in which women would be permitted to go topless. I was shocked! This was news to me. I wasn't about to wear anything translucent let alone nothing at all. Was Val not telling us something?

But, alas, as expected, the charade inevitably fell apart. "Promises of see-through lingerie and hopes of a topless show were dashed when the authorities clamped down on what was supposed to have set a precedent for such shows," reported newspapers. This was no surprise to me. I'm certain the government censors had never had any intention of letting us bare our breasts even if we had wanted to. But it made for a great marketing campaign and assuredly generated interest and ticket sales.

The excitement even interested us enough to attend the HotBod show on our night off. Talk about a double standard. Their show was much more explicit than ours. They used a champagne bottle in ways Asti Spumante never intended, and we weren't even allowed to bend in front of a bar stool. But it was amusing to see them strip down to their underwear, play cowboys and construction workers, and dress for bed in purple velour boxers and robes. They were every bit as buffed as their newspaper ad. The climax of the evening was being invited out to sing Karaoke with the HotBods after their show—just another little perk of being Playboy's Girls of Rock & Roll. While they were so beautiful they could have come to life straight off the cover of a Harlequin Romance novel, they were just too pretty to be attractive to me. Still, it was intriguing to see their protruding muscles up close and personal.

Naturally, after the big media hoopla promoting the hope of indecent exposure, customers were disappointed when we showed up on stage with completely opaque costumes and—except for the new Bunny rabbit, Athena—the exact same decent show. While Athena was certainly highly seductive, exotic eye candy, even her Greek goddess appearance could hardly compete with the allure of actual, bare-naked, private parts. The dashed high expectations caused some of the appeal of our group to droop.

Athena did add an entirely new energy and dynamic to our cast, though. She and Satin were either bosom buddies or in a cat fight. Athena was harmless and friendly enough, and I liked having her around.

In addition to Athena's antics, our new source of backstage entertainment was a very realistic-looking rubber cockroach one of the Girls had purchased back home in the States after seeing so many cockroaches on our first trip to Singapore. The game became to attach it to or hide it in someone's costume to make her scream before or during the show. We'd be innocently putting on our gold sequin blazer only to discover a large, hideous brown insect on the sleeve. "EEEEEEEEEK! COCKROACH! Get it off! Get it off! Get it off!" we'd screech batting at our jacket and jumping up and down like a madwoman. This, of course, was hilarious to whoever deviously planted the roach. Even when it finally became obvious that the bug was bogus, we'd still shiver and shake off just the thought of such a disgusting creature crawling on our personal attire. Although we knew the faux insect was making the rounds, there was still such a high chance of it being the real deal that we got scared and screamed anyway! Plus, after that first prank, we were always paranoid wondering when the next cockroach would turn up, fake or otherwise.

Even more thrilling than the rubber cockroach game was the night that some of our costume pieces were stolen between shows by some American college kids. This was kind of gross and embarrassing, as the apparel were surely sweaty by that point. The criminals were stupid and/or drunk enough to be flaunting the goods in the club, so it didn't take long for Billy, our body guard, to figure out who had done it. After politely asking, "You boys wanna eat your teeth? No? Then you best hand that over NOW," he recovered most of our stuff. Strangely enough, he also collected about $150 that wasn't ours. We all split it and felt a tad less violated. I just loved having a body guard.

Another highlight of the trip was our performance on a Rock & Roll TV show. It just happened to be the night of the Elvis impersonators contest, and there were Asian Elvis's everywhere. It was as surreal as being inside a strange dream image: "There I was, bedecked in sequins, dancing on national television with real Playboy Bunnies, when I am suddenly surrounded by a group of Asian men dressed as the King himself—Elvis—and they are all singing 'Don't you step on my *Brue* Suede Shoes.'" Pinching myself to check if I were dreaming would have revealed that I was very much awake, and Elvis was probably rolling over in his grave.

****

On this return visit to Singapore, we were fortunate to have more time to shop and see the sights. Excitedly, I purchased yards of plain white silk at bargain prices to use for silk painting back at home. With trepidation, we entered strange, ornate Buddhist temples, adorned with lit candles and incense, red lanterns, and what appeared to be cement dog statues cloaked in golden fabric capes, fresh raw meat atop their heads. Billy, Jasmine, Porsche, Satin, Callie, and I took a riverboat tour around Singapore harbor. Billy and I also went to the impressive Jurong Bird Zoo to commune with colorful, exotic birds and throngs of pink flamingos.

What a bonus to discover that Singapore was home to my beloved Tiger Balm—the self-proclaimed "world's best analgesic ointment" and one product that no dancer should live without. Many a dressing room is permeated with the pungent odor of the miraculous pain-relieving remedy that sets sore muscles afire with its healing herbs. Its applications were more far reaching than dance injuries, however. Back in the day, Chinese emperors were said to have employed the magic formula "for aches and pains from the stresses of court hearings, and the strains of the imperial harem." I'd be wanting me some Tiger Balm, too, if I had a harem to satisfy. Every dancer (and harem owner) really should make a pilgrimage to the Tiger Balm factory and give thanks for it. We dutifully drove past and paid homage.

No trip to Singapore is complete without a stop at one of the world's most famous luxury hotels: the Raffles Hotel, opened in 1887 and named after the founder of Singapore—British statesman Sir Thomas Stamford Bingley Raffles. Stepping into the historic hotel was akin to stepping into a set from *Casablanca* with the ceiling fans whirring overhead and the beautiful polished wood bar. Our main mission was to sample the "Singapore Sling"—a famous, fruity drink invented around 1915 by Mr. Ngiam Tong Boon, a Raffles Hotel bartender. His recipe was said to contain gin, cherry liqueur, pineapple juice, lime juice, orange liqueur, benedictine herbal liqueur, grenadine syrup, and bitters. As I sipped the vibrant red concoction served in a tall glass and topped with a pineapple wedge and maraschino cherry, I daydreamed that I was standing in this very room next to Somerset Maugham—the legendary English novelist and dramatist from the early 1900s—during one of his many visits to the Far East. "Legend has it that he worked all mornings under a frangipani tree in the Palm Court, turning the bits of gossip and scandal overheard at dinner parties into his famous stories," declares the Raffles Hotel website. What an exotic life.

We also managed to squeeze in dinner and dancing at the Singapore Hard Rock Café. When the manager discovered who we were, he asked permission to take our picture to hang on the wall with the other famous rock and roll acts that had been there. *Playboy's Girls of Rock & Roll on the wall of fame at the Hard Rock! Cool!*

The final bonus of the trip was awarded us on our flight back home. R&B singers Whitney Houston and her husband Bobby Brown and all of Bobby's dancers were on our airplane! We found out, because Bobby bravely ventured out of the safety of first class and into the dregs of coach, perhaps on some humanitarian mission to entertain the lower class. Or perhaps he was just involuntarily magnetically drawn toward groups of sexy woman, his massive gold and diamond

BBB (Bobby's initials) ring leading the way. Whatever the case, I couldn't believe it when he walked over to us and started chatting. He was very friendly, even flirtatious. Whitney must have sniffed danger, because, before Bobby could say "It's my prerogative," she flung back the first class curtain in search of her wayward husband. I felt better that Whitney wasn't wearing any makeup either, but it made her look even scarier when she gave the evil eye to all us females. Needless to say, it was the most famous evil eye I had ever been given.

****

A month later we received confirmation that the Playboy show was going to go to Japan for the entire summer! Not just one week. Not two weeks, but the entire summer! That was a solid eight weeks of confirmed work, pay, and, more importantly, adventure. With the Japan gig in my back pocket, I decided it was time to leave Adam. I was too young and restless to commit to a relationship; and if I were serious about giving this entertainment career a go, I needed to bite the bullet and get myself up to Los Angeles. Cindy had already made the move there to pursue screenwriting, and my four- to five-hour, round-trip commute from Del Mar to L.A. and back for rehearsals had been grueling. Although it was hard leaving Adam, my Del Martian friends, and my cushy, comfortable life, I knew it was time to commit to my career.

Since I'd be gone all summer, there was no use in getting an apartment right away. Dancers had to save money every chance they got, and paying rent (my biggest expense) while I was out of town for more than a couple of weeks was ludicrous. Instead, I packed up most of my belongings and put them in storage—the cheaper option—and mooched off my sister while rehearsing in Los Angeles.

Singing was still a dream of mine, burning even more brightly after filling in for Rhonda during her malaria crisis, so Val hooked me up with an ex-Playboy's Girl of Rock & Roll lead singer for voice lessons. Formerly known as Melanie, this fantastic rocker had changed her name to "Kali"—the Hindu goddess of empowerment and destruction. She lived, worked, and taught lessons at Michael Sembello's Zendetta Studios—essentially his home with a recording studio in the back yard. Once again, I was oblivious that I was standing on sacred musical ground, treading where a star—Michael Sembello—had tread before me. Had I known at the time that Michael was the artist who performed the song "Maniac" from the 1983 film *Flashdance* (touted as the third highest-grossing song from a soundtrack), I would have flipped out. *Flashdance* premiered my senior year in high school, and I absolutely went crazy over that song, which served as the background for Jennifer Beal's shimmying sweatfest in the movie. As a teenager, I used to put on my favorite turquoise leotard and pink leg warmers, skedaddle down to the dance studio in my basement, pop in the cassette tape, and unabashedly boogie down.

Kali was a musical genius in her own right. With her petite, sexy, toned body and waist-length, cascading sunset of pink-red-orange hair, Kali looked the part of a rock and roll goddess and had the raspy, rough sound to match. Her voice couldn't have been more different from mine, which had, much to my dismay, more of a sweet, innocent quality—the type of tone that gathers wide-eyed, animated bluebirds, bunnies, and deer to a Disney princess's dainty feet. Her voice was raw with grit and gravel and fire and sex, the type that could bring a 350-pound, tattooed bruiser to his knees weeping at its sheer power and passion. In spite of this discrepancy, I loved taking lessons from her and naively held out hope that some of her incredibly cool rock vibe would rub off on me. She was a real rock star in my eyes. She even sang in a band with Michael Jackson's former bass guitar player, Jennifer Batten. Body Guard Billy and I would go to hear her sing at various clubs around Los Angeles. She was incredible.

Kali taught me something called "Vocal Gymnastics" and spent many lessons coaching me on "riffs" and stylistic choices for the songs I chose to sing. For my first demo tape, she actually let me sing lead vocals on top of the original background tracks for the song "I Only Have Eyes for You." This tune and others from the soundtrack for the movie *Corrina, Corrina*, starring Whoopi Goldberg, had been recorded at their studio. I sang the song over and over and over in my car, practicing all I had learned, trying to sound even remotely like Kali.

When the day came to record, I was in heaven, wearing the headset and standing in the sound booth. I felt like a real recording artist! I struggled with the song, however, and got frustrated. We took a zillion recordings that Kali spent hours editing to splice together the best of the takes. The finished product was a quilt of bits and pieces sewn together, which felt like cheating to me. I couldn't have sung the entire song well in one take if my life depended on it. Still, the demo turned out well. I listened to it over and over and over, marveling that I was the one singing. I never did sound like Kali, though, and I never would or even should have. My voice still attracted birds and bunnies and fawns without possessing a speck of grit or gravel or sex, but for me it was another dream come true and worth every penny.

****

For the Japan show, there were again a few cast changes and some shifting around of parts as Rhonda, Porsche, and Kylie had moved on. With Porsche's exit, I was dubbed dance captain. Besides me, remaining cast members were Callie, Jasmine, Satin, and Athena, leaving openings for a lead singer and two dancers. There were also a few costume changes or, more accurately, deletions. Unlike in Singapore and Indonesia where government censors kept making our show "cleaner," the Japanese wanted our show "dirtier" and insisted that some bare breasts be included—a perfectly reasonable request, I felt, considering this was Playboy. Reasonable, that is, until I was the one requested to take one (or two) for the team. "Would you go topless, Kristi? It pays more," Val assured me. "No way," I responded, feeling dirty and offended that she even asked me. What kind of a girl did she think I was? (Although when hanging out on the French Riviera on my post college-graduation backpacking trip, I did contemplate going topless along with all the other European female beach bathers. It was a perfectly normal, acceptable practice for them and seemed so freeing. Alas, just as I was getting up my nerve to disrobe, a team of young male American soccer players showed up, and I got stage fright.)

I became concerned about the possibility of losing my job, but I was willing to let it go if it meant nudity. Going topless didn't pay *that* much more than dancing "covered" anyway. So if it was going to be a life-changing event, "Don't do it!" became my motto. It might be easy for some gals to justify the situation thinking, "It's Japan. These will be complete strangers who don't speak English. No one back home will even know I did it." But they shouldn't fool themselves into thinking no one would find out. Even if they were performing for only one night in the outskirts of Siberia, their uncle's buddy's cousin's neighbor might just happen to be there on a reindeer herding expedition and see them and be thrilled to share his photos with everyone he knows.

If going topless, you must make sure you are perfectly okay with not only the general public but your personal acquaintances, including parents, siblings, friends, schoolmates, teachers, neighbors, postman, bank teller, librarian, gas station attendant, and everyone else seeing your breasts on display. I was not okay with that. Would it be easier if we were all naked all the time like those tribes in Africa? If we weren't ashamed of our bodies so we had to hide them and then create these weird sexual outlets for what we have forbidden ourselves to see under normal circumstances? I'm not sure, but it seems like a silly game we play.

Why not have the actual Playmates go topless? After all, public nudity was their forte, and their breasts were already deemed luscious enough to be endorsed by *Playboy* magazine. Why not display our most desirable, experienced, and happily flaunted, abashedly unashamed bosoms? Well, because Playboy strictly forbade it. Perhaps without photo retouching and the ability to control the environment, they were concerned their product would be diluted or deemed less sexy. Regardless, since the Playmates were out of the running and none of the rest of the current cast would drop their tops, Val hired two dancers who would: Tina and Tasha. Thankfully, Val didn't just replace me, which she easily could have done.

Now all we needed to do was fill the vacant singer spot. Jasmine's younger sister, Marina, had always dreamed of performing and following in her older sister's footsteps, so, being the loving sister that she was, Jasmine encouraged Val to hire her relatively inexperienced sibling. Val agreed. So Callie kept her original track, Jasmine took over Rhonda's solos, and Marina mostly filled in for Porsche's original track with one major exception: "Kali tells me you've been doing well in your singing lessons, Kristi, and I want you to take over the 'Achy Breaky Heart' solo," Val announced. My jaw dropped. I was both terrified and thrilled. Here was my big break! "Plus, you and Marina will sing backup for Jasmine in the Aretha Franklin medley." I was on cloud nine! Finally, I get to really sing! With a microphone!

****

Soon we were back at the LAX International Terminal but this time without bodyguard. Valerie didn't feel we needed one in Japan, so Billy went back to his normal job. This trip we flew Singapore Air, and I had never been so pampered in an airplane. The flight attendants were lovely Asian women in beautiful floral kimonos, white socks, and thong sandals. We received complimentary travel bags with comb, toothbrush, toothpaste, and socks. The food was divine: delicious Japanese noodles and scrumptious blueberry tarts.

Long Legs and Tall Tales

The long overseas flights were old hat by now, we had done them so many times. Our most difficult challenge was to look (and smell) glamorous when we arrived at our destination, as we were often greeted by our hosts who expected us to look the part of sexy Playboy's Girls of Rock & Roll. This wasn't always an easy task when you've been crumpled in a tiny seat for over ten hours, spilling food on yourself, sporting bedhead and drool down your chin from napping, eyes bloodshot from lack of sleep, mascara smudged like a raccoon, clothes wrinkled and stale. Through previous experience, I came up with a few tips for myself:

1. Don't bother wearing makeup on a flight. It just gets smeared everywhere when you sleep. Wait to put it on just before landing. Allowing myself to fly makeup-less took getting over my own vanity and a belief that I had to look hot as a Playboy representative. But if we didn't advertise who we were by wearing the Playboy T-shirt or jacket, no one on the plane or in the airport knew who we were or cared what we looked like anyway.

2. Carry a toiletries bag with makeup, deodorant, perfume, breath spray, toothbrush, and toothpaste so you can primp and freshen up prior to landing.

3. Bring Visine. My eyes were always bloodshot from lack of sleep, so I used Visine to get the red out.

4. Bring a nice hat. My hair was always greasy and pasted to my head by the end of the trip, and there was nothing I could do to improve that situation. Luckily, hats were in style, so I bought an assortment of dressier floppy hats with oversized flowers on the front and more casual baseball caps including a funky sequined one I'd purchased in Indonesia. I figured rock and roll chicks could get away with wearing hats. It was the best I could do under the circumstances. This business of always being sexy took a lot of effort.

****

Oddly enough, I hadn't been particularly excited about going to Japan. Of course, I wanted the work; I just had never thought much about the country itself. But the minute I stepped off the plane at Narita International Airport, before I'd seen a thing, I knew I was going to love the place—call it inexplicable intuition. The warm feeling continued even while we sat holed up for hours in customs trying to sort out our visa debacle (we didn't have the proper papers that allowed us to work in the country). As we sat quarantined in the special customs problems room waiting and wondering if they were going to ship us right back home, Satin whispered to Callie, "Remember that trip to the Philippines where we all had our luggage searched at the airport?" "Oh yeah!" Callie recalled, "All the Playmates had brought their vibrators, and the customs guys were pulling them out of the suitcases and holding them up to inspect them!" "They didn't even know what they were!" Satin exclaimed. The two of them laughed hysterically. I had never seen a real vibrator let alone made it my traveling companion. This customs cock-up was potentially more critical than a sex-toy investigation, but I had a feeling everything was going to work out. Miraculously it did, and we were eventually on our way to get settled into our housing. Tokyo, Japan's capital and largest city, as well as the largest metropolitan area in the world, was going to serve as our home base for the summer.

Driving through Tokyo gave me the impression that this city was incredibly high tech, clean, safe, chic, streamlined, modern, and expensive. Space was a precious commodity and, as a result, the Japanese were quite space-efficient. I saw homes with driveways containing lifts you could drive your car onto; they would rise up and then you could park another car underneath. Ingenious! Given the lack of room, it was good that the people were small. Or maybe the people were small because they had little room to grow, like goldfish that stay small in a tiny fishbowl but grow large when placed in a big fish tank. Perhaps Americans are so big, relative to the Japanese, because we have had the luxury of lots of land to spread out in.

To my surprise, instead of a hotel, we were housed in a tiny two-story apartment building that was comprised of 12 units, six on top and six below. The building stood in the middle of a highly populated residential and commercial area in the Shinjuku ward, one of 23 municipalities that made up the heart of Tokyo, which also boasted what was called by some the "busiest train station in the world." We weren't downtown with the skyscrapers but were instead in an adjacent area chockablock with apartments and homes and little shops, strings of colorful, paper decorations suspended over the streets.

I was thrilled when we were each handed the key to our own teeny-tiny apartment. Privacy! Yay! But when I say teeny-tiny, I mean it. The one-room studio apartment included a teeny-tiny desk facing the only window, which looked out over the back of the apartment building that stood behind and nearly on top of us. A teeny-tiny TV sat atop the desk. Once in a while I would turn it on to see what was playing, but given that the shows were all in Japanese, TV didn't hold my interest for long. I was delighted with the teeny-tiny "kitchenette"—a small sink and countertop, a complimentary electric teapot and rice cooker, and a teeny-tiny refrigerator like college kids use in their dorm rooms.

The only official storage space was a small standing wardrobe closet just tall, wide, and deep enough to hang a couple of outfits one behind the other. The box was the width of a shirt, and it offered me only three hangars. This posed an interesting challenge for me, given that I had packed like an idiot, having brought thirteen pairs of shoes and countless outfits trying to act like a celebrity. My suitcases were so heavy, the handles broke off soon after our arrival. In my defense, however, there was reason to believe that we were supposed to live up to some image in public, especially in front of our hosts. Personally, I wanted to look fab and play the role of rock star. Wasn't that half the fun?

The downside of my overzealous packing was the impracticality of where to put all my clothes. I layered shirt after shirt and pants after pants on top of each hangar and piled the shoes into a mountain beneath the garments. At least we'd be settled here for a while, and I could make myself at home.

There was a futon loft bed that I could access by climbing up a teeny-tiny ladder. The bed was so close to the ceiling that I couldn't sit up without bumping my head. At first I felt claustrophobic and uncomfortable suspended in the air and being wedged between the bed and ceiling, but eventually I adjusted.

The apartment also included a teeny-tiny bathroom cubicle with a toilet, teeny-tiny sink, and teeny-tiny square "tub" that was just big enough to squeeze into in a sitting position so I could spray myself with a shower head. From the shower I could reach any of the bathroom's four walls. It was teeny-tiny, but it was all mine!

Wanting to stay in shape, I brought along a portable cassette tape player and a cassette tape of an aerobics workout I could do in the apartment. The room was so small, however, that I had to get very creative to successfully do the moves and poses, maneuvering my arms and legs above, below, around, and even through the desk, chair, and ladder. Living in a small fishbowl was an adjustment, but there was something comforting and serene about the simplicity of having so little and yet having all the basic necessities.

Our producers had rented an extra apartment to use as our cast gathering room and breakfast room. "What do Americans eat? What do we feed these women?" they must have inquired, almost like trying to care for zoo animals that require diets comparable to that of their native environment. Knowing that we would most likely snub our noses at traditional Japanese breakfasts of fish, rice, miso soup, pickles, and dried seaweed, they kept the community refrigerator stocked with Kellogg's cornflakes and milk for our breakfasts. For lunch, most days they took us to Denny's or Kentucky Fried Chicken for more American chow. "You want to go to Kentucky?" they would ask. I didn't question the restaurant choices back then, but now I would much prefer eating the Japanese food. It seems absurd that we would travel to an exotic location and then dine on mediocre American fare. But that is what we generally did, with the exception of dinner, which was often eaten at our performance venue.

****

Val was right about our not needing a bodyguard this trip, because we had an entourage of people traveling with us everywhere we went. Our escorts included our producer Donald (who was Japanese, so beats me why he had an American name), several business men who seemed to be his partners (Sawa-san, Hayakawa-san, Murata-san, and Isowa-san, to name a few), and then a small group of cute, young Japanese guys who did more of the grunt work and smoked like fiends. These junior gents shuttled us around and were at our beck and call. In addition, we were joined by Bernie—a big, buffed, African-American man—and his lovely American girlfriend, Janice, who resided in Florida. Janice used to be a personal flight attendant for an Arab sheik and had flown the world attending to the wealthy and royal on their private jets. They were both Buddhists and liked to work out. If Bernie and Janice were hired to fulfill any specific function for our show, I couldn't tell you what that might have been. But they were certainly fascinating and fun to have around. Plus they spoke English. I think they may have been good friends of Donald. Perhaps he liked hanging out with them or wanted some Americans on the team to help tame the wild Bunnies. Sometimes others tagged along, but a dozen or so comprised the core circle.

Thank goodness we also traveled with a translator—a sweet, young woman named Namiko. With the exception of Janice and Bernie who spoke only English and Donald who spoke Japanese and hesitant, limited English, our posse didn't speak much English and we, of course, spoke absolutely not a word of Japanese. So Namiko was a godsend.

Being the conscientious Americans that we were, we took it upon ourselves to bridge the cultural divide and the language barrier by teaching our new young male friends the limbo and every American swear word we could think of. In return, they taught us some extremely rude Japanese saying, laughing hysterically when we repeated it. We never did find out what it meant, which was probably for the best. Thinking it a good idea to learn some Japanese that wouldn't make enemies, I eventually attempted to perfect a few key, friendly, respectable phrases: "Konnichiwa" (Good afternoon); "Hajimemashite" (Nice to meet you); "Domo arigatou gozaimasu!" (Thank you very much); and "Ski des" (I like you). I used that last one to flirt with and shock Japanese men, who were easily embarrassed. At first, all Japanese sounded like gibberish or nonsense scatting to me—just a bunch of indiscernible white noise. After a couple months, however, it was as if the smoke cleared and my ears opened wide and I could tune in and pick out certain words.

Just as the Japanese words were indiscernible, the people all looked the same to me at first. They were all petite with dark hair and fair skin. I couldn't tell people apart without more distinguishing features—different hair color, skin color, eye color, sizes. The streets of Tokyo looked like a giant ant farm with black-headed ants swarming about in masses. By the end of the summer, however, I could not only easily distinguish individual Japanese people but I could also recognize who was Chinese and who was Korean.

****

Our first performance location was an exquisite, small, intimate, modern dinner club with a few tables, a small bar, and a stage just big enough to house a small rock band. To our good fortune, they served us dinner each night before the show. Their gourmet food was amazing, including the most delectable Kobe beef—a fat-marbled delicacy from a specific, highly prized black breed of cattle that had supposedly been fed beer and had their backsides massaged. Not a bad life for a creature whose destiny was to end up on a plate. Although I never liked to consume much before a performance (Who needs the extra bloating when bearing your belly?), the meals were much too delicious to pass up.

Unfortunately, this venue had no back stage, so we used the ladies restroom as our dressing room. Like in Singapore, we had to walk through the audience to reach the stage. Val taped a copy of our new show lineup on the wall of our toilet-turned-dressing-room, so we'd remember the order:

1. Opening
2. Free Your Mind
3. Sweat
4. I Will Always Love You
5. Achy Breaky Heart
6. Makin' Whoopee
7. I'm Too Sexy
8. Someday
9. Hot Legs
10. Tribute
11. Erotica
12. It's Rainin' Men
13. Aretha
14. Love Is the Wonderful Thing
15. Closer

My show consisted of seven of the fifteen total numbers. The entire cast performed the opening; then I had a leisurely three numbers to change costumes, after which I sang my new "Achy Breaky Heart" solo, followed by only one number to whip off my chaps and squeeze into my "I'm Too Sexy" lace teddy and fur stole. Doing my little turn on the catwalk with the Playmates was so simple and fun. I then had a whopping four numbers to change into my black rhinestone-studded disco dress, danced "It's Rainin' Men," stayed in the same costume and sang backup for the "Aretha Medley," ran offstage and quickly changed into my gold bikini and sequined blazer, and joined the rest of the cast for "Love Is a Wonderful Thing" and the closer—a reprise of our Girls of Rock & Roll theme song "Opener." The end of the show went by particularly fast as I was on stage for most of the last four songs.

The price I paid for getting to sing the "Achy Breaky Heart" solo was having to wear Jasmine's hand-me-down chaps with the rearview window. Yee haw! Those pants sure were drafty. Having backup dancers and being the center of attention was more exciting than riding a bucking bronco, but I was unsure about my singing. During every show I wondered whether the real singers (Callie and Jasmine) cringed when they heard me howling. *Should I ask them how I sound? Should I ask their advice? What if I'm awful?* Too terrified the truth might break my achy break heart, I kept on doing my best and hoped it was good enough.

I knew I had to start somewhere if I wanted to improve and was grateful to Val for the opportunity. She also let me sing backup with Marina for the Aretha Franklin Medley; I was in Seventh Motown Heaven. Being mostly "oo"s and "sock it to me"s and "re-re-re-re-re-re-re-re-spect"s, I felt fairly capable. Plus I was fantastic with the hair flips and hand gestures, and absolutely bubbled over with personality. So passionate was I about the performing and singing, I could have done it all night long and much preferred it to the straight dancing. If only God had given me an ounce of Aretha's vocal talent.

My singing in the show was certainly a change but nothing compared to our new and improved feature: the addition of topless dancers. Of our two shows per night, the first was "covered" and the second "uncovered." In other words, Tina and Tasha exposed themselves for a few numbers during the later show.

In the opening song, "The Girls of Rock & Roll," Tasha and Tina danced topless, while the rest of us were fully clothed (scantily clothed may be more accurate). Conveniently, the fabric in their underwire push-up bras was removable, so they'd rip out the black leather and only wear the rhinestone-studded underwire. Breasts certainly should be celebrated, and why not glamorized with a bit of sparkle? Still, it was just plain weird having two token topless dancers. I could see how it worked well for Tasha's "Erotica" solo, given Madonna's musical theme. Tina and Tasha also danced uncovered during "Hot Legs"— Athena's solo. Because Athena was the Playmate and soloist, it would have made much more sense for her hooters to get the hoopla. How bizarre. Honestly, did a sneak peak at those four nipples really make or break our show? But that's how our bases were covered (or not).

After the performances, once back at our apartments, we'd walk the few short blocks to our neighborhood 7-Eleven (Yes, a 7-Eleven!). We'd stock up on an array of delicious Japanese junk food, my favorite being wasabi snacks—their version of Cheetohs with a green, spicy wasabi hot mustard coating instead of the finger-staining orange powder. Or sometimes Donald would bring us huge drums filled with an assortment of sushi.

****

Our Japanese hosts treated us like royalty, taking us to every hot spot in Tokyo. The producers and gofers were so dedicated to their jobs that they ditched their families and friends to accompany us for after-hours partying and dancing nearly every night after our last show. All the clubs had exorbitant cover charges—$35 American and up—which we never paid. Take that, Club Tatou in L.A.! Who's a VVIP now? The trendiest of the trendy nightclubs teemed with American and European models. Techno music was the rage, and the petite Japanese girls monotonously bounced to the beat, swinging their feather boas. Their dance moves were limited, perhaps, in part due to their flimsy attire—the shortest skin-tight mini-dresses I've ever seen. Any shorter and the getup would have been called a shirt. The youngsters acted like they were trying to make up for generations of Japanese women who'd been stifled behind stiff kimonos and culturally required politeness.

We, on the other hand, would get out on the dance floor and dance as wildly as possible, holding nothing back. Sometimes we'd coerce our Japanese hosts into joining the chaotic boogie fest. I had never felt anything so cathartic. No one expected us to be prim and proper. On the contrary; we had a Playboy rock and roll image to uphold. Having finally cooled our jets around 5:00 a.m., we'd close the discos only to find it was daylight. I expected Tokyo to be a ghost town at that wee hour of the morning. Au contraire; the streets were bustling with a mix of fresh early risers and stale, late night leftovers.

It's not surprising that the Japanese could keep their engines running all night. Everybody smoked and drank coffee continuously. The entire country must have been on a colossal nicotine/caffeine buzz. One of their more ingenious inventions to stay wired was caffeinated licorice-flavored gum, a treat I bought in bulk in case I needed a quick boost. In the mood for a liquid pick-me-up? Look no further than the nearest street corner for a collection of cold, canned coffee drinks, some sweetened with sugar and milk, easily accessible from one of many vending machines. These ubiquitous, magnificent dispensers catered to your every need, 24/7, including an astonishing variety of drinks, food, and even underwear. Yes, fresh undies. This was a country on the go. Convenience was key.

Long Legs and Tall Tales

The vending machine lingerie was a no-go for the Girls of Rock & Roll, however. For our American-sized heinies, these would've been like squeezing into toddler panties. What a disappointment to discover we couldn't buy any Japanese clothes or shoes, because we were gigantic compared to their women (and men, for that matter). On the other hand, the Japanese were gaga over Western jeans. The denim trousers were in such great demand, we wished we had brought some to sell or trade.

Americans may have excelled in the blue jeans department, but the Japanese were innovative in so many other ways. Say, for instance, we had been dancing most of the night, as we were prone to do, and didn't have time to return home but wanted to catch a few winks without paying for a full-fledged hotel. In downtown Tokyo, special, inexpensive, communal sleeping establishments could be found that catered to business men and women in this very predicament. Instead of having a private room like you would in a real hotel, you got your own private, cushioned cubby hole. It reminded me of a morgue full of coffin-like containers stacked on top of each other. You would slide into an opening at one end and commence getting some shut eye. Each cubby included a little locker for valuables. Each establishment also offered a community shower room and toilets. I had never seen anything like it. Post-party patrons could rest their weary heads for a few hours, shower, grab some vending machine underpants and a canned coffee drink, and be back to work, fairly fresh and refreshed for having painted the town red. We opted to head back to our cozy, little apartments instead.

****

This tour was unlike any other, because Donald and Company took such exceptional care of us, providing not only after-hours entertainment but sightseeing excursions on our days off. The word on the street was this man had brought Michael Jackson to Japan! He clearly knew how to treat his talent. The Japanese, in general, knew how to make a good impression. I never could have afforded a trip like this. Donald was the Genie who granted our every wish, at no expense to us. *Domo arigato!*

One of my wishes, while in Tokyo, was to soak up as much culture as possible. Hence, a group of us got tickets to see Kabuki Theatre—a spectacular, classical dance-drama in which the performers wore elaborate kimono costumes and striking stage makeup. Their faces were completely covered in a white, rice-powder base and were accentuated with dramatic, colorful, sometimes scary features (depending on the character the performer was playing), the end result looking much like a mask. Live music using traditional Japanese instruments underscored the drama. I was most intrigued by strange sounds of the one-string zither and the notion that an instrument could get by with only having one string. Seemed like cheating. Kabuki originally started in 1603 as an all-female production—women playing both the female and male roles—with erotic themes. The actresses were then available for post-show prostitution. Hmmmm... reminded me of the invitation we got in Bandung to "see clients" after our performance. After many incarnations, alterations, and transformations, modern-day Kabuki ditched the ribald themes and ended up with an all-male cast playing both the male and female roles. Sort of like original Shakespeare, I guess. Men in drag always make for good entertainment, as far as I'm concerned.

Another must-do on the sightseeing list was a stop at the emperor's primary residence, the Imperial Palace. I photographed the famous stone double bridges leading to the main gate over the moats. It didn't have quite the pomp and circumstance of Buckingham Palace in London; there was a much more peaceful, Zen feeling about the palace and its lovely gardens.

Perhaps to make sure we didn't get too homesick, some of the tourist attractions we were taken to were very American. For instance, Donald and Company accompanied us to the ice-skating extravaganza produced by Disney on Ice. We also celebrated Donald's birthday lunch at Hard Rock Cafe Tokyo. A good, old fashioned hamburger and fries did hit the spot. And every chance we got, we stuffed our faces with soft-serve ice cream cones. I don't know how we managed to fit into our costumes.

****

Donald ruled the roost, but Valerie was our mother hen, herding her precious little chicks safely around Japan. Sometimes, she tried to act tough and lay down the law, but at heart she was a softie and pretty much let us do whatever we wanted, however bird-brained. Back in L.A. she acted as her own animal rescue mission taking in homeless chicks or, more accurately, Bunnies. She loved her Bunnies that much, even though some of the girls could have attitudes and be hard to control. Occasionally a Bunny would have a diva tantrum; all Val could do was roll her eyes and laugh nervously. Satin seemed to be a special concern of hers, almost like a second daughter. Val would look after her temporarily until Satin once again flew the coop.

Val was kind and generous with a big heart. She lived in Reseda and had us over for a pool party once when we were on hiatus. Quite the modeling agent in her day, Val was always well put together and professional. She sincerely cared for her Girls, especially the ones she'd spent a considerable amount of time working with previously, namely Satin, Callie, and Jasmine.

These three amigos had sung and danced and traveled together so much, they were almost like sisters, close-knit and chummy some days and bickering at other times. Being a relative newbie, I felt more like an outsider, but they were welcoming and nearly always hilarious. They had worlds of show business experience between them, and I loved learning their tricks of the trade. "It's best to keep your hair a little greasy for photo shoots, because it stays in place better when styled," Callie taught me. "Also, it's good conditioner for your hair," Jasmine chimed in. They got a little too into it on this trip and tried not to wash their hair for days, thinking it was healthier for their long manes. We may have been Playboy's Girls of Rock & Roll by night, but during the day we were just normal gals in need of a shampoo.

There were other alliances: the Playmates, Satin and Athena, played fairly nicely together at times until some squabble set off a smack down. They usually made up quickly. Jasmine, her sister Marina, and their mother formed a family trio. Tasha and Tina became unlikely companions; their personalities didn't jive at all, but they bonded based on being the only topless dancers. I clicked most with Callie, who had an outgoing, positive personality and adventurous spirit. Thank goodness everyone was tolerable if not amicable. Otherwise, it would have been a long, lonely, and miserable summer.

Callie and I were the only two Girls always in the mood to go out on the town and explore our surroundings. Several of the others preferred to sleep late, lazily lounge about, and have time alone. Not the two of us. We wanted to squeeze as much juice out of this trip as possible. One day we, along with one of our Junior Japanese chaperones, took an excursion to see Mickey Mouse at Tokyo Disney. Another day, we bravely ventured off all by ourselves to visit an American guy friend of hers who was teaching English in Japan for a living. Negotiating the subway system without knowing the language was nerve wracking. Trying to figure out which stop to get off when the signs were only in Japanese calligraphy symbols proved nearly impossible. We couldn't tell those blasted scribbles apart. Finding someone who spoke English was difficult. And my little Japanese phrase book didn't do diddly squat to help. Even if it had the translation for the phrase, "What the heck does that flippin' sign say?" I wouldn't have been able to understand the person's answer in Japanese. Somehow, by the grace of Buddha, we eventually made it. Callie's friend's one-room apartment was even smaller than our diminutive Tokyo digs. It was an exercise in compact living. He had to put away his bed roll every morning so he could stand at the minuscule kitchen counter to make tea. It had virtually no storage space either. One simply couldn't be weighed down by material possessions in this environment.

After a few weeks in Tokyo, I caught a nasty intestinal bug. Concerned about missing a show, I immediately flagged down one of our gofer guys—Haruyuki Mochizuki. (We called him "Yuki Zuki" for short.) I did charades, pointing to and holding my stomach and making painful faces, hoping my exaggerated motions and expressions were clear enough for him to guess correctly. It was like a scene from one of those old silent films with the melodramatic acting. He shook his head "Yes," made a "Wait there! I'll be right back!" gesture, and immediately went out on a mission to solve my stomach issues. A short while later he returned with a bottle of prescription pills. All I could do was trust that they would make me better, not worse. Don't know what was in those magic capsules or where he got them, but they worked like a charm. What a sweetheart.

****

Our performance schedule for the entire summer left only one long weekend off, and the Dynamic Duo (Callie and I) wanted to make the best of it. "Let's go to Kyoto!" we concurred. After our harrowing day trip taking the subway to see her friend in Tokyo, we decided it would be best to get assistance in planning this much more daring adventure. We went straight to the top—Donald, the man with the deep pockets. In our sugary sweetest voices, wide-eyed and batting our long lashes, we innocently inquired, "Dearest Donald, what's the best way to get to Kyoto? Can you help us?" No sooner had our plea left our pouty lips than Donald had organized and funded a trip for the entire cast, plus himself and his posse, of course.

Woo hoo! We shot off to the historical metropolis of Kyoto—former home of the Japanese Imperial Palace—on none other than the bullet train, a streamlined, high-speed railway resembling, you guessed it, a bullet. Lunch aboard was a bento box with sticky rice and teriyaki eel, eaten with my favorite utensils—chopsticks. Time flew by, and a few hours later we arrived at our beautiful destination, approximately 288 miles from Tokyo. Our accommodations in the fashionable, multistory Hotel New Kyoto were quite acceptable. What I loved most about Japanese hotel rooms were the electric teapots and complimentary green tea, much like American rooms often have a coffee maker. I had little experience drinking green tea before this trip but now I was beginning to acquire a taste for it.

Kyoto boasts 1,600 Buddhist temples and 400 Shinto shrines. That's one enlightened city. We didn't have time to honor all 2,000 holy hot spots, but we hit a few elaborate biggies. Kiyomizu Temple—meaning "clear water" or "pure water" due to the waterfall on the property—was a magnificent wooden structure built in 1633 into the side of a mountain. We climbed oodles of stairs to reach it. It was famous for its pillar-supported stage that jutted from the veranda, where, over time, more than 200 kooks took the proverbial plunge, literally jumping off the stage and falling 13 meters. These cliff divers, so to speak, weren't doing it for the thrill (or suicide attempt). Ancient tradition said survivors of the dangerous plummet would reap a remarkable reward: their wishes would come true. I spent all these years finding ways to get on stage. I wasn't about to leap off.

A second (and much less risky) way to have your wish granted, it was believed, was to drink from the Otowa waterfall, which had been channeled into three streams of water pouring down from the roof for easier access. Tin cups with long handles were provided, so guests could catch a sip of the magic liquid. I took a chance and drank from the cup touched by millions of strange lips before me. *Maybe this wasn't the safest way to have my wishes granted.* Other parts of the complex worth mentioning were the three-tiered red pagoda with the green roof; a shrine of numerous tiny cement statuettes of the beloved Japanese deity Ksitigarbha (I can't pronounce it either), which had all been lovingly dressed in hand-knitted caps and aprons; and the Jishu "matchmaking" Shrine, dedicated to the god who helps one find true love. *That's for me!* There was a magic aura to the place, and I couldn't help but get caught up in the wishful thinking and assistance from the gods.

Kinkaku-ji Temple—the "Temple of the Golden Pavillion"—was the temple to outshine all other temples, literally. A magnificent three-story building, its crowning glory was the top two stories, which were overlaid with gold leaf. An entire two-thirds of the building was completely covered in gold! The gilding lent an opulence and radiance befitting of its spiritual significance. The structure's visual impact was made all the more stunning due to its reflection off the pond on which it rested. This temple was so famous that I actually recognized it, having seen it previously in pictures.

Only 26 miles up the road from Kyoto lay the city of Nara and the Nara Daibutsu, the world's largest bronze statue of the Buddha Vairocana, measuring in at 48.91 feet high sitting down. The ear alone was over eight feet long, the face a whopping 17.49 feet. At the time, Buddhism was about as meaningful to me as a slice of bologna and just as mysterious. *What on earth is it made of?* But even I felt reverence and awe greeting this mighty being perched in his ornate house of worship. In order to reach the Big Buddha, we had to successfully make it past hordes of aggressive, free-range spotted deer. These weren't just any deer; the Shinto religion knows them to be "messengers of the gods." The message I was getting was, "Feed me, tourist, or I'll nip your behind!" We bought them snacks sold right there on the property and doled them out as we worked our way up to safe, stag-free refuge in the Great Buddha Hall.

As if the supersized Buddha weren't breathtaking enough, we were taken to see yet another Buddhist temple: Sanjūsangen-dō, the name translating as "Hall with thirty-three spaces between columns." Designed and built exactly as the name implies, this long, wooden expanse was home to not only the main deity, the Thousand Armed Kannon, but also 1,000 people-sized replicas plated in gold leaf. These "mini-me" Kannons flanked their larger leader in ten rows and 50 columns, forming an impressive army of divine beings. Incredible!

Many of the temples we visited sold small wooden plaques upon which people wrote their wishes. The plaques were then hung on a board outside the temple. It was heartwarming to see how many people wished for world peace. There is still hope!

To balance out all this spiritual stuff, Donald's sightseeing tour tossed in a little Japanese Hollywood. Toei Kyoto Studio Park was a theme park as well as a working movie and TV studio/set. It reminded me of a much smaller, cheesier Universal Studios. We had a ball roaming the streets, each representing a different time period in Japan, watching actors dressed as Edo-era Samurais battling each other with melodramatic flair and harsh Japanese fighting words and grunts. Four of us Girls even got to ride a giant, battery-powered panda.

A real local treat was lunch at a small fast-food joint that served savory Japanese pancakes called *okonomiyaki*, essentially translating as "what you like, grilled." There were griddles in the middle of every table. You chose which ingredients you wanted added to the eggy, floury, cabbage-filled batter (like vegetables, seafood, kimchi, cheese) and then cooked your own pancake. The food could be further embellished with toppings such as bonito flakes, seaweed flakes, sauces, mayo, or pickled ginger. It was like a combination of pancake, omelette, and pizza. Fun and delicious!

That matchmaking shrine back at Kiyomizu Temple must have worked its magic, as, by the end of our trip to Kyoto, it was obvious that Yuki Zuki and I were developing a crush on each other. He had grown up in a tiny fishing village, but had a cool city vibe about him. He wore jeans, nice dress shoes, Hawaiian shirt, blazer, and sunglasses, smoked cigarettes, and rode a motorcycle. I was at least half a head taller than my little Japanese Romeo. Conversation was kept to a minimum, given the language barrier. But in spite of having nothing to say to each other, somehow we found each other adorable and funny. Mostly we toyed with nonverbal flirting—love by pantomime. Satin and Donald had also become an item, but as least he could speak a reasonable amount of English.

Remember when I said I dreamed about transforming like Sandy in *Grease*? One night when we were all back in Tokyo at a Japanese restaurant, some of the Girls were acting extra goofy (after one too many sips of sake) and smoking cigarettes, something they didn't usually do. Seizing this perfect opportunity to further fulfill my fantasy, I tried to smoke one, too. Having only had experience "smoking" fake bubble gum cigarettes that puffed out powered sugar "smoke," I didn't know how to inhale or exhale the real deal. "How do I even hold this thing?" I asked the Girls who were laughing at my ineptness. I finally gave up (my lungs jumped for joy). Then Yuki Zuki took me on my first motorcycle ride, but I was only brave enough to travel less than two blocks. My dream of being the bad girl was quickly going up in smoke.

****

Most of the time, our days were unscheduled and, therefore, free for snoozing or sightseeing. Lord knows, with the late-night shows and post-performance bar hopping (bunnies do a lot of hopping), we needed our beauty rest. Thankfully, we weren't required to do much in the way of daytime publicity. On three occasions, however, we performed on Tokyo-based television shows. The TV studios would hang a giant Playboy logo in the background, and we'd do a number or two from the show.

After several weeks' worth of playing clubs in our home base of Tokyo, we ventured out by bus to perform in other cities: Nagoya, Kofu, Osaka—Japan's third largest city—and Yokohama—Japan's second largest city. Since the Japanese planned opening-night and closing-night parties for each place we performed, we became well acquainted with sake and often ended up toasting everyone and everything in the restaurant.

Other than dancing the night away at Prince's funky live music club, Glam Slam, in Yokohama and getting bedbugs from the sheets in my Osaka hotel, particularly memorable were our stops in Nagoya and Kofu. Nagoya is approximately 220 miles west and a little bit south of Tokyo. We visited the beautiful Nagoya Castle, built between 1610 and 1619, destroyed by the United States in World War II, and reconstructed in the 1950s. I felt guilty knowing that my country demolished one of their national treasures but was glad we were no longer enemies. Another attraction of the castle compound was the Ninomaru Tea House. Here we observed ritualistic tea ceremonies, rooted in transformative Zen Buddhist spiritual practices, in which green tea powder called "matcha" was specially prepared and formally presented. The tea house brochure tantalized:

> *If you would like to taste Japanese green tea in the house, you may buy a tea coupon, and beautiful women clad in kimono serve you tea. It is interesting to sit on the tatami mat, take green tea and admire the castle and beautiful garden. Furthermore, it is said that visitors may strengthen their leases on life five years by taking a bowl of Japanese tea at the house.*

For a modest fee, who wouldn't want to extend their time on earth by simply drinking the bewitching beverage? We all sat down for a cup.

Long Legs and Tall Tales

The bonus of our day sightseeing in Nagoya was a fortuitous star spotting. Three Sumo-wrestling champions! They weren't particularly difficult to spot, as they were multiple times larger than a normal-sized Japanese man. Of course, in their traditional training and tournament togs—naked except for a thong loincloth—they'd be especially obvious. This particular day, they were off duty and, consequently, in kimonos with their rotund rumps well concealed. Naturally, we asked permission to have our pictures taken with these revered, cultural icons. These bottom-bearing behemoths seemed like kindred spirits, given that we all earned our dough donning G-strings and turning loose too much of our respective cabooses.

Another highlight of our time in Nagoya was the night we had to be the Budweiser beer girls, which required us to wear short, skin-tight, sleeveless dresses that looked like giant Budweiser beer cans. Our job was to be photographed as these jumbo brewskis, eating and partying at an outdoor festival, for a magazine spread. I didn't particularly like being squeezed into that sack of suds. The bizarre dinner menu kept me well under my calorie count, however. Now, I generally love me some sushi, and the fresher the fish the better. This joint took fresh to a new level when we watched them slaughter a live lobster, kicking and screaming, then serve us the extracted meat, muscles still a-twitching. The sidekick side dish was an entire baby crab, fried extra crispy so we could munch and crunch the shell, knobby-kneed legs and all. At least I was sure this little guy was dead as a doornail (and just about as pleasant to eat as a doornail). "Bring me another Bud, please!"

Having left Tokyo and our fast-food friends The Colonel and Denny behind, we started eating more Japanese fare, most of it much more palatable than zombie lobster and crunchy crab shells. I adored the sweet potato-filled pastries and the magnificent sushi platters with spicy, green wasabi and pickled ginger. In fact, the many varieties of colorful, little pickle accompaniments were unusually tasty. I also found it fascinating that beans were often treated as a dessert item, sweet beans and cornflakes sprinkled atop ice cream sundaes. The staple foods by far, however, were rice and noodles served in a broth with meat and/or vegetables. I gobbled up so much rice and slurped so many noodles that I nearly collapsed into a carb coma. Like the Indonesians, the young Japanese had terribly rotten teeth, perhaps from too much sugary, sticky starch?

While I thoroughly enjoyed sampling the native cuisine, after a while I began craving fruits and vegetables, which had been noticeably absent from our meals. Starving for nutrition, I stumbled over to the local outdoor market in search of a hit of fruit. The precious cargo was prohibitively expensive—all carefully, individually wrapped, packaged, and nestled in cushy boxes as if to be mailed as an exotic Christmas present. I left, empty handed, as visions of non-sugary plums danced in my head.

****

The show had been running fairly smoothly, but little by little, day by day, an insidious infection crept into the cast. It began as an affliction of a few individuals, but the rest of us were not immune to its toxic effects. First of all, Marina determined that showbiz was not, in fact, the life she desired. (It ain't always glamorous, that's for darn sure.) She no longer wanted to be in her sister's trendy, wedged shoes and was ready to have the whole ordeal over with so she could get back to her normal life. She was one unhappy—though, fortunately, still sociable—camper.

Worst of all, Tina and Tasha had gone off the deep end, through no real fault of their own. The real culprit was the topless factor. Let me explain. Some topless showgirls are quite classy, like the "nudes" in the Vegas show *Jubilee!*, bedazzling and beguiling in their exquisite Bob Mackie and Pete Menefee gowns, slinking down the grand staircase. They were so stunningly gorgeous that I almost wanted to be up on stage with them. These women were like Venus de Milo—their bodies a magnificent work of art. Their elegant, elaborate costumes highlighted and accentuated their natural beauty. Also, a large number of women were contracted as nudes, so they all were able to benefit from a community of support.

Our show, on the other hand, was motorcycle mama minus material. And there were only two topless out of eight. Neither of the girls had gone topless before, and it was messing with their minds. The two grew bitter at being the only ones to have to bare their bosoms. Tasha eventually solved her psychological dilemma by developing a completely different mindset; she seemed to consider herself a special star of the show. In any case, both Tina and Tasha mentally separated themselves from the rest of the cast, and a rift ensued: the topless girls versus everyone else. Although the animosity was unspoken, we all felt their isolation from us, and they were uncomfortable to be around.

Long Legs and Tall Tales

Tina was professional enough not to let her attitude obviously affect her performance. She dutifully went through the motions with a fake smile. The audience probably couldn't detect a problem, but I sensed she hated every moment. Tasha performed with pseudo pride; after all, she was a featured performer. Backstage, Tina and Tasha remained aloof and silent. Awkward.

****

Our tour continued on to Kofu about 80 miles west of Tokyo. On a clear day, you could see the famous, holy Mt. Fuji, Japan's largest mountain, often seen in photographs with its peak covered in snow. *If only we had time to hike it!* Our accommodations at the sizable, sophisticated, Royal Garden Hotel were particularly enjoyable. First of all, because we performed in a big banquet hall in the very hotel in which we were staying, our commute to work was a breeze. Secondly, ours was a dinner show this time, complete with loads of red wine bottles already set on the tables so guests could quickly refill their glasses whenever they were thirsty. After the show, we'd scour the place for full bottles and sneak them back to our rooms to enjoy. Hated to waste good grape juice.

Our gig included a lot of schmoozing with the big wigs, namely the chairman and president, who brought us in to perform, and their cohorts. Consequently, our entourage expanded greatly. These lovely people treated us like gold, fed us feasts, and made us feel like family. The Kofu contingency were so generous they spent an entire day shuffling us through their local pride and joy—an ivory museum, which showcased stunning artifacts made of the creamy-white tusks. (Yeah, I know. We all hoped the animals weren't poached for their parts, too.) A professional photographer followed our every step and documented the day. Our new friends also took us to another beautiful shrine with lovely gardens and a tea room. We sat in traditional Japanese fashion—shoeless on tatami mat floors—and ate from trays with little compartments that housed various, unusual Japanese delicacies. When we inquired what one of the substances was, we received the astonishing reply, "Moss, scraped off rocks." Their culture was clearly more creative in determining what constituted food. On the way back to our hotel, we stopped at a lush vineyard to pick grapes.

An especially delightful surprise was the kimono seamstress who showed up at our hotel rooms to take our measurements. Days later she returned with unique, colorful, custom-made kimonos for all of us, including Janice. Mine was blue-green with big white, pink, and turquoise flowers and a baby blue and pink belt. With help, we were wrapped in the ravishing robes and sash, tied at the waist with a big bow in the back. Beautiful! We all put up our hair, and I added a Japanese flowered hair accessory I'd bought to really look the part. Many photos later, our benefactors took us, still in costume, to a tiny, casual local restaurant for Japanese fast food. It was one of my favorite experiences of the entire summer.

Unfortunately, in the midst of all this merrymaking, tensions were at an all-time high with Tina and Tasha, who by this time couldn't even stand each other. The dressing room was no longer the jovial place it had been. There was an icky, silent, negative-energy cloud floating about. Everybody felt it and wanted to avoid it. As dance captain, having to ask either of them to do anything was terrifying. I half expected to have my eyes scratched out. Tasha, who had previously maintained a mild-mannered librarian exterior and was mostly quiet as a mouse (or a librarian), was a powder keg ready to explode on the interior. One wrong word could set her off. The safest bet was to avoid conversations except when absolutely necessary. Other than a few minor battles between Playmates, everything had been fine until we added topless dancers. *Why couldn't we all just get along?* I can only speculate on what Tina and Tasha were going through that made them so volatile, but I highly suspect this intense drama wouldn't have happened had they been fully clothed like the rest of the cast.

On a nicer note, my birthday arrived while we were in Kofu; when I retired to my room that evening, I found a beautiful blue glass vase filled with enormous red roses from the local chairman of the hotel. He arranged for a special cast dinner to be held in one of the banquet rooms. I was presented with another bouquet of flowers and a card signed by the gang. Everyone sang "Happy Birthday," and I blew out my strawberry-bedecked cake a-sizzle with sparklers. What a nice surprise!

It never ceased to amaze me how respectfully we were treated. At the end of our run there, the chairman presented us each with a beautiful, typed letter. It ended with this lovely paragraph:

We all meet the wonderful people in our lives. Through the Playboy's show, we could get to know one of the greatest people and became friends which we could never forget. We believe that you will continue performing the wonderful show in many cities all of the world. We would like to give all of you as one of our family a heartful cheering no matter where you will be. I felt as if they had been my lovely daughters (sisters?). We hope that we will see you again someday, and may you be happy and successful in your lives. Thank you very much.

****

Our time in Japan had come to a close. Not wanting the excitement to end, Callie, Tasha, and I opted to stay on an extra few days to be tourists with Donald, Bernie, Namiko, and Yuki Zuki after the rest of the group returned to L.A. I stayed, in part, because I wanted to prolong my time with Yuki Zuki. Tasha stayed, because a few weeks earlier, she had replaced Satin in the role of Donald's love interest. Certainly, the tension was far less extreme with the show over and Tina gone, but Tasha remained reticent and close to Donald most of the time. In spite of the strange dynamics, I managed to enjoy my extended visit.

A highlight was our candlelight cave tour by the ocean, where the waves crashed along the rugged cliffs. Callie and I also took a little side trip to visit Rhonda, our former lead singer, who happened to be in Japan at a nearby seaside town doing another show. There was a real tiger in the show; we had our picture taken next to Rhonda who was holding the large, fanged cat by a leash. Standing in such close proximity to a ferocious animal I usually see only at the zoo behind bars or thick safety glass got my adrenaline pumping big time.

Callie and I flew home together but Tasha remained in Japan with Donald for who knows how long. It was the last I ever saw of her. She may still be there. I wish her (and Tina) well, whatever the case. Yuki Zuki and I had a tearful goodbye. It simply wasn't a relationship I could see thriving long distance or otherwise, even though he was cute as a wide-eyed Japanese cartoon kitty and sweet as a sweet bean ice cream sundae. I returned from Japan with the feeling that the world was a very small place.

****

There was no time to be melancholy, because the night we returned from Japan was the infamous annual Playboy "Pajama Party" at The Mansion. You'd better believe I was jumping for joy at seeing that invitation in the mail, although Val had told us ahead of time to save the date. On the front of the card was a drawing of a sexy, 1940s female movie star looking at herself in a hand-held mirror. Wearing only a sheer black sheath, the back of her sleek, naked body peeked through. The inside of the invitation read:

Come join in the fun at
Hef and Kimberley's
Midsummer Night's Dream
Playboy Mansion West
August 13, 1993
8 p.m.
Sleepwear of course.

I am going to the Playboy Pajama Party! But what on earth will I wear? Deciding that boxer shorts and an old T-shirt probably wouldn't do, I made a quick trip to Victoria's Secret for more appropriate sleepwear. I opted for a conservative, classy, forest-green satin pajamas pantsuit and left the top unbuttoned enough to reveal a lacy green, push-up bra. *Sexy and classy but not too trashy. I can live with that.*

I'd never been to an adult pajama party, let alone one at Hef's. *This could be the pajama party to end all pajama parties!* As a youngster, I'd get so excited when invited to a friend's sleepover. But as the night wore on, especially if we turned off the lights to have a séance, I'd get scared and want to go back to my mommy and the comfort of my own home. I was feeling a bit the same way now, not knowing what would go down at this sexy shindig. And there could be a lot going down at a Playboy party. *Am I prepared for this?*

I arrived at The Mansion, left my car with the valet, and was ushered not into the building, but to the backyard. The entire grounds, including the pool and waterfall, were enclosed in a forty-feet-high tent and were decorated like a Middle Eastern harem room with thousands of multicolored satin pillows strewn about the ground. The transformation was astounding. Tall tables stood laden with decadent refreshments. I adored the chocolate-dipped strawberries.

But I abhorred the old geezers in bathrobes dancing with young ladies dressed (barely) in lacy, thong lingerie. (I assume they were models from the magazine.) It just didn't seem right. I was clearly an overdressed prude by comparison. Other than the gray-haired grandpas cavorting with females young enough to be their granddaughters, I didn't notice any particularly sordid pajama games going on. No one was playing "truth or dare," as far as I could tell. I wasn't asked to participate in a séance where some poor victim lies flat on her back and people try to levitate her using only two fingers each while chanting, "White as a ghost. Stiff as a board." No spin the bottle. Instead, hundreds of people in sleepwear were drinking and eating and laughing and talking and mingling much like at any other outrageously resplendent, celebrity, adult pajama party in Hollywood.

Not knowing a soul and feeling awkwardly alone, I scanned the room for any of my Rock & Roll gal pals. They were nowhere to be seen. Surely Scott Baio was somewhere nearby; he was often spotted at The Mansion. What would I say to him? "Hey, Chachi! I used to love wa wa watching you ["wa wa wa" was his catchphrase] on *Happy Days*. Wha wha whatcha been up to since the seventies?" The only face that looked familiar was that of Kareem Abdul-Jabbar, who stood head and shoulders above the rest of the crowd (He was literally a few heads taller than everyone else). But we didn't know each other, and I wasn't brave enough to get the ball rolling with the basketball giant.

Suddenly my attention was diverted from Kareem by a bovine bounding toward me. As it got closer I started to recognize the little heifer. "Holy Cow! Is that you, Satin?" She was wearing white-and-black-spotted cow footie pajamas complete with cow slippers and a hood with cow ears. "Moooooo!" she giggled. There she was, a real honest-to-goodness bona fide Playmate of the Month with the body and professional nude modeling skills to carry off an alluring outfit that would highlight her double features and have every man in the tent eating out of the palm of her hand. Instead, she went totally against convention, put herself into the goofiest pjs she could find, and showed off her teats (the udder ones). That gal had a great sense of humor and could keep me laughing until the cows came home.

Soon, the rest of the Girls of Rock & Roll found us, and we danced and caroused and whooped it up by ourselves. I was relieved to have my friends there to hang out with. Other than them, this wasn't really my kind of crowd. The most memorable part of the night was getting walked in on by a male guest while using the poolside bathroom in the cave and being yelled at to "Lock the door next time!" "I did push the lock!" I shouted back. As if I *wanted* him to see me sitting there with my pants around my ankles. Mr. Hefner really needed to get that lock fixed.

When the party was good and hopping, Hef and Kimberley finally made their appearance, Hef sporting the latest version of his signature silk pajamas, smoking jacket, and velvet slippers. His connection with sleepwear began back in the 1970s, when he pulled all-nighters working on the magazine in his pjs and was still wearing this unusual office attire when his employees clocked in the next day. Eventually, his unorthodox, casual clothing carried over into social occasions, too, culminating in the creation of his infamous pajama party. What an ingenious uniform for a man who had built an empire associated with the bedroom.

While I was in the lavatory unintentionally exposing myself to a rude dude with a full bladder, an old timer in the pool was purposefully exposing himself to Callie and other guests. Rave in the cave! Apparently, he was ready to play party games like he did as a member of Hef's gang back in the wilder and crazier days. However, no one wanted to pin the tail on his donkey. Disgusted, Callie promptly informed Kimberley about the flasher at her bash. She sensibly responded, "Tell him, 'Mrs. Hefner prefers that you keep your swimsuit on in the grotto.'" I agreed with the lady of the household.

Feeling out of place and overly tired from jet lag and the long trip back from Japan, I was ready to leave early. As I waited to get my car, I saw beautiful, blond *Beverly Hills, 90210 actress* Tori Spelling standing next to her date, who was causing a big scene with the valet. Shouting. Finger pointing. Rudeness. Made my skin crawl. Was this considered acceptable conduct in Hollywood? Where I came from, a kid with bad behavior like that may have been spanked and put right to bed. (Of course, this crowd probably wouldn't consider that a punishment.) *I want my Mommy. I want to go home.*

****

The following week we were off on a five-day excursion to Puerto Rico. A white limo transported us from the airport to the seaport of San Juan where we stayed and performed at the Sands Hotel. San Juan was a tropical, oceanside, palm tree paradise, where the ocean water was warmer than the heated pool. It was glorious!

For our cast, we traded in the disconsolate threesome—Tasha, Tina, and Marina—for Lynda—a lovely blond Playboy's Girls of Rock & Roll vet with a beautiful voice and decent dance ability—to fill the vacant singer spot. Thankfully, this production was back to all covered and no topless. Since we had left Tasha behind in Japan, the "Erotica" solo was passed on to me. What bothered me most was not the dance itself, but the exceptionally tiny G-string that highlighted my meager costume. I was petrified about moving too much and exposing more than I wanted to. Like a surgeon careful to keep a steady hand and not slip, doing the splits was a delicate procedure. One wrong move and I'd be operating far outside my comfort zone. I wished I could crazy glue that G in place so my privates stayed private.

Gee whiz, our costumes were high maintenance! I had no idea how much effort would be required to look good in a flimsy piece of fabric. When sunbathing or swimming, for instance, we had to wear thong bikinis so that we didn't get unsightly tan lines. Tan lines and sunburns look terrible on stage and a black thong over marshmallow-white buns with toasty golden brown legs was particularly unappealing. It was hard to find an appropriate swimsuit. Nude sun bathing really would have been the way to go. As far as I was concerned, prancing around poolside with a nearly nude keister was far more embarrassing than singing in a thong on stage. Plenty of Puerto Ricans (and other international patrons) were perfectly at ease wearing next to nothing. But I never felt comfortable with my fanny wiggling freely in broad daylight and always covered up with a wrap skirt when I wasn't lying down on the chaise lounge.

In addition to performing our show, the hotel asked us to be models in a (mostly) swimsuit fashion show by the pool and then sign autographs on our promotional photos. I had to wear an animal print unitard that made me look like a dehydrated leopard, but I attempted to infuse my prowl on the catwalk with some animal magnetism. We were also guest stars on a television show in which we wandered around town, with the *muy guapo* (very handsome) host, asking men, "¿Dónde está mi esposo?" (Where is my husband?) I never did track down my mate, but I sure did find some fantastic dance partners when we went nightclubbing Puerto Rican style. Let me tell you, all the men there can dance a mean Cha Cha and Merengue. *Muy bueno!*

****

When we returned to Los Angeles, I took my belongings out of storage and moved to a studio apartment across the hall from my dear sister, Cindy. Our high-rise building on Venice Boulevard in Culver City sat in a borderline, risky neighborhood. Several of the tenants were surely drug dealers. I didn't feel safe living alone but was comforted that Cindy was only a few doors away. This wasn't the idyllic, small-town, beachfront scenery of Del Mar, but seeing the Hollywood sign in the hills atop downtown L.A. sent a shiver of excitement over the possibility of hitting the big time. This was the place where dreams came true.

In general, Los Angeles had a distinctly different vibe than the San Diego area, and I tried to ascertain and absorb the unspoken rules of surviving in this City of Angels. Rule *numero uno:* You have to look good, preferably stunning. This Pretty Package includes having a golden tan, six-pack abs, well-toned biceps, the most up-to-date trendy haircut, and, for the women, a nice set of perky breasts (for the men, a Fabio-sized set of pecs). If you ain't got the goods, sympathetic locals may pity you enough to help you attain those qualities: "Why don't you come to the gym with me as my guest?" Or "Hey, I know a great hair salon." It's also best to have a personal trainer (and a therapist, while you're at it) if you wish to feel part of the tribe. Tourists, of course, are welcome to have pot bellies, bad hair days, and wear plus-size shirts that don't reveal their belly jewels; after all, TV shows are always looking for makeover candidates to transform.

Much of this obsession with looks had to do with movie star worship. Movie stars were America's royalty and Hollywood was Buckingham Palace. So over the top was our idolization of these über babes that you could start to feel like you were nobody if you weren't somebody. When you lived in L.A., you couldn't help but be influenced by Hollywood. Everywhere you looked were billboards advertising the latest films, movie stars, and wannabe movie stars or rock stars hoping to be discovered. Even if you didn't aspire to be a movie star, you most certainly wanted to look like one. I really couldn't think of a reason to live there unless you were a part of the film industry or servicing the people who were a part of the film industry. It was big business that commanded a lot of attention and admiration, deserved or not. That's why I was there, after all.

Rule *numero dos:* You need a reliable car, because you will absolutely *live* in it, although you won't necessarily drive many miles a day. Mostly you'll just sit in traffic sucking in smog and being honked at and sworn at in various languages by the multicultural community of drivers. Road rage was especially contagious in the overbearing heat of the summer. Automobile outings had to be planned somewhere in the window of about 10:00 a.m. and 2:00 p.m. if you wanted to actually move on the freeway. Otherwise, feel free to park on the 405 and enjoy the cement landscape for a few hours. Even a fifteen-mile drive could take an hour and a half under the right conditions, so you might as well get comfy in your vehicle.

An element of dreariness and danger underscored the vitality of Hollywood due not only to enraged drivers, terrible traffic jams, and oppressive heat waves, but also to shootings, gang violence, riots, smog, and threat of natural disasters including the all-time favorites: earthquakes, wild fires, and floods eroding homes into the sea. I was an impermanent fixture in an impermanent city. In the back of my mind, I recalled all the times scientists warned of the San Andreas fault and how California, in an involuntary act of secession, would one day break off from the contiguous United States and float around like a piece of flotsam and jetsam.

If the city did meet its demise, you could bet Los Angelenos were going to look their best for the occasion. They were on the cutting edge of fashion and fitness trends like Pilates, yoga, oxygen bars, vegetarianism, juicing, tofu, Tae Bo, tattoos, and Doc Martens. To fit in, you should adore a soy caffè latte in the morning followed by carrot-ginger juice and a light salad for lunch. And ix-nay on the smoking, eh? It was illegal in public places and not James Dean cool like it used to be. Breathing the L.A. air was toxic enough; ya didn't need cigarette smoke to add to the lung liability. You could up your trendiness even more by shopping on Melrose Avenue with the other pierced and tattooed patrons. *So that's where rock stars go to buy their spandex hot-pink-and-black leopard-print leggings.* No Midwestern sensible slacks, couch potato, and creamed chipped beef casseroles for me anymore. I wanted to be a non-smoking, smokin' hot, fit, and fashionable Los Angeleno.

****

Not knowing when my next gig would present itself, I thought, "Kristi, you'd better make some money and not just sit around twiddling your thumbs." Friends had told me about a temp agency called "All-Star" that serviced only movie, TV, film, and recording studios. It was a favorite of many wannabe actors who thought they might be discovered answering phones or typing on a computer. *I suppose it is a foot in the door, even if it is the wrong door.* I finally got the nerve up to go to the office and take the spelling and typing test. "You passed. You're hired," the lady announced. All I had to do was be available every workday during regular office hours.

Each morning at six, I arose, showered, styled my hair, and put on makeup. Since cell phones weren't yet affordable or popular, I had to stay in the apartment in case All-Star called. If by noon, I hadn't received a call, I would figure I wouldn't be getting called that day and could leave. I went absolutely nuts waiting. While desperately needing the money, I dreaded having to go somewhere unfamiliar to work and not knowing what my job would require and whether or not the other employees would be friendly. New Line Cinemas brought me in just to answer phones. That's all they expected me to be able to do, which was probably for the best. Mostly I just sat around twiddling my thumbs, but this time for money. Some people excel at it, but I deeply disliked being a secretary.

The day I worked at Warner Chappell Music on Santa Monica Boulevard was a bit more interesting. I seemed to be in the receptionist hot seat as the phones were ringing off the hooks. Apparently, whoever I was answering calls for was someone of great importance and popularity in the music industry. I was so flustered putting a zillion calls on hold and cutting people off while trying to transfer their calls that when the polite, frizzy blond-haired gentleman asked me to let Mr. So-and-so know he was here, I wasn't giving him my full attention. He told me his name the first time, which I forgot. "I'm sorry. What did you say your name was again?" "Sammy." That didn't seem to register either. A few more hundred phone calls later… "Excuse me sir, what did you say your last name was?" "HAGAR," he said with a chuckle. I turned red with embarrassment at my rock and roll faux pas. The man was one of three singers for the legendary rock group Van Halen. Duh! Luckily, he was extremely cool about my cluelessness.

My next experience was as the replacement for the administrative assistant for one of the Head Honchos at Twentieth Century Fox. The H.H. was out of town; I was left instructions to update the A.A.'s Filofax, which meant making all these dreadful calls to people who had no idea who I was and asking to verify their addresses and phone numbers. I hated doing it. Little did I know I'd really be in Hatesville when the boss phoned in. I answered cheerfully as I thought an administrative assistant should do. "WHO IS THIS?!" he yelled angrily. He was clearly offended by my jovial personality. (In his defense, perhaps I didn't sound professional enough.) My tone immediately changed to a woman on the defensive, and I was enraged. He was so rude that I left a note for the A.A.—who wanted me to take over for her once a week while she went back to school (good choice)—that "under no circumstances would I be caught dead working for someone as horrible as Mr. TV!" I was so brain dead and upset by the end of the day that I rear-ended a guy, well, really his car, on the way home. That was my last day temping. I decided I would rather starve.

I nearly did starve. My solution to my employment dilemma was to put as many of my expenses on my credit card as possible and save my dwindling cash reserves to write checks for bills and rent. Who knew how long it would be before I got another show, if I ever did get another show? How long should I hold out before giving up and getting a real job?

****

Yippee! I didn't have to wait too long before booking another Playboy gig, a whirlwind four-day excursion to Taipei, Taiwan. The trip was so short and sweet that our body clocks never reset to the new time zone; hence jet lag wasn't much of a problem. Our hotel, the luxurious Grand Hyatt Taipei, was a gorgeous site, with massive bouquets of fresh flowers welcoming its guests. Upon arrival, we sat down to an incredible, gourmet breakfast buffet. "This is the life!"

Again, our cast changed; this time we traveled with eight: Me, Jasmine, Callie, Satin, Athena, Lynda, Porsche, and our new addition, Kira—a tall, gorgeous brunette, 30-ish woman who had also been taking voice lessons from Kali and sang in an alternative rock band. She and I were backup singers/dancers for Lynda who was singing the sultry En Vogue song, "Never Gonna Get It." It was my job to teach Kira the choreography. Our costumes were black crushed-velvet shorty shorts, black bikini-type tops, and long, white satin gloves. Oooo, la, la! I loved doing that number.

Our biggest concern was Satin, who, after being on hiatus for a month, showed up on the first day of rehearsal considerably plumper than previously. Valerie was fit to be tied. Satin was still a bombshell, certainly, but her skimpy costumes didn't allow much room for expansion. Satin joked, "My boyfriend says I'm storing food for the winter." Val laughed nervously, her mind racing a mile a minute trying to figure out how to deflate her star Playmate's weight in a matter of days. Somehow Satin managed to pull it off (the surplus poundage and a great show). Constant weight-watching was a pitfall of our career; sometimes there was nothing more gratifying than saying, "Supersize it and, yes, I will take a cherry pie with that and an extra large order of fries." But we had to be willing to pay the consequences.

Our performances were held in the Hyatt Ballroom after attendees had enjoyed an exquisite gourmet dinner (duet of salmon, braised shark's fin with shredded abalone and crab roe, stir fried lobster, tangerine sherbet crowned with champagne, panfried beef tenderloin in garlic sauce with prawn and scallops). Sponsored by American Express, the first show was a classy affair; each ticket costing over $400 American. Everyone in our cast was friendly, and I was having a ball. After the performance, the important clients and producers wanted to snap a few photos with us in costume, and we willingly obliged.

Having traveled with Playboy for over six months by now, I felt relaxed, confident, and able to handle just about any performance in just about any costume with grace and style. Not that I endorse Playboy or pornography, but I have to admit that my Girls of Rock experiences definitely loosened me up and made me more comfortable with my sexuality and my body. I read an article in which Hugh Hefner claimed he had started *Playboy* in response to his repressive Midwestern Puritan upbringing, which was far from touchy-feely. Growing up in a loving but conservative, church-going Midwestern family myself, I felt sex as a conversation topic to be totally taboo and excruciatingly embarrassing. I always had the impression that it was wrong. Mind you, I've since realized that *every* person in church was the product of sexual intercourse. Even our pastors. And *every* person in church who had children (who weren't adopted) had actually *done it* themselves. (Except for the few cases of in vitro fertilization. But even in that situation, the father had to produce a sperm sample, and I wouldn't be surprised if a copy of *Playboy* magazine had been provided to help him in his pursuit.) Show business in general revered sexuality (perhaps too much at times). Even backstage, discussions about sex were normal and natural, tolerant and open. Sex was a delightful pleasure of being human and not something to be ashamed of. Love *is* a wonderful thing. Working in an environment in which sex and sex appeal were celebrated, and not a dirty secret, was liberating.

The second show was presented by the Hyatt itself, and the equally delectable meal featured "skillet chicken and corn salad, mussel and spinach mousse parcel in vermouth sauce, sherbet intermission, beef in oriental herb sauce, buttered asparagus, potato pancakes, pear and ginger with mascarpone frot in tulip, coffee, tea, chocolate cookies." They served us this very dinner after our show, and it was lick-your-plate-clean magnificent. Afterwards, we went dancing at a nightclub whose specialty drink was a chemist's container of test-tube iced vodka shooters. Ice, ice baby.

Long Legs and Tall Tales

Before leaving Taiwan, we managed to squeeze in a whirlwind day of sightseeing that included visits to the Chiang Kai-Shek Memorial, Soldier's Memorial, and the National Palace Museum, which showcased representative displays of the country's best ceramics, porcelain, calligraphy, painting, and ritual bronzes. I was disappointed to find that all the bargain Made-in-Taiwan items were already in America. Only outrageously expensive, foreign, designer goods remained in Taiwan. Consequently, I didn't do any shopping for myself this time.

Our hosts took us to a no-frills Taiwanese restaurant for the best Chinese food I've ever eaten. The giant lazy Susan in the middle of the table held a wide variety of individual dishes. We spun the wheel to sample anything and everything. It was all fresh and light and flavorful and delicious—none of those deep-fried nuggets slathered in thick, sweet and sour, super-sugary sauces like we get in America.

When we arrived back in L.A., Kira kindly inquired, "Kristi, do you need a ride home? My boyfriend is sending a car for me, and I'm sure you could come along, too." A sleek and shiny black limo materialized, compliments of her beloved. "What does your boyfriend do?" I asked, noting that this was a particularly elegant vehicle. "Oh, he's a drummer for the band Foreigner. They're rehearsing tonight, so he couldn't pick me up himself." My jaw dropped. "Whoa! Foreigner? I was really into that band when I was a teenager." *This is way too cool. Only in Hollywood.*

****

Now what? I didn't want my job with Playboy to end, but there were no firm show confirmations in sight. My credit card debt was piling up. I'd had it with temping and was going insane holed up in my one-room apartment, doors locked to keep out the supposed drug dealers. I was one slice short of a loaf, two cards shy of a full deck, and nearly out of my mind with boredom. Dance classes would have been a productive way to pass the time, but I couldn't afford them. Instead, I did aerobics in my apartment or rollerbladed along the beach, but it wasn't the same. What do you do when you can't go out and spend money? I did some drawing and painting to keep myself occupied, but I was losing it.

For one thing, I desperately craved social interactions. My sister was busy with her own boyfriend and her writing. My Playboy friends were spread out all over L.A. and the surrounding area. It generally took an hour and a half to drive a mere twenty miles, so meeting up wasn't a quick and easy prospect. Most of my few evenings out were spent with Body Guard Billy going to the San Fernando Valley—also known as "the Valley," where the term "Valley girls" comes from—to hear Kali's band play at classy restaurants with twinkly white lights in the trees. These outings were wonderful—like water for someone dying of thirst—but few and far between. After enjoying such a thriving social life both with Adam and friends in San Diego and then with the Playboy gang on tour, my new, solo, isolated, underemployed, city lifestyle was tremendously lonely. I was down to just enough money to make one more rent payment.

Final Scene: New York City, August 10, 2002

The tourists lined up for photos with the lovely Rockette, who perfectly posed and smiled graciously for each and every request. *I wouldn't miss everything about being a Rockette—the rehearsals and performances could be grueling—but being on the Roster with a guaranteed job, income, and health insurance sure felt great.* Before being hired by Radio City, I never knew where and when my next gig would turn up and, consequently, when I would receive my next paycheck. It could be a stressful way to live if you were the type to freak out about money. "I don't know how I survived all those crazy, uncertain years without having to take anti-anxiety meds," I thought to myself. The whole career was an exercise in learning to trust that the Universe would provide what I needed when I needed it. I had to find the security in insecurity. Still, I didn't look forward to going back to iffy employment. *Remember, Kristi, that somehow a job always appeared in time. Your new life will be different, but everything is going to turn out okay.*

"Would you like a picture, Ma'am?" the Rockette sweetly asked. "Sure," I answered. *Ma'am? Holy cow, it IS time to retire.*

Act 2, Scene 2

Let Me Be Your Sugar Baby

Again, being a bovine's backside with a good attitude paid off. Toni Kaye, the choreographer who had cast me as the back half of a cow in *Gypsy,* called to tell me she was choreographing *Sugar Babies II* and wanted me to audition. My guardian angel had answered my prayers again. The show was to be held in Atlantic City, New Jersey. Fine with me; I was game to travel just about anywhere. I almost had to be to survive. The audition came none too soon, as I was down to my last few hundred dollars in the bank. If I didn't get this show, I would have to find a real job to sustain me. I didn't even know what *real job* to look for. Temping made me insane, so that was out of the question. Waitressing I had never tried and never wanted to; I had enough obsessions with food and certainly didn't need to be carrying it around all day. Plus, the thought of serving rude Hollywood customers sent chills down my spine. *If I couldn't dance, what job would I do?* I choked at the thought of it. There was only one solution. I would have to get the gig.

The audition was held at the Pantages Theatre—a 2,700-seat, Art Deco, former vaudeville venue that opened in 1930 in Hollywood. I felt privileged just to be auditioning in such an amazing, artistic setting. Little did I know, that place would pale in comparison to the theatres to come in my future.

I wasn't so worried about the musical theatre dancing or the tap dancing, but I had to get through my singing audition. The director of the show was there, and instead of the typical sixteen bars, they asked to hear *all three verses* of my song. *Gulp.* Thank God, I was prepared. But I preferred skating by with a quick sixteen. I survived the song (Remember when I could hardly eke out a single verse? By now I was able to belt out over three times that much music!), and was asked to read for the part of the "Soubrette." I had not a clue what a soubrette was (the dictionary defines it as "a minor female role in a comedy, typically that of a pert maidservant") and wished I had researched the show before the audition. No one had ever asked me to read lines before. I hadn't the slightest idea how to act. "Maybe I should take some acting lessons, too?" I chided myself.

Needless to say, I did not get the part, but I did get the job! Including rehearsals, it was a three-month gig running from January 18 through March 17 at the Broadway by the Bay Theatre at Harrah's Casino in Atlantic City. The pay was a mere $450 a week, not enough to get rich off but enough that I wouldn't starve. I was going to be one of twelve "Sugar Babies"—a typical, girlie, ensemble, dancer part that I was comfortable with. I breathed a heavy sigh of relief. It was going to be tricky, but if I could make my last few hundred dollars stretch until rehearsals began a few weeks later, I could survive for the next three months. I put all my purchases including gas and food on my credit card and eagerly awaited rehearsals.

The rehearsals were held at the Alley Kat Studios in Hollywood. Every time I got a job, I had to get used to a new part of L.A., the traffic getting there, and the possible dangers surrounding the neighborhood. Most of L.A. felt sketchy to me in terms of safety, and this location followed suit. I was glad I was able to drive and did not have to take public transportation like in New York. L.A. was desperately trying to initiate a subway system, but people were still too attached to their cars. They chose their cars like they chose their designer clothes; it was another piece of their wardrobe and had to look good. I locked my doors as I drove through certain areas. Even the nice, upper-class neighborhoods, like Brentwood, weren't immune to car thefts. It's just as well people were stuck in their cars most the day, because as soon as a car was left alone for any length of time, someone stole it. I was begging for someone to swipe my old Ford Escort, but it was in such bad shape, all they did was steal the coins and the tools out of it.

I always delighted in seeing a new studio, and Alley Kat did not disappoint. Its interior was spacious with beautiful hardwood floors and red brick walls. When Toni Kaye had mentioned that Nederlander Theatre Corporation of Broadway fame would be producing the show and that it would be starring Juliet Prowse as "Prima Donna" and Rip Taylor as "Top Banana," I had phoned my parents to share my excitement. But it wasn't until I walked into the rehearsal studio and saw Juliet and Rip live and in person standing with the musical director by the piano that it really sank in. I couldn't believe my eyes!

Juliet was a stage, film, and television star, primarily famous for her exquisite dancing. She boasted an exotic background—born in India and raised in South Africa. I adored her in the 1960 movie musical *Can-Can* (her first film role), starring Frank Sinatra, Shirley MacLaine, Maurice Chevalier, and Louis Jourdan. At one time, she and Sinatra had been engaged. During the filming of the movie *G.I. Blues* (1960), in which she co-starred with Elvis, she and "The King" had had a hot, steamy fling. (That meant there was now only one degree of separation between Elvis Presley and me!) Talk about some high-profile ex-lovers. Now, at fifty-seven years of age, she was svelte and toned with perfect breasts and short red hair and was in a serious relationship with the stage manager of our production. I loved that she always carried her needlepoint with her in case she found time for a few, quick, stitches. It made her seem almost regular.

Rip, a heavyset gent with a wiry toupee (his crazy trademark hairstyle) and handlebar mustache, kept *us* in stitches. He was the confetti-throwing, "Crying Comedian" extraordinaire I had seen numerous times on television. His career spanned TV, the silver screen, and stages alike, with numerous spotlights on Vegas stages alongside such entertainment notables as Frank Sinatra, Debbie Reynolds, Sammy Davis Jr., Ann-Margaret, and Judy Garland. At nearly sixty years of age, he still was a hoot and a half. I was in awe of our stars. They were real people.

I scanned the room to see if I recognized anyone else. "There's Georgia from the Starlight Bowl!" I thought excitedly heading over to give a hug and hello. I sized up the other girls to see where I fit in. We were a real assortment of "Sugar Babies"—a dozen of us in all ages, shapes, and sizes. We were a mixed box of chocolates—all sweet but different flavored. The cast also included four youngish men who made up "The Gaiety Quartet," a handsome "Straight Man" (as in comedy straight, not heterosexual), a sexy "Soubrette," and an older gentleman (who reminded me a lot of comedian Don Knotts) playing the "2nd Banana." In addition, Michael Roloff and Company provided a variety act that involved balancing cylinders atop one another and then balancing him on a board like a teeter-totter on top of the rolling objects. It was a dangerous stunt that you shouldn't try at home. (I hope his mother doesn't know what he's up to.)

With Nederlander producing the show and Toni Kaye choreographing, I had no doubts about everything panning out. We even had Ralph Allen, the writer and director from the original *Sugar Babies* starring Mickey Rooney and Anne Miller, writing new comedy sketches for our show. However, the production, which was under A.G.V.A. jurisdiction, was overshadowed by a cloud of union problems and housing challenges. As we got closer and closer to the date of departure, the company manager still didn't have housing secured for us, and we still didn't have a contract.

An A.G.V.A. rep came to meet with us on our lunch breaks to help resolve our predicament. He was a nice guy who would listen to us gripe and then talk in circles and then have us so confused and then accomplish nothing. Or so it seemed. Who knows the calamities he was fighting on our behalf? Regardless, no one wanted to commit to a job when we didn't know what we were getting ourselves into. So we sat in on endless meetings to hear disgruntled union actors demanding a contract and concrete info on where we'd be living once in Atlantic City. One fantastic, beautiful dancer quit because she was a widowed mom and had a toddler who was coming with her. Naturally, she didn't want to take her tiny tot to New Jersey in the dead of winter with no place to stay. With little to lose, I decided it was worth the risk to sit tight and see what happened. Nothing was resolved, so the brave cast boarded the plane bound for the east coast with no inkling of where we'd rest our weary heads that night.

Once in New Jersey, we were taken straight to a real estate agent to look at rental properties. Although we'd be performing in Atlantic City, the most suitable housing they could find for us were beachfront condos on nearby Brigantine Island. Since I was only going to be gone a few months, I hadn't bothered finding someone to sublet my Los Angeles apartment; the thought of a stranger using my belongings didn't agree with me at all. Hence, I would have to pay double rent, which I couldn't afford.

Luckily, I was able to find three other girls in the cast who I barely knew but who were willing to share a three-bedroom condo and split the rent. Ashley was a short, shapely, funny, fetching blond singer about my age. Olivia was a delightful, solid, short-haired brunette and a fierce tap dancer in her early twenties. Brigitte, at a mere 18-years old, was a decade younger than I. She spoke fluent French, because her mother (who had also been a dancer and was even performing when pregnant with baby Brigitte) was French. Still very attached, Brigitte spent a good deal of her hard-earned cash phoning France to *"parler à sa maman"* (speak to her mom).

Other than Brigitte's homesickness, which often kept her alone in her room, the bunking arrangement worked out *très bien*, and Ashley and Olivia and I became *bons amis* (good friends). Our condo was gorgeous, as was the view, because we were situated on the beach. The ocean waves crashed onto the snow that covered half of the sand. My roommates and I spent a short time scouting for seashells in the snow, but it was bitter cold and windy. The winter there was the worst in years. *Brrr*! It was a good reminder of why I loved living in California. Several other cast members entered their condos only to find that their pipes had frozen. They were without water for days.

About three days after our arrival, we awoke to frantic phone calls and terrifying television reports of the L.A. earthquake that killed people in Northridge and left cars and trucks stranded on overpasses that were breaking in pieces. Those of us from the cast who came from L.A. spent the day attempting to contact loved ones. I had a colossal pit in my stomach as I tried to find out if my sister had survived. Learning that she was okay was a tearful, prayerful moment. And, of course, we still had to perform that night with smiles on our faces and be hilariously funny. The earthquake was a reminder of why I *hated* living in California. My apartment was a mess, but I felt so fortunate that none of my posse was hurt. My darling sister cleaned up the dish shards, broken glass, sugar, and water on my apartment floor, which had hardened into a mosaic of sweet cement. Prior to leaving for Atlantic City, a tremor had knocked me off my bathroom counter where I was sitting while putting on makeup. In retrospect, it had been an eerie foreshadowing of the impending disaster to follow. I was glad to be safe on solid New Jersey soil.

****

Sugar Babies Act II was a burlesque-style musical revue patterned after the old vaudeville shows. A combo of old-fashioned burlesque and vaudeville-style comedy sketches and song and dance numbers, it was campy and cheesy and perfect for a casino audience who just wanted to have a good time and not think too hard. A longer version of the show had been originally performed over a decade earlier starring Mickey Rooney and Anne Miller and then again about five years later at Harrah's starring Rip Taylor and Carol Lawrence. Now Rip was back at it with the lovely Juliet as his leading lady.

Our show, set in "The Gaiety Theatre," was pure mirth, jocularity, and clowning around. It opened circus-style with all the cast members dressed as different crazy characters—belly dancer, acrobat, fireman. Lucky me, I got chosen to be an enormously big-busted nurse. The ridiculously buxom, white uniform had the massive mammaries built right in. I was so top-heavy, it's a wonder I didn't fall forward, flat on my face. Had I been a real nurse, that protruding bosom would have certainly gotten in the way of proper medical care.

Our *Sugar Babies* theme song, "Let Me Be Your Sugar Baby," was absolutely adorable. The lyrics let the audience know we could satisfy their sweet tooth like a lollipop, fudge sundae, danish pastry, strudel, or even a crepe suzette. To make us appear even sweeter (and to emphasize the "baby" theme), we wore baby blue and pink, corsette-style costumes with pink lace-up boots and baby bonnets. This cutesy, girlie-girl number included what was to be an applause-generating kick line. However, we could never seem to get our kicks in sync, and the stage manager constantly called us in to rehearse. It became extremely frustrating. *Who knew it was so difficult to do a good kick line?*

The girls also performed "In Louisiana"—a song about travelin' by train back to that marvelous state we loved so much. We did a fun, lighthearted tap dance wearing negligees (what else?) and carrying suitcases for sittin' a spell or tapping upon. Then there was the comedic Salute-to-Sally-Rand fan dance in which we cleverly used giant leaves to strategically cover what appeared to be our naked bodies (but were really nude-colored unitards) in yet another Garden of Eden-type scene. In addition, I got to do a short comedy gag with my "husband"—an actual acting bit! One night I got the hiccups right before going on stage. As we entered from the hotel kitchen, the empathetic waitstaff frantically brought me water, made me hold my breath, and scared me in a series of attempts to stop the spasms. Finally, just in time, the mixture of remedies seemed to do the trick. I was still afraid I was going to blurt out a horrible sound right in the middle of the punch line, but, thanks to the food service workers, I made it through without so much as a hiccup.

Our enormous, full-cast finale was a lively, tambourine-shaking, banjo-strumming "Mr. Banjo Man" number. We wore white gloves, obnoxiously bright red and hot pink jackets and top hats, and lime-green and turquoise-blue striped spandex pants. We did snazzy choreography with the tambourines while, at one point, backlighting added to the excitement and our gloves and pant stripes glowed in the dark. The 2nd Banana did the exhausting Mr. Banjo Man solo. He had to pretend-play his banjo, sing, and dance his heart out all at the same time. Afterward, as he huffed and puffed, he told me, "I always choreograph breaths into the aerobically challenging numbers, so I don't forget and keel over." He was a riot, and I took his good advice to heart, remembering to strategically breathe at certain points in my show.

Our entire production was a ball to perform, the only downside being the Sugar Babies' fast costume change into the "In Louisiana" tap dance. We had so little time, all twelve of us had to strip down in the wings. Oddly enough, over time, the men on stage crew magically appeared just in time to catch a bit of T and way too much A. It got to be so obvious and such a problem that I complained to the stage manager, "This is not supposed to be a free peep show!" The lack of professionalism made me mad, and the stage manager finally made sure we had the privacy we deserved.

****

Harrah's Casino, situated on the water and accessible by boat, sat just over the bridge from Brigantine Island. We had a company van to take us to work, or we could call a taxi, but walking three miles in the frigid cold was out of the question. With only one van at the entire cast's disposal, it was too difficult to go into town for every meal, so we ate brunch at home and dinner at Harrah's employee cafeteria where we dined for free. We also had access to the hotel's tiny, cruddy, workout room, and between shows a few of us Sugar Babies would sometimes ride the stationary bikes or walk the treadmills looking ridiculous in our full show makeup, fake eyelashes, and baseball caps. With two shows a day at 3:00 p.m. and 8:00 p.m., we didn't have enough time to make trekking back to the condo between shows worthwhile, so we filled our break by eating, working out, and shopping at the employee gift store for Harrah's paraphernalia at a discounted price.

Juliet, a devout follower of Bikram, the famous hot yoga guru in L.A., gave herself a yoga class everyday at the hotel and eventually invited the cast to join her. The hotel manager kindly agreed to let us use an empty conference room. Every day, a group of us devoted two hours before the first show to working off our asanas by doing poses such as half moon, eagle, triangle, tree, cobra, bow, tortoise, camel, and rabbit. *Pavanamuktasana*, the "wind-removing" pose, was the most fearsome; Juliet told stories about masses of people involuntarily farting in Bikram's class. But if you purposefully wanted to remove a painful gas bubble, this was a miracle cure. This yoga series was also a miracle cure for my knees, which had gotten so bad from the cement stage that I could no longer even jump. I was really worried until the yoga cleared that problem right up. Juliet was so kind and generous to teach us. She was always trying to coerce Rip into joining in because he had a lot of back pain. He finally did (I hope it helped). I felt privileged to be posing with the stars.

Rip was a character whose humor could be off-beat and unpredictable, making interactions with him perpetually surprising. He had a handsome, young, male assistant who would cater to his every whim and fetch him his fur coat. How Hollywood glamorous! Seeing that Rip was such a wild card, I never knew quite how to handle him. Juliet, on the other hand, could tame even the wildest of beasts with her charming, nurturing ways. She had a soothing quality about her that Rip responded well to, as did the rest of the cast. Rip, too, had a generous, sweet side and was always showering the Sugar Babies with little presents. Every few days some new Harrah's gift store item would appear on our dressing room spots: a clock, a thermometer, chocolate gold coins, a key chain, courtesy of Mr. Taylor.

I was impressed that Rip also joined us before each show for the prayer circle that was started by Georgia. (Showbiz people are very spiritual and superstitious.) The cast members would stand in a circle holding hands and someone would pray to the theatre gods (an all-inclusive, non-exclusive, nonreligious way to be sort of religious) to ensure a good show, or to help someone who was sick or injured, or whatever we felt we needed to pull off that night's performance. I think it helped. At the very least it gave us a positive attitude and made us feel more like a team.

It goes without saying, but I will say it anyway: Rip was a master at physical comedy, and it was a treat to watch him do his thing. In a particularly hilarious scene called "Hearts of Stone," he was a park statue lamenting his life, as real, live, pigeons perched all over his body, leaving their mark as well. A pigeon trainer had trained half a dozen birds (Krieg-James Theatrical Birds) to fly from the wings onto the stage and sit right on Rip's head and shoulders and, well, let rip. His facial expressions were priceless. That he was even willing to be pooped on by a flock of pigeons to get a laugh showed what a great sport he was. He was a terrific performer, and the crowd loved him.

I, too, loved watching his comedy sketches with Juliet including "Bored of Education," in which she, playing the strict school marm, scolded Rip, the naughty, young schoolboy; and "The Court of Last Retort," a scene replete with double entendres in which Juliet, a provocative murder defendant, used her luscious legs to taunt the corruptible, joking judge, played by Rip. Rip was a master of comedic timing and of squeezing as much hilarity out of a gag as possible. While Juliet successfully brought her own brand of humor to the bits, she was mesmerizing in the song and dance numbers.

This woman spelled class, all the way. Always happy and gracious, she never displayed a negative attitude. When the musical director periodically called her in to practice her singing, which wasn't always perfectly on pitch, she never had an ego about it. Instead, she rehearsed with a smile on her face. What a professional. She even went bowling with us and took the entire cast out for Mexican food. She was star quality as a performer and a human being.

****

Working in Atlantic City with two famous headliners was especially fun, because other stars, friends of Juliet and Rip, came to see them in our show, and the cast got to meet some of them. For instance, when famous Broadway musical theatre actress Chita Rivera and screen and stage star Jerry Orbach watched the show, they came backstage. Some of us returned the favor by going to New York City on our day off to see Chita star in *Kiss of the Spider Woman* on Broadway, and she schmoozed with us after the show. She was a class act and very gracious. Another ultra-exciting moment at Harrah's was when former teen idol Davy Jones from the band and TV show *The Monkees* was in our audience. He was my first crush when I was five years old! (Who could resist that charming British accent?) Suddenly, I found myself too busy monkeying around (and singing the Monkees' theme song) to put my enthusiasm for my heartthrob down.

We got so bold that, if the stars didn't come to us, we went to them. When we discovered that Charo was performing in Atlantic City, a few of the Sugar Babies got tickets to see her. Her real name was María del Rosario Mercedes Pilar Martínez Molina Baeza, but she had become so famous (like Cher, Madonna, and Jesus) that people now recognized her by that single moniker. The super sexy, big-breasted, diminutive, Spanish American (famous for her catch phrase "Cuchi-Cuchi!") was also an amazing flamenco guitar player and singer. She was such a stellar performer that I was inspired to buy her CD. We wanted to meet her, so we name-dropped. "We're performing in *Sugar Babies* with Rip Taylor and Juliet Prowse and would like to say hello to Charo." It worked! She chatted with us for over a half hour *in her dressing room*. Just listening to her talk in her thick, Spanish accent with the rolled Rs was entertaining enough. Charo was hilarious and complained, "My see-sterrrr won't let me eat, because eef I weigh overrrr one-hundrrrrred-and-one pounds, I cannot feet into my costumes." I understood her sister's point—Charo's skimpy outfits looked to be stretched to capacity as it was. There was a lot of spunk, talent, and passion in that tiny package. Cuchi-Cuchi!

******

The Sugar Babies were sweet gals who taught me some cool tricks. My roommate Ashley and I became especially close. She showed me how to make a quick, healthy, delicious meal of brown rice topped with black beans and salsa (and shredded cheese for you dairy folks)—one of her staple, go-to meals at the condo.

Maya was the comedy relief in the dressing room; she was always showing off her perfect Arabesque *penchée*—a ballet move in which you lean forward on one leg while raising the back leg high in the air (she was so freakishly flexible, she could make her legs mimic the six-o'-clock position of hands on a clock, like standing splits)—and her grotesquely real, crazed gorilla imitation.

Vivian loved to tap. She had studied with hoofing legend Henry Le Tang in Vegas and taught me a bunch of fabulous tap combos. Before the show or between shows, we'd get on stage in our tap shoes and practice. We paradiddled, maxie forded, flapped, cramp rolled, chugged, shuffled, triple time-stepped, winged, pulled back, and riffed our way to happiness. It really helped improve my tap skills.

June was a flaming redhead and a progressive feminist. She taught us about being goddesses, how a man should please a woman in bed before pleasing himself, and how to sew reusable maxipads out of soft flannel. (Not only were they better for your body and the environment, but rinsing pads off onto droopy plants gave them precisely the pick-me-up they needed. Who knew? I wasn't sure I was that committed to my body, the environment, or my Ficus, but I was impressed that June was.) Once again, the dressing room was a safe setting for discussions of all things girlie and sexy, no matter how intimate.

When a group of us were in NYC seeing *Kiss*, June (an avid salsa dancer) inspired us to go along with her to a Brazilian nightclub. The salsa was so spicy that my dance partner was moved to passionately kiss me smack in the middle of our "quick-quick slow" steps. As a result of having been attacked walking down an L.A. street alone, June had taken self-defense classes and offered to teach us, too. I learned the most effective way to kick a guy in the cohones (and get away with it). Her shocking tips and pro-female perspective took me from feeling like the weaker sex to feeling like an empowered goddess.

One time June auditioned for a singing gig only to get the humiliating feedback, "You might want to use your lunch money to buy voice lessons." How rude. But instead of just going home to cry into her beer, that's exactly what she did. Eventually, she landed a job as a singer on a cruise ship. That's what I call turning a negative into a positive. You hear lots of criticism over time in this business, and you have to learn to separate the good advice from the baloney. Then if it's not baloney, you have to do something about it. June took the "I'll show you who can sing!" attitude instead of wallowing in self pity and admitting defeat. You have to have thick skin for rejection, but be wise and clearheaded enough to examine the comments to see if the casting people have a point.

Marty was the life of the party. For her birthday, the cast presented her with a male stripper-gram. I've never seen anyone more excited about unwrapping a present. Marty and her package hit it off so well, they ended up dating and kept right on exchanging gifts.

Annabelle was one of the older, wiser, showbiz veterans whom I looked up to as a mentor. She knew how to survive in the business, but she also knew how to squeeze the most fun out of it. I was delighted to discover that she traveled from show to show with her little parakeet named Lenny. Her claim to fame was her distinctive, high, squeaky voice that won her commercial voiceovers and even became the speaking voice for toy dolls. She had an apartment in Manhattan where she generously let us stay when a bunch of us Babies went to see *Kiss*.

As a seasoned, union professional, Annabelle kept a close eye on our working conditions and was often alerting A.G.V.A. about some misdemeanor. She knew what her rights were. Many, like me, were just babies and hadn't a clue. For instance, our show run time was always going over the allotted ninety minutes, so our elected A.G.V.A. reps kept a record of what time the show started and finished each night. We got paid extra for overtime, so there was a lot of clock watching.

****

Most of our days were pretty routine: wake up at noon, eat breakfast, go to Harrah's, do yoga, do the first show, eat dinner, do the second show, go back to the condo. My roommates and I could never fall asleep after our second show so we always stayed up until 3:00 a.m. watching reruns of *Thirtysomething* and munching microwave popcorn.

Then we'd sleep until noon, eat something, and start the cycle all over. Without a car, we were stuck at the condo or Harrah's much of the time. So when my family and friends announced that they were coming to visit, I was as happy as a clam (a Florida clam, not a New Jersey clam, because those poor mollusks had to survive the harsh, Northeastern winters, and I'm quite sure they weren't all that cheerful). My mom, dad, grandma, Great Aunt Violet, Aunt Jean, and Uncle Terry came to see the show as did my sorority sister and her husband. It was such fun having them in the audience and then getting to introduce them to Juliet and Rip and the rest of the cast. We gambled a bit, ate salt-water taffy on the boardwalk, visited the Trump Taj Mahal Casino, and picked out the streets found in the Monopoly game. Atlantic City was a happening place after all.

In addition to being a tourist destination itself, Atlantic City was also a great home base because we were close enough to head to NYC or Philadelphia on our days off. Like our show, most professional musical theatre shows were dark only once a week, so performers had learned how to milk every second out of their minimal time off. We considered each day off to start the second the show ended, and even made preparations during the show in order to ensure the quickest exit from the theatre, thereby maximizing our precious free time. What we really needed to do was sleep in until noon, then lounge around in our jammies all day resting our weary muscles, sipping herbal tea, and watching a good movie, followed by a hot soak in the tub and a good night's rest. Instead, we squeezed more activity into those free hours than seemed remotely possible.

On one day off, for example, two of my roomies and I managed to hitch a ride to Philadelphia (only about 62 miles away) with a young couple from our show who had a car—a rare and precious commodity. "Road trip!" We crammed in as many highlights as we could in the short time we were there: We took a carriage ride, saw the Liberty Bell and the site of the signing of the Declaration of Independence, ate the best coconut cake in town at the Old Original Bookbinder's restaurant, toured the Norman Rockwell museum, and feasted on famous Philly cheesesteaks.

In February, we had a rare, couple days off while country music singer Barbara Mandrell took over our stage, so I boarded a bus to the Big Apple (about a two-hour ride) to see my old pal, Jenny. I had a taxi waiting to take me to the bus terminal immediately after the show to catch the late bus to New York City. The characters who rode that night bus seemed creepy and strange, and arriving at the Port Authority terminal by myself in the middle of the night was also creepy and strangely quiet. Thankfully, I felt much more aware and street-smart than when I lived there, and I had no problem hailing a cab to Jenny's. The city felt different to me—less terrifying. It probably hadn't changed much, but apparently I had.

Jenny was currently taking a break from performing, opting instead to serve as executive director of the Broadway Bach Ensemble (a New York City orchestra that offered free concerts) and work coat check at an upscale bistro. We had a ball taking dance classes, shopping, and reminiscing. Best of all was our day of pampering at the Russian-Turkish baths. The steam room, hot and cold pools, and fresh carrot-ginger juice were just what the doctor ordered. Don't get the wrong impression; this was no luxury spa for manicured ladies who lunch. A lot of professional dancers frequented the baths as necessary therapy to rejuvenate their sore and suffering bodies. A lot of heavy, hairy Turkish men also used the baths as part of their regular health routines. It wasn't a pretty place but it was functional. Maybe next time I'll get the special treatment where men in diapers and turbans smack you with eucalyptus branches in the steam room. Maybe not. (Who thought of that anyway?) The Rolfing session I had with the butch, Russian woman was enough of a smack down for one day. Afterwards, I met my friend Bobby, our DJ from Celebration Magnifico, for a wonderful night on Broadway to see *Crazy for You* and have dinner in Little Italy. It was great to be entertained by someone else for once. The next day, I spent a few hours marveling at masterpieces in the Metropolitan Museum of Art, then loaded up on fresh bagels and goodies from Zabar's Deli before bussing back to Atlantic City in time for our show.

****

When *Sugar Babies* ended, the cast had a closing party in which everyone gathered at my condo with their leftover food. We ate strange combinations of lingering tidbits. Annabelle talked me into helping her create silly awards for everyone, and we presented all the Sugar Babies with packages of Sugar Babies candy-coated milk caramels. We ended the evening with a ceremonial ritual in which we decorated the outside of a shoe box with positive words indicating what we wanted in our lives (love, prosperity, happiness, oneness, compassion, peace of mind, charity, hope, tranquility, acceptance, truth, laughter) and filled the inside with personal lists of what we wanted *out of* our lives. Then we tossed it into the fireplace and watched it burn. It was hard saying goodbye to this wonderful cast, but since many lived in Los Angeles, we vowed to get together back home.

I had decided to fly to Michigan first to visit my family for a week before heading to L.A., and my flight was leaving later than the flights of most of the rest of the cast. Juliet, who was also taking a later trip, found out and said, "Kristi, why don't you ride in the limo with me so you don't have to wait around the airport by yourself all those hours?" That was the kind of person she was. Of course, I took her up on her generous offer and enjoyed every glorious minute basking in the light of this shining star.

Final Scene: New York City, August 10, 2002

"Would everyone like to take a peek into the Rockette dressing room?" the Rockette asked, her hand on the doorknob. We all enthusiastically shook our heads "yes," and she obligingly allowed us into her privileged, private, wonderful world. There should have been violins singing and trumpets blaring like a movie score announcing the momentousness of the occasion. *Do these people know how lucky they are to witness this?* The lovely dressing room was neat and tidy; it was clearly the off-season. *If only they could be a fly on the wall during peak performance time. Then they'd really have something to write home about.*

Seeing the ocean-blue carpet with the swirly wave pattern, the rose red walls and matching upholstered chairs, the cloud-white counters, and light-bulb rimmed mirrors made me want to dance there. I was impressed by the Rockettes and other entertainers who could handle Manhattan and make it their home. I had tried taking a bite out of the Big Apple, but it had been more than this mild-mannered Midwesterner could chew. California had seemed much more palatable. Little did I know, New York City's hectic lifestyle wouldn't shake me up nearly as much as a genuine California earthquake.

Act 2, Scene 3

The Love Boat

Long Legs and Tall Tales

Since The Big One hit L.A., I was absolutely terrified to be back there. Driving over bridges, waiting in traffic under overpasses, or entering tall buildings left me shakin' in my boots for fear of earthquakes. I worried about the priceless antiques that might tumble off my shelves, how to secure my kitchen cupboards to keep my fine China from catapulting onto the floor, and whether the pictures I hung over my bed would kill me if they fell on my head during the night. I simply would have done just about anything to leave.

Once again, my prayers were answered and my ship came in. A week after my return home, Anita Mann's office called. "We'd like for you to come in and audition for a cruise ship job. It's a five-month contract sailing mostly around Alaska." Yes! I had never even considered traveling to Alaska, but I jumped at the chance to leave shaky Los Angeles. This was one boat I did not want to miss. The audition gods were on my side, and I landed the gig. The icing on the cake was that I was hired as a *singer*-dancer. At a whopping $750 per week, the pay was considerably higher than the $275 per week I was offered only to dance for another cruising company. Singers generally got paid a better wage. Wasn't I smart to take voice lessons?

The cast consisted of a mere six people—three men and three women. Fortunately, we were all between the ages of 24 and 32. Performers on ships are often much younger, making the atmosphere like the immature drama of high school. Being such a small group, everyone would have to pull his or her weight to pull off the performances. There was no room for slackers.

Our job was to learn two full-length ninety-minute shows, entitled "Let's Dance!" and "Birth of the Blues," and two twenty-minute "bumpers"—basically short, warm-up acts where we bumped up against whatever other headline entertainment was happening. "The Tonight Medley" bumper featured classy, elegant songs like "Tonight" from *West Side Story*. The other bumper was a glitzy, hip-swiveling Elvis medley entitled "Viva Las Vegas."

"Let's Dance!" featured songs and dances from the 1940s through the 1990s. It included everything from an homage to Fred Astaire and Ginger Rogers to a '40s swing dance to a '50s/'60s medley featuring the hand jive, the mash potato, the twist, the alligator, the watusi, and the monster mash (actually, this was basically the same number the singers did in the Playboy show that I had been dying to do) to a country medley, a tropical Latin medley, and a medley from *A Chorus Line*. There were medleys within medleys. Our cruise ship shows were all about medleys, assuming the audience had the attention span of a three-year-old and couldn't listen to a song in its entirety. If someone didn't like a certain tune, they'd only have to suffer through a snippet of it before we moved onto something else.

Choreographers and dancers from previous casts taught us the choreography, some from memory, others by pulling it directly off old videotapes. Learning the dance numbers was a ball. They were high energy and high octane. The show was boatloads of fun. I even got to sing a solo in the *A Chorus Line* medley. It was only a short and sweet few verses from "The Music and the Mirror," but I wanted to shine singing it. I wanted, at the very least, to not completely embarrass myself singing it.

Unlike "Let's Dance!" which was a vintage Anita show that had been successfully executed by many casts before we got our hands (and feet) on it, "Birth of the Blues" was a brand spanking new baby that was created for us and choreographed on us for the very first time in the history of the world, amen. We even got gorgeous, new costumes dreamed up for us by Emmy Award-winning designer Pete Menefee! (This prolific, versatile artist had clothed showgirls, entertainers, and celebrities galore, including Michael Jackson, Kiss, Diana Ross, and Elvis. His jaw-dropping, jewel-dripping, feathered fashions were featured on stage, screen, television, ice rinks, and at the Olympic Ceremonies. Fabulous!)

While performing in the original cast was an absolute thrill, delivering a new production was also a considerable challenge. Starting from scratch and figuring out what works and what doesn't can be a tedious process of trial and error that can have you singin' the blues if you can't go with the flow. "Birth of the Blues" featured an "All That Jazz" tribute, a New Orleans Dixieland medley, a section on George Gershwin and the Blues, Rhythm and Blues, Women and Blues ("I'm A Woman," "Respect," "Lady Is a Tramp"), Country Blues, and a sizzling "Le Jazz Club" finale (including "Le Jazz Hot," "Hit Me with a Hot Note," "Sweet Georgia Brown," "Caravan," "Minnie the Mooch," "Jump Shout Boogie," and more).

Between the two big production numbers and the two bumpers, there were oodles of songs and dances, harmonies, lyrics, and choreography to keep track of. When learning the first number of a show, my brain seemed to be in control. "I can remember this. This is easy." After being taught four or five numbers, however, I'd start to confuse similar parts in different numbers and forget which number started on which foot or from which wing. I bought an oversized three-ring binder to house my sheet music, and on my breaks I'd jot down as much of the choreography as I could for later reference. Sometimes we had choreography shoved at us so fast that we'd learn a number one day and not come back to it until a few days later. After learning several other numbers in the interim, it was nearly impossible to accurately remember the first number. Hence, my detailed notes and dancing stick-figure drawings were a necessity.

Unfortunately, birthing a new show took longer than expected; even laboring overtime past midnight during the final week of rehearsals, we couldn't complete that baby before we had to leave Los Angeles for the ship. "Don't worry. The cruise director promised me you won't have to do the show until you are ready. We'll finish on board," Anita assured us. "There's no pressure to perform it right away. Other entertainers can fill in." We didn't sweat it too much. What choice did we have, anyway?

****

MS *NOORDAM*

Ship's Registry: The Netherlands
Passenger capacity: 1,924
Crew members: 800
Gross Tonnage: 82,318 grt.
Length: 936 feet
Beam: 105.8 feet
Maximum speed: 24 knots

The cast flew to San Francisco to meet what was to be our floating (hopefully) home for the next five months—Holland America Line's MS *Noordam*. First, we'd sail up to our home port of Vancouver, British Columbia. Then every two weeks the ship would sail north from Vancouver along the "inside passage" of Alaska to Ketchikan, Juneau, Sitka, Valdez, and Seward, and back down to Vancouver again.

Walking up the plank to board this monstrous sailing vessel, I thought, "Oh, Kristi. What have you gotten yourself into?" I felt a blend of excitement, trepidation, and outright fear. This was such a strange world I was entering—a floating world with lots of rules and restrictions. I didn't know what to expect but I knew that nearly half a year could go by slowly in the confines of a ship you despise. But there was no way I was going to stay in L.A. Anchors away!

While I knew this was an opportunity of a lifetime, cruising life freaked me out at first. For starters, as is prudent, we were immediately corralled, along with all the newly embarked passengers, to take part in a lifeboat drill. This wasn't just a one-time event. For every new cruise, we were required to attend the drill and assist each fresh group of passengers. Skipping out wasn't an option, as failing to show up meant answering to The Captain on The Bridge. Just watch the movie *Titanic*, however, and you too would put up with wearing the awkward orange life vests each week and directing clueless passengers to make sure everyone has a spot reserved on a boat, even if you already knew the drill. One ship in our fleet actually did run aground in Alaska. It hit an island. How the captain managed to miss seeing such a big chunk of dirt is beyond me, but it just goes to show you that accidents happen, and it's wise to be prepared.

During drills, our ship actually lowered a couple of lifeboats holding crew members into the water to make sure all was in working order. Castmates cautioned me, "Don't let them put you in a lifeboat! People have gotten injured on the way down." Their warning may have been pure hogwash, but those boats did have a long, intimidating vertical drop. If an inept crewmember "controlled" the ropes that lowered a boat, that boat could jerk all over the place or plummet into shark-infested waters at high speed. I was terrified I'd get chosen to take the plunge.

It was scary when I dwelled on all the possible dangers of a ship, like, God forbid, crashing into an iceberg (or island), a fire starting in the kitchen, or someone falling asleep while smoking in bed. If we were out to sea at the time, we'd be trapped with nowhere to go. I hoped and prayed we had a competent captain and crew.

Another big concern of mine was the potential for seasickness. Simply riding in a car sometimes nauseated me. Even swinging on playground swings left me uncomfortably dizzy. The ship was Queasy City. I had to "get my sea legs" before I could begin to tackle any of the other challenges before me. "Keep your stomach full," I was advised, if I wanted to avoid being green around the gills. That seemed counterintuitive, but I did as I was told and armed myself with loads of graham crackers and apples plus seasickness pills and special wrist bands that somehow helped by putting pressure on pulse points. I had a pounding, persistent hangover, but at least this combo of curatives kept me from puking and falling faint. Thankfully, after about four days, I was able to wean myself off the drugs, toss my wristband to the wind, and eat at my leisure.

Those first few days were crazy madness dealing with seasickness and the dreaded lifeboat drills, getting lost among the multi-level maze of corridors, and adjusting to our new quarters in general. Meanwhile, we continued rehearsing "Birth of the Blues," but the only time the stage was available to rehearse was the middle of the night. So we became sleep deprived as well.

Our jaws dropped to the floor when Anita announced, "As it turns out, the cruise director needs the show right away, so we'll be performing 'Birth of the Blues' tonight." *Shiver me timbers!* Panic. Nervous breakdown. Cold sweats. The pressure was on. We had to make it work, make it happen, make Anita proud, and, most importantly, keep from making complete fools of ourselves. Anita could sense we were frozen with fear. "You can do it. You'll be fine," she said trying to instill confidence. But even she didn't know what to expect. This show felt like a sinking ship.

The cast was scarfing down a quick dinner and reviewing the show in our heads when my roommate, Candy, and I had the startling realization that we hadn't even completed one number. "We don't have an ending for 'Twist and Shout!' What do we do?" Thankfully, my Celebration Magnifico training in spontaneity came to the rescue. Candy and I made an executive decision and gathered the rest of the cast. "Let's all improv at the end of the number and watch each other to signal a final pose." All shook heads in agreement.

I've never felt so ill prepared, so mentally taxed, and so panic-stricken at show time. We barely knew how to manage our costume changes let alone perform the show. We were trying to memorize choreography, harmonies, words to songs, how to enter and exit stage, where to preset costume pieces, which costume pieces to wear for which numbers, and the order of the numbers in the show. Our memory banks were overloaded and shutting down. We had no mental storage left.

The girl's costume for "Birth of the Blues" was a beautiful, rhinestone-studded, crushed velvet, royal blue leotard to which we added and subtracted various spectacular skirts, coats, hats, gloves, bracelets, earrings, necklaces, fans, feather boas, and parasols for a clever change of appearance. We rushed to make cheat sheets for all the numbers so we'd know what to put on and what to take off. Every cast member was in some portion of almost every number, leaving literally seconds in which to change costume pieces and return to stage. What were we thinking with the cheat sheets? We had no time to read them and nowhere to put them. There wasn't time to pop in and out of a dressing room, so we'd have to dress at different places surrounding the stage. We preset our quick-change costume pieces in the halls and hoped no passengers swiped them for souvenirs. Working out the logistics of presets and costume changes was a major fiasco of its own.

Adding to the "fun" were the cordless microphones and "micography" (microphone choreography). Remembering which hand to hold our mic with and which hand to have free for choreography was a befuddling brainteaser. In L.A., we practiced with wooden dowel rods as pretend mics. Singing into a real one and hearing yourself through the monitors was an entirely different experience. Plus they were slippery little devils when your hands got sweaty. An exuberant arm flick sent many a mic flying out of someone's hand and crashing down the stairs to the dance floor below all the while amplifying each contact with the ground for the audience to hear.

The clock quickly ticked down. Before we knew it, we were made up and in costume, and the show was getting underway. As the intro played, I felt as if I would actually die from embarrassment right there on stage. During some numbers, I felt I preferred death to performing. Can you imagine the horror of being on stage and forgetting the words to your song? Slam dancing the person next to you who is exiting the right way while you try to dance off the wrong way? Being the only one on stage in only a leotard without the skirt, because you preset it on the wrong side of the stage and had no time to retrieve it? Forgetting your choreography and just standing there dumbfounded? Accidentally flinging your mic into the audience and having to pantomime singing into a pretend mic for the rest of the show?

The show must go on. And so it did. We sang and danced in some form or another to every number. We filled the space of ninety excruciatingly-long minutes with some form of entertainment. We faked it until we made it. We actually lived through that terrifying performance in spite of flubs and flaws. What I learned from that mortifying experience: Chill. You won't die of embarrassment. A year later the whole darn mess will be a funny story in your book of tall tales. You might as well laugh and get on with it and do the best you can. The worst part was that we still had to finish and rehearse the show. We still had ages before we would feel comfortable and get in our groove. We still had to repeat that experience twice a week for the next five months. And we still had "Let's Dance!" to debut that week as well as the two bumpers. Our job was far from over.

High energy seemed to be Anita's secret to a successful show, so all the songs were played at warp speed (any zippier and we would have sounded like Alvin and the Chipmunks), and the dancing couldn't be done big enough or fast enough. Our shows were so dynamic that people could have had heart attacks simply from watching us. Either that or the particularly worn-out patrons would actually sleep through most of the production. You see, the average age of our passengers was about 72. A tuckered-out gent would be snoring away in the front row, and we'd dance over and tap him on the shoulder. Startled, he'd awaken from his dream only to find himself in the middle of a nightmare of forced audience participation. (We could be devilish and sneaky.) Part of me was offended that our show put some to sleep—not exactly the reaction we were going for. But, more likely, they were overstimulated and exhausted by our relentless, high-speed, breakneck movements. Those poor, tired souls deserved to relax and get a decent nap in, and if I could help them in that pursuit, all the better. With so many people wheeling oxygen tanks behind them, I hoped our show wasn't to die for. It would have been awful to hear the announcement of a "Bright Star" over the intercom—code that someone had passed away.

The old folks weren't the only ones who couldn't catch their breath. It took weeks before I could dance full out (high kicks and all) on a moving ship and simultaneously sing full out without hyperventilating. There was almost no down time during the shows. Our costume changes were mere seconds long, so we huffed and puffed then, too. The girls' dressing room was the size of a small storage closet and was so hot and stuffy, we may as well have been three people simultaneously trying to change clothes in a one-seat sauna. My hair was drenched with sweat. The shows were only ninety minutes, but we worked our hardest each and every one of those minutes. The crowd certainly got their money's worth; we packed a pile of exceptional entertainment into that hour and a half.

Performing on a moving stage was an especially difficult task, especially since the shows were challenging for me even on solid ground. Surprisingly, dancing was actually easier than standing still. Trying to balance in a beautiful pose while the floor rocked three feet to the right like a teeter-totter took all my strength. I understood why people have swivel cup holders in their cars to keep their Big Gulps from spilling. Thankfully, I managed to remain fairly upright the entire summer. After the show, we had to lug our own costume racks back to the storage room (a bit of a trek), but my back and the balls of my feet were so sore and tender from gripping the stage so I wouldn't fall over that I could barely walk. Real, hard-soled shoes were out of the question; I had to wear my softest slippers to cushion my aching tootsies. I hobbled through the halls like one of our frail, elderly passengers.

It was stressful enough having to perform a show we barely knew. It was stressful enough learning how to dance on a rocking ship. It was stressful enough adjusting to ship life, castmates, and shipmates. To top it off, we were terribly sleep-deprived from middle-of-the-night rehearsals. Add a persistent, pounding, seasickness hangover to the mix, and jumping overboard sounded like a sensible alternative. The changes and challenges were tremendous.

My job was made all the more painful when Anita dubbed me dance captain/company manager. I appreciated being selected for a leadership position but was so stressed about performing the show and adjusting to living on a ship that I could barely deal with the additional duties of payroll, costume cleaning and repair, and "ratings" meetings with the cruise director. (It was all about the ratings. After each cruise, the passengers rated everything. And if they got a week with bad weather they rated everything down. We could have given the performance of our lives, but it was cold and drizzling while they were in Juneau, so they didn't enjoy the show as much.) Add to those responsibilities clean-up rehearsals, mediating among cast members, and sending weekly videotapes of the show and show reports to L.A. I lasted no more than a couple of weeks, and then fellow castmate Bob bravely took over. Good riddance to that job!

It took the entire first month for us to polish our shows only to lose our two straight, male cast members. One resigned. He was sort of a loose cannon so we weren't totally surprised. He had worked on ships before and, perhaps, realized he just couldn't take another voyage. And one was "released." This guy was, shall we say, "movement challenged" from day one. He had a beautiful voice but two, or maybe even three, left feet. Everyone was hoping that, with enough practice, over time, he'd get in step with the rest of us. Alas, he got canned like a tuna, because even after three weeks, he never did get up to speed. We spent *another month* training and rehearsing two new dudes, Tom and Craig. How frustrating! My lips spewed so many expletives that I sounded like a gangsta rapper. *Would this rehearsal nightmare ever end?* The bonus prize was that these guys were adorable, great performers who were easy to get along with (but both gay, by the way, so no hope for a hook up).

The new boys' friendly, cooperative personalities were probably more important than their talents, because the tempers of castmates could make or break the trip. If you got cast with a bunch of immature, gossipy, back-stabbing monsters, it would be hard to have fun and even harder to last the entire five months without wanting to push each other overboard. Directors casting for ship shows had to take into account attitudes, how the performers got along with others, and whether or not they seemed suited for ship life. The last thing they wanted to do was to have to replace someone three weeks after the shows opened (like we did), but replacements happened all the time. Someone would get injured, they'd have a death in the family, or they couldn't stand being stuffed in a shoe-box size room for half a year. Our new cast had a much better chance of survival than the first one.

After a few weeks performing together, the shows started feeling comfortable. I had improved a lot and could sing and dance at the same time without losing my breath. Moreover, for the most part, I was able to have *fun* performing the shows—something I had previously thought would only happen after hell froze over and pigs flew. "Birth of the Blues," which had been like a ship in distress at the beginning, turned out to be my favorite show. I actually *enjoyed* it, even my little singing solos. Unlike "Let's Dance!," it wasn't all about the quick costume changes. Because we were only alternating accessories on top of one costume, we could focus on the actual performing. After all the chaos and cast changes we suffered at the start, the shows finally pulled together, and I, for the most part, felt confident and competent.

Once our shows opened, Anita and her assistant went back to Los Angeles. She only returned to the ship periodically to check on the quality of the shows, and we'd have to perform all of them for her at midnight right after completing two real shows for the passengers. We were expected to perform full out with stage presence and more energy than the Energizer Bunny. Those were rough, ultra-exhausting near all-nighters. "I can't believe how clean you girls are!" she marveled. "Clean" meant the three of us were perfectly in sync with our choreography. High fives all around. (Physically, we looked very different from one another: short, voluptuous Dana with her smooth, red bob; thin and muscular, medium-height Candy with a shoulder-length black do; and tall, long-legged me with long, blond hair. But our performance skills were well matched.) It was a stressful time when Anita came aboard. We wanted to be at our very best, and, thankfully, our shows were shipshape.

Once out of rehearsal hell, our schedule was pretty easy breezy, especially compared to other cruise ship gigs. Monday night we did two seatings (8:15 p.m. and 10:00 p.m.) of "Let's Dance!" Wednesday nights we did two seatings of "Birth of the Blues." Thursdays we did the "Elvis" bumper before whatever act went on, and Sundays we did "The Tonight Medley" bumper before the main act. A couple hours before every performance, we were also expected to meet and mark through the show we were to perform that night. It made sense that we might need a brush-up since a week went by between shows. We dutifully, robotically went through the motions, but after a few months it felt like a waste of time since we could now do the shows in our sleep.

In addition to performing and rehearsing our shows, we had a few "cruise staff duties." Some ships required the entertainers to act like cruise directors Julie and Isaac from *The Love Boat* and run limbo contests, skeet shooting, and other recreational activities when they weren't on stage performing. We were spoiled, because each of our cast members simply had "library duty" a few hours a week, which involved sitting at a desk twiddling our thumbs or reading, and, on the rare occasion, helping a passenger check out a book or movie. Or, if we wanted a more active alternative, we could teach a few country line-dance classes in the ballroom. I dusted off my cowboy boots and rustled up the gumption to try to wrangle a herd of passengers with two left feet into a troupe that could trip the light fantastic. Many just tripped, and I often preferred to zone out in the lazy comfort of the library.

****

The ship was like a mini floating city, with a population close to three thousand. About two thousand were passengers who stayed for a week or two at the most, leaving little time to forge relationships. Besides my cast, the remaining, "permanent" population included about eight hundred crew members led by a much smaller group of officers. The officers were all Dutch, because the *Noordam* hailed from the Netherlands. I had nothing against the Dutch, having always enjoyed their wooden shoes, tulips, and windmills (although I was never too fond of herring), but these particular Hollanders were stern and, in general, didn't like us. "This is a *ship!*" these seafarers would say with disgust every time we land lovers slipped and called it a *boat*. The men in white uniforms either despised us for having such an easy gig and so many privileges, or wanted to sleep with us. Not always sure which was the case, we walked on eggshells, afraid of angering our superiors, who could make our lives a shipwreck. We decided early that it was best to give a wide berth and steer clear of them or make a concerted effort to stay on their good side. Dana did such an excellent job of getting on the good graces of the officer in charge of food and beverage that they started dating. Consequently, she was able to score refreshments and bakery treats off hours. Bonus! When having a fling, it was a definite perk if the lover could extend special benefits. It was all about who you knew on the ship.

Unlike the officers, a high percentage of the eight hundred crew members on board were Indonesian and Filipino. These folks were hired to do the hard labor, like maid service, cleaning, and waiting tables. They took year-long contracts and sent most of the money they earned back home to their families. When not working, they were banished to the bowels of the ship and even had their own special mess hall, so we didn't have much opportunity to mingle with them. Once in a great while they got permission to go into port and would return with boxes of electronic appliances. Unlike our cast, they had no special privileges and were required to be invisible on their free time. We heard a story of a guy who committed suicide by jumping off the back of the ship into the deep blue sea. I worried that they would be jealous of our charmed life and would want to spit in our coffee. In an act of good will, our cast went down, down, down to their deck and performed our show for them late one night. The place reeked of clove cigarettes—a smell I remembered so well from my trip to Indonesia. It felt good to do something nice for our hard-working shipmates, and I think they appreciated our efforts. I surely appreciated theirs.

****

Life on the high seas was far from normal and definitely not for everyone. It was a cross between prison, an exotic excursion, and a *Love Boat* shagfest. For me, one of the worst parts was my lack of privacy. Because we were confined to the ship much of the time, we could not get far away from passengers, castmates, officers, and crew. Think living, sleeping, eating, breathing, playing, *and* working with your coworkers for nearly a half year without getting time apart. I was extremely fortunate to have an enjoyable, friendly cast, but even being around the best people 24/7 can be too much of a good thing. Occasionally, I needed my space, but I could rarely escape on my own for a moment of peace.

Some of the passengers also proved to be a source of irritation for me. (Although I should have been more thankful for them, because without them, I'd have been out of a job.) Most cruises were a week long, so we took on new passengers every seven days. The first couple days of a new cruising group were the best, because most of the passengers didn't realize that I wasn't just another passenger. Once they saw me perform in the show, however, I was famous. After that, they watched my every move—what I ate, said, wore, and did. I had to be dressed appropriately and behave appropriately at all times. Not that my behavior was bad by any means, but I didn't like being scrutinized and eyeballed all the time. I couldn't leave my room without being observed by passengers who would then report any questionable shenanigans to the officers.

For instance, one night Candy and her new boyfriend Harvey (the adorable spa manager from London) and I went dancing at a fairly empty disco. Dancers move with more passion and abandon than the normal eighty-year-old, and one such conservative senior citizen reported to the cruise staff officer, "Those young people were having a virtual *ménage à trios* on the dance floor!" We got called in to explain ourselves. I was shocked at the accusation, but we had been a pretty frisky threesome. Luckily, I had a good rapport with that particular officer, and we were let off with a warning. There's something to be said for remaining invisible and anonymous.

Certainly, I met some interesting and affable folks, but after a few months, I got tired of making small talk and answering the same questions over and over and over. "Where are you from? What have you done? How long have you been dancing on cruise ships? Where is the poop deck?" I was constantly giving directions, because learning one's way around a big ocean liner was confusing for many at first. Sometimes I preferred to hide in my room and avoid the whole shebang, but if I wanted to eat, I had to brave the crowds and go up on deck. Most of the time, hunger got the best of me and I ventured out.

In addition to the lack of privacy, I sometimes felt imprisoned (certainly, it was a five-star, luxury, gourmet prison) with a lack of freedom and control. We were given pages of rules to follow: "You can't go here. You *can* go here, but only at theses times. You can't wear that. You *have* to wear a floor-length evening gown if you want to leave your room on formal nights. You can't do this. You can't do that. You have be back by this time. You have to let the passengers go first. You have to get a pass to leave the ship." When the ship was out to sea, I was trapped on board. Even when docked in port there were times when I couldn't leave, because I couldn't get a pass to take the tender to shore. If I had library duty, I occasionally missed my window of opportunity by the time it was my turn to disembark, because passengers got first priority. When I did manage to escape and go on shore excursions, I had to constantly keep track of time or face the consequences of the ship sailing without me.

The compact sleeping accommodations also took their toll. My cast stayed in crew cabins, which were much more cramped than passenger rooms but, admittedly, far less awful than the underworld where the poor Indonesians and Filipinos had to bunk. Most of the tiny space I shared with Candy was filled by our bunk bed. Thankfully, there wasn't a soul on earth who didn't like Candy. She was an absolute angel, a godsend since we literally lived on top of each other. Sharing such close quarters could have killed even the best of relationships, but we became close friends. The room also included an itty-bitty bathroom complete with toilet and shower. It was a tight squeeze even for two skinny chicks.

Without the benefit of a porthole to peek at the outside world, I felt claustrophobic at times. The rocking of the ship, the stale air, the dark, windowless room, and the rainy weather made me feel lethargic. I'd have to go to the upper promenade and get some fresh air and take a look at the little pine tree-covered islands and mountains in the distance for a healthy change of scenery.

The puny rooms, lack of privacy, and restricted freedom of choice certainly took some getting used to for us newbies still securing our sea legs. However, with the right mindset, a good set of hiking boots, a camera, a journal, and a large supply of condoms, cruising life could be a rewarding adventure for many. The young, handsome drummer in the ship's resident band had been cruising for about three years (his way of sowing his oats before getting married and going to med school) and had brought along his bicycle and plenty of paperbacks. When ashore, he cycled around exotic ports of call; on sea days, he kicked back and read novels, all while making (and saving) money playing music. What a life! I wished I would have climbed aboard years earlier and taken some world cruises. My best friend from high school took many ship contracts as a singer and saw a good portion of the world, including remote islands that I've never heard of. She'll have to build an addition on her house just to hold her photo albums.

A tremendous bonus of working on a cruise liner was that we were fully taken care of: free accommodations, free maid service, free food, free entertainment, virtually free booze, and free gym. With no living expenses, we could save beaucoup bucks. But the absolute best part of ship life was that we journeyed to some of the most famous and far-flung places in the world *for free*. I fell in love with the romance of traveling the world by sea, sailing the ocean blue, riding the waves of adventure. Water voyages were magical and mystical, full of wonder and excitement. Unfortunately, we were never in port long enough to explore every place it had to offer. Our stops were more like a sampler platter from which I got a tiny taste of a lot of towns but never got my fill. The truncated itinerary left me hungering for more, but because we spent five months in Alaska repeating the same journey every week, I actually got to see and do quite a lot, a little bit at a time. When it was too stormy to take a whale watching tour one week, it was sunny the next.

Alaska was one of the most spectacular places I had ever been. In the heart of summer the sun would still be setting at 1:00 a.m. The wildlife included spawning salmon, killer whales, bald eagles, puffins, sea otters, sea lions, seals, and mountain goats. Once we counted thirty dolphins with white bellies jumping and swimming alongside the ship! We also saw a humpback whale breaching; it would jump out of the water and flop smack on its back playfully. Alaska was a land of majestic blue glaciers, northern lights, snow-capped mountains, waterfalls, colorful wildflowers, fields of magenta fireweed, totem poles, goldmine ruins, float planes, helicopters, fishing boats, quaint towns, art stores, bears, bars, and comforting coffee shops. I adored perusing the ports and combing the countryside.

Sadly, we didn't stop at a new port every day, because some days were "sea days." Sea days meant we were confined on board with limited recreational options, while the ship cruised on to the next town. I had to create my own fun so I didn't go insane. A good portion of my time was spent exercising in the gym, sweating in the sauna and Jacuzzi, walking laps around the deck, reading, painting, writing music with my tiny electronic portable keyboard, watching movies, writing letters, and journaling. (The days and weeks blended together, so journaling helped me remember what happened from one week to the next for when I called home to update my parents.) These were all worthwhile pursuits, certainly, but I much preferred the option of wandering free-range throughout the Alaskan wilderness (and coffee shops).

Some days I would peruse the gift store, but most items were tacky, generously sequined shirts and hats (I never knew I could overdose on sparkle). Then one day I discovered the delightful, chocolatey, sweet crunch of the English Cadbury Crunchie candy bars they sold. After that, I frequented the gift store more regularly and even splurged on a nice, Gucci watch. Some days I attended "high tea" in a lovely lounge where I sipped a hot beverage from a delicate porcelain teacup, nibbled on finger sandwiches and cookies, and learned how to fold cloth napkins into impressive sculptures.

Doing laundry was another way to pass the time. It was a royal pain, however, because we used the same machines as the passengers, and they were always occupied. Why all these people spent their vacation time cleaning clothes (especially the day before they were leaving), I'll never know. My freshly washed wet socks and underwear would have to sit in a laundry basket until a dryer became available. I'd wait and wait and wait and then finally give up after finding out the dryers had already been promised to other passengers.

Since we were sailing for nearly half a year, after a few months I found it necessary to visit the salon to have my hair cut and highlighted. Unfortunately, it was common knowledge among staff that the hairdressers (all young, British women) couldn't cut or color to save their lives and were always hung over from the night before. One of the hairdressers got so drunk so often, the restaurant manager would regularly find her passed out on the galley floor—the ship's kitchen, which was strictly off limits, mind you—with a half-eaten dinner roll in her mouth. She'd be three sheets to the wind, get the munchies, go scavenging for food, and fall unconscious before leaving the scene of the crime. The next day, some poor lady would show up for her hair appointment only to be told her hairdresser was missing in action. Fortunately, by the time my roots were showing and my ends were splitting, Candy had started dating the charming, blond, British spa manager (Harvey) who *did* have a flair for hair. He always took good care of me and my mop.

The primary pursuit on cruise ships was, of course, eating. Mealtimes and snack times set the structure for the day. Each day, our cast queued up with all two thousand passengers for delicious, buffet-style breakfast and lunch in the informal dining room. The masterful process of purchasing, storing, preparing, and serving so many people so much excellent cuisine boggled my mind. Menus repeated like those from the elementary school lunchroom, and it didn't take long before I had them memorized: taco bar on Monday, ice cream sundae bar on Tuesdays, pizza by the pool on Wednesdays, Indonesian chicken satay on Saturdays. The spreads were all-you-can-eat, so I had to be careful not to gorge myself to death like a goldfish. The food was so delicious and plentiful that I could hardly bear to pass it up, knowing I'd be surviving on ramen noodles when I returned home. While oh so tempting, stuffing one's face was not the wisest way to pass time for a dancer who was supposed to appear fit. The pigging out needed to be balanced out with trips to the gym, laps on deck, and enthusiastic club dancing. Nibbling and noshing were enticing ways to amuse ourselves, and it took a lot of will power to not munch my way straight to the fat farm.

Dinner was another story. The crew dined together in the informal dining room, while the passengers were served a sit-down dinner in the fancy, formal dining room. While the passengers enjoyed scrumptious, gourmet meals, we snubbed our noses at "crew food," which we suspected was the excess passenger food that was borderline spoiling, like souring honeydew melon or old hamburger and veggies that had been transformed into an expiration date Shepherd's pie. The young British lushes who worked in the hair salon usually skipped the questionable grub and instead made "chip butties"—french fries stuffed into rolls—a safer, albeit nutritionally devoid, choice. The crew food often turned my stomach, but it was hard to find a healthy, edible alternative. The entrees were saucy and floating in grease. I learned to munch a good lunch and sneak cereal boxes, graham crackers, bananas, and other contraband from the earlier meals to keep a stash in my room for days when dinner was especially unappetizing. Food was not allowed to be taken back to our rooms, so I did so on the down low. After about a month, I got tired of eating even the same *good* food and annoyed with having to wait in a long line to be fed. (I'm ashamed to admit I had those thoughts when there are people starving in the world, but I did.)

In the evenings, when we weren't working, the cast often enjoyed watching whichever visiting headliners were performing on the main stage. They'd come aboard for a few weeks at a time, stay in passenger cabins, and get paid a hefty fee. Our entertainers included singers, magicians, jugglers, impressionists (including Danny Gans, who later made it big in Vegas), fiddlers, banjo players, comedians (including a guy from Juneau who joked about cruise ships), and ventriloquists. Their songs and acts were generally geared toward the senior citizens, but even youngsters like myself got a kick out of them. Afterward, we had the choice of frequenting one or more of the following hot spots:

- The disco, where it was impossible to fast dance without causing elderly passengers to hyperventilate and/or report us to the cruise director (as I noted above);
- The piano bar, where a kind but depressed, married alcoholic had been tickling the ivories for years. (You meet a lot of interesting characters on ships, because everyone seems to have a reason they wanted to escape from their real lives. They are from all over the world, with their own cultural idiosyncrasies, like the Welsh guy who never brushed his teeth, or the Irish radio officer who was terribly afraid to return home in poor drinking condition.);
- The midnight buffet, for which we had to dress in black tie or floor-length evening gown (what a pain in the patootie when all we wanted was a couple of stuffed mushrooms);
- The fancy lounge that served cognac and fine chocolates while a string quartet played classical music; or
- The more relaxed *Officer's Bar* (a.k.a. the "O.B."), where only select staff were allowed, we could dance like floozies, and alcoholic beverages were cheaper than soda pop. It wasn't uncommon for a staff member to develop a drinking problem,

because boozing was one of the few choices available at night, and the ship offered us liquor at ridiculously discounted prices—*pennies*, not even dollars. One night they had a Tacky Party, where we all dressed in our tackiest outfits and drank from a toilet that flushed punch. Tacky!

There was also a small casino on board, which we were *never* allowed to enter—a good thing for many and fine by me.

Sea days could be rough, because we were stuck on the ship with these same old activities. Naturally, they were exciting and new at first, but even the finest amenities became tiresome and old hat after a few months. That's why sex was such a popular pastime; a lot of people hooked up simply due to extreme boredom. New staff members coming aboard were always a big deal, as perhaps some babe would prove to be the source of a hot romance.

That saucy scenario is exactly what happened to lucky me. While I was busy rehearsing the new guys and swearing up a storm, Ron—a handsome Arnold Schwarzenegger look-alike imported from London—joined the spa team as the masseur. I didn't set eyes on him for weeks, as I was entrenched in rehearsals. Candy's boyfriend Harvey (who was not only the spa manager and Ron's boss but the unofficial matchmaker as well) kept bugging me to meet him. I finally gave in just to get him off my back. Turned out Harvey was a pretty good matchmaker, because Ron and I hit it off from the start. Like with Davy Jones, I couldn't resist that endearing British accent. "The Love Boat" theme song played in my head: "Set a course for adventure, your mind on a new romance…"

Having a boyfriend did wonders to lift my spirits, improve my attitude, and provide new forms of entertainment for dull sea days. (Use your imagination.) The risk of on-board dating was that if you eventually discovered yourselves to be incompatible, had a bad break up, and could no longer stand the sight of each other, you would have a hard time avoiding each other. You were essentially living in the same house, albeit a floating mansion, for months on end. Yet I was willing to take the risk and pay the consequences. Ship life didn't permit your typical dating scenario, but our six ports provided plenty of recreational options that I loved exploring with my new chap.

The Canadian coastal city of Vancouver was our home port where we'd drop off passengers and pick up a new group every two weeks. Ron and I strolled through charming, historic Gastown (Vancouver's original downtown) and ate and shopped in the scattered stores that were open early on a Sunday. About a mile away, Stanley Park, with its 1,001 acres of west coast rainforest mostly surrounded by the Pacific Ocean, offered scenic water and mountain views and a perfect place for us to stretch our legs. The onsite Vancouver Aquarium was a guaranteed way to see killer whales, beluga whales, sea otters, and sea lions. We paid the fee and went in even though we spotted many of these amazing creatures out of captivity for free when cruising with the ship.

From Vancouver, the *Noordam* would sail north along the "Inside Passage," a picturesque, maze-like water path around and between the coastal islands and the mainland. This protected route allowed us to bypass rough weather in the open seas. When it wasn't too windy, I'd go outside on the Upper Promenade to enjoy the beautiful view of the tree-covered islands. Sometimes the clouds would stick in the mountain trees like cotton. The water was smooth, and the ride was peaceful.

Our first stop was Ketchikan, Alaska's southeasternmost city. Its most popular tourist attraction was the Creek Street boardwalk—a group of quaint homes, stores, and restaurants built up on pilings overlooking Ketchikan Creek. In the early 1900s, it was infamous for its bootlegging and brothels including the historic Madam Dolly's house (which still stands but as a museum only). It took a hardy woman to survive the Alaskan wilderness and a hardier one still to service its rugged men for a living. I frequented Creek Street not for the illicit Canadian whiskey as they did in days gone by, but to buy the Swedish fish (chewy, red, cherry-flavored gummies shaped like tiny fish) that were sold at the candy store. That was as close as I got to fishing, but a real angler could have his heyday in Ketchikan, known as "Salmon Capital of the World," where "salmon and fishermen go to spawn." Creek Street was the perfect spot to witness schools of salmon swimming upstream.

Ketchikan also boasted a wonderful independent bookstore and a magnificent bead shop for my handmade jewelry projects. Some days I caught up on my errands at Ketchikan's drug store, photo shop, post office, and money machine. When in an educational touristy mood, I'd walk to the Salmon Hatchery or the Totem Pole Heritage Center, which housed 100-year-old totem poles from within a forty-mile radius of Ketchikan. I was especially intrigued by those with "potlatch" rings, which indicated the number of potlatches (huge, prestigious parties that took years of planning) a family had given.

I loved the opportunity to take a break from ship fare, and Ketchikan offered several palate-pleasing restaurants. The 5 Star Café served fresh, strong coffee and excellent brown rice with black beans on top for when I was in a vegetarian mood. Ketchikan Café had minimal décor but it was the place to go for hefty, home-cooked breakfasts served quickly, and it provided a beautiful view overlooking the water. Annabella's had an old wooden bar with happening music; their creamy seafood chowder and soft, freshly baked herb bread kept me coming back for more.

By far the best activity in Alaska was hiking! Ron and I discovered Deer Mountain and decided to take the climb. After loading up the backpack with important supplies (chocolate bars, chocolate milk, and bananas), we tromped up the trail. The beautiful, log and rock and mud path through the lush forest was wet and woodsy and fun and easy (even for a novice like myself). The air smelled so fresh with all the trees and vegetation releasing loads of oxygen. It took us 90 minutes to get up the mountain and 50 minutes to get down. We got a great view of town, our ship, and the surrounding islands from a clearing about halfway up and then again at the top. Near the top, the trees spread out and all was still and spring green. We ate our snacks while the mosquitoes ate us. The weather was in the 70s. Best weather we'd had. I hadn't hiked much before, but I was hooked.

Our second port was Juneau, Alaska's capital city. It was home to some excellent little shops including a great health food store called Rainbow Foods. Instead of always being at the mercy of the ship's kitchen and the specified dining times, I preferred having my own groceries to keep in my room, so I'd stock up on dried mango, chips and salsa, bean dip, banana muffins, sesame-honey sticks, trail mix, organic chocolate bars, whole wheat apricot bars, organic popcorn, soy milk, and power bars for our hikes. On the rare occasion when we really wanted to splurge on an exquisite gourmet dinner, Ron and I would eat at The Summit where they served melt-in-your-mouth halibut medallions in a lime cream sauce. Heritage Coffee shop was my regular stop for a cup of Joe and was right below the enchanting enamel and metal pin shop of artist William Spears. He had hundreds of whimsical, colorful pins of animals, birds, fish, airplanes, and vegetables. I bought a large-mouth bass fish pin.

One of my favorite hangouts with the cast and friends was the Red Dog Saloon. This popular bar had sawdust floors and walls adorned with stuffed bears, moose heads, and mountain goats plus life preservers and flags from different ships. Any leftover spare inch of available wall space was plastered with business cards. Rico, a local singer/keyboard player, kept the place lively singing drunken sailor songs. The Red Dog served huge glasses of Alaskan Amber beer and pucker-your-lips "lemon drops" (a shot of vodka, lemon juice, and sugar that you drank immediately after sucking on a sour lemon wedge). When Monty, the fifty-year-old motorcycle-loving banjo player, was headlining on the ship, he two-stepped me around the circumference of the room!

Somehow managing to pull ourselves away from the cheerful atmosphere of the Red Dog, Candy and Harvey and I hiked the unchallenging but gorgeous Perseverance Trail. The trail was well maintained and took us through forests, past waterfalls and snow-capped mountains, over little rivers, and beside fields of purple, pink, white, and yellow wildflowers. We even passed by old mine ruins and scattered pieces of rusted mining remnants. My calves were aching the next day.

The experience of a lifetime, however, was our helicopter ride to the twelve-mile-long Mendenhall glacier, situated about twelve miles from downtown. It had rained all day in Juneau, and I was certain the trip would be cancelled, but about an hour before we were supposed to go, the sun came out. Eighteen of us (our entire cast plus other young cruise staffers) got dressed in black tie formal wear (not the typical or most appropriate glacier garb) and started by having drinks at the Officer's Bar. I debuted my floor-length, black, stretch-knit Jessica Rabbit-like Japanese designer dress with a thigh-high slit that I bought in L.A. for $300. Ron borrowed tuxedo pieces from various men on board and put together a nice ensemble that actually looked like it matched. I had a glass of Chardonnay before heading to the bus that was waiting to take us to the helicopter port. At the port, we had to take off our shoes and put on clunky black moon boots that looked ridiculous with our elegant gowns. Then we boarded three helicopters with six people and a pilot in each. Ron and I rode with Candy, Harvey, Dana, and Dana's boyfriend Wesley. The whirring of the helicopter blades was so loud, we had to wear headphones and talk into a mic to hear each other.

The three helicopters lifted off simultaneously. Unlike an airplane take-off, this one was so slow and smooth, it took me a while to realize we were off the ground! We cruised over Juneau, its outlying mountains, and finally the glacier that spilled into town through the mountains like a thick, pale blue, ice cream shake river. It was magnificent. We flew over a mountain following the two helicopters before us to discover the glacier field on the other side. Miles and miles of blue ice stretched before us. Then one, two, three, we all descended and lightly touched down atop the glacier.

All hell broke loose. We popped open champagne and sprayed it over each other. My hands were freezing. We tromped around on the ice, avoiding the deep, deep pockets of bright blue water leading down to the depths of the glacier. All, that is, except for Wesley, who purposefully jumped in a puddle up to his waist. The nut! (I don't know how he could stand being in soaking wet pants all night.) We took picture after picture. When the girls egged on the guys for a moon shot, they all bent over and bared their buns to mother nature (who was quite frigid that evening). These men had no modesty.

After about an hour of playing on the glacier, we hopped into our respective helicopters for the flight back. Ron and I kissed the whole night. People made fun of us but it was so romantic and such a great experience to share with your sweetheart. On the bus back to town, we had a cup of hot chocolate to warm our fingers. Next, the entire group headed to Café Verona for pizza. Afterwards, we ran back to the boat to change clothes and squeeze in forty-five minutes of dancing at the Penthouse disco before our 11 p.m. curfew. Then it was back to the O.B. for more drinking and socializing. What a night!

In the panhandle west of Juneau was Glacier Bay National Park, an area of spectacular ice floes between the mountains and toward the water's edge. The ship would cruise the glaciers each week while the passengers would watch expectantly from the deck, hoping for the greatest prize of all: to witness a glacier "calving." If we were lucky enough to be at the right place at the right time, we'd hear the grumble and roar and see a massive chunk of ice break off with a mighty splash into the water. One extremely rare glacier cruising day was so sunny that I was able to lounge outside in my bikini for a while—an odd pursuit when sailing past snow-capped mountains and fields of ice.

Our third port was Sitka, whose claim to fame was that it was the town where author James Michener stayed during the summers when he researched and wrote his novel *Alaska*. Sitka boasted a charming little book store called Harbor Books, which had a Bohemian coffee shop in the back where I liked to order soy milk cappuccino or mocha while hiding out and writing or organizing photos from the trip. The young patrons were hippie-ish with long hair, flannel shirts, and Birkenstocks sandals. Some were in town working at the fish or pickle canneries. A guy from Santa Cruz, California, noticed my glacier pics, and we ended up talking for an hour. He had come to Alaska to make money, but the fishing industry was having a bad season, so he ended up at the salmon cannery filtering salmon eggs for caviar to be sent to Japan. He was an artist and had put together a fountain design he wanted to market and produce back in California once he got the necessary financing. The man had also studied Native American shamanism and Chinese medicine and shiatsu for ten years.

Interesting folks were drawn to this most northwestern state, including wonderful artists. I was captivated by the art of Rie Muñoz and bought a book featuring her work plus her poster of two Alaskan Native women dancing in the sky with the moon and stars. Muñoz was a Juneau-based artist whose colorful, expressionist paintings reflected the daily routine of Alaskans and Alaska's Native people. She had even traveled remote distances in order to observe their way of life. I purchased greeting cards and a T-shirt by Ketchikan-based artist Ray Troll who designed quirky, comical, fish- and sea creature-based scenarios with sayings such as "A woman needs a man like a fish needs a bicycle," or "The Baitful Dead" (a fishy spoof on the Grateful Dead). I also appreciated the distinct style of the red and black Northwest Coast Native American art depicting thunderbirds, orcas, bears, ravens, and eagles. These artists inspired me to do my own painting; I watercolored small pictures of Alaskan scenes I had photographed, like floatplanes docked along the water.

Ron and I visited the Raptor Center where injured eagles and other raptors were rehabilitated and then released back into the wild. It was a moving sight. Afterwards we walked holding hands through Indian Creek trail—a lush, magical rain forest like nothing I had ever seen. I was scared of bears the whole trip, as the trail was covered in berry bushes and took us by the river, a prime eating place for bears, whose favorite meal is fish and berries. We went as far as a clearing where the trees looked charred. Perhaps a forest fire? It was eerie and misty and still and romantic.

Sitka also had a charming, old-fashioned, six-lane bowling alley where you had to keep score yourself on a piece of paper, and cruise ship crews played for only $2 a game including shoes. A group of us went for the youth counselor's birthday, and I bowled with three of the musicians and the ship's naturalist (a young woman who educated passengers on Alaskan wildlife and the environment). I was bad at first but redeemed myself by scoring 110 in the last game, my first and only time breaking 100. We decided the winner should always buy the losers milkshakes. (The alley was known for its excellent selection of flavors: chocolate, fudge, peanut butter, strawberry, vanilla, coffee, mocha, blackberry, peach, blueberry, root beer, and butterscotch.) Our music director won, so I enjoyed a decadent peanut butter-fudge shake on his dime.

Our fourth stop was Valdez—one of Alaska's principal ports and an oil terminal loading site for the Trans-Alaska pipeline (famous for the unfortunate 1989 Exxon Valdez oil spill). When the weather permitted, I enjoyed hoofing it into town, which was 3.3 miles from where the ship docked. On the way, I found a salmon-spawning area with hundreds squirming around laying eggs and hundreds of others dead in the water. It was spooky to think they were all swimming to their deaths. Sometimes an otter would poke its head out of the water and playfully surprise me. Once the wonderful, unique little health food store closed, I didn't have much to do in this small town of less than 4,000 residents. But my friends and I did make the effort to visit the Valdez Museum, which highlighted the 1964 Good Friday Earthquake that wiped out the waterfront and 32 people along with it. (God bless their souls.) Turns out Californians weren't the only ones living on shaky ground. I thought I was on this cruise to *escape* earthquakes. Should have done my research.

Seward, our final port, had the lowest population of all (not quite 3,000) but got the highest marks for incredible hiking opportunities. Mt. Marathon was the most treacherous and difficult hike Ron and I had ever attempted. It began with a terrifying vertical rock-climbing expedition. I had never rock climbed before, and partway up I got scared of heights and decided to go back down. Much to my dismay, reversing looked more dangerous than continuing upwards. (Was this what was meant by being "stuck between a rock and a hard place?") I took deep breaths, didn't dare look down, and kept climbing until I made it to the trees and could pull myself up by their exposed roots.

Long Legs and Tall Tales

The rest of the trail was terribly steep, too. Ron's calves were burning, and my heart rate increased so fast I got lightheaded and had to stop for a while to keep from fainting. It was the clearest day yet in Seward. We saw mountains we never knew existed. The views were spectacular.

Unfortunately, at the halfway mark, we didn't veer left, as we were supposed to do. Instead we remained on the most obvious trail—exactly the route the ranger warned us NOT to take. Soon we were past the tree line and into loose gravel with little to hold onto, confronting wind that was trying to knock us off the mountain. I was on all fours searching for a stable pile of gravel to hoist me up. About every twenty feet we could find a new pile and rest for a few seconds before venturing upward, but the gravel offered no traction, so our legs kept sliding right out from underneath us. I nearly wet my pants from fear and, once again, wanted to go back down, but Ron was determined to make it to the top. I kept yelling at him to stay by me in case I was about to fall. Finally, we reached a massive rock that was nearly impossible for us to climb, and we admitted defeat. Little did we know, the top was just over that big boulder. The trip down was like skiing on gravel. Ron was like a five-year-old jumping and sliding.

Back at the halfway point, we found the right trail and headed back up. This path was no simple stroll in the park either. I whined like a three-year-old the entire journey, once again crawling but with more solid rock to grab this time. The top was unbelievable! It was all soft grass spotted with purple wild flowers. We could see mountains everywhere and the city and the islands and the entire bay. We ate power bars, took pictures, and patted ourselves on the back for our accomplishment.

On our return trip, we had fun sliding down the gravel chute until we reached a fairly dry waterfall. When the waterfall was filled with snow, you could sled down to the bottom of the mountain on your butt. Since it was snowless, that wasn't an option. We also wanted to avoid having to shimmy down the sheer rocks that had scared me so much at the start of the trek up. Instead we found an alternative route where you descended by dangling from tree roots for dear life. We shouted with joy at the end. Hundreds of kamikaze 5K runners race to the top and back every July 4th, some returning muddy, bloody, or wounded. Maybe next year. NOT! With dirt and dust embedded in our skin, nails, and clothing, we trotted off to the Breeze Inn Bar to reward ourselves with beer, nachos, and fried mushrooms.

Mt. Marathon was certainly a memorable and noteworthy achievement, but my greatest day in Seward was the day Ron and I hiked to the Harding Ice Field. We began our day at the Breeze Inn (fondly dubbed "Grumpy Grandma's") for a hearty breakfast of big, fluffy biscuits with sausage gravy. After a quick stop at the Seamen's Mission to make phone calls to loved ones, we took a $20 cab ride to Exit Glacier where the Harding Ice Field trail begins. What a wonderful opportunity to gaze at the magnificent light-blue glacier from a distance so close you could scoop off a chunk and make a dirty, pale-blue snow cone. My awe at nature's beauty was overshadowed by the sign at the entrance that warned us of bears. Ron hoped to see one, but I was scared. What were we supposed to do if we came upon a bear? Seasoned hikers told us just to make a lot of noise while hiking, because coming upon a bear unannounced was apparently a great way to get yourself mauled. Some people carried a little bell with them that jingled while they walked. I thought pepper spray or a Taser stun gun or a rifle-bearing army would have offered better protection. The fact that all we had was our voices didn't comfort me in the least.

According to guide books, the forest ranger, and friends, the hike was difficult, steep, and would take six to eight hours round trip. We didn't have that much time, so we decided to just see how far we could get in a couple hours and then come back down.

The ascent was tiring, but I was on a mission to get as far as possible. Ron admitted that he could hardly keep up with me and almost asked me to slow down. The first part of the trail consisted of creeks with lovely, magenta fireweed and lush vegetation and trees. There were some semi-steep rocky areas, too, but they weren't steep at all compared to Mt. Marathon. Then the trail opened up into fields of white, yellow, purple, and red wildflowers. We even saw fat, wobbly marmots (fuzzy mole-like creatures) perched on rocks and scampering across the path.

After only 1 hour and 45 minutes, we reached our destination, the Harding Ice Field, which consisted of snow, miles of solid ice, and a few rocks to break the white monotony and help lead us back down. It was spectacular! We ran through the snow and over mountain peaks and finally came upon a little log hut. A middle-aged attorney from Anchorage had camped out on the snow the previous night and was hanging out at the mini, one-man cottage. Fortuitously, we had brought three bananas, so we each ate one. Then Ron and I walked for ten minutes more to get a better look at the ice field. The path to it appeared too dangerous to follow, so we made a small snowman and went back to the cabin to warm up. We munched down our chocolate bars, took some crazy photos lying in the snow, and headed back down RUNNING. It only took us 1 hour and 2 minutes to get back down. I felt so healthy and alive! Between the hiking and performing in the shows, I had never been in such great shape with such amazing stamina.

Afterwards, we cabbed back to town, and I treated Ron to his first chile rellenos, with chips and salsa and Corona beer at Niko's restaurant. We were so proud of our accomplishment. Having not brought enough cash to take a cab back to the ship, we power walked the trek in 20 minutes and made it just in time for my rehearsal. I was sore for two days afterwards, mostly from the side of the ankles up the outsides of the legs. But it was worth it, because I loved that hike. I was becoming addicted. I did have to remember to pace myself, however, and take care to make sure I still had the energy and injury-free body to do my job.

****

In August I celebrated my 29th birthday! (I actually remember when my parents turned 29; they joked with their friends about staying that age forever.) Ron took me to Juneau to buy me a birthday present. It was 83 degrees, one of the few days in Alaska that were hot enough for me to wear a tank top and running shorts. I was in heaven. We fortified ourselves for our mission with a cup of java and a flaky blueberry scone from Heritage Coffee Shop. Then we began visiting souvenir shops and art studios. After an extensive search, I finally found an Alaskan artist who made silver whistle necklaces with designs including bears, whales, ravens, frogs, eagles, and other Alaskan animals. My favorite was a bear design, which cost a whopping $140. I didn't think Ron should spend that much, but he wanted the first gift he bought me to be extra special and something I loved. What a wonderful souvenir!

For lunch, we went to Rainbow Foods health store and got two slices of whole wheat veggie pizza, a muffin, and our addiction—dried mango. Then we headed up to a park past the 1913 Governor's Mansion where we had our little picnic by a stream and got bothered by flies. The water was clear but so cold that Ron could barely stand in it. We found a swing set and had to swing a while before traversing a little trail through the woods, across a small bridge, up a dry waterfall, and back to the park entrance. We lay in the soft grass of the cemetery and soaked up the sun's glorious rays. On the way back to the ship, we decided to search for ice cream. It wasn't easy. Apparently there isn't a big market for ice cream in Alaska. We finally found soft serve vanilla.

August was also the month when everyone got sick. It was hard to contain illness in the closed ship environment. I was paranoid that the germs were migrating through the air conditioning's recycled air and infecting the entire vessel. Dana, our lead female singer, got bronchitis and so did Kathy from cruise staff. Craig, our lead male singer, was so sick he couldn't sing, and we had to postpone "Let's Dance!" for a few days. Ron felt awful, too, and a couple days later, I got terribly ill with an upper respiratory infection (perhaps even pneumonia). I woke up with a headache and couldn't get out of bed. It reminded me of when I got mono in high school, and all I could do was sleep. The weather in Sitka was gorgeous that day, and I had hoped to go kayaking. I went into town but was so sick I had to go back to my room to lie down. I hated missing an opportunity to be in port and off the ship, especially on such a sunny day. For most of us, being young and relatively healthy, the worst of it was over within a week or so. Thank goodness! It was a miserable time.

Also miserable was the night I entered costume hell. First, my spandex crop-top that I wore as a bra under my '50s/'60s costume didn't make it back from the ship's laundry service, so I did not have nearly the support I needed up top. (You think you lose a lot of socks in your wash? The ship's numerous professional machines cleaned masses of aprons, uniforms, towels, and sundry items, in addition to all of our costume washables. Talk about the black hole of laundry.) Second, as soon as I stepped on stage for the Fred Astaire number, the top snap of my dress popped open. I danced extra cautiously hoping the dress wouldn't fall down. Third, my skirt came unzipped in the tropical Latin section. Fourth, the hook on the neck of my opening number red dress broke right before second show. What a nightmare! How odd all these mishaps occurred on the very same evening. Coincidence? Or was I the victim of a poorly executed voodoo curse—not bad enough to make me end up naked on stage but enough to keep me uncomfortable, worried, and irritated? Whatever the case, the next day I pulled out the cast sewing kit and fixed my costumes. My seventh-grade home economics class came in handy after all.

The positive aspect of that night's performance was my discovery that if I ate the mic I could hear myself better through the monitors. Not being able to hear myself singing always threw me off. Nevertheless, I could tell I was improving. Hooray for small victories!

A bigger victory than my better vocals was that Ron and I had fallen in love. We had even *said* the "L" word. Out loud. To each other. What was the deal? Was this for real? We spent hours snuggled in bed in his cabin laughing and talking and teasing each other. (Making fun of his accent was a favorite amusement of mine.) But everyone knew that cruise ship romances didn't last. When your contract was up, you went your separate ways, back to your respective countries. My logical mind argued that I was being unrealistic, but being a hopeful romantic, my heart told me Ron might be *The One*.

Come September, the seas got rough. The water splashed over the windows of the crow's nest lounge at the tippy top of the ship. Time to batten down the hatches! We weren't allowed to go outside on deck due to water flooding over. I found it best to stay put in my room anyway, because walking around the ship proved to be dangerous and made me feel even more seasick. The ship lurched so much, I had to hold the handrail in the hall to keep from falling over. My head ached with what felt like a terrible hangover. Moaning in my bunk bed was all I could do to help myself feel better. I could hear (and feel) the ship's belly smacking down onto the sea. We were stuck and simply had to wait out the horrible storm. I felt so helpless.

What a relief when the storm abated and we were safely docked in Ketchikan. Ron and I ran up and down Deer Mountain again, but in the rain this time (idiots!), and I slipped on a mossy, wet rock, and fell on my knee. By evening, that knee was twice its normal size. Luckily I had 2 ½ days before our next big show. Ron played doctor and kept my knee iced but I was bedridden and could barely walk. The ship's real doctor wondered if I'd need to have the fluid from my knee drained. No thanks! I was able to fake all but one number in the show (Candy took over my role in "Porgy and Bess") but still couldn't bend or straighten my leg much. Having to perform with an injury was nerve racking and painful. I didn't know what would happen or if I'd end up crippled on stage and someone would have to come and carry me off like an injured football player much to the dismay of the audience. How embarrassing. Miraculously, when our next show came four days later, I was almost completely healed.

Thankfully, I recovered just in time for Dad, Mom, Grandma, and Aunt Jean to join us for a week cruise. I was afraid my injury would sabotage my week with the family, but in the end my knee was fine. The worst problem was that Bob bailed early on his contract for another gig, and we had to rehearse yet another new guy the week my family was there. I was mad about rehearsals and about the fact that our show wouldn't look as clean without Bob. Plus, I ended up being dance captain again, so I was extra busy.

Nevertheless, my family and I had such fun sightseeing, shopping, and hiking along the glaciers. I loved showing them around the ship and performing for them. Unfortunately, the day after they arrived, summer decided to turn into fall, and the weather turned cold, rainy, and then downright stormy again. It was so stormy that we had to go to a completely different port than planned in order to avoid the worst seas. So, instead of Sitka, we got to see the little gold rush town of Skagway and chug a few beers at the Red Onion Bar to take the chill off. The week went by too quickly, and I was sad to see the family leave. To make matters worse, Ron had to return to London later that same day. After many tears and goodbyes, Ron boarded the train to Anchorage where he would catch his flight home. I was all alone in Alaska wondering if Ron and I would ever see each other again.

The seas went wild once again, and everyone was seasick. The ship was so rocky during the show, I could barely kick without falling over. My back and feet hurt more than normal from working so hard to stay vertical. Thankfully, it was time to leave Alaska and set sail for the Caribbean. On the way, we docked for a few hours in Los Angeles.There, a quick lunch with sister Cindy did me a world of good, as I was lonely and homesick by this time. This stop also allowed me to unload boxes of stuff I had managed to accumulate in my tiny room. I would have never been able to get it all home on the plane from New Orleans—our final port of the contract.

****

Come October, the sun was here to stay, and we had a new activity—sunbathing! Actually I had three new activities: sunbathing followed by burning followed by peeling. It was good to thaw out, and since the weather was warm, I was able to walk lots of laps around the deck at night. I saw the most stunning rainbows and tropical lightning storms. Staring out into miles of nothing but ocean made me feel exhilarated, peaceful, lonely, and isolated all at the same time.

After Los Angeles, we made our way south to Cabo San Lucas on the southernmost tip of the Baha California peninsula. The rock formations were beautiful, but the land was barren. I spent my hour of free time on the phone with Ron. Phoning home, boyfriends, or girlfriends was a big deal when you got to port. You could do it from the ship, but you might as well hand over your entire paycheck. On land, during these Dark Ages before cell phones, you could often find phone centers where they would tell you the rate per minute to call a certain country. I made the call from Cabo through a hotel, and it cost me close to $300. (That was still cheaper than the ship's rate.) Ron and I had so much to say about how much we missed each other, but I had to hang up on him anyway or run out of money.

Next stop: Acapulco! (Why was Mexico so dirty?) I bought colorful Mexican blankets that I could buy cheaper in L.A. just to say I bought them from Acapulco. I quickly got tired of bartering and stopped for an authentic lunch of incredible chicken enchiladas with a deliciously different chocolate-based mole sauce. I was reminded of that lunch for the next few weeks as Montezuma took his revenge. From Acapulco, it cost me $8 a minute to phone Ron in England, so I budgeted for ten minutes. These calls were breaking my bank, but I wanted to keep this long-distance relationship afloat.

We sailed south to Costa Rica. I longed to hike into the rain forest to commune with monkeys and exotic birds and flowers but, having only a few hours free time, I just took a quick trip into town. The town was poor and dirty, but the surrounding landscape was lush and green and gorgeous. A couple friends and I ordered bottled beer in a tiny bar with a dirt floor, a few tables and bar stools, and a hand-painted menu on the wall.

Without this cruise ship experience, I probably never would have traveled to some of the places on our itinerary, especially the Central American and South American ports I would consider slightly dangerous. Costa Rica had become a trendy tourist spot, but any of the places with blatant poverty or Third World country status left me uneasy; I was paranoid they were corrupt and inhabited primarily by drug traffickers, possible kidnappers, and petty thieves who preyed on trusting tourists. I figured the cruise ship industry wouldn't risk taking passengers to a really unsafe place, but once you hopped in a cab and were on your own, you just hoped you were with someone trustworthy. You didn't want to turn the wrong corner and walk straight into a guerrilla ambush. I often consulted with the ship's officers or cruise staff who knew the ports. They'd tell us what to expect and how to get around safely. Being fluent in Spanish would have made me feel better.

These exotic locales were also infused with the possibility of extreme adventure and romance. As I sipped my Mexican beer in this hovel that served as a watering hole, I imagined myself the sexy heroine (unwed romance novelist Joan Wilder) of the comedic murder-kidnapping-treasure hunt movie *Romancing the Stone* awaiting the swashbuckling, bird-smuggling Jack T. Colton to sweep me off my feet for a night of Latin dancing and passion followed by a daring quest to track down a massive emerald before the killer-kidnappers did. The setting seemed perfect for those intrepid individuals who wanted to get themselves into trouble.

Onward to the Panama Canal, which would take us from the Pacific Ocean to the Caribbean Sea. I spent a day sipping rum drinks on deck as we traversed this marvelous feat of engineering. Ships paid quite a sum of money for the privilege of passing through the canal. The trip was particularly fascinating because it was such a tight squeeze. Our ship left little room to spare on either side. We watched as a bunch of small, dark Panamanians boarded the *Noordam* and hooked her up to tiny tugs that guided her through the manmade waterway without a scratch. I soaked in the view of verdant green rain forests and waterfalls.

Each minute passed by like a week, because I was desperately missing Ron and worried about our fate as a couple. He was back in England, and it would be a long time before mail could reach the ship again. We absolutely lived for mail. I never knew that time could pass by so slowly. I was startled to have my sightseeing afternoon interrupted by a visit from the cruise director. He smirked and placed a practically transparent air mail envelope in my hand. I was confused. Even though we never docked, the ship was able to receive mail in Panama, because the Panamanians who came aboard brought it along. It was a letter from Ron telling me how much he loved and missed me. I nearly fainted. I was walking on air the rest of the day.

Our next port was the filthy, poverty-stricken town of Cartagena, Colombia, on the Caribbean Coast. We disembarked to an entourage of fully armed soldiers in camouflage fatigues and entrepreneurs selling Colombian coffee and something that passed as vanilla extract. I bought both but never did spot Juan Valdez. The old architecture and walled fortresses were impressive monuments. A group of us were coerced by a pushy, persistent local guy into touring a historic church/castle for "free." At the end, of course, he put the pressure on us to give donations. We left a few dollars and skedaddled while he was still calling after us for more. Walking around town was scary, because people were shouting and pointing aggressively at us. I ran back to the ship and took refuge well before the last call to board. God forbid I should be late and the ship set sail without me while I'm standing next to irate, Colombian, rifle-bearing militia, wildly waving to the ship to "Come back!" because I don't speak a word of Spanish and only brought along enough cash to buy lunch (half of which I just gave to the assertive tour guide).

My favorite stop was the British Island of Grand Cayman, which is famous for its seven-mile white sand beach with crystal-clear turquoise-blue water. I was so relieved to be in a place where the lifestyle was more what I was accustomed to. Banks everywhere, sporting all different names, suggested to me that this was a perfect place to launder and hide money. Still, Grand Cayman was clean, gorgeous, and high class. I visited the Turtle Farm and the eerie black rock formations known as Hell. At a little gift shop, I bought some scrumptious Tortuga rum cakes.

Our last Caribbean hurrah was our visit to the island of Cozumel, off the eastern coast of Mexico's Yucatán Peninsula. Cozumel (about 30 miles long and 10 miles wide) was dusty and dirty in typical Mexican fashion and full of great shopping "bargains." I bought some pretty silver bracelets with colored stones inset and a bright yellow and red lizard Mexican mask for my collection. I met up with a group of my friends at the famous Carlos and Charlie's bar for margaritas, chips and salsa, loud music, and laughter.

While in the Caribbean, we had periodic coast guard inspections during which they searched our rooms for illegal substances and alien island boys. I was always a little bit afraid. Was there something or someone hiding in my room who I didn't know about? Candy and I checked out clean, but I wondered what would happen if they did find contraband or a stowaway.

The end of the line for the MS *Noordam* was New Orleans, Louisiana, back in my beloved U. S. of A. I left my floating home and gladly boarded a plane to L.A. That trip was an amazing, once-in-a-lifetime adventure, albeit a tad too long for me. My five-month-long work day was finally over. Time to punch out.

****

When we disembarked the *Noordam*, I was sure I'd had my fill of sailing. Probably forever. But Anita had asked our cast to perform for two weeks on a cruise ship currently cruising around *New Zealand*! It was only ten days, after all. And it was New Zealand, for goodness sake! How could I say no? We were home for only one day of repacking before taking our shows across the world to meet the MS *Maasdam* in Christchurch. First we flew to Hawaii for an overnight in Honolulu on the island of Oahu. After a seaside dinner of mahi-mahi and rum drinks, shopping, a walk, and a gorgeous sunset on Waikiki beach, I was rejuvenated and ready for the ten-hour flight to the land of Kiwis and Kookaburra.

New Zealand is twenty-one hours ahead of L.A. Talk about jet lag! To make matters worse, I had also caught some kind of sinus infection and could barely sing my solo songs. I didn't stress too much, as we had only two performances. I was a bit miffed at something else, however. Our "Birth of the Blues" choreographer and another young woman joined the cast, so we'd have more performers to fill the bigger stage. The choreography they had rehearsed by themselves in L.A. before the trip had many slight variations from our show. But since the choreographer was in charge, the six of us had to change the show we had been performing for five months to accommodate the two of them. It's much harder to change a habit than to learn something new, and I simply did not want to have to think that hard and make a bunch of unnecessary changes for a mere two performances. "Get over yourself, Kristi, and just learn the new choreography. You get to see New Zealand!" I wisely told myself.

Once I stepped aboard the MS *Maasdam*, I changed my mind about sailing. This was a "world cruise" for which passengers had paid upward of $20,000 to travel for a few months in absolute luxury. These people were traveling in style, and we had *passenger status*! That meant we had normal cabins like the passengers did, got to eat in any dining room (including the formal one), and could partake of *any* of the activities on board. There was even a real Starbucks on board, and we could order anything we wanted and as much as we wanted for *free*. I think I gained ten pounds just from mochas. The ship had a plush movie theatre and a gym complete with smoothie bar. It offered wine tastings and lectures by acclaimed authors, and a big Octoberfest celebration. The formal dining room was unbelievable. It had two levels that were connected by a grand spiral staircase. The menu offered several choices for each course, all gourmet, scrumptious, and exquisite. And we could order any and all of it at *no charge*. Even steak and lobster. Again, I got so chubby. I don't know how you take a cruise like that and not return home twice your size. Food is available twenty-four hours a day and it's all so enticing. The big dining room excitement was not the spectacular food, however; it was having famous singer and actress Rosemary Clooney sitting at the table next to us. She, too, was performing on the ship. What a star-spotting!

I fell in love with the friendly people of New Zealand and its gorgeous green hills covered with yellow flowers and dotted with sheep. I bought a hand-knit, heavy wool sweater and became hooked on pumpkin soup.

One sea day, we cruised Milford Sound—a fiord in Fiordland National Park on the southwest side of the south island. I could see why it was New Zealand's most popular tourist attraction. Its spectacular icy-blue glaciers were reminiscent of Alaska, but its deep verdant green mountains reminded me of the Hawaiian islands with a dusting of snow on top. Like Alaska, this was one of those places that were so strikingly beautiful they could be considered proof of God.

As we left the shores of New Zealand and headed into the open waters of the Tasman Sea bound for Adelaide, Australia (our exit port), the waters became so rough that trying to do a sit up in the gym was next to impossible. My sea sickness worsened. When our cruise was over, I kissed the Australian soil. I was so happy to be on solid land again.

Bob, Tom, Dana, Candy, and I had decided to stay on and see a bit of Australia before heading back home. After visiting the kangaroos, koalas, and Tasmanian devils at the Adelaide zoo, we boarded a train overnight for the thirteen-hour trip to Melbourne. We spent four fantastic days down under sightseeing. And what sights we saw: Aboriginal art exhibits, botanical gardens, theatre performances, and Queen Victoria Market. (I bought a boomerang and a brown leather, outback hat.) I tasted the best coffee and scones *in the world*. I soaked up the distinctive Aussie accent and practiced saying, "G'day, mate!" Dana and I toured three wineries, too. *Hiccup*! Domaine Chandon served their sumptuous champagne alongside baguette slices spread with herb cheese and their own delicious recipe of tapenade (a mix of black olives, anchovies, capers, lemon juice, garlic, and dijon mustard). Yum! This was one "sheila" (woman) who would have loved to spend more time on walkabout, but it was time to head home to Cali and sort out my relationship with Ron, with whom I had been incommunicado since I left Hawaii.

****

When I arrived at my sister's place in Los Angeles, I found piles of mail and packages from England. Ron had written me every day we were apart and had decided to move to L.A. right away to live with me. Importing a man from London was a risky move, but I had to see how this love affair would play out. This left me little time to search for an apartment. While I was in New Zealand and Australia, Cindy had been on the lookout for vacancies in her neighborhood. Just before I returned home, she found a studio apartment in the building next door that rented for $595 per month. I took it. My parents had to underwrite the lease, because I no longer had a job. It had been stressful knowing I had nowhere to live when I returned. Previously, I had bunked on my sister's couch between gigs, but asking her to house me and my boyfriend was not an option. Imposing stinks and being homeless stinks even more.

I moved into my new place just in time to welcome my British beau to America. With only $1,000 in his pocket, no job, and no work visa, Ron seemed to be more of a financial liability than an asset. Of course, I couldn't see that clearly with all the stars in my eyes. His cash reserves wouldn't last long, and he couldn't legally work unless we were married. (What was I thinking? I wasn't. I was in love.) Plus, I still had $5,000 debt on my credit card, which Ron insisted we clear up ASAP. I had always been worried about how I was going to pay my bills as a dancer who was open to taking nearly any job anywhere. But now, with Ron in the picture, I decided I would not take any gig that would take me away from him for more than two weeks. Otherwise, it would have to be a local job or a job for which he could tag along. With such limited possibilities, I was freaking out about how we were going to make ends meet on my dancer's income.

Our solution: We'd cut our expenses to a minimum until we knew we'd have earnings. I didn't own a TV, so no expense there. For entertainment, we borrowed books and magazines from the library, went to free movie screenings, walked the 3rd Street promenade in

Santa Monica to see street performers, window shopped, biked, hiked, rollerbladed, and attended free concerts on the Santa Monica pier. To keep fit, keep busy, and meet people, Ron joined a nearby gym. He also invested a few hundred dollars on a massage table and started giving massages. It was hard on him (and me) being an alien in a foreign country, unable to get a job, and knowing not a soul except yours truly. But love conquers all, right?

A month later, dear Anita Mann came through for me yet again with a week-long mission in Miami. She hired me as part of a group to perform a Brazilian samba number for the PBS television special "Concert of the Americas." This was no ordinary television show. This mega production was hosted by *President Bill Clinton* and *First Lady Hillary*. (It would be my way of serving my country.) The show's producer was none other than *Quincy Jones*. In addition to the Clintons, the audience members were going to include the leaders of over thirty countries in the western hemisphere, all of whom were gathered in Miami for a free trade summit.

Naturally, for an occasion of such great importance, Anita wanted her *crème de la crème*, A-list dancers. They were the ones she used for the prime television gigs like *The Miss America Pageant*. Lucky for me, many of the A-listers were already booked, and being on the top of the B list (or perhaps just being available), I got to be a part of this amazing, once-in-a-lifetime experience. The A-list dancers were so cool, I could hardly stand it. They all wore sunglasses *inside* buildings and had six packs and buffed arms like all proper Los Angelenos. At first, I didn't feel worthy of being with these dancers and was so nervous during rehearsals that I kept making mistakes. My lack of confidence was becoming apparent to others, making them think I didn't deserve to be there either. Plus, I had never sambaed before, and it took some time for me to get the feel of it, but eventually I got my act together. I kept wondering why they didn't hire real Brazilians to do their native dance instead of hip-hopping Californians.

My traditional Brazilian Samba costume made me feel even more self-conscious, because it was the teensiest-weensiest bikini I'd ever worn or even seen. The bikini bottoms were cut just about as low as they could go in the front, and there was virtually no material in the back. I kept begging the wardrobe people for more feathers to cover my nearly naked, goose-pimpled rear. Eventually, I guess the costumers concluded it wasn't quite respectable to be boogying our bare buns in front of so many prominent world leaders, and they added some extra, strategically placed quills. We also wore a massive feather headpiece and backpack. While our colorful, substantial crown plumage and practically nude body was perfect party attire for Carnival in Rio, I simply felt like a giant bird with a plucked belly.

When we arrived at the venue in Miami, you'd better believe security was tight: metal detectors, bomb-sniffing dogs, and secret servicemen in dark suits, sunglasses, and earphones (Just like in the movies!) everywhere you looked. Of course, we had special I.D. badges to wear around our necks. Had someone chosen to blow up that theatre, they could have rid the world of half its leaders in one go. Talk about killing thirty birds with one stone. I was a little nervous about the reason for all the security, but I had a job to do, and I was more insecure about wearing that microscopic costume on national television.

It wasn't until our dress rehearsal at the venue that we found out who was performing in the show. This star-studded event included Maria Conchita Alonso, Dr. Maya Angelou, Paul Anka, Celia Cruz, Sheila E, Mallory Freeman, Daisy Fuentes, Pat Morita, Tito Puente, Michael Douglas, Liza Minelli, Jimmy Smits, and Bebe and Cece Wynan, as well as singers, musicians, and colorfully dressed folk dancers from the participating countries in North, Central, and South America. What an incredible lineup. I don't know who was more famous—the entertainers on stage or the audience members. While we were standing around waiting to rehearse, Liza came over to talk to our troupe. Just the fact that she took time to acknowledge us was astounding. Then again, she was acting in the best tradition of theatre people, who are used to that cast family rapport.

Anita had worked with this TV producer before and, in traditional TV style, was rushing to finish choreographing our opening entrance two hours before dress rehearsal. She was a last-minute miracle worker, but it put the pressure on us dancers to be quick studies. Our rehearsal went so late, it was eating into our dinner hour, and one of the girls was getting angry. Beautiful, thin, and talented, she looked like she never had a weight problem in her life, but she had learned to keep svelte by not eating or drinking any calories after 7 p.m. She ate whatever she wanted during the day, but after 7:00 her mouth was closed for business. And she was committed: she would have actually skipped dinner had we been released after her self-imposed curfew. That's dedication. My hotel roommate was an intriguing, gorgeous gal, too, who was so cool, she could have given a person frostbite. She dated a handsome, young Haitian politician and dreamed of being the First Lady of Haiti—aspirations much like Eva Perón's. As cool as my fellow dancers were, they finally warmed up to me, but it was all I could do to keep up with them.

The show went off without a hitch; I successfully shook my tail feathers for the President of the United States of America! I just wished there would've been a few more feathers on my tail. President Clinton didn't seem to mind.

Afterwards, a group of us went to town to celebrate, Miami style. "Let's go dancing!" the cool people decided. "At a gay bar!" This seemed to make sense, since our guys were all gay. I had never been to a gay bar, but being in a serious relationship, I liked the idea of going to a place where the men wouldn't hit on me. Well, the people there sure were friendly. As predicted, the gay men steered clear, but (surprise!) I did not anticipate getting propositioned by a heterosexual couple. I politely declined (three's a crowd) but took their offer as a compliment. One club employee bent over backwards to be hospitable to all the patrons; he'd take the shirt off his back for you. Turns out he'd also take the pants off his legs and did so on stage to the delight of patrons. Some people thought he deserved more that a pat on the back for his efforts, and he willingly let them display their affection.

In addition to being approachable, this club went above and beyond to provide the highest standard of cleanliness. Instead of the measly "Employees must wash their hands" signs in the lavatories, they actually provided a *shower*. To assure patrons the employees were rinsing off, they even placed the shower on the second floor balcony in full view. Not a single germ or speck of dirt could have survived that man's exemplary sponging practice. Even the women's restroom was so spotless that men felt comfortable using the stalls for private make-out sessions. Holy cannoli! I couldn't wait to high-tail it outta there, my legs crossed in search of an empty restroom. That bar was far too clean and friendly for me. Salsa dancing in South Beach was much more my pace.

This had been one memorable trip to Miami. How could I possibly top it? Here's how: After returning to Los Angeles, Ron and I decided to get married! And a few months later, we did.

Final Scene: New York City, August 10, 2002

We sailed through our dressing room tour and bid bon voyage to the real Rockette. I didn't know her and she didn't know me, but we'd be forever bonded as part of an entertainment legacy, a select group of glamour gals who knew how to kick high and be spectacular. Once I became a Rockette, I truly felt I'd made it in show business. I was *somebody*. Of course, I had been somebody all along, but it was a good feeling—something no one could ever take away from me. "How that one little audition changed my life," I realized. One tiny decision, one baby step had opened the floodgates to adventure and prosperity. Likewise, simply taking the cruise ship gig had landed me with a husband, and eventually two beautiful children! *Life can transform in an instant*. Joining the Rockettes launched me into another ocean of blessings and lessons that charted a new, even more fabulous course for my future.

Act 3, Scene 1

The Audition

Long Legs and Tall Tales

It was another hot, smoggy, summer day in Los Angeles, and my studio apartment had no air conditioning. I kept the windows open hoping for a breeze, but mostly I let in more noise and air pollution. Santa Monica Boulevard bustled with activity, including the neighborhood drug trafficker and his customers my sister had been spying on from her second-story apartment, kitty-corner from my place. Having Cindy nearby gave me a sense of security, although we rarely saw each other. Usually I kept quiet with the windows closed, so the Jehovah's Witnesses and overly aggressive, door-to-door salespeople didn't think I was home, but today the heat was just too stifling.

I swallowed a breath of stale air and perused the classifieds section of the new *Backstage West* (the California version of New York City's *Backstage*) hoping for a show that would start in the fall after *South Pacific*, the musical I was currently in, ended. With pen in hand, I searched for some enticing, or at least some non-offensive, ad to circle. I was prepared to settle for "Actress needed for independent student film. No pay, some meals, no nudity." At least it would be a legitimate acting gig to put on my resume and to give me more acting experience. And free dinner would be nice. Then I recalled how my sister's boyfriend—an aspiring filmmaker who maxed out his credit cards to produce his own independent film—fed his actors junk food like pizza. Not worth it. I put my pen back behind my ear.

I flipped the pages dreading the thought of having to return to theme park dancing if I didn't find a "real" gig. Theme park shows were considered entry-level positions; many people were thankful to have the work but secretly (or openly) hoped to move on. One really shouldn't knock it, however. Many performers made a decent living for years through the steady work of places like Universal Studios, Disney, Six Flags, and Hershey Park. Some shows were high-quality productions and certainly good performance venues on which to cut one's teeth. They were also more repetitious than prestigious—not jobs we generally bragged about. Even if they started out strong, eventually they morphed into mind-numbing assignments we tolerated only for the financial security they offered.

After Ron moved to L.A., I was desperate for income and had been lucky to land a job at Universal Studios Hollywood working on and off as a replacement performer for *The Flintstones Show*—a surprisingly delightful, well-choreographed, thirty-minute, mini-musical based on the popular, 1960s caveman cartoon starring characters Fred Flintstone, his wife Wilma, and dog Dino plus pals Betty and Barney Rubble.

At first, I was very low on the sub list, meaning about five other people had to turn down the work before I'd get asked. I could have easily been bitter about my status, but I knew that nothing was written in stone. Whenever I did work, I made sure my performances totally rocked, and, as a result, I eventually got promoted to first sub. In spite of my ranking on the totem pole, I always got plenty of calls and made a lot of extra dough. It was my bread and butter between gigs. Never rocking the boat and always dancing my best with a good attitude and work ethic paid off not only in terms of moving me up the sub list, but also in impressing the *Flintstones* choreographer, who eventually cast me in a tour of *South Pacific*—a real, honest-to-goodness musical that I *could* brag about (especially because our leading man, playing the role of Emile de Becque, was none other than two-time Grammy award winning vocalist Jack Jones—the original crooner of "The Love Boat" theme song).

In the busy season, each cast performed six shows a day. I was sometimes crazy enough to accept a double-shift—twelve shows in a row. Holed up in the dark theatre for so many hours, I ached to see the light of day. It was weird repeating the same show over and over and over, back to back to back, like a television rerun marathon. After doing it too many times, I'd get so tired and confused, I'd forget how many shows I'd completed and where I was in the current show. "Have we done the second number already, or was that the last show I'm remembering?" It was like factory work—going through the motions, pumping out identical products. I'd end up either sick or injured—usually a foot problem due to the "raked" (sloped on an angle) stage and unsupportive footwear. It was truly an exercise in mind over matter. If I were lucky, some funny cast member would make me laugh or accidentally goof up or lose a wig or something to help me get through the day.

Being a big corporation, Universal Studios was like no other place I had worked as an entertainer. We went through training with human resources to learn all the rules and regulations, were issued ID badges, had a special parking lot and employee entrance, and received discounts at the gift store and snack bars, as well as several free passes to the park. It was kind of a kid's dream living at an amusement park every day. Still, I had no intention of allowing theme park dancing to become the pinnacle of my career. If I had to keep repeating *The Flintstones Show* a dozen times a day, my health and sanity would surely be on the rocks.

An ad title in the bottom right-hand corner of *Backstage West* caught my attention: "Radio City Music Hall Christmas Spectacular Cast Auditions." The announcement read:

Radio City Music Hall Christmas Spectacular at the Grand Palace in Branson, Mo. will be holding Auditions August 21-23 at the Debbie Reynolds Studio, 6514 Lankershim Blvd. Call backs will be Aug. 24 by appointment. Sign in one hour prior to call. Casting breakdown as follows. Rehearsals begin on or about October 20. Show runs Nov. 10-Dec. 23. Bring two copies of updated photo and resume. ROCKETTES: August 21, 10 a.m. Must be proficient in tap, jazz, ballet, and be between 5'5 ½"–5'9" in stocking feet (no exceptions). Bring tap and jazz shoes with heels. Vocal audition may be required. Bring Broadway uptempo music.

I was in disbelief. Radio City is auditioning for Rockettes? *The* Rockettes? The notice shocked and surprised me as I didn't even know the Rockettes held auditions. I thought they were still using the same dancers they started with back in the 1930s. Well, maybe not in the thirties, but it was pretty common knowledge in the dance community that no one left the Rockettes unless they died or lost a leg. "Why were they auditioning?"

The announcement stated that the Rockettes had another Christmas show in Branson, Missouri, and needed an entirely new cast. Were the Rockettes being franchised like a McDonald's hamburger joint? Radio City was also looking for Santa, dancers, children, singers, and people over eighteen years of age and under 4'6" in height to play elves and special characters. But I didn't care about any of that. "I wanna be a Rockette," I proclaimed to myself. I was 5'8", had great legs, and could kick to my forehead. I was perfect for the part.

When the audition day finally arrived, I threw my dance bag in my little Ford Escort. The audition was at ten a.m., but we were supposed to sign in by nine. It usually took me forty-five minutes to get to the Debbie Reynolds Studios (named after Debbie Reynolds of *Singin' in the Rain* fame) in North Hollywood, but even the psychic hotline couldn't predict with any accuracy how long it would take anyone to get anywhere in L.A. traffic, so I left at 7:45 a.m. to allow a little extra time.

I was familiar with the route as Universal Studios was less than two miles away, but I had my Thomas Brothers Guide in my car in case of detours or in the event that my car should break down. Thomas Brothers Guide—a thick spiral-bound book—was the most detailed and revered map of Los Angeles. Everyone had one. An entertainer without a Thomas Brothers Guide was like a hiker without a compass. It was one of my most crucial possessions.

The trip to Debbie Reynolds was uneventful. Consequently, I arrived about an hour and a half early, a bit earlier than I preferred. While I had plenty of time to collect myself, prepare, relax, breathe, and not feel rushed, I never wanted to arrive too much before an audition because I'd get bored, overstretched, and freaked out analyzing the competition.

The surrounding neighborhood was sketchy at best, but it was by far my favorite studio and the most like the old New York studios I was used to. I felt at home in that well-worn, slightly musty, hardwood floor setting with all the old movie posters lining the walls, many of them starring Debbie Reynolds herself. I much preferred it to the stark, sleek, modern, hip-hop studios that had sprung up to attract the MTV dancers. Thank goodness this was an environment in which I felt comfortable.

Nervous as usual walking into an audition, I found the sign-in sheet but decided to wait to sign my name until I made sure I wasn't going to be in the first group. Audition numbers are typically handed out according to your order on the sign-in sheet. Usually, if you are one of the first five people to sign in, you will be in the first group to dance at the audition. It stinks to dance first, because you have to pick up the choreo faster than anyone else does. An extra thirty seconds of practice time can mean life or death—the difference between knowing what you are doing and not having a clue, food on the table or starvation, and, in this case, fame or obscurity. Alternatively, when you don't dance first, you generally get to watch the groups ahead of you, thereby giving you more time to memorize the steps. You aren't always allowed to dance on the sidelines as you wait, but you can watch and possibly "mark it" in miniature.

Also, the first few groups set the standard for judging. The casting crew don't really know how high to mark you based on the abilities of the group. They will probably score you a little too low to leave room for really spectacular performers, and then realize the rest of the group is at about the same level. By the end, however, they've forgotten how good you were, and your score doesn't really tell the whole story or reflect your relative talent. The only benefit of going first is that you get it over with first. Even the casting people joke about how you got the raw end of the deal by being in the first group. Everyone feels sorry for you and the others who auditioned with you. No, I definitely did not want to be in the first group.

I looked around for anyone I might know and wondered where all the dancers were. It didn't seem too crowded, but I was pretty early. I eyeballed the competition wondering how much better the other girls were. Finally, I spotted a girl I knew from Universal Studios. She was a tall, beautiful brunette and much younger than I. We exchanged greetings, but I didn't know her well and preferred to keep to myself so I could get my mind focused on the audition.

It was time to hit the ladies room to change into my lucky purple audition leotard and tan tights. Knowing that a simple leotard and tan tights were the standard Broadway audition dress code, I figured this attire would probably apply to the Rockettes as well. The high-cut leotard and nude stockings would show off my legs the best anyway. There were a lot of people in black, as it is the most slimming, but nobody else was wearing bright purple. "Perfect!" I knew I would stand out.

I put sweats on over my dance clothes to keep my muscles warm and then touched up my make-up. It was a bit louder than what I would normally wear on the street, but not as obnoxious as what I'd wear on stage. My hair was slicked back in a ponytail with bobby pins securing the smaller strands. I gave my entire head a good, strong shellacking of hairspray. The last thing I wanted was to have bits of hair flying in my eyes and distracting me. It wasn't the most flattering hairdo, but I knew it would stay put and look neat and professional. Other girls wore cute, puffy, stylish hairdos, while mine was plastered to my head. I safety-pinned my bra straps to my leotard, because I hated bra straps sticking out during an audition. Tacky.

My dance bag was stuffed full. I double-checked all the supplies I might need: water bottle in case I got a coughing fit and couldn't sing, tissue in case of a runny nose that would send snot flying while doing turns, hairspray and extra hairpins, Band-Aids in case my shoes gave me a blister, more safety pins in case my bra disobeyed, and Advil for a stress headache. I popped a couple of Advil as a preventative measure and moved the tissue and water bottle to an easy-to-reach position in my bag.

Girls lined the narrow halls, stretching and chatting nervously. Squeezing among them, I claimed a small spot and sat down to locate my headshot and resume, which I set on top of my bag along with my sheet music. Then I stood and slowly unfolded my legs up to my head one at a time, working until I could comfortably kick to my forehead and do the splits in all directions. I had to be very limber for this audition. After fifteen people had signed in, I felt safe to put my name on the audition list.

As ten o'clock neared, a female assistant passed out audition numbers and collected our headshots and resumes. "Come on in, Ladies, and bring all your belongings, please." We gathered in the big studio D and the doors were shut behind us. There were only about forty girls auditioning. I thought there would be hundreds. I was sure in New York there would have been lines out the door. The fewer people, the better chance I have of getting the job, I reasoned.

"We will be measuring first, so please remove your shoes and form a line by the wall," the assistant ordered. One at a time, in our stocking feet, we stood flat-footed, back up against the measuring stick. A girl ahead of me was ousted for being too short. She had tried wearing three-inch heels to boost her height, but when the shoes came off, she was toast. "No one under 5'5 1/2" allowed. No exceptions." Did she really think the casting people would fall for such a trick? The height requirement was strict, at least on the short end of the stick. I measured in at about 5'7". "That can't be right," I said. "I've been 5'8" forever." "No, you are 5'7"," the assistant countered curtly. What possessed me to argue about it? After all, I was well within the zone, so it really didn't matter. "Keep your mouth shut, Kristi," I reminded myself silently. I had passed the first test.

"Next we'll be tapping, Ladies, so please put on your shoes as soon as you've been measured," the assistant instructed. I quickly put on the only tap shoes I owned, the ones I had purchased for my very first New York City audition some eight years earlier. I was slightly self-conscious about wearing them, because, since that time, they had been painted yellow and peach stripes for *No, No, Nanette*, and there were holes wearing through the soles. While ridiculous looking, I didn't have extra cash to spend on new shoes, and they were comfortable. I reasoned that the goofy shoes might actually help the casting people remember me better. Maybe they'd even be impressed that I had tapped in another show.

The tap combination was performed to a Christmas medley played live by a pianist. Having not tapped recently, I was relieved to see it was basic tap—nothing too complicated. I simply had to keep my sounds clean. We performed in groups of five, and everything seemed to go smoothly for me.

After the tap, we changed into our character shoes and learned a tricky, sharp, military version of "Jingle Bells" with some difficult rhythms, not the standard eight counts per measure. We had to be painfully sharp with our head snaps and steps. "Sharper, Ladies, sharper!" demanded the poker-faced woman who seemed to be in charge. It was a totally new style of dancing for me: ultra precise, almost jerky, like time-lapse photography—little snapshots of poses all linked together. Next, we learned a kickline combination linking arms with the five girls in our group. It was a lot harder kicking with a girl on either side of you hanging on, but I felt pretty good about how I did. No major mistakes. Lastly, one at a time, we were called in to sing our 16 bars of music to live piano accompaniment. Prepared and professional, I was well rehearsed and confident that my singing was entirely passable for what was primarily a dance gig. "Please, God, let me get this job!"

My prayers were answered. I made the callback! About thirty of us were asked to return a few days later and do it all again. I was elated to be invited back, but how I wished they would have hired me after the first audition. What if I screwed up the second time around?

For the callback, I wore my same lucky purple leotard, so they would remember me, and went through the same rigmarole with my best smile on. This time David Nash, the producer of the *Radio City Christmas Spectacular* in Branson, appeared at the end of the audition. "I'd like to tell you ladies a bit about the job. If you become a Rockette, you will perform at the beautiful Grand Palace Theatre and make $1,100 a week. Rehearsals start October 19th in Missouri and the show closes December 23rd…"

The more he told us about the gig, the more I ached to get the job. Listening to what might happen to the lucky few in that room was torture. It was so close I could taste it. The $1,100 a week was unheard of. Being a Rockette would be a dream come true. Everybody knew the Rockettes. They were the Big Time.

Once home, I went about my daily business trying to put the audition out of my mind so as not to drive myself crazy with anticipation. When the phone rang, I wasn't expecting anyone out of the ordinary. "This is Myra Longstern, head of Rockette Operations." ("She's from the Rockettes!" I squealed to myself, recognizing the significance.) "Yes," I said trying to sound calm, my heart beating clear out of my chest.

"We would like to offer you a job as a Rockette in the *Radio City Christmas Spectacular* in Branson, Missouri.".

"That's wonderful," I responded, consciously trying to lower my voice, which seemed to have dramatically risen in pitch.

"You will be responsible for transportation to Branson. We have arranged for housing near the theatre. You'll share a two-bedroom condo with another Rockette and split the monthly rent which is $700. Is there someone you'd prefer to room with?"

"I don't know anyone in the show, but my husband will be coming with me," I responded.

"Oh," Ms. Longstern responded coolly, "that presents a housing problem." She was clearly annoyed at the inconvenience, but being newly married, I wasn't budging. "If you insist on your husband coming, then I guess you'll have to be responsible for finding your own housing." Ms. Longstern was all business and no banter; she wasn't full of warm fuzzies. "Your contract and information will be Federal Expressed to your home tomorrow. Please sign it, fill out your W-2 forms, and return it to me as soon as possible. Congratulations."

I took a minute to jump for joy and dance around the kitchen, then phoned my parents to tell them the good news. "I'm a Rockette! I knew I was right for the job. And I'm going back to Branson! Yee-haw!"

Final Scene: New York City, August 10, 2002

The tour guide motioned us forward and continued her monologue as we walked down the hall: "The Rockettes originated in St. Louis, Missouri, back in 1925 as the 'Missouri Rockets,' and later became the 'Roxyettes.' They debuted in Manhattan at the Music Hall in 1932, their name eventually morphing into 'Rockettes.' They were such a sensation that they've been a fixture at this spectacular theater ever since." I could practically give the spiel myself, as I knew this trivia by heart from my extensive Rockette media training. Beginning my Rockette adventures in Missouri was actually fitting since the Rockettes started there, too.

I thanked myself profusely for making this journey to Radio City. I deserved this moment of glory. Rockette life hadn't exactly been a piece of cake. I had survived pain and ecstasy, blood, sweat, and tears. Becoming a Rockette was like joining an exclusive sorority. The whole experience, especially initially, felt somewhat like hazing. After surviving the grueling initiation requirements, I felt bonded into Rockette sisterhood. My induction into Rockette-dom had been more harrowing than my college sorority initiation in which I had to strip down to my skivvies, don a toga, and prance around with flaming torches. Well, that's what my husband guessed happened. I, of course, am sworn to secrecy.

Act 3, Scene 2

Branson

Others may have felt they were being sent to Siberia, but I had fond memories of Buddy and Branson and was thrilled to go back with the Rockettes. Plus, my husband and I were ready to travel again and see something new and different. More importantly, we were down to our last dollar, so this gig was a godsend. We had been nickel and dime-ing our way along with odd jobs since he moved from London to Los Angeles. This job could get us back on our feet.

After the initial excitement wore off, I got down to business and began searching for housing. I hadn't a clue how to find a suitable place long distance, especially one that would take such a short-term rental. Thankfully, after a few, unsuccessful weeks of apartment hunting, I received a phone call from Ms. Longstern, "There is an available two-bedroom condo adjacent to the condos the other Rockettes are staying in. Are you interested?" We gladly took it, although we didn't need the extra room and were concerned about the price.

The dollar signs I had been seeing were quickly fading away. We still had to pay $650 a month rent on our apartment in L.A. and now we had another $700 a month that we would be paying for the housing in Branson. My $1,100 per week paychecks would be quickly spent. Also, the first month's rent on our condo plus a security deposit would be due upon arrival before we ever received any money from Radio City. Things were going to be tight until those first few paychecks started coming in. My cruise ship roommate, Candy, ended up needing a place to sublet for a few months. Since we trusted her with our home, we let her stay for a mere $250 a month. Every little bit helped.

Having decided to drive to Branson so we'd have a car at our disposal, I checked out travel books from the library and eagerly planned our itinerary for the trip across country. Despite some concern whether or not my eight-year-old car would make the trip, we really wanted the freedom of having our own car there. So we decided to take the risk but allowed several days of extra travel time in case of a breakdown.

On October 13, with a packed car, we drove out of the smog and onto old Route 66 eastbound for Branson, Missouri. We took the reverse path of the famous rhythm and blues standard "(Get Your Kicks on) Route 66," traveling through or near San Bernardino; Barstow; Kingman; Winona; Flagstaff, Arizona; Gallup, New Mexico;

Amarillo; Oklahoma City; Joplin, Missouri; and finally "St. Louie." I sang the cheerful song as we passed through San Bernardino to the east of Los Angeles.

With little money to spare, we counted our pennies on the trip. Knowing that it would take a few weeks before I'd get my first paycheck, we couldn't splurge on expensive hotels. Hence, we spent our first night at a youth hostel in Flagstaff—a quaint town on the outskirts of the Grand Canyon. The second day we made our way to the red rocks of Sedona, Arizona (famous for its mystical vortexes), for a hike among Indian cliff dwellings, followed by two nights in Santa Fe, where we stayed for free with friends, drank margaritas, and ate Tex-Mex. Our next stop was Oklahoma City for a visit to the Cowboy Hall of Fame and an enormous steak dinner. Although worried about gaining weight on the trip, I still couldn't pass up the opportunity to sample some of the best cow carcass in the country. We hopped back in the car and didn't stop driving until two a.m. when we stopped for the night at a hotel on the outskirts of Branson. With plenty of time to spare, we had reached our final destination, our car still intact and running. I breathed a sigh of relief and fell soundly asleep.

The next morning we drove into Branson, enjoying the striking fall colors of the Ozarks along the way. Heading down the familiar Highway 76 through the heart of town and past all the theatres, I noticed that a lot of the same stars were still there from my first visit with Buddy Ebsen. When I had been here with Buddy, however, I was thoroughly excited and had normal, healthy stage fright. This time I had a queasy stomach and the uneasiness that comes with self-doubt, insecurity, and not knowing what to expect. I was worried about not being good enough. Dancing with Buddy was small potatoes compared to what was coming. He was the star of that show. We were the stars of this show.

The condos we were going to be living in were situated around a golf course about a half mile from the theatre. We begged the receptionist at the country club to let us into our condo early, but, unfortunately, she didn't know where we were supposed to be staying. Because we had arrived so far ahead of schedule, there were no Radio City people around yet to give us any information. We had no choice but to tighten our belts and shell out the cash, or, safer yet, the credit card, and get a cheap hotel.

Long Legs and Tall Tales

After checking into our hotel, we drove to find the recently built Grand Palace Theatre where I would be performing. It was a 4,000-seat, breathtaking, white, old-southern-plantation-style, monster of a theatre with columns framing the entrance. I got a rush just looking at it. Inside, we climbed the expansive, spiral staircase leading to the second-floor administrative offices in search of the manager to see if we could find a job for Ron. The man in charge was so kind. Without batting an eye, he hired him to help decorate the theatre for Christmas and then usher for my show once it opened. We were relieved to have the extra bit of income, and the job would give hubby something to do. He also gave us free tickets to see the show *Patsy Cline*, which was finishing up its run there. We couldn't believe our good fortune and the generous hospitality. We felt so welcomed. That night, as we sat in the front row, I couldn't help thinking that I would be on that very stage in a few weeks. A chill ran through my body. I had a lot to learn and experience before then.

****

A couple days later, the condos were ready, and we finally moved in. The two-bedroom units were fairly new and tastefully decorated. The master bath even had an oversized Jacuzzi tub, which I was sure I would need after kicking all day. The kitchen was large and fully stocked with dishes. There was even a clubhouse with an indoor, heated pool. We were happy, to say the least. This was absolute luxury compared to our digs in Los Angeles. We grabbed our swimsuits and headed to the clubhouse for a swim and a look around, then hopped back in the car and took a trip out to find the grocery store so we could load up on all the food and supplies we would need.

I pored over my packet of rehearsal information, which had been left at the front desk by the Radio City staff, like I was receiving my secret assignment from the CIA. The rehearsal hall was all the way back in Springfield, so we would be carpooling in vans for the forty-five-minute drive. There was nowhere to buy food quickly on our lunch breaks, so we needed to pack lunches. We were expected to be dressed, warmed up, and ready to kick at ten a.m. sharp. Our rehearsal schedule showed Sundays off, but that was about it. We'd rehearse daily from ten until five with an hour for lunch. I was anxious to get started but scared at the same time.

The following day, one of the new Rockettes pulled up in the van at eight-thirty a.m. with eight other Rockettes. Apparently, my acquaintance from *The Flintstones Show* had gotten axed, as I expected, after she failed to bring her tap shoes to the audition, so I didn't know a soul. I said a quiet, "Hello," and climbed in with my overstuffed dance bag. They all knew at least one other person, because they had at least met their roommates.

I glanced around and immediately was intimidated by everyone. They were all so pretty and, obviously, talented. My teeth clenched and my head began to throb as I thought about the day ahead. We made small talk on the ride through the hills and into town, talking about mutual show biz friends and how they knew each other. I gazed out the window trying not to get car sick, my knuckles white as they gripped the handle of my bag.

At the rehearsal hall, we met up with the rest of the line-up. There were squeaks and squeals as old friends were reunited. About eight girls were returning Rockettes. Some performed in Branson the previous year, which was the first year the show opened there. Some had done the New York show. They had already survived a Christmas show and lived to tell about it. I wished I knew what I was doing like they did, although they all seemed on edge, too.

The veterans were easy to spot, because they all came in carrying Rockette dance bags and wearing Rockette T-shirts, sweatshirts, or show jackets. I couldn't wait to order my show jacket and join the club. All the Broadway kids had show jackets from *Le Mis* or *Cats* or *Miss Saigon* or whatever show they had been in. To me, having a show jacket meant you had made it.

A number of the girls were still finishing their run of *Will Rogers Follies* starring Pat Boone, right there in Branson. They'd rehearse with the Rockettes during the day and perform at night. *Will Rogers Follies* was a perfect show from which to steal Rockettes, as the dancers required for that show were tall, leggy tappers, too. Many of the girls had done that show or *42nd Street* or both.

The girls chatted quietly in the hallway, as they changed into their dance gear and warmed up. There was light conversation, but I could feel the tension, as people readied themselves and started to concentrate on the task ahead. I could sense the mind shift from the small talk on the van ride to the expectation of the rigid drilling to come. This wasn't going to be a light-hearted day of jovial kicking and tapping with friends. This was going to be military boot camp with drill sergeants watching the new recruits' every move. It was intimidating. I wanted to do well not only to make it through this show, but to remain a Rockette for years to come. There was a lot at stake. That guarantee of several months' worth of work at the end of every year was a big boon to a dancer. I didn't want to jeopardize that opportunity by messing up my first contract; otherwise, it might be my last.

A skinny young woman with a serious countenance stepped out of the rehearsal hall and said, "Ladies, we will begin with tap, but we need to take a line-up first, so we need you in stocking feet. Bring all of your belongings with you." Then someone opened the rehearsal hall doors and we made our way in. All chatting ceased and the mood became professional, intense, and focused.

The hall had hardwood floors, brick walls, and mirrors on one end. Two large dolly carts were holding giant alphabet blocks like the miniature version I had as a kid for building towers. I saw boxes of giant foil wreaths, xylophones, and sticks—all props we'd be using in the show. The director, her assistants, the stage manager, and his assistants sat at tables along the front of the hall with their thick notebooks full of choreography and formation notes with X's and O's like a football chart. They were prepared with enough provisions—including coffee, water, and other drinks, cans of nuts, and bowls of hard candy and gum—to get them through the day if not a major catastrophe. The musical director sat in the corner at the baby grand piano, a drummer and his drum kit by his side. All eyes were on us as we entered the room.

Our director, Linda Haberman, was thin, short-haired, and androgynously attired in shades of black. Her voice was low and authoritative with an I-don't-have-time-for-mistakes-so-get-it-right-the-first-time attitude. Her stern demeanor made it clear that she meant business. While she scared the heck out of us, she also commanded our highest respect, because she knew what she was doing, didn't waste time, and got the job done. She made us want to do our best. We did not want to displease her. A former Fosse dancer, she could really cut a rug, and when she demonstrated, we were in awe. She acted embarrassed and annoyed when someone mentioned that the entire cast had just watched the video of her dancing with Ben Vereen in *Pippin*.

Linda had a talented, thirty-something, male assistant, Dennis, who beautifully demonstrated the choreography. Having performed in *La Cage Aux Folles* on Broadway, he had plenty of practice dancing like a woman and could almost do it better than we could, much to our chagrin. He was at Linda's beck and call and tried to act tough and serious, but I could tell he was sweet and a softy inside.

Then there was Julie—the tall, thin, red-headed woman who had ushered us in. She was another assistant to Linda and was also our dance captain and one of our swings. Having been a Rockette for years, she was an excellent teacher and mother hen to her little flock of Rockettes.

Those three comprised the core creative team with whom we had most contact. There was also a music director, stage manager, assistant stage managers, and company manager, but Linda's team ruled the roost at rehearsals. The entire staff was serious about getting the show up to snuff. Apparently, there was a time when the Rockettes were not thought of too highly. Other professional dancers questioned their ability and looked down on them as lacking talent, being able to do nothing more than tap and kick. (What's not to like about great tapping and kicking?) This team was on a mission to change that image and return the Rockettes to their former glory. Their jobs were at stake, too. Teaching all that material, training all those new Rockettes, and getting the girls to gel perfectly before opening night was a daunting task. We had three weeks to look like a team and to learn to dance precisely in unison. The creative staff had a big job to do, and the Rockettes were expected to be no less than perfect in acting out their orders.

The first order of business was determining the all-important "lineup," which refers to the order in which the girls stand in the kickline. The order was critical, because the Rockettes were supposed to look like clones of each other. The great trick to making the Rockettes look the same height was to place the tallest ladies in the center with heights gradually decreasing to either side of center, the shortest ladies dancing at the ends of the line.

We removed our shoes and stood in the order called in our stocking feet. When there was debate about who was taller, the girls in question would stand back to back. Then the entire creative staff rubbed their chins and furrowed their brows and discussed ad nauseam which girl was taller until they came up with a consensus. Great care was taken to make sure that someone a fraction of a hair taller than someone else was not placed out of order. It seemed like a silly detail to me, but it was of utmost concern to the staff.

Our lineup spots were significant not only to the staff, but also to us, because they dictated whom we danced next to (and on which side of the stage) for almost every number in the entire production. Consequently, we were stuck dancing between the same two girls the whole show, and we hoped to high heaven that they'd be easy to work with. We also sat in lineup order in the dressing room, so our off-stage time was affected as well as our on-stage time. Tough luck if we were placed next to someone we really couldn't tolerate. I danced stage left, fifth from the end between a seasoned Rockette and former *Will Rogers Follies* Broadway dancer on one side and a phenomenally talented newbie Rockette—the only African American in the group—on the other side. Thankfully, both gals were nice to me.

After setting the line-up, we began learning the opening of the show, which was a tap number to "We Need a Little Christmas" from the musical *Mame*. Everyone called the number "Wreaths" because our props were giant wreaths, about three feet in diameter. They came up to about hip level when resting on the floor and were made of shiny, gold foil-y stuff on one side and either green or red foil on the other side. When I saw the wreaths come out of the box, the knot in my stomach got a little bit tighter. Having a prop to maneuver was just one more trauma added to the mix. Each of us was assigned either a red or green wreath and everyone made a mad dash to the boxes to claim theirs.

Not only were we learning the choreography, but, right off the bat, at the same time, we were taught our spacing. One of the tech guys had outlined the exact dimensions of the Grand Palace stage, the stairs, and the set pieces with varying lengths of red, green, blue, and white tape. The all-important number line was taped across the front of the room (downstage) and again in the back (upstage) with zero in the center and even numbers spaced two feet out from zero starting with "two" on either side of the zero. It was all very precise. If the numbers were off, our formations would be off as well. We used the number lines at the front and back of the stage to determine our placement stage left and right and the lines of colored electrical tape at various depths going across the stage from left to right to determine how far down or up stage we were supposed to be.

Julie, the dance captain, referring to her Bible of notes, announced, "Holding your wreaths in front of your face, start stage left on the number I just assigned you, toeing the white line, and stomp brush step, stomp brush step, stomp brush ball change, stomp brush step ('shim sham'), in out in out, stomp scuff hop step step. Now flap six times and step feet together moving down to heeling the red line stage left, on the second number I just assigned to you. Lean right, lean left, straighten up, and flip wreath to the colored side. Do two triple time steps and flip wreath to gold on count 8." My brain was filling up quickly and it was only our first day of rehearsal and our first number out of four.

Occasionally, if Linda needed to fix something that we weren't getting right, she would let us gather in front of the mirrors at one end of the rehearsal hall to learn the moves properly. Other than that, we rehearsed facing the tables where the creative staff sat and had no idea what we looked like. It was dancing by Braille. We just had to hope and pray and feel that we were doing the moves as shown. This way of working blindly completely threw me off. I was used to rehearsing in front of the mirror where I could see if my arm needed adjustment or if I looked stupid and needed to amend a move. In my past experience, only after learning the number completely would we perform it away from the mirror (a change that goofs everyone up initially). Using this new method, I was insecure without the mirror telling me what I looked like. No crutch. No way to cheat by watching what the other dancers were doing.

Under such pressure, I found it hard to think with a clear head. Whenever I got that nervous, my brain would simply shut down and the choreography would go in one ear and out the other. Nothing would imprint on my memory. I got so worried about not being able to pick up the choreography that I couldn't pick up the choreography. It was a self-fulfilling prophecy. In addition, a good portion of the women had done the show before, and the choreography was taught at warp speed as if it were all just review—a "brush-up." *Quit doubting yourself and have confidence. Pull yourself together. Relax. Breathe. Focus. You can do it.*

One extra dancer, Megan, stood on the sidelines learning the choreography. Besides Julie, she was our only other "swing." A swing is a person who has to learn every role and yet may perform none of them publicly. She gets that title because she swings in and out of different roles instead of holding her own track; she is basically a replacement person in case of illness, injury, or vacations. This position requires an extreme amount of mental work and memorization in addition to the ability to remain cool and calm in emergencies. On a performance night, for instance, if no one has called in sick, a swing may opt not to put on make-up or warm up that night, but then just as she is ordering dinner, a cast member gets nicked in the leg by the moving ice rink and is forced out with a sprained ankle. All of a sudden, the swing gets paged, and she has to throw off her clothes, put on a costume, grab her notes, and race to the stage. Just when she thought she was free and clear. A swing's job can be very exciting or very boring. She either sits around getting out of shape with a lot of time on her hands to knit scarves, or she is rushing around doing something different every night. To succeed as a swing, one has to have a clear head, do her homework, and be prepared.

Rockette swings had "cheat sheets," tiny little pieces of paper they folded up with mark numbers, L's and R's (lefts and rights), and secret decoder ring Sanskrit clues as to what each and every Rockette's part was. When performing, they shoved them in their cleavage, so they could study them any spare second they had before going on stage for each number. While I was flipping out just trying to learn my own track, Megan had to learn *everybody's* tracks. "Good luck to her," I thought. "She must be a genius!" She was.

In the opening number, we held our wreaths in front of our bodies, elbows bent, with our hands about shoulder level so our faces would show through the middle, encircled by the wreath like a smiley face smack dab in the center of a donut. The director and assistants walked down the line adjusting wreaths, putting us in the perfect position. "Ladies," Linda commanded, "you must get a feel for how high to hold up your wreath so that your face is perfectly centered. And you cannot tilt the wreath forward or backward at all. It must remain absolutely vertical. Now memorize how this feels so you can duplicate this exact posture every show." Easy for her to say.

Throughout the number, all while tapping, we flipped our wreaths from the gold to the green or red side and back for a great color change effect. It was festive and beautiful to watch on stage. The wreaths were so heavy, however, that my arms ached from holding them up for so long, and my fingers became raw from flipping them back and forth. The tapping wasn't difficult, but muscling the heavy, awkward wreath was.

An even greater challenge was the final kickline. Getting the Rockette signature move perfect was, perhaps, the most crucial task during rehearsals. If that looked bad, the rest of the show would be a failure. Hence, we started working on it the very first day. That would give us three weeks to get it right. As we kicked those final eleven, eye-high kicks, we were to flip our wreaths from gold to green or red in a follow-up, down the line and then back to gold in a follow-up back up the line. Keeping our eyes forward, we had to use our peripheral vision to determine when the girl next to us flipped her wreath. Then we were to immediately follow by flipping our wreath. The flipping didn't happen on any specific beats in the music; it was more like an organic wave. But it did have to end on the same beat that the kickline ended, and that was tricky, tricky tricky.

"Ladies," Linda further instructed, "the kicks require the tip of your toes to be directly in front of your eyes, no lower, no higher. Your back must remain absolutely straight. No gooping. You must jump on a stationary dime. In other words, no letting your jumping leg move a millimeter off its designated spot. And NO jumping side to side into your neighbor's space. Yes?" We all shook our heads to say that we understood. "Good. Then let's take it from the kickline."

The drummer set the tempo followed by the musical director's lead in, "A five, six, seven, eight." (A perfect kickline required a perfect tempo. Too slow, and the line would look wavy. Too fast, and we couldn't yank our legs down in time.) We started kicking. Linda watched from the front. Dennis and Julie watched from the sides of the line. My stomach muscles were on fire. This was excruciating. I tried to remember all the notes Linda had given while counting my kicks and keeping watch in my peripheral vision for the wreath follow up. I was trying not to fall down. It was slippery kicking in tap shoes on the varnished wood floor. It was so much to think about at the same time.

"Cut!" Linda shouted. "That was terrible. Marcia and Bonnie, you flipped your wreaths on the same count. It is a *follow-up*. And the kickline was wavy. Ladies, everybody's kicks have to peak precisely at the cymbal crash in the music or the line looks wavy. Those of you with longer legs have to yank your legs down to lower them in time to get them back up for the next cymbal crash. And does everyone know what I mean by kicking *eye-high*?" We all nodded like scared kindergarteners. "Then why aren't you doing it? One at a time, let's see you kick eye-high. That means the *top* of the toe is at your eye level."

Linda got up from behind the table. *Oh no. Not one at a time!* She and her assistants clumped together and with notebooks in hand went down the line examining each girl's kicks. Like a team of scientists, they dissected each and every move, intensely observing every minute variation in each Rockette's performance. A few girls had such elastic inner thigh muscles that when they kicked their legs went over their heads and well beyond the desired "eye-high" destination. Their kicks were spectacular, but they'd be useless as a Rockette until they could get the height right. "You have to control your legs, Ladies." Linda rebuked.

That wasn't my particular problem. It was my non-kicking leg that was going haywire. "Kristi, make sure your base leg stays in one spot and doesn't move forward or backward while you jump," Linda remarked. This was nerve-wracking. Even my gynecologist hadn't examined me that thoroughly.

After every girl was scrutinized, it was time to try it again. "This time forget about flipping the wreaths. Just hold them in place. Focus," commanded Linda. The music began, and we kicked our eleven kicks. Except for Karla. She kicked twelve. All eyes from the creative staff shot daggers her way. "ALWAYS count your kicks, Ladies," Linda warned as if our very lives depended on it. "Kicking out"—kicking when the rest of the line had stopped, or stopping when the rest of the line was still kicking—was a sin worse than murder in the Rockette world. Karla "the Kicker-Outter" cowered and tried not to cry while pulling the knives from her chest. I prayed that would never happen to me. I was mortified for her.

"Better, Ladies. This time let's add in the wreath follow up," said Linda. With no specific counts to the follow-up, we had to feel when the girl to our right flipped hers; as soon as we could feel her starting to flip, we had to flip ours. Then we had to wait for the follow-up to return a second time, going the other direction. All the while we had to keep track of how many kicks we had done and where we were in the music. We practiced over and over, before we ever got it right.

That first year I danced with the Rockettes, I got so many notes I felt like I'd never had a dance lesson in my life. I was afraid to move for fear it would cause the entire creative staff to pull out their pencils and frantically scribble my misdemeanors in their notepads. They were the police squad issuing warnings for our criminal offenses. It was nearly impossible not to take their reprimands to heart.

This type of precision line dancing can be very traumatic. Squelching my individuality and trying to dance exactly like the twenty-plus girls around me was a special skill. As an entertainer, I typically trained to stand out and be noticed. Being a Rockette required that I never stood out. By nature, performers want to attract attention and be different. This job quelled those creative instincts and desires.

Not only was I keeping my artistic passion in check, I was also dealing with the personalities and attitudes of twenty-some other dancers. Every move I made affected somebody else. We were almost always either dancing in such close quarters that incorrectly moving a fraction of an inch in any direction would cause us to invade someone else's space, or we were linked arm-to-arm with the girls next to us in a kickline or some other formation. Then we really had to be careful.

As Rockettes, we couldn't interpret the steps our own way. There had to be no question as to what every move was, what path it would take to get to the next move, and on which beat it would hit. The breaking down of steps was tedious, as was our abundance of nitpicky questions regarding the details. But attention to detail is what makes the Rockettes so awesome to watch. Most everything we did was excruciatingly difficult to master. I doubt I'll ever see a precision dance troupe as polished as the Rockettes, because no one else is crazy enough to try to be that perfect. "So this is what it feels like to dance with the best. This is hard-core Broadway-caliber performing," I thought to myself, impressed. Scanning the rehearsal hall, our high-caliber staff with their high expectations, and the mega-talented Rockettes, I felt like I'd truly made it.

****

Second on the agenda was the "Rag Doll" number, set in Santa's workshop, in which we played adorable, giant rag dolls come to life. Our whimsical costume consisted of a clownish, baby-doll, polka-dot dress over red and white striped candy cane tights; orange foam hair that stuck straight up and fit our heads like a helmet; thick, nerdy, black horn-rimmed glasses; and black tap shoes that resembled a child's best Sunday, patent-leather Mary Janes. It was all giggle and no glamour. The quick-paced, remarkably fun choreography alternated between rag doll floppy and sharp and clean. We were even allowed to make funny faces. Freedom!

In order to surprise the audience, we entered from the back of the house (where the audience sits), half the girls from house right and the other half from house left, holding hands and bumbling up the stairs to the stage. After more comedic rag doll choreography in which we kept pretending to wobble and fall over, we ran upstage to retrieve our assigned giant wooden alphabet blocks from two carts. (I had wondered what those blocks were for.) They were about two-and-a-half feet by two-and-a-half-feet square, and, boy, were they heavy. There were hand holes on the sides and a tiny, one-inch arrow on the top, which had to face specific directions during the show in order for certain sides of the block to be showing to the audience.

We dragged our blocks to assigned spots in two horizontal lines on stage. Then sitting on the blocks, we danced, banging our heels on them in time to the music, whirling around on our behinds, and kicking our legs in the air. My stomach muscles were so weak I could hardly keep my legs up the first few rehearsals. I was so embarrassed.

Next, rehearsal gloves were passed out, so we could get used to wearing them like we would in the show. "You're going to learn how to spin your block. The gloves will keep your palms from bleeding," said Dennis. *Bleeding? I don't like the sound of this.* He and Julie showed us how to balance the block on its corner, with the palm of one hand anchoring the top tip in place. "Give it a good spin. Not too hard or it will fall down," warned Julie, "But you have to spin it hard enough to keep it going for all eight counts. Everybody try."

We all gave our blocks a spin. Some girls were too tentative and their blocks stopped dead still halfway through the counts; others spun with too much gusto and their blocks got out of control and fell over with a loud bang. It looked easy, spinning like a toy top, when Julie and Dennis did it. "You have to control your blocks, Ladies." exclaimed Linda. "Try it again."

After the traumatizing spin section, we had less than a second to stop the block from spinning, locate the tiny arrow, and turn the block to its new position with the arrow facing upstage. This was a crucial move, for if you got mixed up, or couldn't find the arrow in time, the blocks wouldn't reveal the show-stopping surprise at the end of the number. There was no time to dawdle over the problem, because you had only two counts to get the block stopped correctly and then dance away. You couldn't be there still fiddling with your block when the rest of the Rockettes were doing something else entirely.

Later, we had to climb on top of our blocks to tap dance. Our dresses were so puffy that we couldn't see our blocks beneath us to know if we were in the center. Dancing a fraction of an inch in any direction could have put me off the edge of my block and tumbling to the floor. I danced with extreme trepidation.

At the end of the number we did a can-can kickline in which we kicked *heel*-to-eye-high instead of the usual *toe*-to-eye-high. For some reason, as rag dolls we were allowed to kick higher than normal. It felt good to let my legs fly. For "Wreaths" we had already learned how to kick high in perfect synchronization, but because we were holding wreaths while we kicked, it wasn't until this moment that we learned the proper "hook-up" for the kickline. The hook-up was the manner in which the ladies were connected arm-over-arm in a horizontal line. Julie demonstrated and described the process, "Place your left hand directly behind the small of the back of the lady on your left, then your right hand goes just over and above the small of the back of the lady to your right." Julie then took me by complete surprise when she announced the single most important bit of Rockette information ever dispersed. "And NO TOUCHING." "No touching? How can we kick and keep from falling over if we can't hold on to each other?" I wondered, perplexed.

Julie reiterated, "Hold your hands a couple inches away from the girls' backs so it appears that you are linked up, but you really aren't. You have to hold your own weight and use your abdominal muscles to keep you from wobbling. If you press on the girl next to you, she will fall off balance, and there will be hell to pay." Julie meant what she said. Back at Radio City, just about the worst mistake a new Rockette could make was to lay a finger on the older Rockette kicking next to her. It was the quickest path to damnation and a sure-fire way to get blackballed. *Gulp. Please, God, don't let me touch anybody!* This was a new skill that I had better master quickly, or I'd be facing the wrath of bad-tempered, teetering Rockettes. I held my hands as far away from my neighbors' backsides as possible.

After the kickline, two at a time, we jumped into the air and screamed, throwing our dresses up to reveal our bloomers, can-can style, and ended in a split on the floor. This "jump split" terrified me. The correct method required jumping into the air, legs split apart front to back at a perfect 180 degree angle and then letting yourself drop to the floor in that vulnerable position, landing with an equally terrifying "thwack" sound. I wasn't any more reassured about the move when I learned the more truthfully descriptive nickname used in the dance world: "cooter splat." Made my body tingle with fear. I was thirty, just married, with plans to bear children in the near future. My dance career was closer to the end than the beginning. What was the point in risking hurting myself? I wasn't really good at it anyway. When it came to my turn, I jumped in the air in a mini-split and, instead of splatting, quickly and safely slid down into the split. Linda surely saw that I was cheating, but she let me get away with it, thank goodness.

The rag doll costumes and dance were absolutely adorable—to me, it was by far the best number in the show. To top off what already was a colossal crowd pleaser, we did a mini encore, in which we grabbed our blocks, formed a line across the front of the stage, and one at a time lifted them over our heads. Up until this point, the blocks merely appeared as a random assortment of alphabet letters. At the end, to the audience's great surprise and delight, they revealed the message, "MERRY CHRISTMAS!"

We paid the price for such a cute and clever conclusion, because those blocks weighed a ton; after all, they had to be sturdy enough so we could stand and tap on top of them. To lift them we had to first hike them to our chests and then, just like a weight lifter heaving his barbell, use our chests as leverage to muscle them the rest of the way over our heads until our arms were straight. Getting them back down took just as much muscle control and brute strength. Being a new girl, I thought we were being asked to do the impossible, but the others had done it last year. There was no point in arguing. I grunted and shakily lifted my box overhead, my face turning as red as a Christmas bulb. They even made us carry our own blocks off stage when the number was over. I never expected to have to do any heavy lifting. Rockettes were tougher chicks than I thought.

****

Next we learned "The Parade of the Wooden Soldiers"—the most famous Rockette number, having been a highlight of the *Radio City Music Hall Christmas Spectacular* since 1933. Like the kickline, this number had to be dead-on perfect to live up to audience expectations and its long legacy. Dressed as toy soldiers, the Rockettes walk stiff-legged, as if wooden, for the entire song. The choreography consisted of the soldiers performing a multitude of geometric formation changes and patterns that were a feast for the eyes. The Rockettes made it look easy and invariably earned great applause, but getting it precisely perfect was a painstaking process.

To start, we had to perfect the idiosyncratic soldier walk. To accentuate the rhythm of the marching, the number was done in tap shoes. Julie gave the marching orders: "Your legs stay straight and stiff, absolutely no bending or softening of the knees and no shuffling of feet. Take tiny steps, lifting the feet off the ground just enough to make a slight tapping sound when you walk. Your arms stay straight down to your sides with hands plastered to the sides of your thighs, on the stripes of the costume pants. The fingers remain closed tightly together with no thumbs sneaking out. Keep your hands perfectly flat—no 'tea cups.' Take a relaxed position with your upper body, but no slouching. Also, your shoulders need to be perfectly in line with each other, no shifting one shoulder forward. And no craning the neck or tilting the head, or your hat will look out of line. Got it?" I wasn't even close to getting it. "Everybody practice."

The new Rockettes milled about the room, stiff as boards, trying to walk with pencil straight legs. "This is not natural," I thought, the back of my legs aching from the strain. "There's a reason humans have knees."

"Kristi, your shoulders are back too much," Julie told me. I moved them forward a tad, not really knowing what position she was after, and continued my rigid stride. "Kristi, your shoulders are too far back," Julie repeated. Again, I inched them forward and carried on marching in circles. "Kristi, relax your shoulders." I was getting extremely frustrated but kept adjusting ever so slightly until she finally stopped complaining. It took me forever to get the feel for keeping my upper body in a relaxed position; it felt like I was dancing with bad posture.

To complicate the process, we started practicing with our soldier hats right away. They were monstrously tall, heavy, shiny black vinyl hats topped with a big, white feather to make us look even taller. The hat was held onto our heads by a chin strap. Seemed simple enough, but there was definitely more to it. Julie explained, "The brim of the hat has to sit very low—right above your eyes. It needs to be low enough that the audience can't see your eyes, but you can still see where you're going (barely). And the hat has to stand perfectly straight up—no slant." We buckled our hats, trying to follow Julie's directions, and resumed the soldier walk with limited vision. Within seconds hats began sliding down, some completely covering people's eyes, some tilting backwards threatening to fall off, and still others swallowing half the faces of the smaller-headed girls. What a disaster. It was an exact science to get that hat in the proper position, requiring our hair in a low bun at just the right spot to hold the hat in place and our chin straps buckled at precisely the correct tightness to avoid toppling.

Once we got that awkward soldier walk down and learned how to safely secure our hats in a vertical position, the soldier number was, for the most part, math and memorization. It was basically a matter of remembering how many marches to do before changing formations, the order of the formations, what marks to travel to (number and depth), when to "hesitate" (a little musical punctuation in which we stopped with feet together, went up on our toes, and then lowered our heels back down), and when and in which direction to sharply turn our heads. "Getting the correct direction of the head snap is essential," Linda warned. "When everyone's hat with that big, white feather swishes to the right and yours swishes to the left, the mistake is very obvious to the audience."

To aid in the teaching, the formations were given code names: *diamonds, seven-upstage, partner revolve, open the gates, salute, close the gates, nose-to-nose, A's and B's, about face, squads, partner revolve, feed in, form spokes, iris in and iris out, spokes, the huddle, doll turns, the big wheel,* and *the fall.* The real difficulty was getting our bodies in the proper alignment with everyone else's to make the formations look perfect. It was an absolute team effort; whatever one person did wrong affected the rest of the group and had the potential to completely ruin the effect.

In the *opening of the gates*, we started in a horizontal line the length of the stage and split at the center. The end girls stage left and right acted as the pivot points while the rest of the line, linked shoulder to shoulder, marched toward the outsides of the stage to make it look like the two doors of a gate were slowly swinging open. It was hard enough just keeping the line (the gate door) straight the entire time we were marching. The ultimate challenges, however, were 1.) opening the gate at the right pacing so that it was completely open only at the *very end* of the musical phrase and 2.) getting both doors of the gate to open simultaneously—not letting one open ahead of the other. The pivot girls took micro steps underneath themselves while the girls at the opposite end of the gate had to take mega strides in order to reach their respective destinations on time. We had to concentrate carefully to make sure we were moving as a unit and not fighting against each other.

Doll turns, on the other hand, were less of a team effort and more of an individual endeavor. Spread out in three horizontal lines, we had to bend at the waist, still straight-legged, at a ninety-degree angle and salute. Then we stood up erect and spun on one straight leg, like a pencil turning on its eraser, with no wind up, no plie, no help from anything or anyone. We just had to will it to happen. Those turns were dauntingly difficult and downright scary at first. It took just the right amount of force to successfully complete a turn; too much caused you to topple. We had to stop perfectly, sharply, back in place with feet together. No wobbling. I was happy to be placed in the back line where my mistakes would be more hidden.

Soldiers fell over left and right. We practiced and practiced and practiced like troopers. Linda made it a point to examine each and every girl's turns to make sure we were doing it properly. I hated being put on the spot and having to do it all by myself with every single person in the dead-silent room watching me. Being a novice, I relied heavily on prayers and a good bun squeeze to keep me from losing my balance. This show made me more religious.

The *big wheel* was the last, and most spectacular, formation before the end of the number. We started in a horizontal line running the length of the stage, shoulder to shoulder, just barely touching and certainly not overlapping. The stage left girls faced upstage and the stage right girls faced downstage. Everyone guided in to center. The two tallest girls in the center faced each other, eye to eye, breath to breath. The line then made a complete 360-degree revolve, looking like a big wheel spinning. The center-most girls took the most infinitesimal steps possible and the girls on the end worked their tails off taking the biggest straight-legged strides humanly possible in order to cover the distance in time. "To keep the line straight," Linda instructed, "cast your eyes, without craning your neck, to the chest of the girl two spots down and try to stay in line with her. It is imperative that your line remains absolutely straight, or it will look wavy from the balcony seats."

The big wheel was the peak of the performance until, that is, we prepared for the grand finale of the number—the notorious *fall*. We finished the big wheel back in the horizontal line we started from and then turned stage left facing the back of the girl in front of us, our hands placed on the sides of her waist. One of the men, dressed as a soldier, wheeled out a cannon stage left, while another man pushed out a pillow stage right and placed it behind the last Rockette. The first man lit the cannon, which exploded with a fiery and smoky "bang," supposedly hitting its target—the first Rockette soldier in line. That wasn't quite enough force to do the trick, so the male soldier pretended to blow on the Rockette soldier to help knock her over. Slowly she fell backward from the imaginary impact, thereby knocking over the Rockettes behind her in a domino effect, the last one landing safely on the pillow. In theory, anyway.

We spent a day or two just getting mentally prepared for this event. Even the creative staff were scared to make us do it. The anticipation and fear built over time. There were hushed whispers about the fall and what was going to happen. People took out second insurance policies. The heavens were bombarded with prayers for safe passage.

Julie talked us through the process over and over until her voice was hoarse. "As soon as you see the girl two spots down starting to fall backwards, slide your hands (fingers closed, no thumbs sticking out) up the back of the girl in front of you and brace her back (keeping your elbows braced against your own waist as extra support) while she is catching the girl in front of her. As soon as the girl in front of you starts to fall, slide your hands under her armpits, lift and open up your elbows to the sides, go up on your heels, and let yourself fall backwards (remaining as straight as a board), still holding up the weight of the girls in front. When you absolutely can't hold on any longer, roll to the outsides of your heels, let your legs slide down to the floor in a 'V' position, and lie back gently on the girl behind you."

The fear of the first fall in rehearsal was like Ann Boleyn walking to the guillotine in preparation to have her head severed. We talked and talked and talked about the fall. We went through the motions ("slide your hands up, through the armpits, open elbows, go up on heels") until we were like robots. Every day we asked if we were going to do the fall and were relieved at getting to put it off as long as possible.

Finally the day came when we were actually going to try it. It went something like this: The short girl in the very front rocked up on her heels. The next three or so girls kind of got the directions right. The following third of the line turned beet red grunting, swearing, and sweating, while trying to slowly and carefully stop the increasing momentum and hold up the line without being killed by anyone. The final half of the line was pretty much bowled over like pedestrians being rammed by a train at full speed. The last girl prayed she'd land on the pillow behind her for a tiny bit of cushion to stop the intense blow.

It was a train wreck. A portion of the new girls ended up crying; some suffered twisted ankles or knees that were forcefully sat upon, then torqued by the girls in front of them. Our faces still damp with residual tears, Julie only made us practice once more before quitting for the day, but if we were frightened *before* trying it, we were scared to death *after* trying it. It was just as bad as or worse than I had imagined.

By this point, any prior effort one had put forth to make friends with the other Rockettes was diminished, as the fall created instant enemies. There were hushed, secret tete-a-tetes with other Rockettes and the dance captain about what girls in front or in back had done or had not done. Worst of all was getting a note of blame from the creative staff when we knew darn well that if the girl in front of us had done her job properly, we could have, too.

Wronged Rockettes filled with rage. "She didn't hold her weight up. She just sat on me!" "It wasn't my fault I fell on her knee. She dropped me!" "Julie, if the girls up front don't learn to control the speed, by the time it gets back to us, we don't have a chance!" We were quick to point out that "The girl in front of us 'sat down!'" (She didn't stay "pulled up" with a straight spine, thereby creating dead weight making it impossible for us to hold her up.) Or we argued that "The girl behind us didn't brace us enough!" Or "She didn't brace us in time to slow the momentum of the fall, and we got completely knocked over!" There was blame and finger pointing all over the place. Everyone was mad at each other. I wanted to wave the white flag, give up, and surrender.

The fall wasn't the only cause of dissension; the *entire* soldier number was the perfect breeding ground for disharmony in the ranks. Everyone accused each other of being out of line, causing a wavy big wheel, making the spokes go too fast, or wrecking the fall. If we got a note that the big wheel was wavy, the entire troupe of Rockettes would search for the culprit whose shoulder was out of line. The number was absolutely a group effort; what one gal did affected everyone else, and no one wanted to be wrong.

****

Our final Rockette number was a sharp, military version of "Jingle Bells" that was part of the "Carol of the Bells" sequence. Our costumes were tight, white and gold, high-cut leotards that revealed a lot of leg, of course, and extra, extra tall, marching band-type hats. We wore xylophones strapped to our backs like a backpack and held two sticks, one in each hand, with gold balls covering the top ends and rope handles attached to the bottom ends. Hence, we nicknamed the number "Chicks with Sticks" or "Sticks" for short.

Every number had its fear factor, and this time it was the stick twirl-toss-catch. At one point, the tempo of the music sped up considerably, and we each had to grab the rope holding our right-hand stick so we could spin it to the music like a sideways helicopter blade. In a cowboy-rope-trick-lasso-flourish, we were to twirl one of our sticks over our heads and catch it—a nerve-wracking move. If we missed the catch, it was nearly impossible to grab hold of our stick again to finish the choreography. Our rope had to be just the perfect length, or we'd be left holding it, the stick dangling dangerously for the rest of the number. This posed a problem particularly when our arms were above our heads and our sticks were swinging within smack-you-in-the-face distance. In any case, it made you look idiotic and drew unwanted attention your way. To add to the excitement, sometimes the gold balls would come loose and fly like missiles into the audience. Or they'd bounce and roll around on stage waiting to trip an unsuspecting dancer. It was like dancing in a mine field.

The climax of the number was the surprise when we all lined up the length of the stage and turned to play "Jingle Bells" on the xylophone of the girl next to us. That was the first time we revealed the existence of the xylophones to the audience. Had we just been standing still, it would have been easy to play the xylophone. Heck, I'd done that back in music class in elementary school. Here, however, we had to play the song while doing leg poses and turns. The bars on the xylophone were numbered, and we memorized the number pattern as we played: 3 3 3, switch legs, 3 3 3, switch legs, 3 5 1 2 3, turn to face the other direction; 4 4 4 4 3 3 3 3 3 2 2 3 2 5..." The switch denoted the bevel changes in our legs. It was tricky and much more challenging than the pat-your-head-while-rubbing-your-tummy trick.

All the Rockette numbers were brilliantly conceived and superbly choreographed, but the entire rehearsal process was grueling. The highly focused, intense work ethic included little time for joking around. After all, Linda and her assistants were under the gun with a measly few weeks to put the entire package together, neatly wrapped, and tied with a bow. Quickly teaching choreography for a show is one thing; making all your ladies look like mirror images is quite another.

****

Most of the time the Rockettes were sequestered in our own rehearsal room, so it was exciting to finally meet the rest of the cast—the singers, dancers, Santa, Mrs. Claus, children, and especially the "little people" (people with dwarfism or extremely short stature). I had never even seen one little person in person, so seeing an entire group of them was astonishing. I tried not to stare, but they were so interesting to watch. We had seven little people in the cast, all with different movement capabilities depending on the size of their limbs. While the Rockettes were hired for our abundance of height, they were hired for their lack of height. (It's all good.) The little people played the roles of Santa's elves, baby bears, and dancing snowmen. Their part in the show was the easiest by far, apparent in the way they were always light-hearted and laughing, unlike the high-anxiety Rockettes who bore the weight of the show on their shoulders. The little people had a great sense of humor in spite of, or maybe because of, seeing the world from such a low vantage point. They couldn't even reach to put money in the soda pop vending machine, something I took for granted. While they were relatively small, they were certainly big fun.

Little people aside, there was some jealousy from the rest of the cast, because the Rockettes worked a six out of seven-hour rehearsal day (with an hour for lunch) and the rest of the cast worked a seven out of eight. Rockettes also were paid more, received special gifts, and attracted most of the publicity and attention. We were the famous ones—the box office draw. Nevertheless, I was actually a little envious of the singers, as they looked and sounded phenomenal. And while their standards of performance were just as high as the Rockettes, they didn't have quite the pressure put on them that we did.

The entire cast, except the little people, rehearsed and performed together for "The Living Nativity," a scene that required a large number of people to sufficiently dramatize the Christmas story—the birth of Jesus Christ. It was amazing to me that such a commercial production still ended with such a religious finale, but it had been performed at Radio City since 1933 and the crowds kept coming. And they weren't all Christians. Some people loved it more than any other part of the show, and others were bored, but it was a *Radio City Christmas Spectacular* mainstay nonetheless. Unlike the strenuous

Rockette numbers, this number was as easy as a walk in the park with a few simple hand gestures. It was so simple, it seemed uninteresting at best.

Basically, we enacted the main scenes leading up to the birth of Christ, which were narrated to music. People were assigned various roles: Jesus's parents—Mary and Joseph, taxpayers, shepherds, the three kings, and their corresponding queens and royal courtesans. Each of the three kings, queens, and courts had their own color of costumes: There was the gold court, the red court, and the blue court. As a taxpayer and a gold courtesan, I was relieved not to have to think too much or work too hard.

Once we actually started performing the show, there would be live animals: a donkey, sheep, and even three camels! Several cast members were chosen to be shepherds holding a live sheep on a leash. Everyone dreaded being a sheep handler because the sheep could be feisty and buck or wander the set searching for grass to graze. Trying to get out of it, some people cleverly claimed to be allergic to sheep. Linda didn't buy their bull, so they were forced to search for a slightly corrupt doctor willing to write a letter excusing them from their allergy-exacerbating responsibility. The camels came with their own professional handlers, so we didn't have to deal with them.

In addition to "Nativity" and our Rockette numbers, some of the Rockettes were chosen to perform in non-Rockette capacities with other cast members in scenes such as the "Teddy Bear Nutcracker" and a mini-version of the Charles Dickens's classic *A Christmas Carol*. Somehow, by the grace of God, I was the only Rockette not selected for an extra part. This was fine with me, as I was challenged enough by my Rockette duties. Perhaps Linda realized that and kept my show as simple as possible.

My first year as a Rockette was like birthing my first child. I knew it would probably be difficult, but I never dreamed I could withstand such pain. Drugs (ibuprofen and acetaminophen) helped a lot, but I still had to pop that baby out. Many of the new girls ended up crying (myself included), because the whole experience was so physically, mentally, and emotionally stressful, and we got so many notes (corrections) telling us what we had done wrong.

Not only were my body and brain saturated with an overload of bevels, poses, marks, colored tape lines, and kick variations, but, just when I thought I couldn't handle one more task, they'd send me out to do publicity events on my free time when all I really wanted to do was practice or sleep. Let me assure you that we new girls spent our precious time off, which wasn't much, trying to absorb all the choreo we'd learned so far. People who didn't want to be publicly chastised, like me, did their homework. We begged the veteran Rockettes (even offering to pay them) or joined up with other terrified newcomers to pool our resources and practice what we had learned that day.

****

When we moved into tech rehearsals at the theatre, Linda and her staff sat in the audience to watch and critique. We were all relieved when the rare sarcastic joke emanated from the "God mic." This was the nickname for the microphone Linda used, because her deep, authoritative voice sounded like the Lord giving commands from on high. The fact that she had lightened up ever so slightly was a sign that the show was going well. We were adequately prepared once the show finally opened, and more than ready to entertain an audience.

Being a Christmas "Spectacular," our show required a spectacular venue. The newly built Grand Palace did the job exquisitely. With its oversized wreaths, swags of green garland and red ribbon, and plenty of twinkly lights, the exterior of the Grand Palace was properly bedecked for the holidays, enticing people from the get-go. The interior was no less festive. Upon entering the theatre lobby, patrons were overtaken by the smell of sugar-coated almonds roasting. There were treats to satisfy all the senses, not to mention stands bulging with Rockette and *Radio City Christmas Spectacular* paraphernalia including Rockette dolls, teddy bears, mugs, ornaments, and snow globes.

The show itself also lived up to its name and was spectacular beyond my wildest dreams. From every aspect, it seemed larger than life: The theatre was big, the sets were big, the cast was big (fifty-three people in all including twenty Rockettes plus five sheep, three camels, two donkeys, one dog, and a horse), and the costumes were big (370 costumes and 258 hats, so said one newspaper). And, of course, the Rockettes were big, not only in name and history but in size; we were tall, leggy girls wearing high hats that made us look even taller. It was a really big show celebrating a really big holiday. We played to packed houses nearly every show.

The actual scenes were no less impressive. The show began with the gloriously merry opening to "We Need a Little Christmas" in which the singers, dancers, and two children were dressed in satin ball gowns and tuxedos as if at a fancy party. They danced with shiny presents of all sizes, including three gigantic Jack-in-the-Boxes, as tall as the ceiling, that popped open. A real live, fluffy, white puppy dog appeared out of one package for a surprise finish. The set was so festive, one cast member commented, "It looks like Christmas puked all over the stage!"

This cheerful and uplifting opening song segued into our wreath number, which was the Rockettes' first appearance in the show. Dressed to impress, we wore our gorgeous "snowball" costumes—long-sleeved, white and silver high-cut leotards with tiny skirts trimmed in white marabou. The costume's nickname came from the white marabou hat that looked like it was topped with a fuzzy snowball. Add in our big rhinestone earrings, and we were a sparkly winter wonderland on legs.

Each night we stood on our respective sides in the wings waiting for our entrance as the jovial celebration commenced on stage. I liked to get to stage a little early so I could be one of the first to choose a wreath, because they were all slightly different—some more poky than others or with handles not as comfortable. A good wreath made my job easier and lessened my chance of a mishap. My heart started beating faster as our entrance drew near. I took deep breaths to calm myself down.

The Rockettes held our giant green, red, and gold sparkly wreaths encircling our pretty faces as we made our way onto stage. The first time we performed for a live audience was so wonderfully surprising, because four-thousand people started cheering and applauding when we made our entrance. *Whoa! I didn't expect that!*

Near the end of the number, we sang a cutesy excerpt from "Santa Claus Is Coming to Town." Then the music slowed down and trumpets blared "da-da-da-da-da-da-da" as a lead-in to the kickline, which started out slowly as a teaser with waist-high snap-kicks out and in, and then built up tempo into the famous eye-high kicks. The crowd went absolutely berserk. We were good for goodness sake!

Next was a Christmas sing-along followed by the darling "Teddy Bear Nutcracker"—a shortened version of the classic Tchaikovsky *Nutcracker* ballet. It was unique in that it was performed entirely by men and women dressed in various furry bear costumes, except for the main character, Clara, a young girl who dreamed of dancing with teddy bears. Some bears danced in pointe shoes, which seemed impossible in those outfits, because all the bears had to wear bear heads like Disneyland characters. Russian bears did an extremely athletic routine including jump splits and that famous Russian dance move where they cross their arms in front and do fast kicks to the side while in a deep knee bend. Three of the little people played baby bears and did a little dance, which garnered a deserved "Awww!" from the audience for their cuteness. Some of the Rockettes performed as the Arabian bear, the Chinese panda bears, and others. As far as I was concerned, I had already done my animal duty earlier in my bovine career and was perfectly happy to be left out.

Following the *Nutcracker* was the all-time favorite "Parade of the Wooden Soldiers." It had been so difficult to perfect, but it was all worth it, because the audience applauded wildly for every single formation. Their enthusiastic response really energized our performances. They cheered like that for every appearance we made throughout the show, not just the "Soldier" number. Having the audience appreciate us was a thrill.

Ending the first act was the mini-version of Charles Dickens's *A Christmas Carol*, about the transformation of grumpy, heartless, cheapskate Ebenezer Scrooge into a man of joy, gratitude, and giving, thanks to the persuasive visions of the ghosts of Christmas past, present, and future. It's one of my favorite stories, and our sets and costumes depicting Victorian England were spot on. We even featured a real horse pulling a carriage, ghosts flying in on cables over the audience, and a snow fall at the end. It was lovely!

After intermission, we opened with "Santa's Workshop"—a charming scene with Santa and Mrs. Claus, elves (Jiggle, Squiggle, Wiggle, Giggle, and Bruce), life-size dancing toys, and the Rockettes dressed as rag dolls. This was, perhaps, the most delightfully entertaining portion of the entire show. The set was a colorful toy factory with moving gears, talking reindeer, and singing and dancing flowers and Christmas trees. We made our surprise entrance from the back of the house by exiting the theatre from backstage, running outside in the cold and snow, and reentering through a side door, where we waited quietly behind a curtain for our entrance. Then we held hands and flopped down the aisles through the audience and onto the stage. We looked so cute and funny in our puffy dresses with ridiculous bright orange wigs, red circles on our cheeks, and thick black glasses.

The number was charming, and just when the crowd could hardly get anymore excited, we spelled out "MERRY CHRISTMAS!" with our blocks, and they applauded even more loudly. Well, most nights that was what we spelled. One night I got an earful from Julie, because, unbeknownst to me, I had not gotten my block facing the right way, and we spelled "MERRY CHRISTTAS!" Oops.

In contrast to the light-hearted Santa silliness, the following section—"Carol of the Bells"—was a breathtaking, white, winter wonderland scene saluting the tradition of ringing the bells to honor in the Christmas holiday. The cast, dressed in white and silver, performed a gorgeous ballet, dramatically playing giant chimes, bells, and xylophones, while women in white fur coats rode in sleighs. It was magical. As "Chicks with Sticks," the Rockettes performed their staccato version of "Jingle Bells." The reveal of the hidden xylophone backpacks was a huge hit.

For me, "Sticks" was all about the blasted stick-twirl (which I practiced so many times before the number you'd think I had obsessive-compulsive disorder) and the headpiece—essentially a five pound, two feet high, white and gold marching band type-hat with about three feet of furry white plumage on top, enough to coat a good-sized animal. It was like having a high-rise strapped to my head. The chin strap was all-important, as it had to be buckled at just the right tightness to keep the hat upright during the number. In addition, my hair had to be fixed just right (the exact same way every night with the bun in the perfect spot), so that my hat would fit properly on my head. If the chin strap started to stretch a bit, or I inadvertently buckled it too tightly or too loosely or my head was extra sweaty, the entire monstrosity would topple over exposing me in my wig cap.

The trickiest part was our bow at the end of the number. I learned the hard way that if I dropped my head a little too low, that fur ball would come tumbling down, especially once my forehead was sweaty and the vinyl of the hat got slippery. I learned to keep my chin tilted up so the weight of the hat wouldn't give in to gravity and take it down. The kind folks in wardrobe put sticky, no-skid material on the inside rim of my hat to help keep it stuck to my head where it belonged. I think it was the same stuff I lined my shelves with in L.A. to prevent my dishes from sliding off in the event of an earthquake. Still, I was always wondering if I'd end up bareheaded and scrambling to grab my hat off the floor before being trampled by exiting Rockettes.

Chin straps were a problem in the soldier number, too. Worst of all was when the strap broke, and the unlucky soldier would have to do the entire number with a stiff neck, turning her head ever so gently, so as not to lose her hat completely. On occasion, hats also got knocked off during the soldier fall, but at least that was the end of the number.

Even the best performer looked like a doofus and caused unwanted distraction and disruption by losing her hat or wig. It was crucial that we fastened our hats and wigs so securely that a tsunami couldn't knock it off. If we didn't, we'd find ourselves on stage in our wig cap looking bald as a, well, bald person. And then we'd have to attempt to retrieve the fallen headpiece as quickly as possible, or it was bound to be run over like roadkill by other dancers, turn into a dangerous obstruction for the next group on stage (think slipping on a banana peel), or put another performer in the precarious position of having to kick it like an attempted field goal into the wings so as not to trip over it. If we had to wear that same wig or hat in a later number, we were screwed. Performers actually warned each other about impending headpiece danger as in, "Wig down stage left #8. Be careful!" Or they'd whisper to each other, "Can you kick that hat offstage?" "Can you pick that up on your exit?" Once that costume piece fell, every dancer was thinking, "How can we get that off stage?"

To test whether or not a hat or wig will stay on, a dancer should practice doing cartwheels, getting her head caught in a curtain (making sure the curtain rips, but the headpiece stays put), doing somersaults, and having her little brother tug at it. If it doesn't pass the tests, she hasn't attached it securely enough. At that point, she should grovel and beg wardrobe to put horsehair on her headpiece and then anchor that sucker into pin curls with a million hairpins, realizing that the elastic chin strap won't do diddly-squat. Dancers got lazy and cocky, claiming their chin straps would save them. "I don't need hairpins," they'd boast. The next thing they knew, their hats were football fodder, and there was a big nasty note waiting on their spot from the stage manager saying, "PIN YOUR HAT!" A true professional may lose a limb if a tornado were to strike the theatre, but her hat would still be plastered to her head.

The finale of the entire show was our live rendition of the Nativity—a reverent ending befitting the true spirit of Christmas, which brought tears to the eyes and a glow to the heart. In rehearsal it seemed so dull, but with the ornate costumes, sets, lighting, video of the narration, and live animals, it was truly a spectacularly moving experience. "The Living Nativity" was my favorite number to perform, because I could relax and enjoy being on stage without having to worry about making a mistake. My only concern was watching where I stepped, thanks to the animals.

As the crowd of taxpayers going to pay their taxes, we traversed the stage along with pregnant Mary riding on a live donkey, which also happened to be pregnant in real life. We'd be lined up in the wings and hear of poop alerts from the people who were closest to the stage: "Donkey doo-doo #5 stage left. Pass it on," someone would whisper. Then as we did our solemn march to Bethlehem, we had to sneakily glance down without the audience noticing in order to avoid treading in a fresh pile. Some of the taxpayers walked with their sheep, creating even more opportunities for poo on the shoe.

After we made our faux trek to Bethlehem, we ran downstairs to change into our sparkly, colorful courtesan costumes. While we were changing clothes, there was a scene in which Mary, Joseph, and newborn baby Jesus (a fake baby nestled in a little hay-filled manger) sat serenely atop a small mountain with shepherds and their sheep admiring them from below. One night, one of the sheep decided he was sick and tired of being stationed at the bottom. He wanted to be on the very top of the mountain, so he took a hefty leap, dragging his poor shepherd on the leash behind him. Tug as he might, the shepherd could not control his stubborn, runaway sheep and had no choice but to hang on and follow him up. Wait a minute…aren't sheep supposed to be the followers? This was one faux pas that even the crowd knew wasn't supposed to be happening. Everyone in the cast and crowd howled hysterically. It wasn't the only time the sheep got feisty, but it was the funniest.

During one show, our littlest little person surprised Mary and Joseph by hiding in the wooden manger that was supposed to hold their baby Jesus. They had to keep a straight face the entire number while he was goading them. They had to gaze upon him as if he were their beloved son, while he was making goofy faces. They had to keep from laughing for what seemed like an eternity. Now that was a miracle. The rest of the cast was dying with laughter knowing that Mary and Joseph were in a sticky situation.

After the previous scene, the gold, red, and blue courts walked across stage as if on their way to see the Christ child. This part was extra special, because it was when the camels made their first appearance. We'd be waiting in the wings for our entrance and feel the draft of the cold air wafting through the loading dock, as the three camels were ushered from their pens outside into the backstage area. There was one camel for each of the three royal court processionals, and they and their handlers were dressed in costumes to match their assigned court.

It was bizarre and awesome to be standing right next to a real camel and to be performing in the same show. We were not allowed to mess with the animals backstage for fear of spooking them, and they were usually well behaved if we left them alone. But one night, one of the more daring Rockettes decided she wanted to ride one. She fell off and was nearly knocked unconscious. That squelched any dreams of wild camel races.

Again, we had to be aware of camel patties as we followed in the camels' footsteps from stage left to right. Once we reached the opposite side of the stage, we had to run like crazy to exit the theatre and reenter through the back of the house, where we would pass through the audience and march up the stairs to the stage to stand before the Christ child behind our respective kings and queens. All the courtesans knelt on the floor as the lights went out, and video screens dropped down for a reading of "One Solitary Life"—a short but moving summary of the story of how Jesus's one, humble, solitary life was more powerful than all the armies and kings of the world. This is the time when we cast members could plan our grocery lists, think about what to buy our families for Christmas, or even close our eyes and take a short siesta.

Almost every night, on cue, as soon as the lights dimmed, one of the camels would relieve himself right on stage. As you probably know, camels can store some serious water. I don't know what moved that humpbacked mammal to empty his bladder at that very moment, but that is what he did without fail. Gross! Anyone in the puddle's path would try to walk around it without diverting too much from the choreography. The last thing you wanted was your gown trailing through a pool of camel piddle. It seemed sacrilegious to be dodging urine and excrement during the most sacred part of the show, but I guess that's part of the point—Jesus came to teach us how to deal with the dung of life and still experience heaven by putting our faith in him.

After we bowed in respect as the kings presented their gifts to the Christ child, we took our final pose—a stunning snapshot of the three kings, their extra-long, regal capes extended behind them on the floor, the three queens, and the courtesans standing to honor baby Jesus who, flanked by his proud parents, was still sleeping in the manger on the top of the mountain, unaware that he was going to change the world. It was a tear-jerking moment.

I was really proud of our show, and my family was really proud of me. As soon as I found out that I was selected to be a Rockette, my family quickly started making plans to come see me in Branson. My sisters, grandmothers, parents, aunts, and uncles traveled days to be there. They seemed as excited as I was. My grandmothers even submitted photos and articles to their local newspapers about me being in the show. One of the best benefits of performing was the many family gatherings it spawned all over the country that would have otherwise not taken place. It was wonderful to perform for an audience of strangers but even more fantastic to perform for the people who loved me.

****

Our spectacular show called for spectacular promotions. It would have been more fun to do publicity and media events, which were a relatively new experience for me, if I weren't so completely exhausted and uptight about the show. A publicity expert from New York flew in to give us media training during which we had to learn sound bites and pat answers to reporters' questions about the show and the history of the Rockettes. More memorization. "Make sure you are in control of the interview and always bring it back around to 'the *Radio City Christmas Spectacular* starring the Radio City Rockettes at the Grand Palace running now through December 23rd,'" our trainer instructed us. Thankfully, most of the important interviews were given to the veterans, so we newbies could get our act together.

There always seemed to be a radio, TV, magazine, or newspaper interview happening as well as photo shoots and publicity events. Sometimes reporters photographed us during rehearsals, so we had to be looking and acting our best even then. For the majority of our publicity events we wore our snowball costumes from our opening number.

After every show, a couple of Rockettes, dressed in snowball costumes, were assigned to "Meet and Greet" (sign autographs, schmooze, and have our pictures taken) with patrons in the lobby. The people were thrilled to talk to us in person. We were truly stars in Branson. "Where do you perform the rest of the year?" they'd ask. They couldn't understand that we all went our separate ways and scrounged for work. We were rich (for dancers) at Christmas, but the rest of the year we may starve!

One of our grandest publicity events was kicking off the Branson Area Festival of Lights with a Christmas tree lighting ceremony on the steps of the Grand Palace. The official switch was thrown by none other than the great comedian and humanitarian Bob Hope. The ninety-two-year-old entertainer arrived in a tinseled golf cart, to the delight of the fans. Along with famous singers Anita Bryant and Tony Orlando, the Rockettes hosted the event with Mr. Hope in front of a crowd of about 5,500 people. It was an honor to be paired with this legendary showman. I remembered watching both Bob Hope and Tony Orlando on television when I was young. Of course, the papers published wonderful publicity shots of the event, including one of us doing our kickline in front of the theatre.

Our most large-scale publicity event, however, was performing "Sticks" for the St. Louis Thanksgiving Day parade—not exactly the Macy's Thanksgiving Day Parade in New York City, but a big deal in this part of the Midwest all the same. Plus, we got paid a good chunk of change for doing it. The downside was that just when we had some sort of control over our bodies and the choreography, we had to learn a slightly different version of the number for the parade. The choreo was different enough to really mess us up. Since our every mistake would be aired on television for all to see, the stakes were high for a clean performance. I coddled, cajoled, and then downright threatened my brain and body to remember the new information while keeping the old in storage for later use. I can't begin to describe the pressure.

As if our schedule wasn't full enough already, the night before Thanksgiving we were shuttled to St. Louis after our Wednesday evening show. We rode the bus for five hours overnight, got to the hotel in St. Louis, and slept a few hours, only to arise at five a.m. to be transported to the parade site. We performed, got back on the bus by about nine a.m., and returned to Branson just in time to do two Thanksgiving shows. We were so tired, we could have slept standing up.

It was a bitterly cold winter day, and we weren't exactly dressed for it. Our costumes—skimpy white leotards with legs covered in nothing more than paper-thin tights—may have been bikinis for all the warmth they provided. Julie was terrified that we would get injured trying to do high kicks with frozen muscles, so she kept us bundled up in winter clothes and warmly tucked inside a nearby building whenever possible.

When our time came to rehearse, we were escorted to our performance space—a section of the street along the parade route. Stiff with sweats and coats and hats and mittens and scarves, we marked our moves on the temporary chalk lines and portable number line that had been set up so we could keep our formations clean and precise. Sometimes we had to use cracks in the street as a guideline or just fend for ourselves in trying to keep our lines straight.

The street was bumpy and uneven making it extra treacherous, hard to turn on, and easy for tripping. It was far from ideal performance condition, but we did the best we could to make it work. Then we scurried back into the building to thaw out a bit before we'd have to do it for real in costume.

At the last minute, when we were to perform, we dropped our winter clothing and ran outside in our little leotards. My fingers were so numb I could barely move them let alone twirl a drumstick. Our saliva froze our lips to our teeth, and we couldn't smile unless we smeared Vaseline on our pearly whites. I struggled to keep my choppers from chattering. We were Rockettes on ice.

As painful as the experience was for us, it was nearly as painful for the cameraman as well. He crouched down to get a leg shot while we were kicking and barely missed getting walloped in the head. I was relieved when it was over, and I hadn't made a mortal mistake or killed the cameraman. Finally I could dump that goofy choreography out of my brain so I could perform the regular shows later that day without having to keep straight which version I was supposed to be doing.

While dancing half naked on the frozen tundra wasn't really my idea of a good time, it was exciting to be there for the festivities, and some of the girls got to ride in a limo on the parade route and wave to the crowd. I wished we could stay and see more of St. Louis than just the hotel and the street, but we had to get back to Branson in time for our shows. I did manage to get a photo of the famous St. Louis arch on our drive out of the city.

Since we had to work all day, the company was nice enough to throw us a Thanksgiving dinner party (including turkey and all the trimmings) at a local steak house after our last show, which ended about ten p.m. It was better to pig out when we had overnight to digest than it would have been to perform looking and feeling like stuffed turkeys. These couple of days had been crazy and exhausting, but I truly had reasons to be thankful.

My favorite publicity promotion was our photo and article in the magazine *Midwest Living*. We were all lined up on the grand spiral staircase in the lobby of the theatre in our sexy snowball costumes. Appearing in a gorgeous picture spread in a national publication was so exciting!

Naturally, with every P.R. event it was fun to be the one featured. We all scrambled to see how we ended up looking in the photos and hoped each photo was flattering. If we looked fantastic, the bigger the shot, the better. If we looked pudgy or ugly, we wished to God we hadn't been captured on film. Photos could go either way, and it was always a gamble.

****

Ron kept fairly busy ushering at the theatre while I was working, which was good, because our work schedules were pretty much in sync. Ron's job wasn't particularly challenging for him, but it gave him something to do and brought us in a little bit more cash. Plus he got to watch the show for free. Over and over and over again. He knew the show better than I did. Ron used to tell people seated in the front row, "Make sure you duck when the Rockettes kick, or you might get kicked in the head." Of course, it wasn't true, but joking with people made his job more entertaining.

Our condos were so close to the theatre that we could walk to work, and I often did. At the backstage entrance, I'd flash my laminated *Radio City Christmas Spectacular* backstage "ALL ACCESS" VIP pass that hung on a lanyard around my neck. Having a badge that says "I am a very important person and can go wherever I want" was quite the novelty and made me feel extra special. Backstage, the Rockettes were separated into two dressing rooms: The nine stage left girls were in one room and the nine stage right girls were in the other. Because of these logistics I got to know the stage left girls I danced next to better than the others. It was harder for me to make friends, however, because I was also nurturing my new marriage and not rooming with another Rockette.

Ron and I did mix and mingle at the occasional cast parties—both preplanned, lovely restaurant gatherings sponsored by Radio City and/or our producer and spontaneous soirees hosted by cast members in their condos. The little people threw the wildest parties and could drink a big person under the table. One little person favored wearing a Scottish kilt in the traditional fashion (underwear optional) and could be counted on to flip it up and flash us as the night went on. Showbiz parties encouraged wildness and wackiness. Everyone was expected to kiss and hug each other and tell them how hot they looked. It was well within good manners to dance with total abandon and be a goofball and make everyone laugh. No one cared if a cast member dressed overly crazily or wore a funny hat. The more entertaining and attention-getting the better. Zaniness was encouraged. With performers, practically *everyone* was capable of being the life of the party.

Otherwise on my off time, I felt I needed to spend alone time with Ron. We didn't have a lot of free time anyway—Monday was our only day off; on the other days we had an afternoon show and an evening show. A few weekends we even did three shows in one day. Sometimes we also had publicity events. Still, Ron and I managed to make the most of what little time we did have. We took in as much of Branson as we could, and there was a lot to take in.

Many shows were still offering free tickets to performers from other shows, so we saw every show we could fit into our schedule: Glen Campbell, Tony Orlando, Andy Williams, Dino ("America's Piano Showman"), *Pump Boys and Dinettes*, the Osmonds, Jim Stafford, the Oak Ridge Boys, Yakov Smirnoff (a Russian comedian who had a morning show at the Grand Palace before our show each day), *Jennifer in the Morning*, Wayne Newton, *The Lawrence Welk Show*, the Branson Belle showboat dinner show on the river, and more. It was fun to see so many stars I recognized from my childhood. We couldn't pass up Dolly Parton's Dixie Stampede—a musical dinner show in a 35,000 square foot arena in which you ate chicken and ribs with your hands as you watched performers on horseback enact a Civil War-era North versus South competition. Of course, we had to see the popular Branson icon Shoji Tabuchi—an exuberant Japanese violinist who created a name for himself with his musical showmanship, family participation, and overly ornate restrooms.

Sure, all the shows were wholesome and hokey, spewing a hefty dose of family values, patriotism, and Jesus, but there was something soothing about it all the same. Part of me really loved living in a corny hillbilly world where fiddling was fine art, you didn't think twice about frying your food, and a flannel shirt and overalls were suitable attire for any occasion. Still, I sensed the undercurrent of hatred and intolerance sliding beneath the surface of it all, remnants of the Civil War. This became apparent when one of our castmates was forced to move out of his condo and into another when the owners discovered an African American man was staying in their rental property. Southern hospitality? Yikes. Not for that guy.

Ron and I whooped it up at Silver Dollar City—a country/hillbilly-themed amusement park with rides, country craftsmen, country music and bluegrass shows, kettle corn, and plenty of old-fashioned vittles. We brunched at Big Cedar Lodge, a wilderness luxury resort replete with stuffed animals—a real taxidermy-fest, and gorgeous grounds. We gorged ourselves on home-cooked fried chicken, biscuits and gravy, and thick slices of pie at country cafés with floral tablecloths and gift shops selling apple butter, rock candy, and fake, canned roadkill. I found myself saying "possum" more than usual. Our biggest outing was the fifty-mile trip to Eureka Springs, Arkansas—the quaint Victorian bed and breakfast town famous for its hot springs and charming art galleries and boutiques. We entertained ourselves with all that Branson and the surrounding area had to offer. It was good, clean fun.

****

More amusement was to be had backstage at the theatre. Many of the Rockettes loved to take creative Christmas card photos in costume using the actual stage set. I dressed in my rag doll costume, and Ron borrowed a toy soldier costume from one of the male dancers. How we got away with that, I don't know. I'm sure it was strictly forbidden. We took pictures on stage next to a set of giant presents so we looked like little toys. Very cute! Some of the other cast members wanted their pictures taken with all the Rockettes for their Christmas cards. We were constantly taking photos and having our photos taken.

One day the gift shop offered an employee discount, so the Rockettes went into a frenzy buying Rockette-related gifts for ourselves, our friends, and family. Many of us bought Rockette dolls, show posters, teddy bears modeled after the "Teddy Bear Nutcracker" characters, and rag dolls that looked exactly like us in our rag doll costumes. Everyone wanted their purchases signed by all the Rockettes, so we were constantly with Sharpie pen in hand signing stuff until our wrists ached.

The Rockettes were also constantly getting gifts. Cast members left all kinds of trinkets and goodies at our spots: chocolate fudge, homemade ornaments, candies. I baked frosted gingerbread soldier cookies and made rag doll ornaments for everyone. Myra Longstern (the director of Rockette Operations) overnighted bagels and cream cheese all the way from New York City. Radio City sent giant gift baskets laden with sweets and treats. The Rockettes would arrive at the theatre and find beribboned boxes on our dressing room chairs—gifts from the Higher Ups at Radio City with red and gold embossed cards wishing the Rockettes a "Merry Christmas."

Being a Rockette certainly had its perks, and while it was the most widely recognized of my performing accomplishments, it was also the most difficult. Performing precision dance could be used as prisoner of war torture. Repeating the same movements over and over until they were precisely the same as the twenty people next to me (and maintaining that meticulousness show after show) was excruciating. Having to be perfectly on my mark at all times and not a hair to the right, left, downstage, or upstage was an exacting, mentally taxing task. To top that off, it was done under conditions of extreme exhaustion and sleep deprivation.

To make absolute certain that we didn't let our guard down and our perfectionism slip, our dance captain Julie sat in the house with a notepad and tape recorder noting any mistakes she could find. She gave notes every single show. "Move your left pinky finger one-half-inch higher." "Your kicks are a millisecond slower than everyone else's." "You were a millimeter too close to the girl next to you." "Your smile was too big." "Your smile wasn't big enough." Mistakes were not tolerated. Error was not an option. The quest for perfection was taken to such an extreme that I sometimes felt paralyzed with the fear of doing it wrong. This took Type A to a whole new level. The stress was draining and took some of the joy out of performing. I was relieved when our run was done, and I had successfully made it through the season without any giant goofs beyond the one "MERRY

CHRISTTAS" blunder. As much as I hated the pressure to be perfect, I also wanted the show to be fantastic. I wanted to work hard, have the cast be amazing, and impress the audience. The show was a high-class production with extremely talented performers.

So it was with mixed feelings that I left the Rockettes, the Grand Palace, and Branson. It was December 23, and we had completed our seventy-two shows for that season. We had experienced such a whirlwind of emotions, excitement, fame, and fantasy. We had worked so hard and performed so well. Our show had received rave reviews not only from our audiences but from the head honchos at Radio City as well. "You ladies were more polished than the New York Rockettes!" they said. Our fabulous director Linda and her cohorts had accomplished their mission and whipped us into shape. I felt on top of the world and deflated at the same time, similar to the let-down I felt as a kid when the hoopla of Christmas was over. My stardom was over. For the time being, anyway. But I did finally have a *Radio City Christmas Spectacular* show jacket! And I had earned the right to wear it.

As a Rockette, I had definitely gotten my kicks, but it was time to return to Route 66. Ron and I loaded up the car and made that long (but hip) California trip.

Final Scene: New York City, August 10, 2002

The corridors of Radio City were filled with framed photographs of famous entertainers who had played the Music Hall. There were also oodles of pictures of the Rockettes from over the years. I searched each one, until I finally stumbled upon more recent photographs containing a few of the older gals I actually knew personally. I gasped excitedly as I recognized some of the ladies I had met while dancing in Las Vegas. Ahhhh, Vegas. Now that was a trip. They say "What happens in Vegas stays in Vegas," and for good reason. Okay, so I didn't do the whole New York Rockette thing. But I wouldn't have given up my Rockette days in Vegas for the best poker hand in the world.

Act 3, Scene 3

Vegas

Long Legs and Tall Tales

I resumed life with my husband in our tiny studio apartment in Los Angeles. With no upcoming shows on the horizon, I jumped right back into subbing in *The Flintstones Show* at Universal Studios Hollywood. Since we only had one car, and I needed it, Ron searched for a job he could walk to from our place. The nearby Honda dealership needed car salesmen and presto! He was hired. I also decided to try more movie extra/background work for some easy cash until I could get into a legitimate show. All I had to do was take my photos to the offices of Central Casting—the nation's largest extras casting company—and sign up.

Except for star spotting and free food, being an extra kind of stunk. The long days (sometimes as long as fifteen hours) of mostly sitting around waiting were so wearisome that the all I gained from the experience was weight from visiting craft services so often. The extras spent the majority of the day lounging about, waiting to see what would appear next on the snack table. "Cheetohs and Tootsie Pops!" Everyone made a mad dash towards the latest junk food addition—the highlight of our day. The holding rooms were often cold with terrible lighting and inadequate seating, so I learned to take a sweatsuit to keep warm and a flashlight for reading to pass the time. Folding beach chairs were popular among the regulars, who had gotten tired of having to park their behinds on the hard floor for hours on end. The extras were a strange breed, and I learned to either keep to myself or carefully screen before striking up a conversation. Most of the call times were ungodly early, and the work was especially irritating when I had to drive to a remote location for, say, a 6 a.m. call. Oftentimes, I was required to lug my entire closet along so that wardrobe could pick out something suitable for me to wear. Add in the fact that I'd be unlikely to ever find myself in the movie, and I had myself a pretty miserable job. Still, it beat temping.

The highlight of my extra career was being chosen to be a flight attendant in a scene at Los Angeles International Airport for the hit movie *Jerry Maguire*, starring Tom Cruise, Cuba Gooding Jr., Renée Zellweger, and Kelly Preston. I got to wear a real costume and have my hair french-braided in the hair and makeup trailer while Kelly Preston sat next to me getting her hair styled. I didn't even realize it was her until she walked onto the set all made up and started making out with Tom Cruise (for the scene). As extras, we underlings were strictly forbidden to talk to the movie stars unless first spoken to by them. It was a mistake worthy of getting us fired on the spot. When filming *Jerry McGuire*, I stood within a few feet of Tom Cruise at one point. He didn't utter a peep in my direction, but it was all I could do to not gasp aloud at his superstar presence. His handsome costar, Cuba Gooding Jr., however, did single me out for some small talk. He was cheerful and chatty and made me feel like a fellow human being instead of a lowly untouchable. I was also an extra on the 1996 movie *Mad Dog Time* (a.k.a. *Trigger Happy*) with Jeff Goldblum, Gabriel Byrne, and Ellen Barkin. Jeff was friendly and talkative with all the extras in an attempt to recruit new students to his acting school.

The menial background work and drudgery of theme park dancing were starting to drag me down, so I was elated to finally get cast in a real musical—*Evita*. My beloved Don and Bonnie Ward from the Starlight Bowl summer stock were the directors. We took the show on the road for a small tour from Glendale to Thousand Oaks, California, and then out of state to Phoenix, Arizona. It was the most intense and emotional musical I had ever done, and I was thrilled to break out of my comfort zone and into deeper theatrical territory.

But the real bonanza happened shortly after *Evita* ended, about six months after leaving Branson, when I received a phone call from my Rockette friend Jan. She and several of the other Branson Rockettes were now performing in *The Great Radio City Spectacular* at the Flamingo Hilton in Las Vegas. "Kristi, I've got the inside scoop that one of the girls is going to give her two-week notice soon, because she's pregnant. We want you out here. Call Radio City right away and let them know you're available." Whenever there was even a hint of someone leaving, the girls back at the Flamingo wasted no time in taking matters into their own hands. They wanted a girl they could get along with, spend hours rehearsing with, share their most intimate dressing room secrets with, and dance next to twelve shows a week without wanting to kill her. I had been selected as a suitable candidate. It was my duty to go. I mustered up my courage and called Myra Longstern to tell her I was available if any spots opened up in Vegas.

Having a direct line to Radio City made me feel powerful. I could hardly believe I had the ability to personally call the most famous of dance troupes in one of the most famous theatres in the world and request a job. And they would actually accept my call! Not that they would necessarily give me the job, but since I now had a working relationship with the head of Rockette Operations, such a request was well within acceptable conduct. It was not in my nature to be so bold in asking for what I wanted, but Ron and I wanted to leave L.A. It stressed us out—the crime, the traffic, the gangs, the mud slides, the brush fires, the riots, the earthquakes, the smog. This opportunity could be our ticket out.

I had initiated "Operation Vegas" and continued my campaign by sending letters to Radio City reminding them that I was ready to work. With such a large pool of Rockettes, I knew I had to be in Myra's face and in her memory when the time came to find a replacement. I had to be the first one she thought of, the easy way out. After all, who wouldn't want a simple solution to her problem? No hassle searching. Kristi to the rescue.

Sometimes you get the job because you fit the costume and your friend begged the stage manager. Sometimes you get the job because you are available at the right time. After three weeks of advertising myself to Radio City through phone calls and snail mail, the golden call from Myra came in. "We have a spot for you in Vegas. You have to sign a six-month contract and after that you can stay on as long as you want, but we ask for four-weeks' notice if you decide to leave. You'll be making $1,200 a week, with two shows a night and Fridays off. We need you there in two days."

I was elated and terrified at the same time. Two days to completely move to an entirely new state? I pleaded for more time. "Be here in five days, and that's my final offer," Myra compromised. In show biz, you don't always get time to ease into gigantic life changes. One day you could be in L.A., down to your last dollar, slurping Ramen noodles for every meal, and the next day you could be whisked off to Vegas to make $1,200 a week indefinitely. Your home is where your top hat is, and you need to be able to pack up your life and leave town at the drop of a hat if you want to survive.

Such was now the case. So, with little warning, Ron and I began to box up our belongings and prepare for our next adventure. Luckily, we were on a month-to-month lease for our apartment so we wouldn't be losing out on too much rent. I called my Vegas connections with the good news, and Jan came to the rescue and offered to let us stay with her until we found an apartment.

What about our little, blue Ford Escort with eighty-thousand miles on it? Old Not-So-Faithful probably wouldn't make the trip across the desert. She was falling apart one piece at a time. I envisioned us stranded on an endless stretch of sand, under the scorching sun, crawling on our stomachs, my arms outstretched toward what was, alas, only a mirage, and uttering my last dying word, "Water!" Even if we didn't break down in No-Man's Land, we might very well sizzle up driving through Death Valley with no air conditioning. My air conditioner was long gone—a faint memory. There were no gas stations, Denny's, or 7-Elevens for ninety miles. No Slurpies to quench our thirst. We could perish on the four-and-a-half-hour trip across the parched desert and become fodder for rattlesnakes and vultures. No doubt about it, we'd have to get a new car. The next day, Ron quickly scored us a two-year lease deal on a sporty, white Honda from his dealership. I looked good in it. My old beater was fine for a theme park dancer, but I needed something sophisticated and sexy to match my spectacular show on the Las Vegas Strip. I could feel my luck starting to change.

Ron loaded the U-Haul we'd rented, while my sister helped me clean the apartment. Cindy and I cried and cried. Leaving Cindy was by far the worst part about leaving Los Angeles. At least I'd have Ron and several Branson friends there, but I really didn't know them all that well.

Towing the U-Haul behind the new Honda, we set off to Las Vegas. Heading east on highway 215 through San Bernardino, we could see ourselves driving right out of the smog, which sat like a slathering of light-brown chocolate frosting atop the San Bernardino mountains. I hadn't realized how disgusting the air really was until we drove out of it. I took a breath of the fresh air and sensed the new life that lay ahead.

We approached Vegas from the northwest down a long stretch of deserted desert highway. The pink and purple sun setting in the mountains was breathtaking and alluring just like the infamous neon lights of the Strip. We were drawn into Las Vegas—"the meadows" long since dried up—like so many others desperately seeking their fortune, the big jackpot win that would change their lives, perhaps their only chance.

The wind stirred up dust devils—tiny tornadoes of sand and dirt—and actual tumbleweeds rolled across the road. Cowboys rode on horseback, their tiny ranches giving way to cookie-cutter, terra cotta housing developments ever pushing farther out from the center of the

Long Legs and Tall Tales

city. This was a booming community; some said thousands of people a month were moving in to work at all the new casinos being built and to enjoy the relatively low cost of living compared to California. Schools weren't being built fast enough to keep up with the influx.

We drove past Mt. Charleston, about thirty miles from downtown, a tiny alpine village similar to those in the Colorado Rocky Mountains, where you could ski in the winter and horseback ride or hike the rest of the year. I never knew Vegas had snow let alone a ski resort nearby. Even closer to town, just west of Northwest Vegas where Jan's home was, we passed the magnificent Red Rock Canyon where people mountain biked, hiked, and discovered remains of buried Mafia hits.

It was July third, the heart of the summer. McCarran Airport registered one hundred thirty-two degrees on the tarmac. It was a hot, dry heat, which Las Vegans say is more tolerable than a humid one hundred thirty-two degree day. Whatever the case, humidity or not, it was stifling. We were thankful for our reliable, new, white car with air conditioning.

We arrived at Jan's house at dinner time. She had already left for the theatre, but we found a note on the table telling us where to put our stuff, as well as hotdogs, corn on the cob, and watermelon that Jan had prepared for us to eat. What a great friend. After shoving food down my throat, I began rummaging through my suitcases for a sundress and sandals. My dress was wrinkled, but it would have to do. Lara, the dance captain, wanted me at the theatre to watch the show and get a tour of backstage. I phoned backstage at the Flamingo and talked to Lara, who gave me directions to the casino.

Off I set, in my new Honda, heading for the lights of the Strip. I didn't have a map, but with such huge landmarks as the high-rise needle of the Stratosphere, the pyramids of the Luxor, the monstrous MGM Grand, and Caesars Palace, I knew I would find my way eventually and without too much difficulty. Approaching the Flamingo, I noticed the large neon sign advertising the "World Famous Rockettes starring in *The Great Radio City Spectacular* and featuring Susan Anton." I got a chill looking at the picture of a line-up of Rockettes. I was going to be "starring" on the Vegas Strip like so many famous performers before me: Sammy Davis Jr., Frank Sinatra, Dean Martin, Wayne Newton, Liza Minnelli.

I parked around back in the employee parking lot and entered the casino recalling that familiar smell of smoke and alcohol and the sound of the coins falling out of the slot machines. The whole atmosphere had disgusted me when I first came to Vegas six years earlier with my mother, but I wasn't so shocked by the debauchery this time. In fact, I was excited, especially seeing our show posters hanging everywhere in the casino. I found the theatre and the inconspicuous door to the right of the theatre near the deli counter, just as Lara had instructed. As I stood mesmerized by the flashing lights, the clanking of coins, and the intoxicating nicotine wafting through the air, the secret passageway door opened. Out peeked Lara—a brunette, slightly shorter than I, who looked to be in her mid thirties. Her face looked sweet and kind, and the voice that came out of it sounded like a New York City cab driver. She was obviously a Jersey girl. I recalled the accent from my days in Celebration Magnifico.

We climbed the stairs and walked through stark, white tiled hallways—secret employee tunnels running through the casino—until we reached the backstage door. She called the girls out of their dressing rooms and, as it was near show time, five girls in wig caps and show make-up filtered out in various stages of undress. I got quick hugs and squeals of recognition from the Branson girls I had danced with, and then it was down to business.

"Take your line-up, please," ordered Lara. The girls quickly fell into place in a horizontal line, shoulder to shoulder. Lara eyeballed me and then the line. I took off my shoes and was shoved between two girls. "Now, Kristi and Mona switch. Now Mona switch with Trisha. Hmm. Switch back again." Lara debated with herself. After a few more manipulations and changes, Mona and I stood back-to-back to see which girl was a hair taller than the other, and I was finally given a spot in the line-up. The girls were dismissed. As they scattered to their dressing rooms, they muttered their approval or disdain of the new line-up, assessing how my placement would affect their show. "Shoot! This means I have to do the mirror section of Diamonds," grumbled Trisha.

Lara quickly introduced me to the stage managers and then ushered me to the VIP booth, for the show was about to begin. This was the only remaining dinner theatre in town, and the audience sat around little tables and in booths, unlike traditional theatre seating. This show room only seated about nine hundred people—so small compared to the Grand Palace in Branson. I got two free drinks with my ticket and was glad to have them. What was I getting myself into? The printed program gave me a clue:

> *For more than 60 years Radio City Music Hall has been home to the nation's most spectacular live entertainment. Now, for the first time in its history, Radio City is taking the greatest scenes ever produced on its famed New York stage directly to the Flamingo Hilton Las Vegas, presenting them together in one special evening. Tonight, you will experience a new look at the greatest dancing, scenery, costumes, and show-stopping entertainment enjoyed for years on the Great Stage at Radio City. Here are the highlights, back-to-back, in an unprecedented array of pageantry and spectacle. So...sit back and celebrate the magic of Radio City entertainment—a night you will never forget!*

The description sounded so impressive! I scanned the program to see how many numbers the Rockettes performed. I had just tallied eight Rockette numbers when the house lights dimmed and the announcement about "no flash photography and video recording" was made in English and then Japanese. An arc of lights framed the stage. Then, as the music—an arrangement of "Come On Get Happy" (made famous by Judy Garland)—swelled, the curtain opened, exposing a long sign, running the length of the stage, made of red lights spelling out "THE ROCKETTES." Below the sign, forty of the longest, most gorgeous, bare legs in the world stood posed, beveled, and ready to tap dance. The sign lifted up into the rafters, and the upper halves of the World Famous Rockettes were revealed in all their sequined and feathered glory.

Holy cow! They're practically nude! Are those bikinis? I nearly choked on my bitter, cheap red table wine. The costume was essentially a rhinestone-studded bikini with some long, red feathers going up the back like an unopened peacock and an elongated red sequined top hat also adorned with long feathers to make the Rockettes look even taller. *Every little flaw is going to show! You can't hide anything in those costumes.* My mind spontaneously began creating a new workout regimen: seven hundred sit-ups a day, four hundred push-ups, three hundred butt squeezes, and five hundred leg lifts. I was going to have to up my game if I wanted to look as gorgeous as the other gals.

I could hardly focus on the choreography, as I kept recognizing my friends, picking them out of the crowd like a *Where's Waldo* book. There was no missing the girl I was to replace with her basketball stomach protruding between her bikini top and bottom. She was all skin and bones and boobs and baby. I couldn't believe how bold she was to dance pregnant in a bikini on a stage in Las Vegas for all the world to see. I could never do that, I thought.

At the end of the number, as the Rockettes exited kicking off into the wings, none other than Susan Anton made her grand entrance. She was currently filling the show's "star spot"—a singer who had reached enough stardom to be a box-office draw. This star was usually contracted for three months and then a new star would take her or his place. Susan Anton—the larger-than-life, beautiful, blond, singer, actress, and second runner-up to Miss America (1970)—filled the spot and then some. At 5 feet 11 inches tall, this glamazon seemed to tower above the Rockettes. Her mere size made her a stunning presence; she owned the stage.

Susan skillfully belted out "Too Tall to Be a Rockette," her strong, savvy voice steeped in the style of vintage Vegas headliners like Judy Garland and Frank Sinatra (in fact, she toured with Sinatra in her younger years). Her jazzy vibe made me want to be at a classy nightclub in a slinky red dress sipping martinis alongside a handsome gentleman in a tuxedo. She was a well-seasoned performer having been, as her program bio reported, "entertaining television, theatre, film and nightclub audiences for almost 20 years." This versatile artist had earned gold records and a Golden Globe nomination, toured with Kenny Rogers, co-starred on Broadway in *The Will Rogers Follies*, and even starred in her own television series. For three years, she had been on the cast of *Baywatch*—the international hit television series, starring David Hasselhoff, about Los Angeles County lifeguards who spend their days patrolling beaches in red swimsuits that accentuate their toned, tan, sexy bodies.

I remembered her first and foremost from my teenage years; my date to my 9th grade dance had a poster of Susan (baring her flawless physique in a Hawaiian bikini top and sarong) hanging on his bedroom wall. She was every guy's fantasy, and every girl wanted to look like her. But tonight Susan was no longer simply a two-dimensional sex symbol in a pinup; she was my real live coworker!

After Susan's solo, the six young men comprising the male ensemble joined her for a tribute to Fred Astaire followed by the Rockettes returning in gold and silver gowns to perform "The Gold and Silver Waltz." In this elegant, balletic, Sally Rand-style dance, the women waved huge, white-feathered fans. They glided gracefully around stage using the fans to create beautiful visual effects, like a flower blooming and closing up its petals again for the night, or a circular, flowing wave of water cresting and falling. They had obviously had solid classical ballet training. Having been a devoted ballerina myself for many years, I was eager to join the lovely ladies.

As is customary in Vegas, in between big production numbers specialty acts often perform, giving the rest of the cast time to change costumes. Our first act, Nino Frediani, a diminutive Portuguese juggler, now exploded onto the stage. He was a power-packed fireball, his wispy, black, curly hair shooting out of his head like out-of-control flames. The man spoke seven languages, all with an Italian accent. Nino's specialty was tossing small hoops over the heads of standing audience members like that carnival game where you try to land the ring on a Coke bottle. When Nino said he wanted to "ring your neck" he meant it literally. The successfully nailed audience members would then reciprocate by trying to Frisbee-toss the hoop to encircle Nino. They were all terrible shots, of course, and to milk all the hilarity out of the situation that he could, Nino would scream and run like hell across the stage, diving like a baseball player determined to make the catch. In Nino's case, however, it was his head and not his arm that was outstretched. Wild applause ensued as his head poked through the flying hoop and his mission was accomplished.

"How would anyone ever think to do such a strange thing for a living?" I wondered. My question was answered when I read his bio and learned that he had been born into a traveling circus family. Having myself come from a highly academic family with Ph.D.s and Masters degrees, I felt pressure to go to graduate school. Had he felt pressure to walk the tightrope, swing from a trapeze, or stand on an elephant's head?

Following Nino's crazy human ring toss was the "Big Band" number, hosted by Ms. Anton. She sang a snippet of "Sentimental Journey," then served up some witty banter, as four couples appeared—the girls in 1940s-style red, white, and blue short dresses and the boys in World War II dress khakis. Susan then emceed a dance contest in which each couple tried to outdo the other with flips and spins and tricks. In the background, the Rockettes formed a fake band sitting on platforms. They did choreography with their various instruments—drums, trombones, trumpets, and saxophones—while watching and cheering on the couples. It was hard to tell if they were really playing or not. They wore short red and blue dresses with wigs and hats that reminded me of Lucille Ball in the *I Love Lucy* TV show.

As the couples left, the "band" came down off their stands and did a forties-style, cutesy tap number. In the middle of the number, the music stopped, and an a cappella challenge tap took place. The Rockettes' silver shoes moved fast and furiously. The steps got more and more complicated, the tempo speeding up to a frenzied riff at the end. It sounded really difficult. After the applause, the music resumed, and the rest of the number seemed harmless enough.

The second specialty act to make an appearance was Stacy Moore and his "Mess of Mutts." Having been established by his uncle in 1939, the act was billed as the "oldest performing dog show in the country today." Stacy's mess of dogs, about ten in all, were rescued from Humane Societies. These endearing mongrels easily won over the audience with their spectacular tricks: mailing letters, jumping rope, jumping through hoops, and even balancing standing upright on hind legs on a tightrope. Adorable!

Ravel's "Bolero" provided a Spanish twist to the evening, the Rockettes sizzling in tight, red sequined, floor-length skirts, matching red-sequined halter tops, and oversized red saucer hats that looked much like the top half of the planet Saturn. The dancing seemed simple enough for me to pick up quickly. Also part of the number were three "Infantas"—a designation given to daughters of the king of Spain or Portugal. These regal women were buckled into enormous, ornate, horizontally protruding skirts and did simple formation changes (which was all they could do in those monstrous structures) and demure choreography with their small, decorative hand fans. To add even more excitement, a soloist appeared in an even sexier costume and enchanted the audience with her exotic flamenco-inspired moves, as the remainder of the Rockettes danced around her. Since when did Rockettes use soloists? I was transported by the emotionally moving music. The snare drums' repetitive rhythm in three-quarter time kept the dramatic intensity pulsating throughout the piece. Its smoldering, romantic melody was etched in my memory from the passionate 1984 Olympic gold-medal winning, ice-dancing performance by Torvill and Dean.

As the Rockettes bolted off stage to change costumes once again, the third specialty act appeared like magic. Actually, they were magic. Tim Kole, the magician, was a black-leather wearing, dark, foreboding,

David Copperfield lookalike. In stark contrast, his beautiful blond sidekick, Jenny-Lynn, was an angel in white. As often happens to magicians' assistants, she found herself lying flat-back on a table. The menacing music swelled, and we all realized something exciting was about to happen. Sure enough, using his miraculous powers, Mr. Kole somehow levitated her clear above her perch! Knowing some audience members would still be skeptics, he dramatically waved his hands over and under the airlifted assistant to prove there were no wires or hidden support. She really appeared to be defying gravity!

Tim supernaturally brought the mysteriously floating woman back down to earth, and, as they left the stage, the familiar tune of "Parade of the Wooden Soldiers" began to play. Having spent so many nights with that music, I knew it better than I knew my own husband. Soldier huts appeared on both sides of the stage, and the Rockettes, dressed as toy soldiers, hobbled out. My eyes kept doing a double take as the formations were slightly different from those I had done in Branson. "That is going to goof me up," I predicted. It's hard to relearn something after you've already performed it another way hundreds of times. I closely monitored the fall. *The fourth girl sat, the middle section is trying to muscle it, and the back section is getting killed. Typical.*

After "Soldiers," Susan returned to sing a beautiful, belty ballad in front of the curtain. When she finished, the curtain rose. Running the length of the stage was a series of gigantic light-bulb and diamond-studded mirrors in front of which the Rockettes stood frozen, reflecting their own gracefully poised images. This was the grand finale entitled "Rockettes in Diamonds"—a ten-minute-long showstopper bursting with kicks. The Rockettes wore dreamy costumes by Bob Mackie, the acclaimed designer famed for dressing many of the most glamorous and captivating superstars of all time, including one of my favorites—Cher! (This Emmy Award-collecting "sultan of sequins" had built a fashion empire by becoming the man to turn to if you intended to turn heads, light a room on fire, and make audience members audibly gasp at a glimpse of you. Our outfits were not as outrageous, daring, or belly-baring as Cher's, but I was over the moon at wearing Bob Mackie, nonetheless.) They were essentially elegant black leotards embellished with loads of silver and diamond studs. The leotards were sleeveless on one side, sexily revealing a bare shoulder, while the other arm was completely concealed. A swag of diaphanous black material dripping with silver beads draped from the covered shoulder to the opposite wrist. The headpiece was an exotic, turban-style hat with the required, height-enhancing feathers. The costumes sparkled like a star-studded night and revealed lots of leg.

The music started out slowly, the girls emulating it with some flowing moves and snappy poses. It wasn't until I noticed that the images of some of the girls weren't quite matching up that I realized they weren't looking in mirrors after all. They were looking at a second row of Rockettes pretending to be their mirror images. As the tempo increased, the music signaling that something exciting was about to happen, the front row of ladies moved forward and their "images" stepped through the "mirror"—actually just an open frame—breaking the illusion. As if that weren't surprising enough, more and more Rockettes kept filing out through mirrors. Soon the stage was filled with Rockettes.

By this time, the music was loud and lively, and the choreography followed suit. There seemed to be a kick every other second. I kept waiting for down time, but they kept on kicking, and the number seemed to go on forever. At the end, all the girls chasséd down to the front of the stage for the final kickline. I applauded wildly and smiled profusely knowing that as much as I was watching my friends up there, they were watching me.

The Rockettes exited and the male ensemble came back to do some Fred Astaire-type tapping in black tuxedos and top hats. Man, were they great tappers. A spiral staircase appeared upstage. It looked like a multi-tiered wedding cake topped with six Rockettes all dressed in different revealing hot pink, black and silver showgirl outfits with huge headpieces. The ladies all had perfect six-pack abs, which were also on display. Each of the men escorted a showgirl down the treacherous stairs to present her, her unique costume, and her beautiful, buffed body to the audience.

The Rockettes returned, still in their "Diamonds" costumes, and everyone sang, "The world is a stage; the stage is a world of entertainment!" Pyro went off on the cake like giant sparkler explosions, and it was over. The show was highly entertaining even though it didn't have the spectacularly large set pieces, massive stage, or huge cast of the Christmas show. It was Vegas. It was hot.

My head was pounding as I thought about all I had to learn and perfect in such a short time. All I wanted to do was go home to bed to forget about the whole show for a night. But I needed to say a quick,

"Great show!" to my friends. Lara met me at my table and took me backstage to greet the girls who, also anxious to get home, were already out of costume and wiping off the final smudges of make-up.

"Hey, girl!" shouted Missy, my Aussie friend from the Branson show. Jan and Ginny came running over for hugs followed by Wanda and Leslie—more pals from Branson. "You all looked gorgeous! The show was wonderful!" I gushed, truthfully. "Did you see me mess up in 'Diamonds'?" Ginny asked, a tone of annoyance in her voice. I assured her I hadn't. (Ginny had danced in Paris at Le Lido—the world famous, extravagant and exotic, cabaret/burlesque showgirl show to rival all showgirl shows since 1946. Even when she messed up, she looked magnifique.)

Lara showed me my dressing room spot. I felt so out of place. It's different when you are the only new person to join the show than when everyone is starting a show at the same time. They were all used to the routine. I hadn't a clue what to expect. I was just glad I had friends there to help.

****

The following day, Ron set out to search for apartments while I went to the Flamingo to rehearse from ten until five. Lara, the dance captain, was already backstage when I arrived. We rehearsed right on stage so I could learn my choreography and spacing all at the same time. "Let's start with 'Diamonds,' because it's the longest and most strenuous number. That'll give you ten days to build up your stamina and let the choreography sink in," Lara decided. "It worked out that you don't have to do the mirror section, so that'll make life easier for you." She took me by the hand and led me upstage. "Stand here and wait during the intro. The mirror set piece will be here, and you'll be hiding behind it until you step through the mirror. Remember from the show last night?"

I shook my head yes, and was glad to have that much less choreography to learn. I liked having the one-on-one sessions with Lara, because she was friendly and let me ask all the questions I wanted. I felt more relaxed about learning, and at the same time she shoved that choreography down my throat so fast I thought I was going to choke. I had a lot to learn in ten days. *Ten days.* I spent a month in rehearsal preparing for the Branson Christmas show. Was a week and a half really going to be enough time?

After dancing for an hour and twenty minutes in my two and one-half-inch character shoes, my feet were already starting to ache. "How am I ever going to survive another five hours today?" I moaned. When the stage manager came down to notify us that it was time for our ten-minute union break, I was more than ready. Lara offered to take me with her to "the caf," as they called the cafeteria, to grab a cup of coffee. It was almost directly across the hall from the backstage door of the theatre. How convenient. Everything in the caf was complimentary! Free food. Twelve hundred dollars a week. I could feel my financial burdens disintegrating. We grabbed big, white Styrofoam to-go cups and filled them with thick, dark, overcooked coffee from the dispenser before heading back to the dressing room to sit for a minute and take a load off our feet.

I liked Lara. She was a good teacher with a good heart, who didn't scare me like the stricter, Branson creative team had. Working one-on-one made the sessions much more informal than rehearsals with an entire cast had been. I was astounded when Lara informed me that her mother had been a Rockette. The Rockettes had always been an important part of her family, and Lara had literally followed in her mother's fancy footsteps.

When we resumed rehearsing, she tried to explain the formations, traffic patterns, and my positions relative to everyone else, but I really wouldn't get to see the whole picture until the day of my put-in, which was also the day I'd first perform the real show.

As the dinner hour neared, the wait staff came in to set the tables for the show. The clink-clank of the sturdy white porcelain dishes being set out was distracting, not to mention the fact that I now had an audience. We put "Diamonds" to rest for the day, so I wouldn't be completely overwhelmed and burned out, and moved on to "Soldiers," which was much less taxing. I felt completely stupid being the only one up there doing that stiff-legged soldier walk with my arms glued down to the sides of my legs, turning my head sharply on the appropriate counts, marching all over the stage. I was like a toy robot gone haywire. When I thought about how ridiculous I looked, I burst out laughing.

My excruciatingly long, first day of rehearsal was finally over. I had lived through it and was free to go back to Jan's to relax. Lara, on the other hand, after having taught me all day, was going to swing two shows that night. Lara appeared to be as exhausted as I was; when I left to go home, she curled up in a sleeping bag underneath the costume racks in the dressing room to take a nap before the first show.

****

Finding a place to live as quickly as possible worried me about as much as learning the show. Jan was more than hospitable, but the house she was staying in was really owned by her roommate, a singer in Cirque du Soleil, that mind-boggling, imaginative show of acrobatic impossibilities. She and Jan met in Branson doing *The Will Rogers Follies* with a bunch of the other Rockettes. I felt bad imposing on them. Plus every day we kept the U-Haul was costing us money, and I didn't feel comfortable with all of my life's possessions sitting on someone's driveway, especially in Vegas. It was July fourth, and everyone was off for the holiday, so our search would have to wait another day.

I was desperate to get some rest, but Jan and her roommate had planned an after-show Fourth of July party. There was no way I was going to sleep through it, and I felt rude not hanging out with my friends anyway. The Flamingo cast and some Cirque people filed in around twelve-thirty a.m. bringing food and drinks. I tried to put on a happy face but I was overwhelmed by the crowd of new people to meet. We stood outside twirling sparklers in the heat of the night.

The following day was our day off, thank goodness, so Ron and I anxiously continued our apartment search. First we looked in Northwest Vegas where Ginny and Jan lived, but we found no apartments that were available right away and waiting two weeks wasn't an option. Eventually we gave in and looked in Green Valley on the southeast side of downtown. We did find a nice place on a golf course, but why pay extra if we weren't golfers?

Finally, we discovered an apartment building on Las Vegas Boulevard, otherwise known as the "Strip." It was located a couple of miles south of all the big casinos and not far from McCarran Airport, in a newly growing area dubbed "Enterprise," although I doubt that anyone would have had the faintest idea what I was talking about if I said I lived in Enterprise. The location was perfect; my daily commute to work was just a few miles up the road.

Our place was close enough for convenience yet far enough away that we weren't living in the hubbub of the Strip. The stucco and terra cotta-roofed apartment buildings that made up our complex were brand new. They were so new, in fact, that some apartments hadn't even been cleared of construction debris, because the crew had just left the premises. One unit was available for rent, but it still needed cleaning. I begged the manager to let us in that afternoon. "We'll clean it ourselves!" They finally gave in. Whew!

For seven hundred dollars, we got a gorgeous, never-been-lived-in, one-bedroom, one-bathroom apartment. It had a nice-sized living room, high ceilings, gas fireplace (fake like everything else in Vegas), oversized Jacuzzi bathtub, tiny dining room, and a kitchen with plenty of counter space. We were on the second floor (better for avoiding break-ins) and had a small balcony overlooking the pool, gym, and tennis courts. All the new apartment buildings were loaded with recreational amenities. We weren't paying that much more for it than we paid for our crummy closet-sized studio apartment in Los Angeles. Jackpot! I returned to rehearsal the next day less stressed since the apartment situation had been resolved. Ron unpacked while I was at the theatre.

Lara and I plugged away daily at "Diamonds," which included so many variations of kicks that I needed to build up my stamina. The number even included a "sit-down drill," a kick sequence we performed while seated on a long bench running horizontally the length of the stage. Sit-down drills were incredibly hard, because they took tremendous abdominal strength, and I didn't currently have it. It would take time for me to develop killer abs.

When I needed a break from the rigors of "Diamonds," Lara would introduce other numbers. Luckily, I was just a hair too tall to be in "Gold and Silver," which only required a subset of the smaller girls. That was one less number to learn. I was a little sad but a lot relieved. The opening tap number was the second most strenuous dance, but I could handle it. "Bolero" utilized simple choreography (mostly a lot of running around holding our arms up in a Spanish-style, "Ole!"-type pose), partially due to costume constraints. The oversized, flying-saucer-like hats restricted arm movements, and the tight, mermaid-mimicking skirts limited leg movements. I was happy to take a break from kicking and primarily concentrate on looking pretty.

"Big Band" was fun and cutesy, and I was perfectly capable of doing the dance, even the challenge tap that had sounded so difficult. The hardest part was the intro to the number where I had to pretend to be part of a band. Luck of the draw landed me a trombone, which felt like a monstrosity. I had to swing it side to side and up and down pretending I was playing, but I couldn't really touch my lips to the mouthpiece or I would mess up my cherry-red lipstick. This cumbersome arm stretcher was a bit weighty for my weak arms.

****

As the evening approached, the wardrobe crew began filing in to do repairs and prepare for the show. Lara led me down the hall from my dressing room and around the corner to a room tucked away in the back where I would have my costume fitting. The pregnant momma I was replacing had left the show, so her costumes were finally available for alterations. I couldn't figure out how they were going to make that tiny bikini fit me, because, even with child, she was decidedly smaller than I was.

We walked into the wardrobe room where a small group of polite females in their forties and fifties were hand-stitching strands of beads that had fallen off back on the "Diamonds" costumes. In a tinier room behind the worker bees sat the Queen Bee of Wardrobe himself: Raoul. Lara made the introductions: "Raoul, this is Kristi. Kristi this is Raoul, Head of Wardrobe."

"I know who she is; who else would she be?" Raoul snapped. "Well, get undressed, and let's get this over with." His Highness tossed me a package of nude tights to put on.

I discreetly tried to change, while he mustered the motivation to buzz off and retrieve my opening costume. My guard was up; I could see his stinger was poised to prick.

I was standing there in my G-string, nude tights, and sports bra when Raoul handed me the red bikini bottom. It was so small it terrified me. I had bigger underwear. I stepped my feet through the holes and then yanked and tugged to pull it up. I held my breath as I fastened the hooks on the side. The tight costume piece was cinching me below the waist and squishing me in unflattering ways. I tried pulling the sides of the bikini up as high as possible to hide my love handles and make my legs look longer. But I knew it would never stay in place once I started dancing. I didn't think Rockettes ever had to show their midriffs. They didn't, except in Vegas. I started to panic. "Don't you have anything bigger?" I pleaded. "Ha ha. Right," Raoul retorted, rolling his eyes. I cursed myself for all the pub trips Ron and I had made on our recent vacation to visit his family in England and decided I'd better start that workout routine right away.

On the back of the bikini bottom was a pocket (we called it a "butt pack") into which a giant, red, tail-feather plume was velcroed. Add a skimpy, nude-colored, rhinestone-studded bikini top, sparkly neckband and arm bracelets, and a tall, red top hat also adorned with a feather on the side, and that was about all there was to the opening outfit. Fully dressed in the costume, I felt only slightly less vulnerable than when I was standing in my G-string, bra, and tights. I don't know which was more frightening, that minuscule costume or Raoul. Thankfully, the rest of the costumes were less traumatic, and Raoul was more bark than bite (or buzz than sting).

****

As if I didn't feel insecure enough about my body, Lara informed me that I had to see a professor at the University of Nevada, Las Vegas for my official weigh-in and body fat testing. "Not to worry, if the results show that you are over or underweight you have a whole two weeks to make the necessary adjustments," Lara said. *Two weeks? How healthy can that be?* I grudgingly dragged myself in to be weighed, to have my love handles, back fat, thighs, arms, and stomach pinched with barbeque tongs, and then to sit in a water displacement tank. The measurements were combined and scientifically manipulated, graphed, and calculated to determine what it would take to create the perfect woman's body for my body type.

A few weeks later I received an assessment in the mail. My overall body fat composition was thirteen percent, well below that of a healthy female—a surprise to me. The section carrying the most fat was my stomach. Duh. My interpretation: "I have a beer belly!" Measuring in at 5'8" and 125 ½ pounds, they would have considered me three pounds underweight for my height, but, due to the low body fat percentage, I was deemed proportionately fine. My ideal weight was considered 128. I was allowed to be six pounds over or under that ideal weight without getting a warning. Future weigh-ins could happen with only twenty-four hours' notice. "I can weigh up to 134 pounds. That shouldn't be a problem. I haven't weighed that much in a long time," I reasoned. My weight was okay, but I still felt the need to tone up and lose that extra, little bit of padding around the middle.

We were lucky that Radio City had relatively professional, fair, and safe guidelines for weight requirements. With other jobs, the producer just eyeballed you and insisted that you needed to lose five pounds. My girlfriend who worked a lot of cruise ships with the same producer said that every time she booked a gig with that producer, the producer would tell my friend to lose five pounds even though she was five pounds thinner than she had been the previous contract. A stage full of dancing skeletons may be good for a Halloween show, but I didn't see the appeal otherwise. It wasn't unheard of to find a girl using laxatives to control her weight only to end up with an atrophied sphincter muscle incapable of pushing out a normal bowel movement. And that's one muscle you can't rebuild at the gym.

The issue of weight is huge among female dancers. I saw girls try to survive a whole day on a single bagel, or on grapefruit, or sushi and Metabolife (a dietary supplement that was later banned by the FDA for adverse side effects including *death*), or on lollipops for dinner. I saw gorgeous, thin women beat themselves up over being "fat." And fat in the dance world was not fat in the normal world. A fat dancer was one who needed to drop five or ten pounds, but we'd feel chubby after gaining only one or two. If you were "fat," people would talk about how you would be such a great dancer if you would only lose ten pounds. If you did lose ten pounds, they'd start to worry about whether or not you had an eating disorder. Or they might even become envious that you were now skinnier than they were.

Regular folks shouldn't be jealous of dancers because they have perfect bodies. Few are born with them. Dancers agonize more than anyone else in the world (except maybe models) about how they look. They have taken a gazillion dance classes a day since they were three years old to get those bodies. They do sit-ups, push-ups, yoga, and Pilates, and they lift weights to get those bodies. Some have breast implants, face lifts, and tummy tucks. Others starve themselves, count calories, and go on every diet you can imagine. They occasionally do terrible, irreversible damage to those bodies in the name of perfecting them, and they still may obsess about their weight constantly.

Mind you, nobody else in their right mind would have called me fat or flabby or said I had love handles, but dancers aren't always in their right minds when it comes to their bodies. I was overly critical of myself. But let's get real. Dancers don't just have to look svelte in a suit or skirt and blouse. No, they have to look picture perfect in a skintight, high-cut-in-the-legs, low-cut-in-the-bust leotard. They have to have flat stomachs, ripped abs, thin thighs, and toned arms. Any sign of a spare tire, back fat, cellulite, saggy buns, or any wiggly jiggly bits is forbidden. Dancers' bodies are thoroughly analyzed and sized-up by employers, directors, choreographers, costumers, and audience members. Talk about an unhealthy pressure to look good. Being successful at my job included having the audience scrutinize my every body part and conclude that I looked marvelous. In a *bikini*. Next to other totally toned, gorgeous gals. Wouldn't you be self-critical?

****

Time flew by, and I couldn't believe it when opening day arrived a mere ten days later. Dancing all those hours in character shoes had been murder on my feet. My stamina was building, but I had yet to perform the show in real time and sequence with costume changes. Technically I had learned all the material, but I still didn't feel prepared to perform. Until the put-in, I had no opportunity to practice with the other Rockettes or to get a feel for the timing of the show. God help me with the traffic patterns; I didn't want to crash into anyone on stage. This afternoon's put-in would be my only chance to have any idea what to expect on stage that night and to see what surprises my costumes might have in store for me. Usually, we had a week of tech and dress rehearsals to work out all the kinks. My show might be kinky. Very kinky, indeed.

The Rockettes all dragged their tight, perfect tushies into the theatre four hours early for my put-in. This was the moment I had dreaded ever since that initial costume fitting left me feeling totally insecure. They were all sitting on stage chatting in their sweats and leotards when I came down the stairs in my opening costume. There I stood, in front of that group of gals, the lone peacock poured into that bikini, holding my breath, sucking in my stomach for dear life, and pretending to be invisible. It wouldn't have been so bad had they been in costume, too. But all attention was on me; all eyes were surely checking me out, sneaking a peek at my unwanted spare tire. I felt as ugly as Quasimodo, tarred and feathered in an itsy-bitsy-teeny-weenie-rhinetone-studded red bikini. I simply wanted to get this over with as soon as possible. I couldn't wait for the day to come when I had a hard body like the other girls did and could perform the show without fear.

We rehearsed the opening number once, and Lara asked if I wanted to do it again. "No, that was fine," I responded. The girls cheered. I could have done that number all day long, and I still wouldn't have felt ready for the show that night. Why prolong the misery for everyone? I changed costumes, and we continued on to the next number. I did each number only once even though I was desperate for more rehearsal. What could I really accomplish running the numbers another time? I knew it would take weeks for me to feel good in the show. I figured I might as well win points with the girls by making the put-in as quick and painless for them as possible. And I did. "This was the fastest, smoothest put-in we've ever had," Lara commented cheerfully after it was all over. "You are all excused." All the girls applauded as they ran up the stairs to enjoy the extra free time they hadn't expected.

I change into my sweats and went to the caf to get dinner before the first show, although I was too nervous to eat much. As show time neared, I was in absolute disbelief that I was actually going to be performing on stage that very evening. What possible embarrassments lay ahead? I knew I could make a fool of myself in myriad ways. I had to stop thinking about it and just get on with it. Time would pass and the shows would be over in a few hours.

When the stage manager called, "Half hour!" I already had my make-up on, so I stretched and marked through the numbers one last time. It was strange to be the only nervous one in the entire cast. The other girls were busy gabbing away, well into the routine of the show, and I was sweating. Lara came in at fifteen-minute call. "Kristi, I'm not going to watch the show tonight, because I don't want you to feel pressured." I didn't know whether or not to believe her, but it did take the edge off. I was ready well before the rest of the group, because I wanted some quiet time on stage to calm my nerves and focus. The Branson girls all stopped by on their way to "places" to give me a hug or whisper, "*Merde!*" (*Merde* is the French word for "shit" but it means "good luck" or "break a leg" to dancers. Some say the tradition started in France back when a lot of *merde* from horse-drawn carriages meant a big audience.) Once the curtain opened, the show was a blur, and all of a sudden I was standing on stage in the finale. First show, a success! Yippee! One down, one to go, and no major screw-ups.

The second show was going just as fast. What a relief that my debut was almost over. I was in the home stretch. I could see the light at the end of the tunnel. Everything was hunky-dory. Until the very end of "Diamonds" that is, when I made one single, solitary faux pas. It was a Big One. A Doozy. The Granddaddy of Rockette Mistakes.

Somehow in all my anxiousness and exhaustion I lost count in the kickline. Something distracted me for a millisecond, and I realized I didn't know where we were in the music or in the kicks. My body started sweating. My face burned with fear. *Oh no! When do I stop kicking?* I tried listening carefully to the music to feel the end of the phrase, but I couldn't be sure. I attempted to feel the vibes from the girls next to me, but they didn't give any indication either. Instead of trusting my instincts and my legs to stop at the right time, I freaked out, second guessed myself, and stopped *one kick too soon*! My brain had failed me. I should have let my muscles do the thinking, but my nervous mind got in the way.

Mortified, I exited the stage, holding my breath as I waited for someone to let me have it. *Should I just beat them to the punch and convict myself? What if no one noticed?* I decided to keep my mouth shut. If anyone did call me on it, my back-up plan was to feign innocence and surprise. "Are you sure I did one less kick than everyone else? If you say so."

Amazingly, no one said a word, and I *sure* as heck didn't tell anyone. I decided not to beat myself up over the mistake. It was a monster, but, under the circumstances, I could have made a lot more. I'd just pretend it didn't happen. If a tree falls in the woods, and no one is there to hear it does it really make a sound? I figured if I goofed and nobody on the Radio City staff saw it, it never happened. None of the Rockettes ever mentioned it. And if Lara had fibbed and actually watched the show, she either missed or blew off the blunder. True to her word, she didn't give me any notes that night.

****

While being thrown into *The Great Radio City Spectacular* in record time, I eventually eased into life as a Vegas Rockette. As I had earnestly anticipated during my debut, my life soon fell into a routine. About four o'clock in the afternoon, my brain went into "show mode." For the next two hours, I started getting mentally prepared for the evening while keeping a close eye on the clock. I put my hair into a ponytail, slipped on a sundress and a pair of chunky, high-heeled sandals, grabbed a magazine, and left my apartment every evening at 6:20 p.m. so as to arrive at the stage door at 6:37 p.m. That gave me just over an hour to get ready before the show. Officially, I didn't have to be at the theatre until half-hour call at 7:15, but I felt too rushed with only a half hour to get made up, warmed up, and focused.

In the apartment parking lot, I hopped into my brand new, white, sporty, Honda Civic. White was the preferred car color in Vegas as any other color just soaked up the heat and fried you upon entry. A foil windshield cover to reflect the sunlight away from the car was absolutely imperative, because the heat was brutal. From the lot, I turned right onto Las Vegas Boulevard. I drove past sporadic apartment buildings; past Vacation Village, a no-frills little casino for the locals; past Sunset Boulevard and McCarran Airport on the right; then past a few more small casinos, until I reached the famous retro, fifties-style "Welcome to Las Vegas" sign, the official introduction to the famous casinos of the Strip. The Strip was ever pushing southward with more and more casinos all fighting over the business of the tourist industries and some of the locals. Could this boomtown keep booming forever? It certainly gave that appearance.

On my left, I passed the black, glass pyramid of the Luxor with the concrete Sphinx replica guarding the entrance; the pink and blue and gold turret-topped castle Excalibur; New York New York with its rollercoaster encircling the famous New York skyline and the Statue of Liberty; and the construction site for the grandiose, ostentatious Bellagio. On my right, I passed the turquoise-blue glass MGM Grand with the giant gold Lion head entrance, the Middle-Eastern Aladdin, the construction site for Paris, Bally's, and finally the Flamingo.

The original Flamingo was built by mobster Bugsy Siegel in 1946. This new version, adorned with pink flamingos, sat at the intersection of Flamingo Road and Las Vegas Boulevard in the heart of the Strip directly across from the monstrous Caesars Palace. A little thrill buzzed through my body every time I saw our show advertised on the giant video screen out front. I still couldn't believe I was in it.

Attempting to turn right toward the employee parking lot in the back was a challenge, due to the steady stream of drunk, oblivious tourists crossing the road or inadvertently stumbling off the curb, intoxicated and transfixed by the lights. They seemed to think sidewalk and street were synonymous, and they weren't the least bit worried about stepping in front of a speeding vehicle. Waiting for a clear path so I could make that right turn took half my travel time to work. I cursed the sauntering pedestrians who were slowing me down. *Why don't they build a walkway over the road for goodness sake? This is ridiculous.*

Finally, my car made a bold dash across the intersection during a brief lull in the people moving and zoomed over to the multi-tiered, employee parking lot on the left. As I slid my security badge into the machine, the gate magically opened. I always parked in roughly the same spot, especially when we had to come in a second time for rehearsals during the day. Otherwise it was easy to forget where I parked, as each day blended into the next.

A secret employee entrance took me past Human Resources and down a maze of stark, white hallways, unmarked doors, storage closets, and freight elevators. My nose could sense the employee cafeteria, with its combination of industrial dishwashing steam, coffee, and overcooked food wafting through the hallway. In general, employees weren't supposed to take food or supplies from the caf. Somehow our cast was given the green light to munch lunch backstage—but only backstage. A security guard at the exit to the parking lot ensured that employees weren't stealing anything on the way out. Before I knew better, I took a couple of ham and cheese croissants home one night, but I mended my ways after one of my castmates got busted for pilfering toilet paper.

****

Opening the unmarked door to the backstage of the theatre, I headed down the hall to sign in. Entering through the stage door was always exciting for me. I felt like I was part of an elite club going through a secret entrance into a magical world, like Alice discovering Wonderland. Backstage was a world of its own, like some remote island where exotic, scantily clad natives performed secret rituals, dances, and customs, and spoke a secret language. "You go, girl! Fierce solo, Diva! Work that feather." Being allowed backstage was like winning the golden ticket to visit Willy Wonka's Chocolate Factory.

As a guest, you, too, may have been lucky enough to wander the halls of backstage, view the actual stage, the wings, sets, fast change rooms, and props. But rarely would you be allowed into the dressing rooms. Seldom, on a special occasion, after the cast had cleared out, you may have been given permission to take a look, although that was not encouraged. It was a sacred place where our possessions were not to be seen or touched. It was our home, after all. All visitors had to vacate by half hour call. You would *never* get to be in the dressing room, in the wings, fast change room, or on stage *during* the show unless you were cast or crew or a fly on the wall. And it was the stuff that happened during the show that would really knock your socks off. Only the select few who "break into" show biz get to witness the magic and madness behind the scenes. Perhaps that's why the term "break into" is used; you have to get past all the closed, locked doors.

The Flamingo's backstage was dingy. The carpet may have once been a garish, dirt-disguising, colorful hotel pattern but it had become well worn, dirty, and faded by the time my feet graced the floors. The hallway smelled of must, fog machine, stale smoke, coffee, hairspray, and the thick, heavy stage curtain that soaked up the essence of the theatre and its patrons. I was now a part of the history of the hotel, one of a long line of shows and performers to call this place home.

On the immediate left was a stairwell that led down to the stage left entrance to the stage. (Yes, we had to run downstairs to get from the dressing rooms to the stage.) As you continued down the hallway, on the left was a high shelf that housed our soldier hats and hangers for some of the larger costumes, like the showgirl headdresses and the Infanta costumes. On the right were two tiny dressing rooms for the specialty acts, followed by the Big Rockette dressing room, the Green Room, the Small Rockette dressing room, the boys' dressing room, and the stage managers' office. At the end of the hallway on the left was the stage right stairwell to enter the stage. Around the corner to the left were the star spot dressing room, the magic act dressing room, the wardrobe department, and the tiny sound booth with a view to the stage.

I headed down the hall to the callboard where there hung the cast list on which we had to sign in for every show under the appropriate date. I usually signed in for both shows at the same time, as I rarely had plans to leave the theatre between shows.

Around half-hour call, backstage at the Flamingo became a hubbub of activity from tech crew, stage management, company manager, dancers, specialty acts, stars, wardrobe, sound and lighting technicians, and dance captains. On special occasions, directors, choreographers, producers, or Radio City visitors might show up, too. Nino Frediani and his unobtrusive Japanese wife arrived as well as magician Tim Cole and his South African spouse and assistant, Jenny-Lynn.

The energy was electric; the buzz of excitement escalated as showtime neared. Girls wearing wig caps and white bath towels flitted through the halls. Dancers stretched in every square foot of available floor space, each girl holding the wall with one hand, her leg pulled over her head with the other, all the while talking away with the other girls. At the last possible minute, the stage door would fling open, and Stacey Moore would be yanked into the hall by his happy, yappy "Mess of Mutts," an assortment of ten medium to smallish adorable rescue dogs all on leashes he held like a bouquet in one hand.

At five-minute call, I'd go by the stairwell to have a dresser put the feathers in my butt pack and top hat, and then I'd walk down the flight of stairs to the stage. A couple of early-bird Rockettes were already on stage, sitting face to face and feet to feet, both in the Russian splits, legs spread apart at a nearly perfect 180 degree angle, gossiping in hushed tones. Little peacock cliques, mostly in pairs and trios, swarmed in, stretched, and caught up on the day's events.

At "Places!" call, the stage filled with the rest of the flock, all yakking while kicking to warm up. It was hard to believe that, after working together six days a week, the girls could still fill up every second with chatter, but we could. Why do married couples run out of things to say to each other, but girlfriends don't ever have enough time to share everything that is on their minds? The noise often reached a deafening level; our two stage managers constantly reprimanded us for talking on stage, but it was a losing battle.

Once the overture started and the announcement came over the loudspeakers in English and Japanese about "No flash photography," we all lined up side by side across the width of the stage behind the long, heavy sign that read, "THE ROCKETTES." Our bodies were hidden from the waist up, so all the audience could see when the curtain opened was the sign and twenty sets of gorgeous gams, poised to dance. Still whispering to each other, we stood there, arms linked behind without touching any body part of the girls next to us, our right feet beveled against our left ankles, our lower bodies remaining perfectly still, even though our mouths were going a mile a minute. Only at the very last moment when the sign was lifted into the rafters, revealing us in our bikinis and feathers, did we finally stop gabbing and start smiling, as we flapped downstage. It's a wonder we were (mostly) able to keep our mouths shut during the dance. We always had so much to say.

Slowly but surely, I gained control over my show and got used to the routine, the stage, the traffic patterns, the costume changes, and the timing between numbers. I ended up setting a bathroom break between "Bolero" and "Soldiers." Whether I had to go or not, I would try so I didn't end up jumping and kicking with a full bladder during "Diamonds." Plus, I didn't want to alter my routine for fear of the superstitious retributions. I always went down to the stage at the same point in the music before each number. I always put on my red cheeks for "Soldiers" as soon as I got off the stage from "Bolero" so I wouldn't forget them. I got a drink from the water fountain on my way to "Diamonds." Entertainers may possibly be one of the most superstitious groups of people in the world.

Between shows, most of the cast members, including myself, would throw on sweats, baseball caps, and flip-flops or slippers and bring back dinner from the caf or relax in the Green Room or dressing room. Occasionally, I'd take off my wig cap and let my hair down to breathe, but I never took off my false eyelashes until after the second show was over. If I had to run to the box office to buy a ticket for someone, or to meet someone between shows, I always felt conspicuous in my garish makeup. But Vegas is about the only place in the world where you can blend in despite looking that scary. Our small Green Room was nothing fancy, but, with a refrigerator, a microwave, two couches, chairs, a coffee table, a TV, and some bookshelves, it was a homey enough place to hang out.

At fifteen-minute call, I would prepare for the second show. I'd touch up my lipstick and powder and get my Opening costume on. Fifteen-minute call was also the time we celebrated cast birthdays. Our cast took birthdays so seriously, we actually had a "Cake Marshall"—a Rockette in charge of buying the cakes and cards for everyone. I'm not sure where the money to pay for all these goodies came from, but I think it was our generous producer, Richard Martini of KL Management Inc., who footed the bill. With a cast of over thirty and fifty-two weeks in a year, there was a new cake about every other week. One cake would just be getting eaten up when the next cake would arrive. My thirty-first birthday happened less than a month after joining the show. I was shocked to arrive at the theatre and see my dressing room spot filled with gifts, many from girls I barely knew. It made me feel very loved and welcomed.

Women are notorious shoppers, ultra caring, and easily guilted, so we felt we had to buy every Rockette a present for her birthday. The gift expense got so outrageous that I started to break out in a cold sweat whenever someone mentioned the word "birthday." Hence, I helped kick-start the "Group Gift Initiative" in which we all chipped in from $2 to $5 and got one fairly nice gift for the birthday girl without breaking our individual banks. My favorite group gift was my idea for our ice cream fanatic, Leslie. The entire Big Dressing Room pitched in and bought her a pint of every flavor of Ben and Jerry's ice cream our grocery store sold (about fifteen kinds). Leslie was thrilled.

Celebrating birthdays became a part of our regular routine, so much so that, over time, we got so jaded that half the time we'd yell the "Happy Birthday" song from our dressing tables and never actually get up. When we got to the part in the song where you name the birthday boy or girl, we'd all look at each other, as we refreshed our mascara, and ask, "Whose birthday is it?" With cake constantly available and my muscles adequately stretched from the first show, my second show warm-up evolved into two knee lifts, two high kicks, and a few bites of cake. Then I was sugared up and ready to do the show all over again.

The show finished around midnight. I'd rinse off in the dressing room shower and scrub off my make-up if I were going home or tame it down a few notches if I were going out on the town. Sometimes I'd join friends for drinks (loved those $1 margaritas at the Hard Rock Cafe), dancing, bowling, sushi, or birthday celebrations. Parties started around 12:30 a.m. (goodbye parties, Halloween pumpkin-carving parties, Christmas parties). When those of us in the cast were participating in a fundraising show for Golden Rainbow—an organization "dedicated to providing housing and direct financial assistance to people living with HIV/AIDS in Southern Nevada"—we had middle-of-the-night rehearsals. Late night was also a nice time to go grocery shopping, because the stores were less busy. After-hours activities and socializing made sense, because it was hard to go right to sleep while still wound up, our blood pumping from performing.

On average, I went to bed at three in the morning and woke up around noon. Having to be anywhere before noon the next day was torture. Entertainers are in their own little time zone. The Rockettes knew that calling each other before noon was taboo, because we'd probably be deep in slumber. My apartment groundskeeper, however, did not get the memo. "Stop that racket! Don't you know people are trying to sleep around here?" I wanted to shout out the window. "The nerve of him mowing the lawn at ten a.m.!" Even doing lunch with friends was a chore. Far better was to schedule a rendezvous around two p.m. or later.

My beauty rest was Essential with a capital "E." If I didn't get my full nine hours of peaceful slumber, my body ached and I was miserable. After my put-in rehearsals were over and I had adjusted to the show, I tried to resume my previous workout regimen, but my body would not have it. Extra physical activity left me with no energy for the show. On my day off each week, I made attempts at hiking or mountain biking or snow skiing, but my body wanted to be a couch potato. My first month in the show, I was so sore and tired all the time I didn't know how I was going to survive my six-month contract. I had so much to squeeze into my precious, one day off that I couldn't possibly do chores and errands, and socialize, and spend time with my husband, and make room for rest in that tiny amount of time.

Eventually, our wonderful producer brought in a yoga teacher to give us on-stage classes on Wednesdays before the first show. Yoga helped me to relax and stay flexible, but maintaining my health for the long haul was a challenge. Like final exam time in college, during a short-running show, you can burn the candle at both ends, pull all-nighters, push through the pain while surviving solely on junk food and a good caffeine buzz, and then collapse when it's all over. That approach doesn't work so well with a long-running show. I felt like I was running a perpetual marathon.

****

Being my first truly long run, working at the Flamingo was unlike any gig I'd had before, and not only because I had to pace myself to stay in the race. The show, a bus and truck tour whose final stop was an indefinite stay in Las Vegas, had already been running there for a year. The cast had settled into their dressing rooms and made them home, the result of which created an interesting backstage dynamic. Learning and getting comfortable with the show was one challenge; acclimating to the hodge-podge of personalities, backstage protocol, and dressing room politics was another.

As might happen in a town where people tend to associate only with those living on the right side of the tracks, the layout of the dressing rooms and the characters associated within created divisions that necessitated certain alliances and obligations. First and foremost, there were two distinctly different Rockette dressing rooms: "the Big Dressing Room," which housed eighteen women, and "the Little Dressing Room," which housed seven. I was involuntarily placed by Raoul, who held jurisdiction over matters related to who sits where, in the Big Dressing Room.

The Big Dressing Room was basically a long rectangle with a bathroom and a shower room at the far end of it. Running along the entire perimeter of the room, save the doorways, were counter tops with lighted mirrors above them and shoe racks below them. These counters served as our dressing tables. We called our portion of the counter our "spot." The room was divided in several significant ways. First of all, a large costume rack ran straight down the middle, which prevented us from seeing the girls on the other side of it. Secondly, blocks of dressing spots were separated from each other by either partial walls or the bathroom or shower room door. These separations became important, as each section became its own entity with its own name, atmosphere, and identity.

As you entered, to the immediate right was an L-shaped section lining the corner of the room and dubbed by the girls "Kiddie Corner." My guess is that the founding sisters were more childish acting, but no one ever told me the origin of the nickname. Kiddie Corner contained five dressing spots, the last of which bordered upon a small partition wall that separated it from the spot to its left.

Past the wall on the left and continuing down that same side of the room ending at the wall by the shower room were six spots decorated with red hot chili pepper lights, called the "Hot Tamale Row." Many of my best Branson buddies congregated there, all of them known either by their Rockette nicknames or by their last names, like we were on a sports team: Ginny (a.k.a. "Gyne"—as in "gynecologist"), Wanda Squillante (a.k.a. "Squally"), and Jan Safford (a.k.a. "Safford"). The partition wall served as the dividing line between Kiddie Corner and Hot Tamales. The Hot Tamales were known as the fun, talkative, happy subset of the dressing room. They were a crafty group, in general, who engaged in a lot of cross-stitching (or, as we used to say, "cross-ball-stitching"—a play on the dance step "cross-ball-change"), except for Kristen, a rebel redhead (a.k.a. "Fathead"—thanks to her massive head of hair). She was the black sheep of the herd, shunning crafts and instead shouting her mantra, "Drink Beer!"

Continuing counterclockwise around the corner on the other side of the shower room door were two isolated dressing spots (sandwiched between the bathroom and shower room doors) that never really had success forming their own identity. They had a few different names while I was there, but none really stuck. They were in a kind of No-Man's-Land, not close enough to Hot Tamales on one side or to the row on the other side of the bathroom to feel like a part of either. Once, in a great act of empathy and generosity, Hot Tamales tried to annex them. They were too far away to hear the conversations and participate in the fun, however, and ended up retreating back into their own little lonely twosome.

Directly opposite from Hot Tamales, on the other side of the costume rack, were five spots that comprised by far the scariest section of the dressing room. "Death Row," as it was known, housed the dance captain, who sat on the far end next to the bathroom, as well as the jaded ladies, who had been kicking too long to enjoy it anymore but still wouldn't quit. These negative Nellies lived to gossip, but couldn't always do so freely with the dance captain nearby. So they were often seen leaning into one another for secret conversations in hushed tones and whispered words. Death Row was generally somber and deadly silent. They preferred to read quietly with scowls on their faces when not complaining to each other about whatever irked them to death. Their grim perspective cast a pall over that portion of the room. Eventually, the aggrieved dears departed and some "New Age-y" women moved in. With their fresh blood, they made a concerted effort to revive Death Row into a more cheerful space.

When you walked around the Big Dressing Room, you could sense the different energies emanating from each section: from Kiddie Corner's childish monkey business to the frivolity and camaraderie of Hot Tamales to the gloomy stillness that lingered over Death Row. I felt bad for the innocent girls who were involuntarily sentenced to Death Row and cursed with its cynical legacy. For the most part, I stayed away from the dark side. It was all too easy to get lured into a noxious gripe session.

Last was a single dressing spot nearly the size of two normal spots that was called "The Condo," because it was so much larger than the other spots. It was the first spot you saw on your left as you entered the room and was sandwiched between the entrance and Death Row with another small partition separating it into its own entity. The Condo always had a waiting list of people who wanted their privacy and a little extra room to spread out. The girls who moved there were happy and The Condo held no negative connotations.

The Little Dressing Room was down the hall from the Big Dressing Room on the opposite side of the Green Room. It took on the name "Bellevue," after the famous insane asylum, which was supposedly indicative of the mental state of the dancers who were admitted there. It developed an entirely different atmosphere than the Big Dressing Room, acting almost like a small, exclusive club. Bellevue contained one row of seven dressing spots, and you knew if you lived there that you would have no privacy and had better get along with all the others. Because of its library-like atmosphere, you could actually read there uninterrupted. On the down side, it was a confined space with poor ventilation and no bathroom.

Moving to Bellevue was a big commitment that required careful advance consideration not only due to the aforementioned features, but also because you were expected to help host several events throughout the year. Bellevue became a haunted house at Halloween and held regular "Popcorn and Kool-Aid Nights" as well as bake sales to raise extra cash to buy community items for the dressing room (a coffee maker or an ab roller, for instance). When one Bellevuean got engaged, her wedding shower was held in Bellevue between shows. Her cake was like none I've ever seen. Leave it to Vegas to have an adult bakery specializing in anatomically correct genitalia desserts. It was so real looking, I could hardly eat it. Bellevue was also home to the "Stinky Sock Contest," a kooky game in which participating Rockettes would keep their soldier socks unwashed for weeks. Once sufficiently ripe, the socks were judged to determine whose were the stinkiest. One had to be really brave or really crazy to be a judge, but some people were just that bonkers.

Mona McDonald (a.k.a. "Mac") and Rhoda Mado (a.k.a. "Jado"—a play on the word "jaded") were the unofficial masterminds of Bellevue. They were in their terribly late thirties and had been Rockettes for about seven years. Having both recently been put on the Roster, and therefore guaranteed work as long as they wanted it without needing to audition, they claimed their status and seniority and weren't going to be pushed around by anyone. Mac was a Midwestern, blond Barbie doll almost exactly my height, so we often danced next to each other in line-up. She was so flexible a pretzel would be jealous and could hold her leg suspended in the 6:00 position by her ear for days. In the past, she had made a good living dancing with a male partner on cruise ships. Mac served as the Bellevue cruise director of sorts, planning all kinds of events and activities.

Jado was a brunette, Jersey girl with a thick accent and an infectious laugh. She had battled it out in New York and survived being a Rockette at Radio City Music Hall, so she must have been tough as nails. She had even performed in 42nd Street on Broadway the first time it came out. Jado was the foremost Gossip Queen of the cast and kept in close and frequent communication with her contacts in New York so as to always be up on the latest talk or "T." "What's the T?"

she'd always say, a twinkle in her eye. If the Rockettes had their own CIA, Jado was surely a lead member. Gathering information and spreading it around on a need-to-know basis was her forte. If you wanted to know what was going down, Jado was your woman. She was in cahoots with the men's dance captain, who also had connections and good "dish." I've never been good at dishing the dirt and have always been last to hear the latest scuttlebutt, but luckily for me, this time I was friends with Leslie, and she was friends with Jado, so I got the "T" earlier than usual. The only person to get remotely close to rivaling Jado for info was Fathead. Fathead was excellent in sussing out the Vegas dish, but couldn't come close to touching Jado when it came to the inside intelligence from Radio City in New York. "Ya gotta have contacts, Girls." Jado was also a strong competitor in the Stinky Sock Contest, her socks coming about as close to smelling like vinegar as anyone's could.

Mac and Jado, a strong united front to be both feared and respected, were also founding members of the F. of I. (Fear of Intimacy) Club. Although both had no shortage of suitors over the course of their lifetimes, neither Mac nor Jado pursued marriage at that time. Their biological clocks may have been ticking, but they both chose to remain single due to their so-called "fear of intimacy." Over the course of the run, many other Rockettes joined the F. of I. Club, but once officially hitched, they were required to resign their membership pins. It was the odd Rockette who didn't have a man clambering for her affection, but not everyone was ready to commit to the old ball and chain.

In general, the girls in Bellevue were the older, more seasoned, been-around-the-block Rockettes, and they were particular about with whom they wished to cohabit. As such, it was imperative that they keep tabs on everyone's potential comings and goings so as to be the first to know when one of the Rockettes planned to quit her job. Jado's super-sleuth skills came in especially handy in this regard. At the first buzz of a departure, Jado and Mac secretly discussed which girls they deemed worthy of joining the esteemed ranks of the Little Dressing Room. That lucky person then received a hush-hush visit during the show to meet them at a certain time and place away from other listening ears. "So and So is leaving the show, and we want you to move to Bellevue. Think about it, and let us know ASAP. And don't say a word about this to anyone else."

By the time someone in Bellevue gave notice and her spot opened up, the Bellevueans had already been secretly lobbying for weeks in advance for a certain person to move in. It was a serious, clandestine affair involving Raoul, who made the final decision regarding seating assignments. As soon as one of their top picks agreed to move in, Mac and Jado dashed off to the wardrobe room to secure first dibs on the spot for their chosen lady.

Finding your niche in the dressing room was a big deal, because the location of your spot and the neighbors surrounding it could mean the difference between loving, tolerating, or downright disliking your job. This realization became apparent to everyone, not just the wily Bellevueans. It was, therefore, crucial to be in the loop when it came to hearsay about who was leaving, in case her exit would affect who would be sitting next to you. For instance, what if rumor had it that Lucy was quitting the show, thereby leaving her spot in Bellevue up for grabs, and Squally who sat next to you desired to be in the Little Dressing Room? That would leave the spot next to you open. One of two things could happen: 1.) If any of your current castmates heard that Squally's spot was probably going to be available if Lucy left, they might wish to leave wherever they were sitting and take the spot by you; or 2.) The new girl would be automatically placed there. If you were afraid of a wild card person sitting next to you and wanted to be in control of who your neighbor was going to be (especially if you didn't know the new girl at all), you needed to quietly convince someone you knew you got along well with to move into Hot Tamales. Then you had to get her to okay it with Raoul and stake a claim before anyone else did or before the new girl moved to Vegas.

Hence the importance of befriending the cast Gossip Queens, especially Jado and Fathead, because they nearly always had the scoop before anyone else. They and their spies continually bugged dressing rooms for inside information on anyone remotely considering vacating. In addition, Jado regularly phoned her NYC Rockette contacts to suss out what was going down and who might be the next replacement sent to Vegas. The new girls got stuck wherever there was an opening and had to make the best of it.

Likewise, in those instances when *you* yourself weren't happy where you were sitting and contemplated moving to another section, your antennae had to be up and running at all times, so that you could pick up any signal that one of the girls might be giving notice. Then you had to race to get to Raoul before anyone else. Herein lay the importance of getting on the Queen Bee's good side; he could blurt a big fat, "No way, Jose!" to your request to relocate. After all, it required moving all your costumes to another location as well as teaching a new dresser about all your costume changes. If Raoul was in a bad mood or didn't like you, he could make your life difficult backstage. He not only overruled seating assignments but also okayed or denied requests for costume changes and repairs. So if you desperately wished to move to Bellevue, you had better start bowing down to and buttering up not only Mac and Jado but Raoul.

The other tricky part to such an ordeal was that you didn't want your dressing room section to know too far ahead of time, because leaving was like being a traitor. "You don't want to sit with us anymore?" When changes were made, it was sometimes in a big flurry and uproar with hard feelings. Having someone leave your section could feel like she'd personally slapped you across the face, ripped your heart out, thrown it on the floor, and stomped on it. Or you could just shrug your shoulders and peacefully let the person go. Other shows I've done prevented that whole dressing room problem from ever happening by arranging girls in alphabetical order or, as in the Branson Rockettes, by your lineup on stage. Raoul's tolerance for our spot-shifting shenanigans was unnecessarily generous. It would have been within his right to lay down the law and make us sit and stay put wherever he wanted.

As the new girl, I did not have a say in where I wanted to sit and was assigned by Raoul to the last seat of Kiddie Corner, where I butted up against the partition wall. Luckily, Ginny, my dear friend from Branson, sat in the Hot Tamale Row spot closest to Kiddie Corner, so if we leaned back in our seats we could see each other and talk. Kiddie Corner housed an interesting potpourri of people, starting with Dorrie who sat on my right. Dorrie was one of the older girls in the group, a contemporary of Mac and Jado and a New York Rockette and tour survivor. Thankfully, she loved to chat and, having paid her dues, had earned her right to an opinion on anything Rockette-related. Because she had seniority over me, I was relieved she wasn't one of those terrifying New York Rockettes about whom I'd heard rumors. While she certainly could have pulled rank, she never did, and we got along fine and even became good friends.

Occupying the first spot next to the dressing room door was Joann, who had joined the touring Rockettes and settled in Vegas when the tour ended there. A fashionista, music buff, and shopper extraordinaire, she was also mothering and responsible. Next to her sat Missy, the totally buffed and beautiful Australian I had danced with in Branson. She was the only person in my section who I already knew. Missy and Joann, best friends and both nearing thirty (my age at the time), lent an air of maturity and "been there, done that" to Kiddie Corner, but it was the one and only Bobbi Sue with her childish antics who infused the section with personality befitting its name. Bobbi Sue was sandwiched dead in the middle of us all, and it was probably for the best that she had a safety buffer on both sides.

Dorrie was the eldest member of Kiddie Corner, but Joann was the matriarch, especially to Bobbi Sue, whom she best-friended in a big-sisterly, even motherly way. Joann would cook lasagna or pot roast and bring the leftovers in a Tupperware for Bobbi Sue to make sure she was eating well. Bobbi Sue was one of the few Rockettes who was considered underweight, a condition that earned her the nickname "Skinny Chick."

Skinny Chick was a twenty-two-year-old, 5'10", paper-thin, drop-dead gorgeous, firecracker, southern gal with silky, light-brown, waist-long hair. If she liked you, she was as loyal a friend as they come. If she disliked you and had the urge, she could punch your lights out in a second. Her unbridled passion for dance absolutely poured out of her every pore. She didn't touch booze or drugs, and God knows there wasn't a drug out there that could match her energy anyway. Bobbi Sue turned heads. Always sporting some sexy dress that started four feet up her gams, she caused traffic jams on the Vegas Strip. She made it known that she wasn't big on anything educational, including reading, but who needs smarts when you've got a bod like that?

Every night at precisely half-hour call, Bobbi Sue would come bounding in, boisterous and full of spit and vinegar. Then she'd spend the next twenty-five minutes laughing and parading about, eating her take-out food or modeling her latest shopping purchases. While I needed a leisurely hour or more to prepare myself for the show, Bobbi Sue could sit down at her dressing table at five-minute call without a stitch of makeup on and be ready on time, which she did regularly. When she was in a real hurry, she'd smear on lipstick and lashes and finish her make-up *after* the opening number.

Bobbi Sue's one self-proclaimed flaw was that her breasts were too small. As such, she joined the "Itty Bitty Titty Committee"—a backstage club that was formed by women first on the alphabetical bra scale (size As). I thought she looked stunning as is. But some women are naturally like computers: As soon as they see another female, their brains scan her body, process the information thoroughly, and assess how they compare. The Rockettes were familiar with each others' parts down to the last detail. We all knew perfectly well who had the tightest abs, most toned legs, best buffed arms, and most beautiful breasts. We were always begging the girls with the sexiest stomachs to spill their secrets to getting that perfect six-pack. (Wouldn't ya know it? Sit ups.)

I saw perhaps half a dozen breast augmentations (some exquisite and some gone terribly awry) on Rockettes over the years. Some members of the Itty Bitty Titty Committee pondered openly about enhancing their bra sizes, and many of us would try to talk them out of it. After carefully surveying all the naked gals in the room, Skinny Chick announced, "Kristi, if I ever get a boob job, I want them to be just like yours. My boyfriend should come and check yours out." I was floored! Boy oh boy, was I honored to have the winning mammaries, because we had some doozies in the cast, both faux and natural. I soon became known as "Kristi B-Cups," because it was determined in the dressing room that I had the ideal size B-Cup breasts. That nickname morphed into "Krystal B-Cups," and from that moment on, the girls almost always called me that or just "Krystal" or just "B-Cups." When I was a modern dancer in New York, I thought my breasts were too big. When I was in the Playboy's Girls of Rock & Roll, I felt my breasts were too small. Now, as a Rockette, my breasts were just right! Go figure, Goldilocks. I should have just accepted my body from the very beginning.

Skinny Chick and I were polar opposites in several ways. I would sit quietly at my perfectly organized, tastefully decorated spot reading a book or quietly working on some craft project or another while she bounced off the walls, taped junk to her mirror, or searched through her pile of dance shoes and dirty clothes under the dressing table. Her spot was so messy it's a wonder she could find her make-up. She could barely view her face in her mirror, because it was covered with magazine cutouts, photos, lipstick graffiti, and other types of trash. Being the consummate professional, I routinely did a fifteen-minute ballet warm-up using my chair as the barre every night before the first show. I never *ever* witnessed Bobbi Sue warming up. It would have been a redundant gesture, as she ran around so much her muscles were constantly on fire anyway.

It didn't take long for Bobbi Sue to discern and become annoyed by our opposing idiosyncrasies. After I'd been in the show for several months, Miss Skinny Chick went so far as to issue me an eviction notice:

Why Kristi Should Not Be in Kiddie Corner!
- *Too neat*
- *She does ballet warm ups*
- *Boobs!!!*
- *Reads (not just looking at pictures)*
- *Too crafty*

She also complained that I was too smart and used big words. Then to really stir things up, one night I came off stage from dancing in "Big Band" to discover her sitting demurely at her perfectly clean and neat dressing table pretending to write a letter, while my spot had been ransacked, garbage thrown everywhere and all my stuff strewn about. She was a wild card. I don't know how any of us would have gotten through the shows without her.

Kiddie Corner was full of surprises, but when a Hot Tamale gave her notice, I jumped at the chance to move closer to my Branson buddies—Gyne, Safford, and Squally—where I could cross-ball-stitch without guilt, where "read" wasn't a four-letter word, and where I was not only allowed but encouraged to do crafts. Several of us openly worshipped Martha Stewart, and Squally could make a masterful butternut squash risotto and work a glue gun like nobody's business. Eventually, even Fathead gave into peer pressure and cross-stitched Christmas gifts for her entire family. My people! While I still dearly loved my Kiddie Corner compatriots, I found my happy place in Hot Tamales and stayed the remainder of the run.

Later, I had the tremendous honor of being secretly asked to move to Bellevue when one of their residents was leaving the show. But after careful consideration, I decided to remain in the Big, wild, Dressing Room. After all, it did house the bathroom and shower room—a huge plus. More importantly, I didn't want to miss out on any of the hilarious, backstage entertainment. Bobbi Sue was reason enough for me to stay put. I could have just popped a bag of popcorn and watched her all night.

****

By the time you perform a show about thirty times, you are generally comfy with the choreography, you have calmed your nerves, and you have adjusted to the pace (you no longer hyperventilate after every number). The choreography has gone out of your brain and into muscle memory so you don't have to think about it anymore. At this time, your eyes and brain become free to focus on other activities, like scoping the audience for, say, cute guys. I couldn't believe how much we could see from stage, especially after the show became routine, and the cast loved to spread the word. "Did you see the lady breastfeeding her baby in the front row?" "There was a couple making out stage left, five rows back around #8!" "That dude center stage, third row hasn't clapped the entire night!" Let that be a lesson to you, audience members. If you don't want to be seen, don't do it. These were welcome diversions, however, as they kept the gig interesting for us.

Additionally, most of your costume kinks have been ironed out. You've gotten extremely efficient with your costume changes and have memorized your entrance music including exactly the number of counts needed to get you from the dressing room to your place on stage. When I first started, I had to listen carefully for all of my cues; I couldn't even make small talk for fear of being distracted. But after a while, I barely needed to pay attention to the music on the monitors. My body automatically got up at the appropriate time in the music, started putting on my hat, and headed downstage, like Pavlov's dog salivating to the ring of the bell. Sometimes my internal alarm clock failed, and I found myself spewing profanities while dashing down to make my entrance, but for the most part, I was running on automatic pilot.

By this point, your show has become so streamlined that you have freed up precious seconds, even minutes, of time in which to do something other than focus on the show. Even during the most hectic periods of the night, we'd find micro-snippets of time to fix lipstick, flirt with a stagehand, read a note on the call board, or grab a chocolate. I was living life on high speed, and every moment counted. Maximizing time was a game we played to the fullest.

Lots of performers, myself included, cross-stitched, knitted, or crocheted because we could always sneak in a few stitches if we had a couple extra seconds. Plus we could gossip while doing it, a pursuit that proved most difficult when trying to read a book. Reading wasn't the best way to pass the time during the show, as you could become so engrossed in the story that you'd nearly miss your cue to go on stage. And you most certainly had no business concentrating on your history exam in the dressing room, as that would prevent you from being available for questions, bantering, and complaining. Our favorite way to fill time and our natural default activity was loads and loads of chewing the fat, tittle-tattling, and dishing the dirt. Nothing wasted time as well as some serious scuttlebutt.

During this particular show, we were lucky enough to have a few long breaks of seven minutes or so while the specialty acts performed. Seven minutes is an absolute eternity in backstage time; you wouldn't believe what an actor can accomplish in those few instants if prepared. I'd bet my tap shoes that if God had been an entertainer, she/he could have created the world in seven minutes. Much like the "New York minute," only considerably faster, is the "Entertainer's minute." What entertainers can accomplish in three seconds, one minute, or a whopping seven whole minutes would astound you. It did me.

It's no wonder we became masters of the clock. Our entire job revolved around tick-tock: We had to be at the theatre at precisely half-hour call, start the show at exactly the same time every night, be on stage at the start of each number, change costumes in record time, perform choreography perfectly to the beat and timing of the music. Time waited for no one in the theatre. The show would go on with or without you. It was a regimented lifestyle; to be successful, you had to keep good time.

In addition, the show was completely scripted and choreographed. Can you imagine having a job in which every day, at the same time, your every motion and utterance are done in the same way and in the same order with the same people while wearing the same clothes and saying the same words verbatim? And doing a good job meant repeating this exact same protocol every single day without the slightest deviation? It was robotic and unnatural. After repeating our performance time and time again for days, weeks, months, and years on end, we became so intimately familiar with the show that we were desperate for variety and something refreshing to mix up the daily routine. We loved to find ways to break up the repetitiveness and inject a touch of the unexpected.

Consequently, out of sheer necessity, the combination of tedium and seven glorious minutes of free time catalyzed the creation of some fantastic backstage entertainment. If preplanned, we could squeeze in the world's fastest "Talent Show" or "Showing." One Rockette would announce, "Everyone meet in the Big Dressing Room after 'Big Band' for a Showing!" That meant that someone had put together entertainment for us. Yippee! As soon as our number was over, we'd sprint off stage, unzipping each other's dresses and eschewing costume pieces along the way. We'd quickly put on the costume for our next number and gather for the special event.

A showing could be any silly spectacle presented by one, two, or several people. Bobbi Sue, the Queen of Backstage Entertainment, periodically dressed up like the female lead dancer in *Riverdance*—the "Irish Dancing Phenomenon"—wearing a leotard and wee little skirt, her hair down in long, wavy, flowing locks, a wreath of sparkly ribbons around her head. She would mock Irish dance and parody the show to much laughter, cheering, and applause.

After dating Russian gymnasts from Cirque du Soleil's bizarre "Mystere" extravaganza at Treasure Island Casino, Bobbi Sue and pal Sunshine showed off the "hand-to-hand" routine their grotesquely flexible, burly boyfriends taught them—a series of ever-so-slowly changing formations where they'd balance on each other in gravity-defying, contortionist poses. Sometimes the showings were as simple as Ivana (a.k.a. "Ivy") doing her famous, fantastic Russian jump splits in which she'd spring up, straddle-split her legs out to the sides, and touch her toes with her hands, all while suspended in midair. This airborne move was a favorite request for showings, talent shows, or just for a quick pick-me-up.

Talent shows were a much grander affair involving numerous contestants and even judges. Given that this was an exceptionally talented group to compete against, participants dug deep and pulled out their best, most unique skills. Gyne wowed the crowd with her super-soprano imitation of Snow White singing her bird-calling trills. A couple ladies got together behind a chair to make an adorable tap-dancing mini-Rockette in which one person's hands went in the shoes to be the feet and another person did the arms. They pulled off a hysterical, miniature, high-speed version of our "Big Band" number.

The showings and talent shows were met with great excitement, and all the dressers, as well as some of the male dancers, rushed in to watch. As a rule, men and women were not allowed in each other's dressing room except with permission from all performers present and almost never during the show. But exceptions were sometime made for talent shows, especially if the guys had whipped up some juicy entertainment for us, like a sexy dance routine performed in black leather lingerie (think Harley-Davidson meets Victoria's Secret). After the talent show, we had to rush like crazy to make the next number in time. We'd hightail it down to the stage, still guffawing, our spirits lifted and energy renewed.

Although the audience thinks entertainers are only there to entertain the audience, I learned that entertainers expend a considerable amount of energy entertaining themselves. Backstage was where the prime entertainment happened. Ticket price to see *The Great Radio City Spectacular*? $50. Backstage Talent Show? Priceless.

****

Backstage was also an excellent place to make a little money on the side, as we were a captive audience. With two shows a night close together, we didn't always have time to leave the theatre, but we usually had time to shop. Here we were, twenty-five mostly single women with healthy, regular paychecks, trapped at the theatre with time on our hands. Consequently, we did a lot of catalog shopping. Most intriguing, however, were all the little side businesses that sprang up. Squally and one of the dressers sold homemade G-strings made of fun material (M&Ms, shimmery silver disco, plaid flannel, holiday themes) adorned in lace and rhinestones for anywhere from $2.50 to $5. We all went crazy over the new G-strings. Somehow knowing that under your costume you had on a sexy, red sequined Christmas G with dainty, red lace ruffles just helped put you in the holiday spirit.

Skinny Chick offered eyebrow shaping and mani and pedi appointments between shows. Her specialty was painting tiny designs (flowers, hearts, stripes, Christmas trees) on toenails. One night, I had her paint pink and white flowers on my bright purple toenails. She did a beautiful job; my tootsies had never looked so spectacular. But I had little time to let them dry sufficiently before the second show. Stuffing my feet into tights, fishnets, and tap shoes wasn't the best way to preserve my fresh pedicure. The entire second show I worried about my nails getting messed up and tried to tap dance ever so softly.

"Momma" (whose real name was Marlene, but her nickname stuck) was the most ambitious money maker. She sold Avon, and we all looked forward to getting our new catalogs. She also ended up repping Mary Kaye cosmetics and offered makeovers between shows. Momma

Long Legs and Tall Tales

even started a resume-typing business and sold gift baskets at Christmas time.

If we had the munchies, we needed look no further than our very own Big Dressing Room, thanks to Thalia's entrepreneurial spirit. She sat in The Condo and used her extra space to house "The Condo Café," where she sold baked goods. Thalia, Trisha, and Barbara, our primary bakers, tempted us with delectable cookies, brownies, Cheerio Bars, and other tooth-decaying treats, which were offered for a modest fee, paid on the honor system into a coffee can. We were always excited to see treats for sale and were disappointed when the gals hadn't had time to bake.

Bellevue was also a good source for treats and sweets, thanks to their regular Popcorn and Kool-Aid nights and bake sales. Mac was the one person into health food; we could count on her to make her famous, healthy, mini carrot cakes. In addition to founding The Condo Café, Thalia (a Bohemian, holistic, New-Agey girl) took health a step further by offering ear wax removal. The somewhat dangerous process involved sticking "ear candles" from the health food store into your ears and lighting them with a match. Supposedly, the hot vacuum melted and sucked out the nasty wax buildup. I was shocked the first time I walked into the dressing room between shows and saw ladies lying on the floor with smoking cones protruding from the sides of their heads. Those were some smokin' hot Rockettes. Thank goodness nothing unintended caught fire.

Eventually even I jumped on the entrepreneurial bandwagon and set out a basket of my original watercolor greeting cards. The Rockettes shopped till we dropped, or at least until the show ended, whichever came first.

****

The dressing rooms weren't just a source of silly amusement and random small business pursuits. They were a hotbed of information gathering and exchange. If I needed a one-dish dinner I could stir up fast to feed my visiting in-laws, Joann was ready with her five-minute "Miracle Lasagna." If someone needed to find a reliable babysitter, Trisha was on the case. If I needed a good headshot photographer, a Pilates instructor, or a dentist so darling he would make Superman drool, I could find someone through the gals in the dressing room. (There was this drop-dead gorgeous, melt-in-your-mouth dentist who a few of the Rockettes started using. When word got out about how handsome he was, we all suddenly realized our mouths needed check-ups.)

Attempts were also made to engage in productive activities. For a while, thanks to Ivy, we had a Vocabulary Club. Ivy came from an academic family out East (Dare I say "Ivy League?") and was the intellectual of the cast. To prevent her brain, and ours, from absolutely rotting away, she started a Vocabulary Club in the Big Dressing Room. Daily, she posted a new Word of the Day, like "onomatopoeia" or "fiduciary," along with its definition. At the end of the week, Ivy gave us a test on all our words. A Bible Club met, too, if we were so inspired.

If you were a fly on the wall of the dressing room, your ears (if flies even have ears) would have burned upon hearing the hot topics that were discussed. A good Catholic fly would have turned red with embarrassment at the talk provocative enough to rival that of a men's locker room. No topic was too private, too intimate, or too personal to be off limits. Husbands and boyfriends knew less about their own sex lives than the Rockettes did. We talked about anything and everything. We consulted each other about anything and everything. We kicked up a fuss about anything and everything. Just ask a dresser.

****

The Big Dressing Room had three dressers assigned to it: wardrobe women hired to zip and unzip, hook and unhook, and hang up our costumes for us. Weren't we spoiled? Maria, the dresser for Kiddie Corner, was in her fifties and had a strong Spanish accent. She was well liked and acted as a pseudo mother figure to Rockettes. Yvette and Julia served the other sections of the room. Yvette, also in her fifties, was sweet, kind, and well respected. Julia was an ex-exotic dancer and a thirty-something single mom. She was also a seamstress, which came in handy for any tailoring we wanted done.

It was important to have a good dresser; people actually considered which dresser they'd be getting or leaving in deciding whether or not they wanted to change spots in the dressing room. It was even more important to befriend your dresser, not only because it was nice to do, not only because she could help your show run as smoothly as a baby's bottom or as bumpy as a road full of potholes, but because she knew your most intimate secrets. Like the president of the United States and his secret service men, dressers should all have to sign a contract stating that they are sworn to secrecy. For the stories they could tell could certainly cause grave embarrassment. We tipped our dressers and always gave them either bonus money or presents at Christmas time, because we loved and appreciated them, and we knew full well that it was best to have them in our court. These ladies truly became a beloved part of the family and were always included in special events at the Rockettes' homes.

The Rockettes' differing personalities were reflected in the manner in which they changed costumes, and our darling dressers adapted to our individual, quirky patterns. There were the anal-retentive, Type A people (me) who were organized and, like good Girl Scouts, always prepared with plenty of time to spare. Immediately after coming off stage from one number, I changed into my costume for the next number, except for the hat, and sat down at my dressing table. I wanted to be ready to go and not feel rushed. And if my costume broke there might be time to fix it.

Then there were the saunterers who would go from friend to friend chatting and s-l-o-o-o-o-o-w-l-y disrobing one costume piece at a time. They'd be standing there topless in their tights, blue trunks, and tap shoes, holding their "Big Band" headpieces, one talking about her new, sexy, boyfriend with the long, wavy black tresses, another about her photography class, or the new puppy she just bought. They'd stretch out the undressing and re-dressing process across the entire break.

Then there was Skinny Chick, who came right from the stage and remained fully dressed in costume bouncing around backstage like a Mexican jumping bean, stirring things up until just seconds before the next number when her autonomic nervous system would kick into panic mode and finally propel her to get changed in a big whirlwind of energy and looming deadline. Didn't she ever get nervous about missing her cue? She seemed to be one of those people who thrive under pressure, who actually require stress in order to get anything accomplished. I wanted to be more like her. It was fortunate that all the Rockettes didn't try to get dressed at the same time. Otherwise, there would have been a mad scrambling, and the dressers wouldn't have known who to zip up next.

The one exception to our individual robing and disrobing regimens was the change into our white soldier pants on those dastardly days when they had just returned from the dry cleaners, freshly starched. That was an occasion in which it behooved everyone to start getting dressed early. In order to make them look wooden, our pants were so heavily starched that we had to lie down on the floor to put them on. It was like stuffing your legs into two hollow planks. A couple dressers had to help because we couldn't get back up by ourselves. If the floor routine seemed too daunting, sometimes we'd stand on a chair and jump into the pants from above. The trousers were so stiff, they could actually stand up on their own.

We cursed dry cleaner day not only because of the difficulties posed by the starch, but also because the pants seemed to shrink two inches at the waist. "I swear these aren't my pants!" we'd shout, dead sure there must have been a mix-up. We'd have to suck in our stomachs and hold our breath while it took an entire team of dressers using all their strength to pull the sides of the pants close enough together to zip us up. Oh, it was painful, and we didn't want to breathe for fear we would burst open the pants. They gave us such wedgies, we called them "baby killers," worried they were permanently damaging our reproductive organs.

In addition to allowing plenty of time to get into the pants, we needed to remember to try the "doll turns salute" before going on stage. During the "Soldiers" dance, we discovered (the hard way) that when we bent over at the waist to salute before the doll turns, those super-starched slacks would sometimes split at the butt seam. It was, therefore, imperative we do a practice salute with time left to change into a spare pair of pants in case of a blow out. Dry cleaning day was a day to take seriously.

The second component of our "Soldiers" costume that provided the most amusement was the red circle "cheeks" cutout of cloth that we taped to our faces to make us look like dolls. After the number, we pulled off our cheeks and stuck them on the theatre wall or on other performers. If you forgot your cheeks, and someone noticed just before your entrance, you could often find a couple on a wall somewhere. Sometimes we would reuse the same cheeks from the previous show and realize that the tape had lost some of its stick. During the number you'd feel a cheek loosen its grip on your face and flutter to the ground, and then you'd see the audience members pointing. Used cheeks were also a source of backstage amusement—some ingenious Rockette discovered that the cheeks made perfect pasties.

Other costume conundrums presented themselves during performance. For instance, the neck clasp on the sequined bikini we wore for the opening number was occasionally a trouble maker. After too much wear and tear, the hook and eye popped, down fell your top, and out breasts would plop. I learned to periodically double check clasps, snaps, and hooks on my costumes, so I didn't end up with involuntary indecent exposure. If you were one of the unlucky ladies who had a top pop while tapping, there wasn't much you could do except cross your arms in front of your chest and sprint off stage. Sure, this was Vegas, but we weren't getting paid to go topless.

Our footwear caused quandaries, too. To keep track of all my shoes, I would line them up on the shelf under my dressing table in the order they were to be worn. To confuse matters, we wore silver *tap* shoes for the opening number and silver *character* shoes for the closing number. The shoes were identical except for the taps. Inevitably, one of the Rockettes went on stage for "Diamonds" in her taps instead of her character shoes or, even worse, in one tap and one character shoe. As soon as the music started, and we heard the click-click of the taps, we'd all start to snicker, whisper, and look for the poor soul who would be next to receive "The Dork Award."

"The Dork Award" was an ugly, little rubber guy presented to whomever made a big flub on stage. As if messing up wasn't bad enough, you had to keep that hideous dude on your dressing spot until someone else pulled a boner. Then you gleefully gloated "Ha ha! You get The Dork!" and ceremoniously passed it on to the new winner. After performing in a show long enough, you live for other entertainers to make mistakes, because it breaks up the monotony. The goofball is generally ticked off, but everyone else thinks it's hilarious. (Excepting when you have friends or family at the show; then you want everyone to perform perfectly.)

Being the only one clicking in taps was embarrassing. Everyone in the audience was watching *you*. (I know; it happened to me.) Also, kicking in taps was extra slippery and especially difficult with only *one* tap shoe, as the tap made that foot higher off the ground than the foot wearing the plain character shoe. Not to mention the fact that you were so distracted by the taps and all the stares that it was easy to lose track of the choreography and goof up.

The Grandmommy of costume calamities, however, was our "Diamonds" outfit. The main culprit was the swag of beaded fabric that hung down from one arm. It was a terrible nuisance because the dangling strands of beads would get caught in the beads adorning the front of the costume, and you'd end up like a spider snared in its own web. More often, your beads would entwine with the beaded swag of the girl next to you, pulling you together like Siamese twins needing to be surgically separated. The other dancers would be off leaping around in a circle, while you and your neighbor were still yanking on your swags in a tug-of-war, trying to pull the blasted bead strings apart. The final pull that successfully disentangled you would send stray beads flying all over the stage, leaving potential slipping catastrophes in the wake of all the dancers. A tiny, unnoticed bead could be more dangerous than a discarded banana peel. The poor wardrobe people spent a great deal of their time sewing strands of beads back onto our costumes.

Much like loose beads, a runaway earring posed another real disaster. Because it was so small, a performer was likely to overlook the sparkly sphere resting innocently upstage left, poised and ready to be underfoot during a jump kick that could land you back-smacking to the floor or twisting an ankle. If you perchance had the good fortune of noticing the earring or bead and planned to kick it out of your path, you'd better be confident about your ability to lob it all the way off stage, because if you moved it directly into someone else's spot, you were bound to get an earful. Unless you were a sure shot into the wings, the best bet was to boogie around it and warn everyone you passed as you danced by.

"How did we warn each other without the audience knowing?" you might wonder. On stage, Rockettes could relay information, virtually undetectable by the audience, to other Rockettes using the most minute eye signals and/or ventriloquist-type whispering while maintaining the requisite, toothy smile. We used this covert communication to transmit messages like "My zipper is coming down! Can you zip me up?" "Look at that hot guy in the front row." Or "Watch out for beads!"

Eventually, most of us, myself included, dropped our dread of the free-range earrings and beads and dealt with these diminutive nemeses as a fun challenge. I'd be chasséing downstage for the final "Diamonds" kickline and catch a glimpse of a bead sitting smack on number 3 ¼—the exact mark I was heading towards. "I see you, you little bugger!" No longer a newbie, instead of cowering in fear, I'd hone in on my target with determination and laser-like focus and launch that missile, whizzing past a group of jet-lagged Japanese. Some of the girls became absolute masters at punting the small objects without compromising the choreography. They were like soccer pros, kicking the ball without missing a beat.

Thanks to these destructive and dangerous little orbs, we developed a "Rockette Showgirl Revenge Kit," which consisted of an Altoids box filled with single beads that had fallen off our costumes. Inspired by the movie *Showgirls*, which depicted jealous underlings sabotaging lead dancers to steal their limelight (by pushing them down stairs, for instance), the Revenge Kit was ostensibly to be used to derail an irksome dancer by tossing a bead in her path while on stage. Of course, no one would ever purposely jeopardize a fellow Rockette. It was all in jest. But we all recognized the hazards inherent in those peewee pellets.

****

One of the big challenges of *The Great Radio City Spectacular* was that we often found ourselves burning the mid-day oil in rehearsals. Our contract specified that we could be called in to rehearse anytime after noon (except on our day off, which was sacred) with only twenty-four hours' notice. Consequently, it was difficult to plan a life during the day (except before noon, but come on, that's when we snoozed), because, like doctors, we were "on call."

Our job required an assortment of rehearsals. Regularly scheduled "clean-up" rehearsals were run by the dance captain to keep the choreography and formations in tip-top shape. "Put-in" rehearsals were essential to accommodate the revolving door of new Rockettes coming in. Rehearsals were held to plug new stars into the star spot, to take out "Gold and Silver," to reinstate "Gold and Silver," to put different soloists into "Bolero," and to insert special Christmas numbers at holiday time and then reinstate the original numbers once Santa had returned to the North Pole and the tinseled trees had been taken down.

Clean-up rehearsals were not my favorite; it was hard to get enthused about rehearsing a show you'd done hundreds of times and would do again twice that very evening. But Radio City was intent on making sure we were functioning at our highest level, and there always seemed to be formations that needed fine tuning or moves that some of us were interpreting slightly differently than the others or spacing that needed a tiny tweak.

We were watched and evaluated not only during clean-up rehearsals but during nightly performances as well. We even had to meet on stage every Monday before the first show for notes. When the dance captain dispersed her list of peccadilloes and transgressions, I held my breath, hoping that I wouldn't get any and bristling when I did. The worst part was getting notes to make minor changes in the choreography, because I was now performing fully on autopilot, and if I had to think about what I was doing again, I was bound to make mistakes. None of us particularly enjoyed being critiqued and scrutinized, let alone singled out for dancing out of line, but this kind of painstaking attention to detail is what makes the Rockettes the household name they are today. They strive for a level of excellence that necessitates fastidiousness, so scads of rehearsals and corrections were a part of the whole shebang. I had to learn not to take it personally.

In addition to clean-up rehearsals with the dance captain, we also had random visits and clean-up rehearsal calls from the show's various choreographers and directors. For instance, Violet Holmes, the visionary seventy-some-year-old choreographer of our magnificent "Dancing with Diamonds" number, dropped by with plans to polish her fading jewel back to its original glory. It was a real treat to have this legendary choreographer working with us live and in person. She was a superstar in the Rockette world, and we loved to watch her shake her groove thing. Her way of moving was so stylistic, however, that it was difficult to imitate precisely. Come hell or high water, she intended for us to get her little hip bump right. "No, Ladies, it's like this," she'd insist, popping her pelvis in a manner totally unnatural to the rest of us. We couldn't argue with her; she created the dance, after all. After a heavenly afternoon with Violet, we shined brightly and were no longer diamonds in the rough.

Rehearsals with our show's director, Boris Leghorn, on the other hand, were hell on heels. I trembled in my tap shoes at the mere mention of his name. Based in New York City, he wasn't around much, but when he did fly out to Vegas, he returned to the stage with a vengeance. Most directors and choreographers were grateful to work with the Rockettes and treated us respectfully. He was not one of those people. To minimize any chance of provoking his ire, I came into rehearsal exquisitely made-up, with hair perfectly pulled back, and danced at full performance level with a smile plastered on my face. Otherwise during rehearsal I kept my lips zipped and mouth shut. "Zip it. Clip it. Collect it," was my motto (as well as that of many other Rockettes) about refraining from complaining so that I could collect my paycheck and keep my job. The best way to handle any and all personalities, I decided, was to take the high road, remain professional, and, as a last resort, submit a formal complaint to Radio City if a leader truly stepped out of line. Eventually, karma caught up with Mr. Leghorn, and he got the boot, while the Rockettes remained employed.

Every three months we also had rehearsals with the dance captain to adjust for the incoming star spot. This injection of new star-power energy always created a lot of backstage buzz, curiosity, and excitement. The striking Susan Anton was a regular in the rotation, but we also shared the stage with the lovely Paige O'Hara and the legendary hoofer, Maurice Hines. Paige O'Hara was a lead Broadway actress (*Les Miserable, Showboat, Mystery of Edwin Drood*), most noted for being the voice of Belle in the acclaimed Disney movie *Beauty and the Beast*. The girls were happy to have her and her powerful, three-octave, bona fide Broadway voice on the bill. "She'll be a perfect fit with the Rockettes!" we cheered, insistent upon a star whose professionalism and perfection matched or exceeded our own. But it wasn't until we heard her belt out her solo, "I Want to Be a Rockette" (from *Kicks: The Showgirl Musical*, lyrics by Tom Eyen and music by Alan Menken, who also created the music for *Beauty and the Beast*), that we were moved to tears, fell to our knees, and kissed the glittered ground on which she glided.

That song was about us! Being a Rockette was our dream, too, and we were living it! Made me want to kick myself for all the times I had taken the gig for granted. This wasn't just a job. This was a *dream come true*. Being just a little squirt, Paige played up her petiteness compared to the towering Rockettes. She was clearly too short to fulfill the fantasy, but her song hit me right in the heart. And she was as sweet as she was short.

Maurice Hines, a charismatic song and dance man, leant an entirely different vibe to the show. He was also an actor, director, and choreographer and had been discovered by his tap teacher, the famous choreographer Henry LeTang, way back when he was a wee, little tyke growing up in New York City. He and his brother Gregory Hines (film star, Emmy Award-winning television star, and Tony Award-winning Broadway star) started performing professionally as young children. The brothers had even served as the opening act for the real Gypsy Rose Lee, the actress about whom the musical *Gypsy* was written! I knew the dynamic dance duo from the 1984 film *The Cotton Club*, a gangster flick set in a 1930s Harlem jazz club (choreographed by their mentor LeTang). I was in awe of Gregory from the dance films *White*

Nights (1985), in which he co-starred with ballet master Mikhail Baryshnikov, and *Tap* (1989). Gregory even came to see our show once when Maurice was headlining! Like his brother, Maurice was a shining star whose radiant personality captivated audiences and our cast alike. His fancy footwork and jazzy vocals were pure pizzazz. He made us look good.

The Rockettes always loved performing with Susan Anton, who was not only a real class act but also tons of fun. Prior to settling down in Vegas, she had toured the country for two years with *The Great Radio City Spectacular*. Hence, she was so comfortable with the show (and us) that she was able to goof around a bit. Occasionally, during the "Big Band" dance-off between couples, she'd play a secret "Guess the Theme" game, purely for the amusement of the performers on stage. She'd introduce the guys or gals with different names according to some particular theme that she had secretly chosen. For instance, "Please welcome Mr. Johnson, Harry, Richard, and Peter!" Of course, the audience didn't have a clue that any hanky-panky was going on, but the cast was in stitches at the inside joke. Every one of our stars was delightful to work with and treated us well.

In spite of our wonderful stars and stellar production, an internal stigma had been attached to the Vegas show from the get-go. Our show wasn't nearly as spectacular in scope or size as the one at Radio City. And our theatre seated only about 800 people compared to the Music Hall's 6,000. Perhaps size *does* matter. We seemed to be the black sheep in the family of Radio City Spectaculars, and it appeared that our parent company didn't quite know how to handle us. At times, the attitudes from above made us feel like we were slightly flawed (behind closed doors, we jokingly labeled ourselves "The Factory Outlet Rockettes"). A lot of us had been well-respected Rockettes in other shows or eventually left to do the show in New York and became favorites there. So it wasn't the individual Rockettes who were inherently defective. Something about that show made our superiors continually want to fix it.

The production was constantly in flux, a perpetual work in progress, and Radio City was always searching for ways to improve it, whether by cleaning up and fine-tuning our numbers, revamping them, or going back to the drawing board and creating entirely new numbers. So while it may have appeared to some that our job was easy (after seeing the show, my brother-in-law said, "You're only actually on stage working for about a half an hour!"), I can assure you it was not. The behind-the-scenes rehearsing was substantial. Couple that with twice-nightly performances, and we spent an insane amount of time at the theatre, on our feet, in heels, kicking.

Being a Vegas Rockette was both mentally and physically demanding. Great stamina and emotional tenacity were required to survive intense and frequent rehearsals and the rigors of a twelve-show work week for years on end. The strain and pressure gave me so many headaches that I kept a stash of bright red, Excedrin headache tablets in my makeup case that I fondly entitled "Rockette Reds." This was a spoof on the specific shade of lipstick we were required to wear, nicknamed "Rockette Red," that fire engine red, not brown, not pink, but flaming, bright red like the babes of the 1950s wore. If they haven't created a real lipstick of the same name, they should. Several friends of mine relied heavily on Advil to get them through the show, masking their injuries, aches, and pains. The job was so stressful, we joked about how Radio City should give us a free week of rehab at the Betty Ford Clinic when we left the show. It was not a gig for the weak.

Part of the reason the job was so taxing was that we were playing in the Big Leagues where the bar was set much higher. Falling under the jurisdiction of MSG Entertainment (Madison Square Garden) and Radio City, this was *big business*. This was no rinky-dink operation. The Rockettes are a *national institution*, and they earned that distinction because they are masterful at what they do. A dance troupe that has the capacity to bring in over a million audience members a year since 1933 and wants to continue to expand that tradition has to constantly maintain and improve its standard of excellence. Consequently, expectations were high and the talent had to be extremely high caliber at all times.

I was not accustomed to working for a big corporation. The environment was much more formal, and we had to deal with strata of superiors. Being stationed in the Wild, Wild West, far, far from the Motherland—our beloved Radio City Music Hall—most of the time we were governed by our two stage managers and our dance captain. But periodically, some Radio City bigwigs would fly out from New York City to check up on us, and we'd jump through hoops, have meetings, and pay our respects. We'd get visits from all manner of higher-ranking authorities including several Radio City execs, our producer, the head of Rockette Operations, the creative director, artistic director, choreographers, and the human relations lawyer. This army of Higher Ups marched in and out with pomp and circumstance but never stayed too long. Their different personalities, various perspectives, and corresponding policies were a lot to contend with. But we put our best foot forward and tried to please everyone.

Our organizational structure included rankings not only within the off-stage talent mentioned above, but also within the Rockettes themselves. Barely one month after I joined the show, the Rockettes were strongly encouraged to participate in a Roster Placement Audition. As you may recall, the "Roster" was the group of 38 golden gals who were permanent Rockettes, guaranteed work as long as they wanted it (without ever auditioning), and got first dibs on all gigs. Getting a spot on the Roster meant prestige, job security, uninterrupted health insurance, a 401(k), and cashola. Spots had always been filled according to seniority, so, as a newcomer, I knew I didn't stand a chance. No one ever left the Roster if they were still alive and kicking. A deadly plague would have had to wipe out the entire Roster and more before I had an inkling of a hope of getting a spot. Far too many people stood in line ahead of me because they had danced with the Rockettes longer than I had, so I never gave it a thought, never worried about it, never cared a whit.

This particular year, however, Radio City sent shock waves through the Rockettes when it decided to abandon the old seniority system in favor of *auditioning* for the positions. I can only imagine how upsetting that must have been for the girls who were next in line, who had been kicking until they were blue in the face, biding their time for years and years until someone older retired. The newer girls, however, knew that this opening could be their big break. Still so stressed out and exhausted from adjusting to a brand new show and a new city, I was simply grumpy that I had to go through the motions of an all-day audition when we had two shows to perform that same night. Even with the new audition process, I didn't think I had a hope of getting on the Roster, so I almost didn't go. But Radio City put the pressure on all of us to attend. They flew out a panel of six non-Radio City professionals to judge us in tap, ballet, jazz, singing, and on-camera media interviews. It was so intense that, by the end of it, I had a wicked migraine headache. Straight afterwards, we all had to rush to the theatre for showtime. I was so glad when it was all over.

A few days later, I got a phone call from the head of Rockette Operations congratulating me on making the "Temp Roster." I didn't know what she was talking about and had to ask my friend Jan. "The Temp Roster is made up of the next three people in line to move up to the real Roster when spots open up!" she explained, incredulous at my ignorance. I was dumbfounded. Of all the Rockettes in the country who auditioned, four of us from Vegas had been chosen for a promotion. Now I was thankful that Radio City had insisted we all audition. I didn't feel so much like a black sheep after that.

****

Being in a long-running show, working six nights a week plus oodles of afternoon rehearsals (sometimes we had twelve-hour days or longer), the Rockettes spent a lot of time together in close quarters (backstage, on stage, and shoulder-to-shoulder in the kickline). We had to learn to get along and live peacefully, day in and day out, year after year, arm in arm and side by side. As is often true of those who have survived a lot together and shared the same experiences (both groovy and rotten), who have faced common adversaries and accomplished a common goal, our bonds ran deeper and deeper with passing time. In spite of little spats, in spite of (or maybe because of) the challenges of dancing in the line and practically living at the theatre together, we grew to be like sisters. This Rockette Sisterhood turned into the world's most amazing support system. We saw each other through thick and thin, through boyfriends and break-ups, marriages and divorces, failed pregnancies, successful pregnancies, and birthing of babies, through injuries and illnesses, college graduations, home buying and foreclosures.

In fact, we became such a large "family" that we were constantly planning and throwing birthday parties, baby showers, wedding showers, holiday parties, party parties, and going-away parties. The extracurricular activities got to be overwhelming, especially since we only had Fridays off. That's what happens when you get twenty-five high-achieving, creative, intelligent, kind-hearted women working together six days a week. We could have ruled the world (in three-inch heels) and still found time to bake cookies.

The Christmas season was when our extracurricular activities got most out of control (including baking cookies). It was an exceptionally busy time at the theatre, especially because we put up a slightly different show for the holidays. The fabulous Maurice Hines choreographed a festive and merry new Christmas-y opening number in which we, in sumptuous, red velvet costumes trimmed in fine, white feathers (like a mega-sexy, skinny, young Mrs. Claus), exploded onstage out of a giant present. The special number required many additional rehearsals, but when it was all said and done, it put us in the holiday spirit and rejuvenated our pride in the show. After all, Christmas and the Rockettes are synonymous. What a gift to be working with the legendary Mr. Hines, whose enthusiasm for us rivaled Santa's love of Christmas.

Extensive rehearsals didn't stop us from enjoying our annual holiday festivities. The cast always decorated a Christmas tree in the Green Room. For ten days, we also played "Secret Santas," and our men's dance captain dressed up as Santa and passed out the final presents. Since we worked on Christmas Eve, every year on that evening, as our gift to the rest of the cast and crew, the Rockettes cooked and served a full Christmas dinner (turkey, ham, mashed potatoes, sweet potatoes, green beans, corn, rolls, drinks, and pies) for about seventy people. I made all the mashed potatoes, and that was a crazy amount of spuds. In between the first and second show, we set up long tables in the hallway backstage, and everyone would gather for the feast. I couldn't believe the amount of stage and tech crew who came out of the woodwork. I didn't even recognize most of the guys who showed up to chow down. It felt good to spread Christmas cheer and support the people who supported us night after night.

The Rockettes also organized an annual Christmas Cookie Exchange amongst ourselves and even printed out a cook-booklet of all the recipes. They included Trisha's Peanut Butter Blossoms, Leslie's Grandma's Sugar Cookies, Mona's Chocolate Oatmeal Bars and Health Carrot Cake, Ginny's Chewy Butterscotch Brownies, Anna's Lemon Bars, Heidi's Peanut Butter Balls, Sandi's Chocolate Chip Toffee Bars, Barbara's Chocolate Pretzels, Alexis's Chocolate Chip Oatmeal Cookies, and my Cappuccino Shortbread Cookies. Yum!

As if our schedules weren't already packed enough, our dance captain even organized a Christmas caroling group of Rockettes and guys from our show to sing for her grandmother and her fellow residents at her Las Vegas nursing home. We got together ahead of time to practice our harmonies, then went out and sang classic Christmas carols for the homebound seniors. Not too many people got house calls from the Rockettes, but Christmas was a time for miracles.

****

After about a year, as I moved up in the ranks, I was invited to become a swing for "Bolero." Although it seemed a scary proposition, I decided to accept the challenge. Preparation was key. I created detailed charts showing the various formations (like football plays with X's and O's), as well as each girl's marks, choreography, and traffic patterns. With enough practice, I enjoyed being a swing, as I never knew what was going to happen or when I'd be called for duty. It offered an element of fear, surprise, and the unknown that the routine of having my own track did not. When performing, I didn't get terribly nervous but I was always thinking hard about where to go, on what counts to dance, whom to follow in which direction, and which marks to hit.

For the benefit of the entire production, it behooved the swings to keep the show running smoothly for the rest of the cast on stage, and it behooved the rest of the cast to assist the swings. For instance, a swing might rush up right before a number and beg the girl they knew they were supposed to dance behind, "Will you please glance my way, so I remember to follow you in the circle formation?" If a swing had time, she'd usually warn the people she was going to dance alongside, "Watch out for me!" Who knew if she would accidentally head in the wrong direction and mess up your show? It was helpful to be alert and aware of a swing in your vicinity (like knowing there's a student driver on the road). In turn, if a swing were on stage going the wrong way, a cast member would help out by whispering, "Over here!"

I worked with some fantastic swings who never missed a beat. You knew they were excellent because you never noticed them bothering you in the number. They blended right in as if nothing were different at all. When other swings messed up, their blunders had the potential to throw you off your game as well. One of our Vegas swings, LeAnn Bramble, did a blooper that earned her the nickname "Scramble." In "Bolero" there was a formation in which a big circle of dancers ran in a clockwise direction while a smaller, inner circle of dancers ran counterclockwise. Scramble got confused about where to go and frantically scrambled to find her place. Unfortunately, she ended up forming her own circle *outside* the big circle and sprinted around it all by her lonesome. We laughed so hard. Yes, she most certainly deserved and received The Dork Award.

The cast and crew always got excited when a new swing was on. They made it a point to gather in the wings and watch, so as not to miss out if the swing did something horrendously funny or stupid. Hence, the pressure was on when I started swinging, because I knew everyone would be watching and waiting for me to flub. Fortunately for me, but disappointing for the backstage crowd, I never did goof enough to be entertaining.

****

Not only was backstage at the Flamingo Hilton a world all its own, topsy-turvy Las Vegas was a world all its own, and each took some getting used to. Everything in Vegas was open twenty-four hours a day, even the grocery stores. Night was day and day was night. On my mother's first trip here, she marveled at how the multitude of lights on the Strip made it appear to be daylight outside when it was really the middle of the night. Inside the casinos, you couldn't tell the difference between day and night either, an illusion casino designers created on purpose so you wouldn't leave the gaming tables to go to bed. It could be a confusing world out there, and many people didn't know which way was up.

Vegas was sometimes referred to as "Adult Disney Land," and in a way it was true. Every adult vice, fantasy, and pleasure ride was available for the taking, and it was all acceptable. One could almost become numb to the sleaze. The lewdness could get tiring and depressing, but during the time I lived there, it became cloaked in more and more of a theme-park atmosphere in order to lure the whole family's money. Vegas dressed itself up like a place that would make all your dreams come true, but it held an underlying sadness from all the desperate people who had come to win but lost everything and all the women who had bared their bodies for the moola of seamy men.

Playboy's Girls of Rock & Roll helped prepare me for life in this town rife with strippers and hookers; I was not as prone to being shocked into a stupor from all the sordidness of Sin City. If Playboy were a lesson in "Smut 101," life in Las Vegas could have practically earned me a Ph.D. in Obscenity. After the silver and turquoise mines of the 1800s were depleted, the state of Nevada turned to gambling and prostitution to keep the place alive. Oddly enough, prostitution was illegal in Vegas, but you could still legally sow your oats at the Chicken Ranch just outside nearby Pahrump. I'd see prostitutes now and then at various casinos. They were all dressed up and classier than the NYC 42nd Street streetwalkers, but I could tell they weren't just ladies out looking for a good time.

It didn't take me long to discover that if I called myself a "dancer" in Las Vegas, everyone assumed I was a stripper. As a legitimate dancer, I didn't want to be associated with strippers, but I wished I made as much money as they did. My neighbor at the apartment complex was a "dancer," and she raked in a fortune. Something shady was going down with her, however, because in the middle of the night once, she and her kids and boyfriend cleared out of the apartment with their belongings and never came back.

Most of the real dancers in Vegas were underpaid and generally not on a union contract. It was a "right to work" state. Word on the street was that other dancers were jealous of the Rockettes because we made considerably more money than they did. But those who got into a long-running show like *Jubilee!* at Bally's could practically keep dancing forever. (Perhaps the most fantastic showbiz name I've ever heard is that of *Jubilee!'s* well-loved and respected director/choreographer Fluff LeCoque. Hers was a household name among Vegas entertainers, who referred to "Fluff" without batting an eye. And she's not even a drag queen.) Some people had double careers like one guy who was a police officer by day and dancer by night. Some of the women stayed home and raised their families during the day. Others went to law school. With University of Nevada, Las Vegas (UNLV) and two campuses of the Community College of Southern Nevada right in our backyard, dancers enjoyed plenty of educational opportunities. I myself ended up taking college watercolor classes two mornings a week. Many dancers also worked the busy convention seasons during the day to really cash in. Plenty of performers stayed in Vegas indefinitely and hopped from show to show.

I made it through my first six-month contract and, despite the tiring schedule, decided that the gig was too good to give up. So I settled in and made Vegas my home. After living there a year or so, however, I contracted island fever. Unlike Michigan where you could travel a few miles in any direction and be in a new town, the closest places we could go to really get away were a couple hours' drive. Having only Fridays off, we didn't have time to journey far. Plus, while mini-mini-vacations provided a much-needed change of scenery and a short respite from the daily grind, they also often left me more fatigued than if I had stayed home and rested. With so little free time and such long drives to escape the craziness of this tourist town, it was easy to feel like I was trapped in the desert.

Nevertheless, sometimes I simply couldn't stand being cooped up any longer and had to hit the open road. Ron and I made several 2 ½ hour drives northeast to the breathtaking Mt. Zion National Park in Utah and stayed at a bed and breakfast or camped in a tent and hiked among the towering rock formations and trickling streams. On one occasion we joined Squally, Gyne, and Gyne's hubby for a trip to Laughlin, Nevada (about 90 minutes away), for a hot air balloon festival. Laughlin was like a miniature, trashier version of Vegas, full of people traveling by RV. The casinos were so smoky I thought I was going to keel over with lung cancer on the spot. We dragged our tired tuckuses out of bed at 6:30 a.m. for the balloon launch, but it was so windy that only one balloon attempted the takeoff. The crazy old captain wearing a motorcycle helmet crashed almost immediately into the nearest lump of dirt, barely high enough to classify as a hill. That grounded hot air balloon festival was not worth losing my beauty sleep over.

Occasionally, we escaped all the way to the Grand Canyon or Los Angeles, but both trips were about five-hour drives, depending on traffic. One Thursday in October, Ron and I decided to go camping at the Grand Canyon the following day. We rushed over to the sporting goods store and bought a tent and some sleeping bags before I went off to work. The next morning, we arose early and drove the five hours to the North Rim, which was about a week shy of being shut down for the winter season. We pitched our tents in the sunshine, took a little hike in our shorts and T-shirts, and grilled gourmet sausages for dinner. It was lovely. That night, I tried to sleep, but the hard ground was compressing my muscles into a dull soreness. Just as I was about to conk out from sheer exhaustion, the sky opened up and the thunderstorms rolled in; they continued one after another all night long. I've never heard anything like the sound of that ear-splitting thunder reverberating off the canyon walls. Only after the rain water crept into our tent and approached our sleeping bags did we give up and take refuge in the car. When we awoke, the sun was back out, the birds were chirping, snow was covering the ground, and after a near-sleepless night, we had to drive straight back to Vegas in time for me to do two shows. I was so very, very tired. Taking a trip on our day off

Long Legs and Tall Tales

was a risk, as it probably meant returning to work unrested. That was a difficult way to start the week.

For times when we weren't willing to take on a big outing but knew we would go insane if we stayed in the city, we could take advantage of the old local standbys. Within a thirty-minute drive of the Strip, we could snow ski at Lee Canyon, hike or horseback ride at the Alpine-esque village of Mt. Charleston, mountain bike or hike at Red Rock Canyon, and search for petroglyphs at Fire Canyon. For those so inclined, myself not included, there was golf available and also boating, windsurfing, sailing, water skiing, and jet skiing at Lake Mead. People usually only think of the Strip when they think of Vegas, but the greater Las Vegas area offers a lot also in the way of nature and outdoor activities.

Thanks to all the casinos, we were absolutely spoiled for entertainment. There were a gazillion fine restaurants and shows galore. Not only could we always count on seeing the long-running mainstays like *Jubilee!* at Bally's or *Les Folies Bergere* at The Tropicana any time we wanted, but many of the big-name headliners came into town, either to MGM Grand or Caesars Palace. Some shows were quite affordable; it only cost me $35 to see the bawdy Bette Midler at the MGM Grand. Mind you, I was in the nosebleed section. (A Rockette friend of mine was one of Bette's back-up dancers.) The Strip also offered plenty of free entertainment: lounge acts, the Bellagio fountains, strolling minstrels at the Venetian, the *Parade in the Sky* show at the Rio, the Pirate Show at Treasure Island, the laser light show on Fremont Street. Simply wandering through and marveling at the various themed hotel-casinos made for a fun-filled outing.

Of course, we could gamble all we wanted, if that's what tickled our fancy, including at Fremont Street casino's 25-cent tables if we wanted the thrill without the risk. Thankfully, it didn't tickle our fancy; neither Ron nor I took up gambling as a hobby, passion, or obsession. Some smaller casinos were built away from the Strip to cater to us locals and to take our hard-earned cash. Living in the midst of so many temptations can cause tremendous problems for people with addictive personalities. If you're the type to have trouble controlling your gambling habit, I'd suggest moving to Branson where "casino" is a dirty word.

When we tired of fighting the crowds and the clink-clank of the slot machines, we found amusing diversions off the main drag. Within a short driving distance from downtown was an art museum, an outdoor amphitheater offering family concerts and picnicking on the lawn, and several noteworthy restaurants and wine bars. Within an hour, we could be at the Pahrump Winery sipping sherry and enjoying a steak lunch.

Vegas was a transient town with a massive influx of people hoping to score jobs or beat the house at gambling so they could claim their fortune. Unfortunately, the promise of easy money brought criminals. When Skinny Chick first got into the show and didn't have a car, she rented an apartment a couple blocks off the Strip so she could walk to work. Seemed like a smart idea, right? Wrong. You never wanted to live within walking distance of the Strip unless you were comfortable cohabiting with drug dealers, strippers, hookers, and crooks. Skinny Chick found out the hard way when she was robbed during the night while home sleeping. That story scared the bejeezus out of me.

Another Rockette had such trouble with a Peeping Tom spying on her from one of the other apartments at her complex in Northwest Las Vegas that the police had to intervene. To top that off, once during a show, she made eye contact with a young, handsome, exotic man in the audience. He sent her a note backstage and they met. His sexy accent, worldliness, and good looks got the best of her, and she agreed to go out with him only to discover he was Romanian mafia. He made it known that he wielded physical power and had an entourage of cohorts with him to either protect her or make sure she did what he wanted. The man visited Vegas on a regular basis, and she was always having to make herself scarce so he wouldn't find her. Vegas attracted some creepy, sordid, scary scoundrels.

There were also shootings now and then on the Strip, especially on New Year's Eve. Occasionally, a dead body would be found in a casino, but those types of events were hushed up quickly. Wouldn't want to hurt tourism with the news of violence. New Year's Eve was a survival game and a challenge all its own. After a couple Vegas New Year's Eves, I just wanted to hole up in my apartment with a bottle of champagne and a good movie, and avoid the crazy crowds altogether. Unfortunately, this wasn't an option, as the Rockettes had a 10 p.m. show that finished soon after the midnight countdown to the New Year. To complicate matters, the city closed off many of the streets surrounding the Strip in order to accommodate the rowdy, drunken swarm of pedestrian partiers. Hence, our escape route had to be planned well in advance if we wanted to be able to drive home.

One year the cast walked to a nearby cheap and cheesy hotel lounge where we stayed up until dawn singing karaoke and nursing our beers. By the time the sun came up, the creatures of the dark had slunk back into their holes, the streets had reopened, and we could drive home in relative safety. Another year, the cast had a party at the theatre until the wee hours of the morning when most of the intoxicated wackos had dispersed. One year, we heard a rumor that the Crips and Bloods (infamous, violent, rival Los Angeles gangs) might attend the festivities. Yikes! While Vegas was one of the prime places to celebrate New Year's Eve in excess, the mobs of dangerously wild celebrants made me uneasy.

Everyone we knew seemed to want a weekend in Vegas at least once a year, and not just on New Year's Eve, so Ron and I found ourselves getting visitors galore. Family, college friends, sorority sisters, show biz friends, childhood friends—we housed and entertained them all. There was never a dull moment living in this prime vacation spot.

During the three years we were there, Vegas changed faster than a chameleon. The cheap hotel rooms and all-you-can-eat, ridiculously cheap buffets still existed, but they took a backseat to the new five-star restaurants like Le Cirque and exclusive suites at places like the lavish Bellagio. Old, has-been casinos were imploded and magnificent, new structures took their place, including The Venetian, Mandalay Bay, Paris, and more. It seemed as if this boom town would never quit booming.

My first trip to Vegas years earlier with my mother had left a poor impression on me. However, once I got over the initial shock of the place and spent some quality time there, I kind of liked it. Like the first time you open a can of Spam, because someone dared you to try it. At first you almost pass out from the smell, but then you decide it sort of tastes like ham if you fry it and slather it with mustard. We cooked up plenty of activities and outings to keep Vegas palatable.

****

Life went on, and I, along with a good chunk of the cast, settled into our steady jobs. The show ran a glorious year after year after year with no visible end to the run in sight. We ensconced ourselves in the comfort (and discomfort) of our theatre home at the Flamingo and all the activities, backstage shenanigans, and traditions that had developed.

Working in one place for so long garnering a regular and substantial paycheck allowed and encouraged many of us to start putting down roots. Cast members bought homes. Some took college classes. Rockettes got married. A few gals even tied the knot with our stagehands, thereby knitting the cast and crew together even more so. Rockettes got pregnant and, eventually, birthed babies. The Rockettes, our dressers, castmates, and stage crew became our extended family. Unlike many entertainers whose lives resembled those of gypsies, we were able to have close to normal-ish, stay-in-one-place lives.

One night in spring, in the Big Dressing Room, we had a mysterious, charades-like showing in which we had to guess the scenario: Leslie stood, legs apart with a hula hoop in front of them while Kitty Cat (her real name was Katrina), beginning crouched in a little ball, wriggled her way through Leslie's legs and out the circular hole. Did you guess? This pantomime was Leslie's announcement that she was pregnant! Shortly after Leslie's dramatic enactment and just shy of two years after joining the show, I, too, discovered I was pregnant! Both of our babies were due in mid to late December.

Naturally, we turned to our resident New Age Guru, Thalia, and her magic crystal to find out the sex of our unborn babies. While we were at it, we also wanted to know how many children we would birth in our lifetimes. The crystal hung on a string and Thalia held it still over my palm. She asked it the burning questions I wanted answered. The cosmic forces then caused the stone to swing a certain number of times indicating the number of children and in a certain direction (clockwise or counterclockwise) indicating the sex of the children. "You're going to have two children—a boy and a girl," Thalia predicted. The crystal indicated that Leslie would have two boys. This process was all the rage with the married girls. Before long, ultrasounds confirmed the crystal's predictions: Our first-born babies were boys!

Not really knowing what to expect when expecting, I decided to continue dancing until my fourth month of pregnancy. Most days, I was so tired that I felt like I was run over by a truck. I'd sleep until noon, eat breakfast, do errands, and then nap from about four until six o'clock. Then it was time to get ready to head to the theatre. Unfortunately, my "morning sickness" arrived in the evenings while I was doing the show. Sucking on candied ginger between numbers helped me combat the nausea. Luckily, I never got really sick during the show, but I was always a little concerned about the possibility that I would turn green smack in the middle of a number and have to dash off stage. I was also terrified of my little guy getting squished from people landing hard on my stomach during the soldier fall. In addition, I worried about how quickly I would plump up with a belly bump. After all, our costumes left little to the imagination. As luck would have it, I took maternity leave just before wardrobe would have had to alter my costumes to make room for baby. By this time, my ballooning breasts were absolutely bursting out of my opening number bikini top. Even though Vegas audiences tended to prefer and celebrate big bosoms, I was too self-conscious to flaunt mine. (Remember how I claimed I could never dance pregnant like Momma did?) All in all, I fared fairly well performing with a bun in the oven.

During my final show before taking maternity leave, I was given a proper Vegas send-off: a little song-and-dance extravaganza we fondly called "Big Butts." Instead of "For She's a Jolly Good Fellow," our traditional farewell song for exiting Rockettes was Sir Mix-a-Lot's "Baby Got Back," a tune touting the sexiness of curvaceous women. (I didn't have a lot of "back" at the time, but I did have more than enough "front.") This was a wild, emotional, celebratory tradition everyone expected and enjoyed. Right before the second show, we'd all gather in the Big Dressing Room in our opening number bikinis. The girl leaving (in this case, moi) would stand on a chair, and we'd all dance with total abandon, twirling towels and shouting the lyrics loudly. It was a touching goodbye.

Ron and I took the opportunity to visit family and travel for a few months in England, Paris, Scotland, Michigan, and Florida. We then returned to Vegas so Ron could resume working while I became homebound with child. Ron had easily scored a job as a used car salesman. It helped pay the bills, but these Vegas salesmen took used car sales to an entirely new level of shadiness. Ron was the only one at his dealership without a parole officer, and the stories he heard at work of meth labs and salesmen stealing the cars they were supposed to be selling made the hairs on the back of my neck bristle. He found them highly entertaining, however, and couldn't wait to go to the office to see what would happen next. I stayed home and nested, preparing for baby.

Our beautiful son, Kieran, was born in Henderson, Nevada, eight days after his due date: Christmas day! He was the best Christmas present ever. One of Ron's coworkers at the car dealership, who was a bookie in his off time, kindly presented Kieran with a birthday gift: He had bet on a football game on Kieran's behalf and had won him $50. Albeit an unusual baby present, it seemed befitting for a bookie. The instant I gave birth, my life changed forever. Suddenly I was on mommy duty 24/7, always at Kieran's beck and call. And he called a lot. Poor little thing had terrible colic and screamed for hours each day. His only comfort came from motion, so I bounced him much of the time. My days and nights became consumed with this precious, tiny, needy creature.

Leslie's son had been born five days before Kieran, and we decided we'd return to work when the babies were about three months old. Wowie, was that too soon! Being a new mom, I didn't realize how challenging going back to work would be. By the time I gave birth, I had gained thirty-eight pounds and been out of the show for about six months. Having to get back in bikini shape and develop the stamina to do a couple hundred kicks a night while recovering from childbirth and getting adjusted to caring for an infant was a lot of pressure to put on myself and my body. Thankfully, I had Leslie by my side to muddle through it with me. We busted our behinds to lose the extra pregnancy weight, pushing our babies in their strollers for miles and miles around Sunset Park. In my apartment, I also did aerobics and kickboxing videos, sometimes with Kieran in a baby backpack strapped on to me to stop him from crying (the motion soothed him). On days when we needed to get out of the house, Leslie and I would meet at a coffee shop with the boys and discuss all our baby issues. Having a friend to share new Mommy-hood with helped a lot. I don't know how I would have gotten through it without her.

When I finally returned to work, I felt chubby and self-conscious, because I was definitely not back to my pre-pregnancy shape or strength. Stuffing myself into that opening number bikini was pure torture, physically and emotionally. Thankfully, after a couple of weeks, the weight fell off. My first week in the show was especially nerve-wracking, because I had to be a swing until my regular spot opened up again. Luckily, I only got called in to cover the Infanta spot in "Bolero." There was no way I was going to learn everyone's tracks when I was only swing for a week. It was probably best that I wasn't dancing too much right away, because my tendons and ligaments hadn't returned to normal yet since giving birth. I snapped my Achilles tendon simply walking around my apartment complex in medium-high heels and had to go to Pilates and get acupuncture to help it heal. (My Achilles heel was my Achilles heel.) Probably not the smartest idea, I stayed in the show and continued dancing even though I was hurting for quite a while.

If I thought doing twelve shows a week was taxing pre-pregnancy, doing it while raising an infant made my previous fatigue seem laughable. I danced two shows a night, got home around 12:45 a.m., and tried to catch a couple hours sleep before Kieran woke up to be fed and cared for. Some days he was up for the day starting as early as 5 a.m. He wasn't one of those babies who slept all day. He required constant attention and stimulation. Any time he actually slept, I had to avoid the temptation to get something done (including taking a shower) and instead dropped everything and took a nap myself. Adjusting to the needs of this little angel, who kept me on my toes night and day, was a challenge like no other.

****

Just as I was learning to cope with and somewhat manage both baby and work, we got word that there was going to be a major renovation to our show, thanks to Maurice Hines, the Rockettes' biggest fan. After performing with us, his creative juices began flowing and he became inspired to add more sizzle to his beloved Rockettes. Maurice's master plan included revamping "Bolero" and creating a new number to "Luck Be a Lady" from *Guys & Dolls*, with Maurice singing and the Rockettes, his "sidekicks," dancing backup. Exciting!

Most rehearsals required an afternoon or two of our time, but Maurice's grand vision was going to mean *weeks* of daily rehearsals in addition to our nightly performances. Maurice's magical touch was sure to turn our production into a tour de force, but the impending rehearsal schedule threw a huge wrench in the works for me. With Ron working during the day, I had to find childcare. I wasn't keen on having a stranger in charge of my newborn, especially since he needed extra loving patience. Plus, now I'd have to pay for a babysitter. My solution was to fly my mom out from Detroit to stay with us until the process was finished.

Substantial overhauls like this one left us camping out at the theatre, day and night. We practically *lived* at the Flamingo. Surviving it intact required tremendous physical and emotional fortitude. And plenty of coffee, donuts, bagels, and cream cheese at our disposal at all times. So essential was this convention that we had an official Bagel-

Donut Dictator—the persuasive Mac. Mac toted a clipboard with a list of names; when it was your turn to buy bagels or donuts, she showed up at your spot and dictated your duty with supreme authority. You didn't have a choice. Mac's system was all very organized and you were expected to do your part. Capiche? I don't know what would have happened if someone had mutinied and refused to buy bagels and donuts. Since the contracts were a minimum of six months, I guess no one thought being ostracized for that long was worth saving the $20. The girls descended upon the treats like vultures to a carcass.

On a typical rehearsal day, we would roll out of bed, groggy and sore from the night before, and stumble into the theatre. Seeing the sugary glaze glisten on a box of fresh Krispy Kremes assured us that we would make it through the day. We bedraggled Rockettes would be plopped down on stage, still wiping the sleep out of our eyes, and cajoling our weary muscles and brains into waking up when Mr. Hines came flitting into rehearsals, assistant choreographer David at his heels, sporting his baseball cap and toting his steaming cup of Starbucks coffee, gesturing grandly, smiling broadly, and calling out, "How are my divas today?" He was caffeinated, energized, and brimming with grandiose ideas of making the Rockettes spectacular enough to befit the name *The Great Radio City Spectacular*. His enthusiasm was infectious, and you had to admire his passion for his art. And for us. We were lucky to be ladies working with this remarkable and appreciative guy.

Maurice had such a flamboyant, improvisational style all his own, however, that it was nearly impossible to translate his grooves into our rigid, precision-dance moves. Stylistically, we spoke two different languages. Like a master musician, off the cuff, he'd spontaneously create some show-stopping dance riff. We'd all stand and stare with our mouths agape, stunned by his showmanship and simultaneously not having the slightest clue how to begin trying to match him. This was not how Rockettes were used to working. His assistant had the excruciating task of trying to break down Maurice's motions into tiny fragments we could duplicate in such a way that we all looked exactly alike doing it. Transforming his free-flowing, jazzy pizzazz into precision-dance felt like trying to box in a butterfly. To top that off, keeping us in height order was a mathematical nightmare. The Rockettes couldn't be moved around willy-nilly because returning us to height order for the requisite final kickline would then be like solving a Rubik's cube. Formation changes took considerable preplanning. It was a painstaking process, and we had to be alert and focused at all times if we were going to absorb the groove of this Grand Master Dancer.

After an intense day of rehearsing plus our regular performances, by the time we neared the end of our second show, we were either loopy and slaphappy or monstrously grouchy or both. If we were really lucky, someone would make Jell-O shots to be passed out right after the finale of the last show. Often it was my dear friend Heidi, who became famous for the fantastic margarita Jell-O shot she created using lime Jell-O, triple sec, and tequila—another reason she quickly became one of my best friends. She was a gorgeous blond with stylish, short hair and a flawless body including that coveted six-pack. I should have been jealous of her, but instead I just thought she was the cat's meow. She grew up on a dairy farm in Grand Island, Nebraska. "Who ever heard of an island in Nebraska, let alone a 'grand' one?" I'd tease her. When standing next to her in the wings waiting to go on stage, I would pretend to milk a cow, quietly making udder-squirting sounds.

Heidi and I started our own private wine-tasting club. Every Thursday, we would stay at the theatre after the second show, drink wine, eat cheese and crackers, and chit-chat in the dressing room until about 1:30 or 2:00 a.m. It was easier to hang at work since we lived on opposite sides of town—too far to drive that late. One memorable night, we walked out to the employee parking garage to head home and couldn't find Heidi's car. Being tired, we figured she had just forgotten where she'd left it. After doing several laps around the garage, we enlisted a security guy to drive us around. Sure enough, her car was AWOL. The man escorted us to an obscure, stark, plain, closet-sized room in the bowels of the casino to fill out a report with security. It looked like an interrogation room where casino goons would rough up patrons suspected of card reading and cheating the house out of money. About a week later, Heidi's car turned up, stripped and trashed. Apparently, a couple of teenagers had taken it out for a joy ride. Vegas. Good times.

Anyway, Heidi's margarita Jell-O shots were a big hit after a drawn-out, devil-of-a-day at the office. The Rockettes relied heavily on caffeine, sugar, the occasional slurp of gelatinous agave liquor, and lots of laughter to help us survive rehearsal marathons. Thankfully, through all the trials and tribulations, Maurice didn't give up on us or his grand vision. We all persevered, and the final product was a smashing success.

The bonus prize was that Radio City sent new costumes! Actually they were used, pink and silver "Singing in the Rain" costumes, but they were new to us. I think they were hand-me-downs from the *Radio City Spring Spectacular*. Even more fun was choosing whatever color short-haired wig we wanted to wear with the hat. I went peroxide blond. The Rockettes convened on stage in our new costumes and took group photos to commemorate the special occasion.

The Super Deluxe Ultra Grande Supreme prize was that Kilpie (real name Karla Kilpatrick) and I were the two Rockettes chosen to dance with Maurice for a special intro to "Luck Be a Lady." I was shocked, humbled, and honored. As Maurice's two sidekicks, we had this fantastic, sexy choreography that showed off our long, luscious legs. We'd be wearing a long purple coat with fur trim over our pink and silver costume and then dramatically strip it off before joining the other Rockettes for the rest of the number. Unfortunately, when we finally tried our newly sewn coats for dress rehearsal, they restricted our movements so much that we could only perform a substandard, miniature version of the actual choreography. What a disappointment. As sometimes happens in showbiz, the costume killed the choreography. This is why it's so important that the choreographer and the costume designer communicate well with each other.

My proudest moment was the night Maurice told me, "Kristi, I love performing with you, because I can really feel your energy on stage!" The heavens opened, the angels sang, and I was silently shouting, "Hallelujah!" Talk about a compliment. I should have typed it up, laminated it, and carried it with me wherever I went. My second proudest Maurice moment was when my son was about five months old. I brought him to the theatre and was pushing him around backstage in his stroller. He often seemed to be pointing his toes. Maurice said, "He's got great dancer's feet!" I felt like my son had gotten the stamp of approval from the King of Dance himself. Hallelujah, indeed.

****

Rehearsals were over, for the time being. Our new, improved show was a winner. Maurice was over the moon with my performance. Nevertheless, even with a heaping dose of Jell-O shots, caffeine, and Krispy Kremes, those positive results weren't enough to make up for the fact that I was dangerously sleep-deprived and exhausted. Little Baby Kieran and I were on different schedules—mainly he was awake and screaming when I desperately wanted to sleep. My mother had come to the rescue for this rehearsal session, but I couldn't keep flying her in from Detroit on a moment's notice. Last-minute rehearsals made it difficult to have a babysitter ready and available. Yes, the show had just gotten a beautiful face lift, but, based on past experience, odds were that it would continue changing and changing and changing. I could bet on more rehearsals somewhere down the line. When? Well, that was a roll of the dice. Even without rehearsals, performing six nights and week while raising a finicky newborn was outrageously difficult. I couldn't handle both the rigors of the show and the demands of taking care of a baby. It was time to throw in the cards.

Final Scene: New York City, August 10, 2002

After the tour ended, I had just enough time to run to the gift shop to see if they had any new Rockette memorabilia. Did I really need anymore stuff? The memories were worth a lot more. I scoped out the latest Rockette doll thinking that someday my baby girl would enjoy playing with it. "Better yet, I'm going to buy one for her to play with and a second one to keep in the box as a collector's item," I told the sales lady. I adored my little rascals and had learned a lot about parenting since my son Kieran was a tiny tot.

I went back up to the green room, changed into my dance attire, and began warming up. As I was stretching, the nice man entered with that morning's *New York Post*. "Thought you might want to take a look at this," he said, tossing the paper on the coffee table. The cover read "KICKED OUT: Radio City gives Rockettes the boot." The Rockettes were front page news! Anxiously I read on: "The Rockettes are getting a kick in the derriere from Radio City Music Hall. Cash-strapped Cablevision, which owns the Rockettes and the fabled music hall, is trying to dissolve the current roster of 41 New York dancers."

August 10, 2002, the very day of my first Rockette appearance at Radio City Music Hall, the paper claimed I was being kicked out. This official news made the day all the more poignant. How ironic that I had finally hit the big time, and now my time was up. The fat lady was singing. My heart sank to my bunioned and battered feet.

Act 3, Scene 4

Detroit

In addition to the prevailing, mother-of-all-Rockette-shows in New York City at Radio City Music Hall, there were *Christmas Spectacular* franchises running at several locations simultaneously around the country. These were dubbed "Christmas Outside New York" or "CONY" shows. Being a member of the Roster, I could choose where I wanted to perform, including the highly coveted NYC gig. I agonized for some time about whether or not I wanted to dance at Radio City. Finding adequate, affordable, temporary housing and relocating with a baby seemed daunting and difficult. What would Ron do all day in New York City in the winter with Kieran? The *Radio City Christmas Spectacular* happened to have a show in Detroit that year, and the thought of performing in my hometown was especially enticing. We could stay with my parents for free, and they'd help with the baby. Ron might even be able to find temporary work. Yes, Detroit sounded like a much less stressful and financially better option, so baby Kieran and Ron and I packed up our belongings, vacated our apartment, bid a teary goodbye to my dear friends in Vegas, and headed to my parents' home about thirty miles west of Detroit.

I felt something incredibly special about returning to perform in "The Motor City," near where I grew up. New York was the Rockettes' city, but Detroit was *my* city. I rooted for our precious "Motown"—an underdog with latent potential and plenty of soul. Amidst a depressing array of abandoned homes, burned-out buildings, dilapidated structures, graffiti, liquor stores, grungy bars, and pawn shops were shining jewels like the Masonic Temple, where we rehearsed. The magnificent Detroit Masonic Temple was hailed as the largest Masonic Temple in the world. Its fourteen floors contained a whopping 1,037 rooms including three theatres and three ballrooms. Built in the 1920s, its lavish lobby hearkened back to a time of glory and grandeur. Rehearsing in this unique, historical space thrilled me.

On the first day of rehearsals, I was elated to discover that the director of our production was none other than our assistant director from the Branson show, Dennis. He had a cheerful disposition, as did our dance captain, and the rehearsal atmosphere was more relaxed than it had been in Branson. The quality, however, was intended to be just as stellar. All parties seemed to coexist and work together as happily as Santa and his elves.

Aside from Dennis, the only other people I knew in the show were Mac, my fellow ex-Vegas Rockette sister (also a southeast Michigan native) and a male dancer from the Branson show. It was wonderful to see a few friendly faces, and I was particularly thrilled to have Mac in the cast. Mac and I were by far the oldest, most well-seasoned Rockettes of the bunch and the only Roster gals. Being very close in height, in Vegas Mac and I usually danced next to each other in the line-up. This time I was placed alongside a considerably younger-looking lady. One day, I got the nerve up to ask her how old she was. "Eighteen," she replied. I quickly did the mental math. "I'm old enough to be your mother!" I exclaimed, horrified.

We ate, slept, and breathed the show for the next three weeks. My mind felt like a computer overloaded with too much information for its memory capacity. After a few days, choreography started spilling out my ears. I couldn't process one more bevel, arm pose, or kick. The moves became a jumble of mishmash, and there came a point at which I couldn't assimilate any more information. It was like cramming for college final exams, trying to memorize an entire book on art history in one evening. Fortunately, I wasn't the only one on overload. When the dance captain and director noticed that everyone was melting down, they stopped teaching new material for the day.

What made it so difficult was that the choreography for the various dances was too similar. We had to learn so many different bevels, kick combinations, and arm poses, we'd get mixed up from one number to the next. "Was that the left hand on the hip with the thumbs forward or thumbs tucked behind? Does the right arm lift from the wrist to get straight above the head, or did it push through with a bent elbow?" There were hundreds of these poses with minute variations and no rhyme or reason to them. It wasn't like one number required the thumbs forward every time it was on the hip. With no consistency and no rules to cling to, the choreography was a mind-boggling brain teaser. Like learning for a foreign language which nouns are masculine and which are feminine, we had to flat out memorize it. It seemed a miracle that our muscles and mind would ever work together to retain it all, but eventually, with enough repetition, the entire routine became second nature and stuck in our muscle memory. Much of our choreographic consternation could be attributed to the brilliant artistry of our former Branson show director, Linda, who had created more complex, show-stopping numbers to beef up the CONY shows. I thought the Branson show was arduous and a lot to learn. The Detroit show had all the same Rockette numbers in it plus two new, colossal, Linda masterpieces. The first was "Christmas in New York," a magnificent, festive, city scene that utilized the entire cast. It served as the grand, climactic finale of the first act and was by far the Rockettes' most back-breaking, leg-breaking, heart-stopping number in the show. It was a kick fest with a gazillion kicks throughout the number (including a sit-down drill and "circle kicks," which featured the Rockettes linked arm to arm, facing out, forming a giant circle, and kicking while rotating the circle around), a massive kickline at the end, and an encore kickline afterward.

The second was "Bizzazz," a snappy number we did with Santa, about Santa having that "extra kind of special something" that let him "sparkle and fizzle-fazz," and this wonderful stuff was "bizzazz." The Rockettes called the number "Candy Canes" because we wore sweet and sassy, hot pink costumes trimmed in candy cane stripes (I was so sweet on this Pete Menefee masterpiece of fabric and feathers that I begged him to let me put his sketch of it on the cover of this book) and danced with three-foot, ten-pound, wooden, glow-in-the-dark candy canes. The candy canes were cumbersome, heavy, and hard to maneuver. Holding them in such a way that they looked uniform among us at all times was an excruciating task. Whenever we rested the end of our canes on the ground, for instance, they had to be exactly straight up and down at a ninety-degree angle to the floor with the top arc of the cane facing the exact same direction as everyone else's. We also tossed and twirled the canes and had to be extremely careful not to toss or twirl too hard, or we'd drop them. This was one of the few numbers in which we sang, this time a duet with Santa from "The Holiday Season." It took a lot of breath support to belt out the tune, dance full out, and lift our weighty, striped, candy sticks at the same time. This long and taxing number started off the second act right after intermission.

The addition of these two monstrous numbers to our workload meant rehearsals that demanded an even faster and more furious learning curve and a greater ability to perfect our performance quickly. The process was extremely intense, and our thinking caps had to be on at all times. Once real performances started, we'd only have intermission during which to recover from "Christmas in New York" before having to be back on stage to bust out some "Bizzazz."

For our final week of tech and dress rehearsals, we relocated to our performance venue—the historic Fox Theatre. The Masonic Temple was certainly a gem, but "The Fox" was known as Detroit's "crown jewel." Less than a mile from the Masonic, it was located on Woodward Avenue in the Grand Circus Park Historic District, directly across from Comerica Park—home of the Detroit Tigers major league baseball team. Built in the late 1920s as a movie palace, its exceedingly opulent, overly ornate mélange of Burmese, Chinese, Indian, and Persian decor was a spectacular setting in which to house our spectacular show. So excessive and impressive was the ornamentation that it almost competed with our show for the audience's attention. The ostentatious lobby and the theatre itself were a breathtaking display of lavishness. Of all the theatres in the world, The Fox was my absolute favorite, hands down.

Opening night at The Fox was a grand event. Before the show, the Rockettes, dressed in our white snowball costumes, arrived in vintage automobiles to the delight of the crowd. Colorful streams of confetti streamed down as we lined up for photographs in front of the theatre's massive marquee. We ceremoniously paraded through the lobby and made our way to our dressing rooms to prepare for the show. Backstage in the hallway, we signed the "Wall of Fame"—the designated place for entertainers to leave their mark. For the Rockettes, there was a painting of a kickline of ladies, and we each autographed our respective line-up spot.

After not performing for such a long time, it took a few shows to get used to dancing in front of an audience again. Ten thousand eyes on a person can really get the adrenaline going. I had so much nervous energy, I felt uncomfortable with stage fright. A brilliant idea came to me, "Why don't you *pretend* you've already been in the show for weeks, Kristi, and breathe as if it's old hat?" My entire nervous system settled down, and I felt fantastic.

****

After the big opening night hoopla was over, we settled into more or less of a daily routine for the remainder of our approximately seventy-show run. While some aspects of the job were repetitive, my typical day (and night) at the office nearly always included something new and exciting happening.

For instance, we did tons of publicity: radio shows, newspaper interviews, television segments, photo shoots, appearances, and charity events. Some of us even went to a Detroit Red Wings hockey game in costume and schmoozed people. A handful of Rockettes were Detroit-area natives, and publicity played heavily on the use of local ladies. Another Rockette, two young girls who played Clara in our "Teddy Bear Nutcracker," and I all hailed from my same childhood dance school, so a newspaper article covered that angle. Being the only mom in the bunch and a local gal to boot, I got loads of attention and was personally featured in newspaper articles, radio shows, and even on television. One television station featured me on their "Working Women" segment. They came to my parents' home and took footage of me playing Mommy to Kieran and then filmed me at the theatre being a Rockette. It was terribly exciting. In addition, I participated in some charitable community outreach events, including an in-between-shows appearance at a home for battered teen girls in Detroit (we hung out, autographed stuff, and handed out Rockette dolls) and visits, in costume, to cheer up patients at a local hospital. Our biggest publicity event was probably performing the "Rag Doll" number for the televised Detroit Thanksgiving Day Parade.

Sometime we had local celebrities (like famous newscasters, radio personalities, or athletes) read "'Twas the Night Before Christmas" to the audience before the show started. Select Rockettes had the honor of escorting these special guests onto the stage. I had the good fortune of being chosen to host two handsome Detroit Red Wings hockey players. Score!

Other thrills included finding presents from Radio City at our dressing spots. Over the years, I was gifted an assortment of Rockette paraphernalia including snow globes, ornaments, an umbrella, a gift basket of lotions (from Vaseline, our sponsor at one time—official lotion of the long-legged ladies), a plush burgundy robe embroidered with a Rockette kickline and personalized with my name on it, an embroidered black leather jacket for the Rockettes' 75th anniversary, a Rockette windbreaker, a Rockette dance bag, a Rockette warm-up suit, Rockette dance clothes, a Rockette over-the-shoulder bag, an engraved silver compact, Rockette lapel pins, a Rockette-embroidered denim shirt and denim jacket, a Rockette instant camera, and Rockette figurines. The company even sent gifts to my home during times I wasn't working. How's that for a great job?

The best gift, however, and a big bonus of being back near my hometown, was that my typical day often included the delight of having old friends and family in the audience. Tons of people from my past and present attended the show—parents, grandparents, aunts and uncles, old school teachers, dance teachers, childhood friends, high school acquaintances, sorority sisters, and college pals. It was a fantastic homecoming and always thrilling to be surprised by a blast from my past. Many wanted to visit with me after the show, so I was constantly spending extra time greeting people. For really special folks, I'd ask permission to give a backstage tour or take them outside to the animal tent behind the theatre to pet the camels, sheep, and donkeys. I loved being able to give them the VIP treatment.

****

In addition to the excitement of seeing expected and unexpected guests after the show, plenty also happened *during* the show to stir things up. For instance, I ran out of luck and got stuck being one of three oversized panda bears in the "Teddy Bear Nutcracker," so I had to wear a giant panda bear suit and a huge fiberglass bear head. Those particularly dangerous costumes were a recipe for disaster and/or comic relief. The body suit was so heavy I could hardly lift my arms. The head offered such limited visibility that a dresser had to hold my hand like a two-year-old and lead me to my stage entrance, because I could barely see where I was going. When left to my own devices, I bumped into set pieces, knocked over crew, and tripped over cables. I could do little else but grin and bear it. Dancing in those costumes took a leap of faith; each show I prayed I could find my marks and see well enough to discern my exit path when my dance bit was done. I had nightmares about being stuck on stage, blindly wandering in circles trying to find my way off.

Just like in the real *Nutcracker* ballet, our production also included Russian dancers who did athletic jumps and leaps and turns and kicks. In our case, however, the three men were disguised as bears and had their faces covered by those dastardly heads. It was a feat for me to just walk in my cumbersome costume without killing myself or someone else, so I marveled at their ability to perform such outrageously difficult maneuvers under the circumstances. They weren't always successful. One particularly exuberant yet visually impaired Russian bear leapt his way right off the edge of the stage and onto the lap of a surprised audience member seated in the front row. That was not your typical lap dance. Luckily, no one was seriously injured.

Surprisingly, being a bear ended up one of my favorite parts of the show due to a special spot we called "The Bear Room." This was a makeshift fast-change area set up behind the stage for all the performers who had to be bears in *The Nutcracker*. The Bear Room was the place to be for entertainment. It all started when one guy and gal created a little impromptu dance to a portion of the music of the number happening on stage at the time. They showed off their turns, high kicks, hip-hop moves, leaps, and fancy lifts. The other bears and our dressers cheered with delight. Not wanting to disappoint their fans, the couple kept coming up with new, amazing routines. The panda bears judged their various dances, going so far as to hold up score cards. The dancing duo expended a lot of extra energy each night to entertain us (and themselves). It turned out to be too much of a cross to bear for the long term; they got burned out and had to take a break. Once in a while, however, they'd surprise us and bring back reruns of our favorite high-scoring routines.

The dance extravaganzas weren't our only amusement in The Bear Room. Three of our little people played baby bears, and one of those cubs was always playing practical jokes. Once he hid inside a new girl's big bear costume. The rest of us were in on the secret and made sure to be there to watch her get initiated. When she stuck her feet into her costume, she screamed, because a live creature was inhabiting it! We lived for stuff like that at the theatre. It was highly entertaining, and the high jinks broke up the monotony.

Sometimes we added a dash of spice to our official routine to make it more amusing. In "Candy Canes," for instance, one night I accidentally caught the glance of one of the male dancers standing offstage in the wings within eyeshot of where I was dancing. I smiled right at him. Afterwards he said, "You saw me looking at you and you smiled back! Wasn't that great?" Of course, he was standing in the same spot the next night, and I couldn't *not* flash him a smile and a look. That would be rude. It became our "moment," and we did it every night without fail. This little connection was important to both of us and made our show special. Once you started something like that, you couldn't just stop it willy-nilly or it would throw off your show. It became part of our choreography. It also became a superstitious ritual that we knew better than to quit. One time I had the great fortune of being swung out of the show—our swing had family there and wanted to perform, so our stage manager let her take my spot—and I got to watch the show from a seat in the audience. A spectacular swing will even cover the "moments" of the person she is swinging out, so I asked my swing to cover my moment with my guy friend. She did, and he was thrilled! It made the whole experience more fun for all three of us.

Another ritual developed during "Nativity." I was standing in the wings waiting to go on, and a stage hand held out both fists and asked me to pick one. Inside was a chocolate candy that he gave me. The next night I returned the favor and had him pick a hand. If you did something like that twice, it was bound to turn into a ritual, and it did. Every show, we'd take turns giving each other chocolates at that precise moment. "Nativity" was the only number in the show during which the cast could get away with eating (as long as we kept it on the down low from stage management and our dance captain), and several of us regularly (discretely, of course) munched chocolates and peanut butter cups on our walk to Bethlehem. There was no shortage of chocolate and Christmas candy floating around backstage. Between that and the abundant supplies of coffee, cookies, and doughnuts (which you were required to bring in if you had gotten "lucky" the night before), we'd all be due for a caffeine and sugar detox after the show closed. Treats sweetened up the routine.

****

Besides spontaneous backstage entertainment, rituals, and superstitions, live theatre always had its share of unpredictable mishaps that kept things interesting. Props and costumes were always helpful in this regard, and the giant candy canes from "Bizzazz" were no exception. When dropped on stage, they would make a thud to wake the dead. Whenever the Rockettes heard that awful sound, we'd quickly eyeball the stage to see where the runaway candy cane had landed in case it was about to trip us. The poor Rockette who dropped it had to scramble to pick it up and catch up to the rest of the girls who, by that time, had probably changed formations. God forbid the cane should go flying more than five feet away. Reminiscent of my childhood baton recital fiasco, it was nearly impossible to make one's way through all the moving dancers to pick it up again without causing a huge scene. If it seemed too difficult to retrieve, a girl might leave her cane on the floor and pantomime the rest of the number with an invisible cane. (That was embarrassing.) Some dancers gave up altogether, ran off stage, and cowered in the dressing room in shame. Everyone else felt really bad for the poor soul who dropped her prop. After the number, there would be hushed whispers in the dressing room asking, "Who lost her candy cane?" We could tell by tracing where the whimpering and quiet sobbing were coming from. Generally, that would be a new girl. The veteran Rockettes were more likely to shrug it off with a "That's show biz!" attitude.

What made dancing with these striped sticks especially treacherous were the slippery, white satin gloves we wore as part of our costume; they made it nearly impossible to hold onto the canes. Wardrobe's solution was to glue-gun hundreds of tiny, sticky glue dots onto the palms. This approach worked well, but over time the dots wore down. It was imperative that the Rockettes be vigilant about monitoring the level of our glue dots, or we'd be in for a treacherous show. If we told our dresser that our dots needed replacing, and by the next day it wasn't done, there was trouble (for us and our dresser). Before the number, we'd have to get to the stage early to talk lovingly to our candy canes and say a dozen "Hail Mary Tyler Moores," or whatever worked, because we knew we needed all the cosmic forces on our side, or that cane was going down. When the prop master repainted the stripes on our canes, which he did periodically, our canes were even more slippery. Minute changes could mean the difference between a dynamite show and disaster. What might seem like a triviality to the layperson could mean serious injury or mortal embarrassment to a performer.

Thankfully, I never flat out flung my cane on the floor. On the contrary, my worst cane experience was when it slipped out of my hands as I was lifting it over my head, and it walloped me in the face. I thought I had broken my nose and was sure it was going to start bleeding right there on stage. It didn't, but my eyes watered so much for the rest of the number that I could hardly see where I was going. It was like being smashed in the schnoz with a baseball bat. The accident report filled out by the stage manager hardly did justice to the incident: "Performer was hit in the nose with a candy cane," it read. "Can't you at least write that it was a *three-foot, ten-pound*, wooden prop?" I retorted. I didn't think the insurance company would believe my claim, as how badly could one be injured by your average candy cane?

To avoid the aforementioned dangers, the smart girls massaged, smooched, pep-talked, and said silent prayers over their candy canes before each show. It was a superstitious ritual that we never missed for fear of the consequences. Props needed a lot of love and attention.

My most spectacular mishap was so unexpected, unheard of, timely, and far-reaching that it goes down in the record books as my all-time favorite. The set-up is important to get the whole effect, so here goes: Because there wasn't safe, adequate housing within walking distance of the The Fox, the entire cast had to commute by car. Being winter in Michigan, this often meant driving in snow. One Saturday morning, I awoke to discover that there had been a blizzard all through the night, and the snow was still coming down. Like a school kid hoping for a snow day, I prayed that the show had been cancelled and envisioned myself spending a cozy day in my pajamas sipping hot cocoa in front of the fireplace. A call to my stage manager quickly killed that fantasy. The show was a go. I had a matinee performance and a thirty-mile drive downtown from where I was staying. That dreamy winter wonderland became an instant nightmare, as I realized I'd be lucky to make it to the theatre at all, let alone on time. At show time, the curtain would go up with or without me. I'd better be on stage when it did, or I was apt to be out of a job.

Hence, it was with great concern for my personal safety and career that I embarked on the treacherous trek through the tundra. I left hours early to allow for the perilous, unplowed roads. Gripping the steering wheel so tightly made for a white-knuckle journey, as I drove past car after car after car in the ditch, some slipping, sliding, and spinning out uncontrollably right in front of me. What a relief to finally pull into the theatre parking lot. I hadn't gotten into a wreck, but I *was* a wreck after that harrowing commute. My muscles were so frozen in fear, I thought they'd never thaw out and relax again.

Adding to the tension, backstage was abuzz with worry over how many of our cast and crew would make it. A good portion of the performers were New Yorkers who rarely drove cars on a normal day let alone in blizzard conditions. I recalled the time I visited a friend in Washington, D.C., when a freak snow storm caused people to abandon their cars on the highway, because they didn't know how to drive in snow.

Our show had a huge cast, and each person had a valuable and unique role to play. No one was easily expendable. Usually, soon after half-hour call, the stage manager looked to see who was missing and assigned swings to go on in their place. In this case, too many people still had not arrived to make a call. We didn't know if all the swings would make it in or if enough would make it in to cover all the missing people. The stage manager waited anxiously, hoping more performers would show up, as the clock ticked down to show time. This was an especially tense waiting period for those of us present, as we knew that, right before we had to go on, we might be asked to learn new choreography, spacing, and traffic patterns to adjust for gaping holes in the show. It was torture! Fortunately, in the nick of time, enough people rolled in to complete the show without major changes, but everyone was shaken and rattled to say the least.

To make matters worse, most of the audience members had been smart enough to stay safely snuggled up at home; only a few brave, Christmas-loving, diehard fans had ventured out into the storm. Consequently, we were playing to only about one hundred people in a 5,000-seat venue. The house was virtually empty. Performers feed off the energy and enthusiasm of audience members, and this place was dead. Not only were we anxiety-stricken from the dangerous drive and the potential of missing performers, but we had risked our very lives to perform for a mere handful of patrons. We became a group of Ebenezer Scrooges thinking, "Bah, humbug! We don't want to be here!" But the show must go on, so I gritted my teeth, plastered on a fake smile, and waited for the whole miserable day to be over.

Then it happened—the straw that broke the camel's back. (Animal lovers, not to worry. This is just a figure of speech. The real camels in our show remained unharmed.) It was during "Christmas in New York"—our massive, magnificent, musical masterpiece that teemed with jolly singers toting colorful, beribboned packages in a festive New York City shopping scene. Real ice skaters skated on an ice rink as fake snow fell from the sky; and, just when the audience thought the number couldn't possibly get any more exciting, out came the Rockettes, dazzling in our sexy little red velvet costumes with white fur trim.

"Christmas in New York" was a real crowd pleaser, but it was also the Rockettes' most grueling number in the show. It was a marathon of kicks so strenuous and brutal that my legs and abs got sore just thinking about it. This dance was so taxing that one night, one of our young new Rockettes, thinking she could get by on Coca-Cola and cigarettes alone, passed out in the wings before our encore and the paramedics had to come and revive her. This was no walk in Central

Park. The number built up to the Rockettes' spectacular entrance in which a yellow New York taxi cab drives on stage, the driver opens the door, and out steps a Rockette followed by another and another and another until the entire stage is filled with Rockettes. It was like that circus illusion where a big bunch of clowns somehow spill out of a teeny tiny car. The effect was superb.

We each then pranced our way over to our partner and did a few cutesy moves side by side. Unbeknownst to me, my partner and I had gotten a little too close for comfort and the buckles of our shoes had hooked together. Oblivious, we continued the choreography in which we jumped back to back in preparation for one of those famous Rockette eye-high kicks. The buckles were attached to the shoes by a short elastic band, so as I jumped away from my partner, the elastic band stretched, and stretched and STRETCHED, and when I went to kick my leg.... Remember shooting rubber bands as a kid? You make a gun with your hand, stretch the band around your fingers and let it fly?

When I kicked my leg, my shoe exploded off my foot like a rocket ship blasting into outer space. The Fox has extremely tall ceilings, so it was free to fly high. One hundred audience-member heads and two hundred eyeballs traced the path of the projectile as it made a colossal arch all the way over to the opposite side of the stage and landed with a thud somewhere in a galaxy far, far away.

This left me with a problem of cosmic proportions. I'd have to dance the remainder of the number (and remember, we were at the beginning of a very long and difficult number) wearing only one shoe. "What should I do?" The choreography kept moving along fast and furiously, so, even though I was somewhat in shock, I had to make a split-second decision about how I was going to fix this problem. Since I couldn't see where my wayward shoe landed, retrieving it to place it back on my foot was not going to happen. Even if I quickly found it, it wasn't a shoe I could easily slip back on, especially with a broken buckle. Running off stage was an alternative, but my exit would have drawn a lot of attention, as I dodged dancers on my way out. And my absence would have left my colleagues one woman short, messing up all the formations and spacing.

My best bet, I decided, was to keep right on dancing. Here's the kicker: In order to make us look even more long and luscious, the Rockettes danced in high heels. Try simply walking in one high heel and one flat foot. Awkward. I had to dance on tiptoe with the bare foot in order to maintain fairly equal footing with the shod foot. Put yourself in my shoes (or "shoe"), for a moment, if you will. Embarrassing? Yeah. Distressing? You bet. Pretty? Not at all.

The audience continued to point and giggle, following me throughout the dance. To top that off, word spread like wild fire backstage that "Kristi lost her shoe!" Soon every cast and crew member possible flooded into the wings and joined in chuckling and watching to see how I was going to manage to finish the number. The day had been a disaster even before my shoe went airborne. And now all this to boot? I felt like I'd been kicked when I was already down.

As I waited for the other shoe to drop, however, I suddenly had an awareness: I had a choice in how I was going to respond. I could become even more upset and stressed out than I already was, or I could decide, "Shoe fly? Don't bother me!" After all, it was downright hilarious. A huge grin spread across my face—a wider, and certainly wackier looking, smile than the Rockettes were legally allowed. Then I burst out laughing and didn't stop until well after the number was over. That footwear "fiasco" didn't break the camel's back after all; it broke the ice. Everyone—audience, cast, and crew alike—relaxed, had a good laugh at my expense, and lightened up. We finished the show in true Christmas spirit.

Another favorite backstage event, which wasn't a mishap by any means, happened near the end of our "Soldier" number. We had just lined up like dominoes, facing stage left, in preparation for the famous "soldier fall." Audrey, being the shortest girl, stood at the front of the line, close to the wings. At that very moment, her boyfriend (a stage hand), who had been waiting in the wings, got down on one knee, diamond ring in hand, and held up a sign that read, "Audrey, will you marry me?" Of course, Audrey had to wait patiently until the fall was over to jump his bones and say, "Yes!" Those special backstage moments were precious.

****

Christmas was my favorite holiday, and I was elated to be doing the Christmas show again. For two solid months, we were absolutely inundated with Christmas—music, costumes, decorations, merchandise, gifts, parties, and events. It was Christmas on steroids, and I was high with the holiday spirit. Since Christmas also happened to be my son's birthday, it was an exceptionally magical time as well.

The Rockettes almost had to perform for half-time for the Detroit Lions' football game on Christmas day, our day off. I nearly cried when our producer, Brian Kauffman, brought up the idea. "It's Christmas! And it's my son's first birthday! Please, don't make us do it!" I begged and groveled. Enough of the Rockettes also preferred to have Christmas off, so Brian (who was not only highly professional and respected but kind as well) nixed the idea and I was off the hook. Some days should be sacred in my book—Christmas and my kids' birthdays being top of the list. (By the way, Brian was so thoughtful that on occasion he even cooked homemade soup for the entire cast. We adored him.)

We did have Christmas Eve performances, however. As soon as I got home from the theatre, I went into Mommy mode, stuffing stockings, wrapping presents, and baking birthday cake. My wonderful mother stayed up with me until the wee hours of the morning making ladybug cupcakes for Kieran's birthday. Juggling motherhood and career was a challenge that certainly took its toll on me, but I was determined to bring home the bacon and fry it up in a pan.

With daily matinee and evening performances (as well as some *three-show* Saturdays), plus publicity events before or between shows, holiday festivities, and family obligations, I was running on empty. Unfortunately, I was hardly ever home and neither was Ron, because he had gotten a job working as a stage hand for the Detroit Auto Show. We were raking in the dough, but my fabulous parents were the ones babysitting Kieran most of the time.

A few days after Christmas, our show came to a close. Even though I had consistently pigged out and pumped my body full of chocolates and sugary treats, I still got down to skin and bones by the end of the season. My B-cups deflated, and my clothes fit me like I was a wire hanger. The entire month of January my body craved meat and proper food. I couldn't get enough. It was as if I had starved myself and my body was trying to replenish its fat supplies. Some Rockettes didn't like to do the show specifically because they'd always lose so much weight. Others did it precisely so they could look good naked. Whatever the case, although part of me was sad to see the show end, I needed to recover, rest, nurse my scrawny body back to health, and spend quality time with my family again.

****

Ron and I had no solid plans for what we were going to do with our lives going forward. We simply knew we wanted to rejuvenate somewhere warm by the water. "California is so expensive," we grumbled. "What about Florida?" Ron had dug the Ft. Lauderdale area in the past, so we targeted south Florida on the Atlantic coast for some fun in the sun. After a week of apartment hunting and driving around the southeast side of the Sunshine State, we settled on Del Rey Beach, a small, charming seaside town boasting four miles of beautiful Atlantic beachfront, north of Ft. Lauderdale and south of West Palm Beach. Ft. Lauderdale was a fantastic site for some drunken debauchery during spring break from college, but sleepy Del Rey seemed a more appropriate setting for raising a youngster. We found an apartment within walking distance of the ocean. Ron and I flew back to Michigan, packed our stuff into a moving van, and drove down south to set up house. Then Grandma and Grandpa flew with baby Kieran to meet us in our new home.

Moving so far from friends and family with a toddler and no secured employment was risky. Thankfully, Ron soon found a job as the pool manager at an exclusive, private yacht club in Palm Beach. I became a stay-at-home mom for the next nine months. While not particularly in dance shape, at least I stayed skinny from chasing after Kieran, who constantly ran away from me. Every day I also power walked several miles pushing Kieran in his baby jogger on the paths along the beach. When he napped, I would work out to yoga or aerobics videos in my apartment. Finally I found an adult ballet class I could take once or twice a week. My body didn't want to do what it used to do, and I was frustrated by my backwards progress. Dance takes daily discipline and regular practice, and I was rusty.

When October rolled around, Kieran and I returned to Detroit, so I could do the *Radio City Christmas Spectacular* again. There was no quicker way to whip myself into shape than by plunging into rehearsals seven hours a day, ready or not. The process was painful and exhausting, but eventually my muscles adjusted to the rigorous routine. I was proud of myself for being able to keep up with the youngsters and perform such intense choreography at age thirty-five after birthing a baby. As we continued into performances, however, my body was on the verge of rebellion. The jump splits and repetitive kicks were taking a toll. I felt like I was on the brink of getting injured. "How long can my hip flexors hold out?" I worried.

I had to face the facts: My body was aging, and it was hard to age gracefully in the world of entertainment, especially if you were a woman. Women in general feel the pressure to look young, and entertainers feel it a million times more. After about age twenty-seven, we didn't want to admit how old we were anymore. We had to practice telling our "showbiz" age—the one we made up (and it should never be older than twenty-nine)—with a straight face. Although I looked younger, I had just turned thirty when I joined the Rockettes, but I was told that Radio City preferred their dancers to look about twenty-three.

The Rockettes had a reputation for harboring "old" ladies (forty-plus years of age), so the media loved to pry and ask our age, especially if we looked old enough to buy our own alcohol without getting carded. Five years and a toddler later, I didn't look like I had any recollection of being twenty-three. So I was always skirting the age issue and having to say to reporters, "I'm old enough to have children and young enough to do those eye-high kicks!" It got to be a little depressing. What I really wanted to say was, "I'm thirty-flippin'-five. I popped out a baby, lost thirty-eight pounds, and was back on stage dancing in a bikini in less than three months. I can still work a skin-tight leotard cut up to my waist. I'm up at 6:00 a.m. (after finally getting to bed around one a.m.) changing diapers and making bottles. I'm still dancing with the most famous precision dance troupe in the world and keeping up with eighteen-year-olds, and I look pretty darn good. You put on this skimpy costume and see how sexy you look!"

Realizing that this might well be one of the last opportunities for Kieran to see his mommy perform as a Rockette, Grandma and Grandpa brought him to the show. Two-and-a-half hours was a long time to expect an energetic, not-quite-yet-two-years-old toddler to sit still and be quiet. Kieran lasted the entire production. He loved the show but cried every time I left the stage. I don't know how he could even find me in that line-up of ladies who all looked the same. At times he got restless and complained during "Nativity," but many adults can't sit through that one either. When he saw me perform with the Rockettes on television for the Detroit Thanksgiving Day Parade, he ran up to the TV, banged his fists on the screen, and screamed, "Mommy, no!" Apparently, he thought I was stuck in that box and was not coming back.

On the final day of our run at The Fox, I knew that this might be my last show as a Rockette. Constantly relocating my son was getting harder and harder. Being a full-time mom and staying in competitive dance shape was difficult. While performing that final show, I made a conscious effort to take it all in. I gazed at the audience. I studied the gorgeous, gilded Fox Theatre. Tears welled up in my eyes, as I listened to the applause and tried to memorize how it all felt. I didn't want to take any of it for granted. "This may be the last time I get to be on this side of the stage," I acknowledged woefully.

Back in the dressing room, my Rockette friend asked me, "Where are you planning on doing the show next Christmas, Kristi?" "Maybe I'll be on maternity leave," I answered with a twinkle in my eye, surprising myself at the statement that had spilled out of my mouth. My husband and I hadn't planned on having more children yet. Slowly and methodically, I removed my make-up, savoring the ritual. I gathered my belongings from the dressing room and pulled my name and photos off my mirror. I was one of the last to leave, not wanting it all to end. I walked out the stage door and heard it close solidly behind me.

Kieran and I returned to Daddy and our rental place in Florida. We decided it was time to put our money to good use and buy a house. Soon after we started looking I found out I was pregnant! It looked like my career would be slowing down for certain. I contemplated doing the Christmas show that year, but with the baby due in September and rehearsals starting in October or November 1 at the latest, I realized it would be impossible for me to get back into shape in time.

Instead, I took a year off for maternity leave, and that September, I gave birth to a beautiful baby girl named Kara! (Thalia's crystal's prediction had been correct, not only for me but also for Leslie who had two boys.) By the time she was four months old, I was eager to work again and started taking ballet classes to get back in shape. The Christmas show was still nine months away. I phoned Radio City to let them know I was available to teach the Rockette Experience. It was a long shot, as the waiting list of interested teachers was a mile long and most of them lived in New York. But I had to try. Then I ordered a subscription to *Backstage* to see what other kind of work options I had. "Maybe I could fly to New York to audition for something. Maybe a show will be coming to Florida. Who knows the possibilities?" I just knew I desperately missed performing and needed to get back to it.

Like a virgin, reliving the excitement and anticipation of the very first time I touched a *Backstage* newspaper in search of performance opportunities, I eagerly turned the pages only to be rudely awakened to the discovery that everyone wanted eighteen to thirty-five-year-olds. "But I was thirty-five just last year before I had the baby! What happened?" I blurted aloud, my tykes wide eyed over their ranting mommy. Time had flown by faster than I could count "a five, six, seven, eight." That's what happened. Somehow I had forgotten or failed to realize that, like a carton of milk or a can of tuna, a dancer came with an expiration date, and I was already spoiled goods. One moment I was reaching my peak and the next I was over the hill. "At least I still have the Rockettes," I reminded myself, temporarily relieved.

But no sooner had I recommitted myself to my show business career than all hell broke loose and loads of information started pouring in regarding Radio City's mission to disband the Roster. My phone rang off the hook, the Rockette hotline dispersing gossip cross country. My computer was bombarded with conflicting and confusing e-mail from various sources. My mailbox was loaded with persuasive letters from Radio City and Cablevision, opposing rhetoric from A.G.V.A., the union representing the Rockettes, and retaliation from enraged Rostered Rockettes. Our boisterous battle made the morning television news shows and CNN. Matters were coming to a head and the tension was thick. There was even talk of a strike. I breathed a heavy sigh, sensing that my time as a Rockette was nearly over.

As an almost thirty-seven-year-old mother of two, who was apparently too old to audition for other dance gigs, I also knew that once my Rockette contract ended, my dance career was completely kaput. This was a devastating prospect. Retiring from show business isn't like retiring from most other careers. You aren't just losing your job, you are losing your identity. You are relinquishing the consuming passion that drove you to risk rejection time and time again at auditions; that caused you to miss countless holidays, birthdays, and weddings with family and friends; that kept you dieting, taking ballet class, and doing an absurd amount of sit-ups; that drove you to risk financial ruin just to get the chance to *audition* to dance as a giant M&M in a candy commercial. You are giving up an enormous piece of your soul.

And so it was under such suspenseful circumstances that I received a crucial call from Rockette Headquarters at Radio City. "Kristi, you're next on the list to teach the Rockette Experience. Can you be in New

York in two weeks?" The opportunity had arisen just in the nick of time. Heeding the call from H.Q., I mustered the troops and briefed them on my upcoming deployment. "Kids, Mommy is being sent on special assignment and has to go bye-bye for a little bit." In response to this entertainment emergency, I left my precious progeny in the hands of my husband and boarded a flight to JFK International Airport in NYC to do the divine deed, most likely my final duty as a World Famous Radio City Rockette.

Final Scene: New York City, August 10, 2002

Another Rockette arrived in the Green Room. She was younger and newer to the Rockettes than I and, as such, was slated to teach the Rockette Experience in the small rehearsal hall, while I was assigned a bigger group in the big rehearsal hall. We did the requisite, traditional bonding ritual of name-dropping in search of mutual dancer friends, then compared choreography notes and ideas for how to run our respective sessions. After running through the dance combos several times, I stretched so I could kick to my head. It had been nearly a year and a half since I had danced in the Christmas show, and the choreography did not feel second nature anymore. The nice man returned to get us. "Ladies, you're on!"

The rehearsal hall hummed with eager, nervous students from all over the country, stretching and anticipating the afternoon ahead. They weren't the only ones who were nervous. This was a massive, unfamiliar undertaking for me, and I wanted to live up to their expectations. It was strange realizing I had accomplished something these dancers dearly wanted. I was living their dream: I was a Rockette. At least I was for one more day. Before I could set my dance bag down, I was approached by three scholarship students from Broadway Dance Center, the place where I had attended my first professional dance audition. "We're your dance assistants for the day and will help you with whatever you need," a young lady explained. The trio was at my beck and call. They would fetch water, handle my sheet music, and organize my audition score papers. I had been a scholarship student once myself years ago, and now I had students assisting me. Fantastic!

Then a friendly, middle-aged man walked up and extended his hand for a handshake. "I'm Gordon, the musical director for the Christmas show. I'll be your accompanist for today. Have you got your music with you?" I handed him the score, and we discussed where I'd be starting and stopping. The actual musical director and orchestra conductor for the *Radio City Christmas Spectacular* was *my* pianist, kindly taking orders from me. I was overwhelmed at my sudden change of status and loving every minute of it. Like Cinderella, I was Queen of the Ball for a day, all the while aware that, at the stroke of midnight, this fairy-tale existence would end.

"Hello, Ladies! Welcome to the Rockette Experience. I'm Kristi, your instructor. Today, I'll be teaching you excerpts from two numbers in the Rockette repertoire and, of course, we will work on performing the famous kickline. We'll start with a tap number we call 'Wreaths' and will then change into our character shoes to learn a section from 'Christmas in New York.' Sound good?" The young dancers were focused, attentive, quiet, respectful, and hanging on my every word. Within the group were varying levels of dance abilities, but everyone seemed to be trying their hardest. Their relative lack of skill and experience made me recognize how far I had come since my first time dancing in New York.

The afternoon flew by. The participants weren't yet comfortable with the choreography or polished, but they'd have to get used to performing well despite lack of practice when auditioning in the future anyway. To start our mock audition, my dance assistants gave each girl a number to pin onto her leotard, just like she'd get in a real audition. Then smaller groups of six or so performed the choreography, one group at a time, as I scored them on their own personal score cards. This time I was the expert. The dancers tried to impress me like I had tried to impress so many casting people over the course of my career. "So this is what it feels like to be on the other side of the table," I thought. I was rooting for them all to do their best and didn't want to judge any of them. I simply wanted to tell them, "Have fun! Enjoy dancing! Sparkle! Shine!" Which of these starry-eyed girls will take my job, fill my tap shoes, and be able to meet the challenges, survive the hardships, and stay passionate about show business? Which one of these young ladies has the entertainer's gene? Is destined for fame? Has performing in her blood? Time would tell.

Sadly, we ran out of time for the question-and-answer session. I was disappointed, because I wanted to share my story. I had so much I wanted to say about pursuing your dreams despite fear or failure, enjoying the journey, and not taking any of it for granted. Having learned so much about show business, I could have filled an entire book, maybe two. Instead, I briefly answered a few simple queries, as the girls lined up for photographs. Pulling out my special black marker, I signed my autograph on dance bags, T-shirts, audition score cards, and commemorative programs in indelible ink. For one final instant, I was famous. I thanked my lucky stars, my Fairy Godmother, my parents, and myself for making my dreams come true. This had been one spectacular, wacky, sexy adventure.

Encore

"Was that really your last day as a Rockette?" you may be questioning. Alas, that was my final public appearance; I never kicked up my heels as a Rockette again. A new day was dawning and the Roster disbanded. In exchange, however, I accepted a sizable retirement package. Surprisingly, that Roster audition I had thrown a hissy-fit over in Vegas years earlier yielded me financial benefits beyond my wildest expectations. Stay open to the miracles, friends. When one stage door closes, another door opens. Luckily for me, that new door led right into the bank.

However, while grateful for the substantial severance pay, I still felt a colossal pit in my stomach and a crack in my heart upon hearing the news that we had officially lost our contract negotiations. That single phone call signified the end of my dance career. Getting kicked out of the Rockettes meant more than relinquishing my vocation; I was simultaneously stripped of sequins, status, stardom, security, insurance, and my self-identity. So were many of my fellow Rockettes. Even our parents, spouses, boyfriends, children, and friends were lamenting the loss of our fame, as it was indirectly their fame, too. I didn't want to go back to being the regular Joe Shmoe (Josie Shmosie?) I had worked so hard not to be. What was I going to do with my life now? I grieved. Heavily. This was not an uncommon reaction; every performer I knew went through a mourning period of at least a year after they retired; for some it was devastating. Dancers often don't have the same desire or passion for their next career as they did for performing. Would I?

Fortunately, days later, in spite of the grief, I began to feel relief. For this was also a time of self-reflection. I realized that I had accomplished my goal of being a professional entertainer of the highest caliber. Along with that realization came a sense of contentment I don't ever recall feeling. I had actually accomplished my dreams! BIG dreams! A weight had been lifted off my shoulders. All these years I had put pressure on myself to be competitive in jazz, tap, ballet, modern, singing, and acting. To be in shape, thin, and beautiful. To keep myself looking in my twenties, or at least my early thirties. Who can do that for long? I begged to age gracefully and naturally, to not fight every pound, wrinkle, crease, and crow's foot. Part of me was simply relieved to let go of the stresses of performing and arriving at the theatre on time every night. No more glancing at my watch every two minutes to make sure I didn't miss the show.

In truth, by the time I turned thirty-five, I also wasn't nearly as willing to embarrass myself playing dorky parts. I resisted performing knee drops, jump splits, or any move that could permanently damage my body. I felt silly having to act like a sex kitten at an audition. (I was married with children, for goodness sake!) I no longer desired being cast in the chorus and was over living from paycheck to paycheck. I envied my "normal" friends who had scored real nine-to-five careers right out of college, had gorgeous homes, cars, retirement plans, and college funds for their children to show for it—and could afford to pay full price to see the show that I was in.

The starving artist thing had been adventurous, exciting, and motivating when I was young. Now I was less enthralled with the gypsy life. I wanted a real home where I could hang my top hat and tap shoes. A place where I could permanently display all the trinkets I had picked up on my travels. Because as much as a showbiz career fulfills you for twenty years or so, by the time you are thirty-five or forty, you will probably be craving stability and relationships. At least I was. In the past, I had never wanted to spend more than a few months in the same place and certainly didn't want the responsibility of owning a house. Today I covet those very things. Even mega stars reach a point in their lives where they want to nest with a mate and some offspring. Despite all they've got, they still aren't fulfilled without someone to love and a place to call home.

So the transient life style got harder and less appealing to me as time went by, especially after I was married with kids. The logistics of packing up the family to travel from job to job became increasingly difficult, expensive, and exhausting, and it certainly wasn't in the best interests of my little tykes. Plus, theatre gigs are generally nights and weekends—prime family time. The older I got, the more important it was to me to be free to spend holidays, birthdays, and special events with loved ones.

Given all this ranting and raving about the positive side of retiring from an entertainment career, I will now declare that I will never completely leave showbiz. You'll have to pull me away from the stage kicking and screaming. I don't care to wear an itsy-bitsy-teeny-weenie-rhinestone-studded red bikini anymore, but you can bet that I'll find some way to perform, entertain, choreograph, direct, teach, or create. I may be behind the scenes (with my behind fully covered, unseen), but I still love the theatre and don't intend to completely bow out (gracefully or otherwise).

Before aspiring entertainers make that faithful leap into showbiz, we don't always adequately ponder or premeditate the realities of the future, how short our careers could be, or what we will do when they're over. We are so compelled to be dancers, singers, or actors that nothing will stop us—no amount of reasoning, depressing statistics, or pleas from our well-meaning families to be practical and realistic. Consequently, this forced retirement left me high and dry without a Plan B.

So, I settled down to focus on my family and squeeze as much joy out of my precious time with them as I could. Having a baby and a three-year-old to raise kept me plenty busy, no doubt, but my life couldn't have been more opposite to the free-spirited, highly social, world-traveling life of fame and entertainment I had known. Although I adored my tiny tots and was grateful for the opportunity to stay home with them, I sorely missed the life of glitz and glamour I had attained and then abandoned.

And so I started writing this book. Writing gave me a way to stay connected to show business while I was home changing diapers and making bottles. Whenever I had a spare moment, I'd type away, laughing and reliving the memories, cherishing the adventures all over again. I had so much to say! My sister —a successful, savvy screenwriter—told me I shouldn't write a book if my goal was to make money. That advice derailed me for a spell. While I absolutely loved my time writing and had much to share with the world, why go through all the effort for nothing?

So, playing Mommy became my main role and writing a pleasurable pastime. But to earn income, I started teaching dance classes in the evenings at a wonderful local dance school. Choreographing and fostering our next generation of performers was rewarding, but I realized it wasn't what I wanted to do full time.

Most unfortunately, a few years later (hate to break the sad news), my Love Boat romance capsized and my marriage sank. With my relationship with Ron on the rocks, my showbiz career (as I knew it) over, teaching dance not a full-time option, and making money on my book a long shot (or so I thought), I decided I'd better go back to the drawing board and envision a new plan for my talents and passions. Time to reinvent myself.

Somewhat magically, I was introduced to the field of *drama therapy*—a type of psychotherapy that purposefully uses theatre and drama techniques for personal growth, behavior change, and healing. Wow! Who knew this fantastic modality existed? This career path combined my interest in psychology (you might remember I got a psych degree back in 1987) with my love of theatre. The stars seem to be aligned. I set the book aside, went to graduate school, and trained to become a *drama therapist*, so I could use theatre, creative arts, and holistic health education to inspire people to overcome obstacles, pursue their dreams, and become the happy, healthy, loved, and wealthy superstars they were designed to be. Of course, I continued to teach the odd dance class and choreograph a musical now and then to get my theatre fix!

"But what about the book?" you are wondering. Thanks for asking. After three years of writing grad school papers (including a whopping 350-page Master's thesis), I couldn't bear to type one more syllable. Yet, amidst divorce, eight years of single motherhood, serious health challenges, graduate school, several moves, a tornado destroying our home (I didn't meet Glinda the Good Witch or the Wizard of Oz, how twisted is that?), unemployment, starting a business, a new marriage, and loads of laundry, grocery shopping, cooking, and dishwashing, the book kept calling to be written. It tugged and tugged and tugged at my sleeve. It begged to be birthed. I had to appease this pesky publication once and for all. The book is finally finished and is in good hands—yours. I hope you got as much of a kick out of my wacky, sexy journey as I did.

Although I am retired, the Rockettes have remained a special part of my life. Not only am I a member of the fabulous Rockette Alumnae Association (where I actually met a woman who had danced in the 1940s!), but I also stay in touch with many of my guy and gal pals from the Vegas and Branson shows. To this day, we continue to support each other during tough times and celebrate each other's happy life milestones, many flying across the country to attend weddings, baby showers, college graduations, and fortieth or fiftieth birthday parties during which a sparkling birthday tiara gets passed on to the next glamour girl to be crowned ten years older, wiser, and more beautiful. We may no longer be linked arm and arm, but we are still connected heart to heart. To this day, I'll phone my Rockette friends to ask their advice just like I used to back in the dressing room. I don't know how I'd survive without them. (Another update: My once-rival, childhood dance teachers are now very good friends. Spread the love!)

A creature of habit, I still pencil my eyebrows, wear Egyptian-like eyeliner, bat my overly mascaraed eyelashes, and smile too widely. I wear high heels when it is absolutely ridiculous to do so and find any excuse to don glitter, rhinestones, or a feather boa. I use my kitchen counter as a ballet barre, secretly tap dance when waiting in line at the grocery store, and sing at the top of my lungs when driving in the car. There's no business like show business, and I have no business letting go of my inner (or outer) showgirl. Times change, but whatever challenges are before me, I've learned that the show must go on. And until the final curtain falls, I intend to keep creating spectacular, wacky, sexy adventures. Encore! Encore!

Kristi Lynn Davis

Photo by Doug Coombe, 2015

About the Author

Kristi Lynn Davis is an author, speaker, entertainer, choreographer, and drama therapist. As a trainer and coach, she works with individuals and organizations who desire to dream bigger and think and act more creatively. Pairing her professional background in show business with extensive graduate studies in psychology, drama therapy, and psychoneuroimmunology, Kristi offers a unique, holistic, creative approach to activating the power of the mind, body, and spirit. She particularly enjoys inspiring audiences to entertain new thoughts that will mess with stress, kick out obstacles, and "Rockette" them into spectacular success. In her signature keynote speech, *Kick high! Be spectacular!: Showgirl Secrets to Tap into Your Potential and Get a Kick Out of Life*, Kristi transforms into a Rockette right before your eyes as she shares stories of sparkling success and fortuitous "failure" from her rocky journey into showbiz, to assist you in discovering your dreams, dancing with fear, and becoming the star you truly are. Kristi thrives in the beautiful state of Michigan with her wacky, sexy husband and two spectacular children.

Please visit www.kristilynndavis.com to
- Learn more about Kristi
- Hire her as a speaker, trainer, or coach
- Read her blog
- Shop at her store
- View photos and videos
- Sign up for a free gift
- Leave a message

Made in the USA
Middletown, DE
22 November 2015